A RELUCTANT WELCOME
FOR JEWISH PEOPLE

A RELUCTANT WELCOME
FOR JEWISH PEOPLE
Voices in *Le Devoir*'s Editorials,
1910–1947

BY
Pierre Anctil

Translated by
Tõnu Onu

University of Ottawa Press
2019

University of Ottawa Press
Les Presses de l'Université d'Ottawa

The University of Ottawa Press (UOP) is proud to be the oldest of the francophone university presses in Canada and the only bilingual university publisher in North America. Since 1936, UOP has been "enriching intellectual and cultural discourse" by producing peer-reviewed and award-winning books in the humanities and social sciences, in French or in English.

Library and Archives Canada Cataloguing in Publication
Title: A reluctant welcome for Jewish people: voices in Le devoir's editorials,
    1910–1947 / Pierre Anctil; translated by Tõnu Onu.
Other titles: Chacun ses Juifs. English I Container of (work): Devoir (Montréal,
    Québec). Selections.
Names: Anctil, Pierre, author.
Description: Series statement: Canadian studies collection I Translation of: À chacun
    ses Juifs. I Includes bibliographical references.
Identifiers: Canadiana (print) 2019010418X I Canadiana (ebook) 20190104236 I ISBN
    9780776627953 (softcover) I ISBN 9780776627960 (PDF) I ISBN 9780776627977
    (EPUB) I ISBN 9780776627984 (Kindle)
Subjects: LCSH: Devoir (Montréal, Québec) I LCSH: Jews—Québec (Province)—
    Montréal. I LCSH: Editorials—Québec (Province) I LCSH: Antisemitism in the
    press—Québec (Province)—History—20th century. I LCSH: Québec (Province)—
    Social conditions—20th century.
Classification: LCC FC2950.J5 A2213 2019 I DDC 971.4004/924—dc23

Legal Deposit: 2019
Library and Archives Canada
© University of Ottawa Press 2019

Copy editing   Robert Ferguson
Proofreading   Susan James
Typesetting   Édiscript enr.
Cover design   Édiscript enr.
Cover image   Alexander Bercovitch, *Vue du port de Montréal*, gouache, charcoal
                    and pencil on paper, 36,7 × 50,8 cm, circa 1934. Collection of the
                    Musée national des beaux-arts du Québec, acquisition (1987.16).
                    Reproduced here with kind permission from MCBAQ.Photo
                    credit: MNBAQ, Patrick Altman

The University of Ottawa Press gratefully acknowledges the support extended to its publishing list by Canadian Heritage through the Canada Book Fund, by the Canada Council for the Arts, by the Ontario Arts council, by the Federation for the Humanities and Social Sciences through the Awards to Scholarly Publishing Program, and by the University of Ottawa.

ONTARIO ARTS COUNCIL
CONSEIL DES ARTS DE L'ONTARIO
an Ontario government agency
un organisme du gouvernement de l'Ontario

Canada Council   Conseil des arts
for the Arts   du Canada

Canada

u Ottawa

Table of Contents

Translator's Note

There is little I can add to what two eminent historians, Ira Robinson and Pierre Anctil, have written in the preface and introduction respectively about the present volume. I shall, therefore, limit myself to some brief comments on the challenges of translating *Le Devoir*'s editorials written 70 to 100 years ago. Apparently, Boris Pasternak once stated that, "The usual reliable translator gets the literal meaning but misses the tone, and … in poetry tone is of course everything." The editorials in this volume are not poems and I am neither a historian nor a poet, but I believe Pasternak's quote still has some relevance to the translation of the editorials from *Le Devoir*. The editorials addressed crucial issues in Canadian and Quebec history, therefore, as with any translation it was necessary to get the literal meaning right. Language has evolved and the nature of editorials has also changed significantly since the time that these were first written. Compared to the editorials of a few paragraphs, in most newspapers today, the editorials from *Le Devoir* of the period covered here were veritable social or political essays. Furthermore, they expressed views that were controversial and often appealed to and raised emotions. Therefore, in the translation it was essential, not only to get the literal meaning right, but also the nuances that reflected the tone of the editorials. In such cases the choice of words is always a challenge and is open to question.

Although the task of translation was challenging, it was also a stimulating one, facilitated immeasurably by Pierre Anctil's patient and knowledgeable explanations of the meanings of numerous expressions that no dictionary could provide. His support and encouragement were invaluable in grasping and translating the ambiguous and obscure references that popped up in texts written long ago. The translation was much improved by his wise counsel. Any shortcomings in the translation remain mine alone. I can only hope that this translation will provide the reader with some of the same enlightenment and matter for reflection which I found in the original French version of the book.

Preface

One of the most important tasks facing scholars of the Jewish experience in Canada is making sense of the phenomenon of anti-Semitism. This is a task fraught with difficulties, not the least of which is the recognition and overcoming of numerous mythologies that have developed around this issue. In particular, the complex and fraught relationship between Jews and French Canadians in Montreal in the first half of the twentieth century has become the subject of controversy that has, unusual for issues related to Jewish studies, become a public issue debated not merely in scholarly journals but in the op-ed pages of the Montreal daily press in both French and English.

In attempting to create an appreciation of this historical relationship in all its complexity, Pierre Anctil has contributed much. He has been, for many years, a strong voice within the Quebec intellectual community, arguing on many levels and in many places that the Jewish community of Quebec is an important constitutive element of the historical and intellectual heritage of contemporary Quebec. Practically single-handed, Anctil took upon himself the task of translating the intellectual heritage of Jewish Montreal, expressed in the Yiddish language, to French and he has succeeded in creating a veritable library of such works, as well as a series of significant essays and books designed to make this heritage contextually understandable to contemporary readers.

Yet another crucial aspect of Anctil's work has been to help us understand the myriad ways in which the Jewish community of Montreal was understood—and misunderstood—by the French Canadians of Quebec in the early twentieth century. He has, with great justice, characterized this relationship as a "rendez-vous manqué." In examining this relationship, he has rightly focused on *Le Devoir*, a major intellectual force within the French-Canadian community for more than a century. In 1988, he published a book entitled *Le Devoir, les Juifs et l'immigration*, in which he attempted to contextualize the stance of *Le Devoir* on the Jews and, without denying its negativity, sought to mitigate the negative reputation it had received, especially in the Montreal

Jewish community. For this, he received considerable criticism in Esther Delisle's book, *The Traitor and the Jew,* which strongly condemned the French-Canadian intellectual, Lionel Groulx, and *Le Devoir,* for their anti-Semitism. Anctil was thus also implicated in Delisle's evaluation of French-Canadian anti-Semitism. Among the many results of this public controversy, Anctil ceased publishing directly on anti-Semitism in Quebec and began in earnest his project of translating the cultural heritage of Montreal Jewry from Yiddish to French.

Some twenty years later, Anctil has returned to the subject of *Le Devoir* and the Jews. He began this process with the 2010 publication of *'Fais ce que dois'; 60 éditoriaux pour comprendre* Le Devoir *sous Henri Bourassa (1910–1932),* which dealt with the newspaper under the editorship of its founder, the distinguished French-Canadian public intellectual, Henri Bourassa; followed in 2013 by *'Soyons nos maîtres'; 60 éditoriaux pour comprendre* Le Devoir *sous Georges Pelletier (1932–1947).* In the present volume, Anctil attempts to focus on *Le Devoir* and Jewish issues in the era from the journal's founding in 1910 to the aftermath of the Second World War. In light of the importance and the sensitivity of this issue, and especially because of the previous scholarly controversy on this specific subject, this attempt takes on a special importance.

In approaching the reading of this book, it is important to understand what this book does and what it does not do. It examines the editorial policy of *Le Devoir.* Anctil has read through nearly four decades of editorials in a daily newspaper, some 11,000, and extracted for analysis all those dealing with Jews and Judaism, however obliquely. This in itself is a monumental task. What it does not do is to examine the news reporting of *Le Devoir* on Jews and Judaism. This is of some importance because the tone of news reporting is itself influential in creating the readership's understanding of and reaction to a given subject. Early on in the history of *Le Devoir,* in 1912, Jewish community leader Samuel W. Jacobs wrote to Henri Bourassa complaining not about editorial policy but about prejudiced news reporting:

> It is a matter of almost daily occurrence for the "Devoir" to publish items of little interest to the public respecting Jews, the only object, so far as I can see, to bring to the attention of the public the fact that some Jew has offended against the law. Does the "Devoir" wish to hold our people up to the hatred and contempt of French speaking citizens?[1]

Systematic examination of this area of *Le Devoir* remains a *desideratum*, but is of greater scope than any individual scholar can readily undertake. It would be an important investigation that should not by any means be confined to the pages of *Le Devoir*.[2] Even the rival Liberal journal of French-Canadian opinion in that era, *Le Canada*, which did not share *Le Devoir*'s reputation in the Montreal Jewish community for negativity toward Jews and Judaism, was not free from articles denigrating Jews and Judaism. Of *Le Canada*'s apology for such an article that appeared in 1945, Montreal Jewish writer and journalist, A.M. Klein, wrote

> ... the management of *Le Canada*... repudiated Mlle Oligny's sentiments, saying that those were but an expression of her personal opinion.... *Le Canada* in its apology, if it is intended as an apology, makes reference to favorable articles about Jews that it printed. We must admit that it does not seem much of a defense to us for a newspaper to state that it does not spread its Jew baiting all over the journal, but reserves it only for a special department.[3]

Within the editorials of *Le Devoir*, Pierre Anctil finds a complex situation. He has discovered that *Le Devoir*'s editorial attention is not constantly or consistently focussed on Jews, as was the case with Quebec's openly anti-Semitic press of that era, especially those newspapers edited by Adrien Arcand. Of the 11,000 editorials published in these years, just a little over 200 qualified for analysis. Many of these were concentrated in the 1930s and 1940s, and the most negative were those firmly opposing the immigration to Canada of Jewish refugees from Nazi persecution.

A reading of the sixty editorials Anctil chose to present to the reader in their entirety enables us to approach the comprehension of this subject in a way we were unable to do previously. What do we find? Among other things, we begin to comprehend the individuality of the editorial writers. Henri Bourassa, for instance, hardly referenced Jews at all in his editorials, and then with little or no negativity. This is certainly a remarkable change from his public stance in the debate in the Parliament of Canada on the "Lord's Day Act," in 1906, during which Bourassa stated:

> They [the Jews] do not adapt themselves to the customs of the people among whom they live, but on the contrary, they conduct

xiv   A RELUCTANT WELCOME FOR JEWISH PEOPLE

> themselves in such a way that they are vampires on the community
> instead of being contributors to the general welfare of the people.[4]

By contrast, Georges Pelletier was often negative in the tone of his editorials and was not above referring to a Jew as "un circoncis."

It is both interesting and highly instructive to see that the editorialists of Le Devoir did not wish to identify or to be identified as anti-
Semites, possessors of an anti-Jewish hate that was characterized in one
editorial as "odieuse et stupide." At the very same time, the editorial
page of Le Devoir maintained in a relatively consistent form throughout the period the assumption, shared by many Canadians of all origins in that era and beyond, that "the Jews" were powerful; that they
had financial power as well as a powerful influence on the press. These
attitudes tended to remain constant even when Le Devoir had something positive to say about Jews, often in the context of how French
Canadians should emulate Jews, in such areas as communal solidarity.
In all of this area, including its ambivalences, the editorials of Le Devoir
closely parallel the thought of Lionel Groulx, who had this to say:

> We do not prevent anyone from living; but we also want to live;
> and I believe we are not taking anyone's place by taking our own.
> Is it necessary for me to say that I am neither anti-English nor
> anti-Jewish. However, I see that the English are pro-English and
> the Jews pro-Jewish. And as long as such an attitude is neither
> uncharitable or unjust, I will certainly not criticize them. Why
> then, I wonder in the same vein would French Canadians be
> everything except pro-French Canadian.[5]

A second factor of importance was that "the Jews" were considered
practically inassimilable strangers who could be truly at home only
in Palestine. In relation to "Canadiens de vielle souche," Jews were, in
Editorial N° 9, characterized as a "foreign group that is more or less
impossible to assimilate."

Yet a third factor of capital importance is that Le Devoir in that
era upheld a perspective on the ideal life for Canadians that Jews
could not live up to. Though the newspaper itself was headquar-
tered in urban Montreal, its ideal was rural. The ideal Canadian was a
farmer, whereas Jews in Canada were almost exclusively urban dwellers. (Editorial N° 5) They were characterized by "proverbial fertility"
and were "one of the most prolific races of the world" (Editorial N° 10)

who threatened a major invasion of immigrants that might result in a decrease of the percentage of French Canadians in the population of Canada, and hence the political influence of French Canada.

A fourth factor that comes to the fore is the notion that Jews simply seek to take up a disproportionate share of society, or, as Georges Pelletier put it, "They are too prominent for who they are" (Editorial Nº 16). Editorial Nº 33, likewise, adds "the economic influence of the French Canadians, the English and the Jews normally should be an approximate reflection of their numbers. One need only look around to see that this is far from the case." To say the least, this attitude has had great lasting power in Quebec, as when Quebec entrepreneur Pierre Peladeau caused a furor in 1990 when he was quoted in *L'Actualité* magazine saying that Jews "take up too much space" in Quebec.

A final factor that editorialists focused on was the religious difference between Jews and staunchly-Catholic French Canadians who had learned from highly ambivalent pre-Vatican II teachings of the Church that Jews were simply not to be trusted. Thus in 1943, when the magnitude of Hitler's Final Solution of the "Jewish Problem" was just beginning to impinge on public consciousness, a *Le Devoir* editorial commented on the magnitude of the catastrophe, but added the caveat "If the Jews are not inflating figures in the Western or Talmudic way." In the end, as Editorial Nº 7 characterized Jewish leader Samuel W. Jacobs, so it could be said of *Le Devoir*'s stance toward the Jew: "he is not of the parish."

In conclusion, Anctil's analysis of *Le Devoir*'s editorial policy on Jews and Judaism in the period 1910–1947 leaves us first of all with a deep appreciation of the complexity of the issue. It also helps us to understand in more subtle terms the newspaper's negativity vis-à-vis Jews, often perceived clearly by the Jewish reader of this era. In the last analysis, *Le Devoir* was not marked by an obsessive or unmitigated attitude to Jews and its opinions on the subject were for the most part coloured by the times. *Le Devoir*'s editorials were part and parcel of a climate of opinion existing in Canada that—directly or indirectly—made it virtually impossible for Canada's political leadership, both Anglophone and Francophone to materially aid the multitude of European Jews put in harm's way by Hitler's "final solution" when that aid was literally a matter of life or death.

IRA ROBINSON
Concordia University

Notes

1.   Letter from Samuel-W. Jacobs to Henri Bourassa, September 5, 1912, Bourassa family fond, Bibliothèque et Archives nationales du Québec, Montreal.

2.   Marc Hébert's study on this subject should be noted: "*Le Soleil, The Quebec Chronicle Telegraph* and Jewish Immigration 1925–1939," *Canadian Jewish Studies/ Études juives au Canada,* n° 3, 1995, p. 55–91.

3.   A.M. Klein, "*Le Canada* and 'This Hatred'" (November 16, 1945), in *Beyond Sambatyon: Selected Essays and Editorials, 1928–1955,* dir. M.W. Steinberg an Usher Caplan, Toronto, University of Toronto Press, 1982, p. 251–2.

4.   Cited by Paul Laverdure in: *Sunday in Canada: The Rise and Fall of the Lord's Day,* Yorkton, Saskatchewan, Gravelbooks, 2004, p. 32. Laverdure notes that Bourassa had soon changed his mind and supported the idea of a "Jewish exceptionalism" p. 49.

5.   Lionel Groulx, "L'économique et le national," public speech offered by abbé Lionel Groulx on February 12, 1936, before la Chambre cadette de commerce de Montréal. The text was published in *Directives,* Montreal, les Éditions du Zodiaque, 1937, p. 70.

Introduction

The position of the newspaper, *Le Devoir*, respecting the Montreal Jewish community and Judaism in general constitutes one of the most discussed and most important historiographical issues in Canadian Jewish history.[1] This applies particularly to the period between the two world wars when an oppressive climate of suspicion and inter-ethnic tensions spread throughout the country owing to the unprecedented economic crisis. Taking into consideration the political influence of *Le Devoir* on decision makers, the paper took on the role of a paradigm in the complex relationship between the Jewish and French-Canadian populations of Canada. Over the last fifty years, the subject has been examined in a large number of works by numerous commentators without our knowledge of the issues really advancing. In fact, the impression left by these studies is that authors often do little more than repeat previously-expressed opinions which have become canonical. This tendency is particularly noticeable in English-language works on the historical evolution of Canadian Judaism that view *Le Devoir* as a patent example of French Canada's ideological and nationalistic defensiveness during the 1930s, if not the instrument of choice in the expression of the anti-Semitism of Francophone elites. Such a perception is not necessarily false, but it has often been presented without any nuance. The perception goes back to the immediate post-war period when the first monographs on Canadian Judaism were published in universities.

However, many aspects of this now-standard analysis are problematic. First, these historical reflections on *Le Devoir* were often produced by researchers who did not read French. Several of them, for example, were not able to quote any significant passages from the newspaper or the main editorialists to corroborate their affirmations. The same authors also often repeatedly displayed an ignorance of the history of French Canada and of Catholicism in general. Clearly, the conclusions that they reached were based on data which was far from complete and often unverified. In fact, it can be stated without fear of being mistaken that *Le Devoir* crystallized, among some historians, perceptions that came from sources other than university research, and now we must rethink the whole evolution of these perceptions. The treatment of the issue is made even more difficult since Canadian Jewish historiography in general contains a perception of French Canada that has its roots partially in the rather negative and sectarian opinion held by some British Anglo-Canadian authors regarding their Catholic Francophone compatriots. When the time came for historians of Canadian Judaism to examine the complex, and at times perplexing, relations between Jews and French-speaking Canadians, many did not question the prevalent biased opinions, nor did they approach this difficult subject from a new angle. Consequently, the conclusions reached by these authors were either outdated or incomplete.

Furthermore, the methodology used to analyze the content of *Le Devoir* left much to be desired in several works dealing with Canadian Jewish history. Often, the texts amount to no more than an examination of very short periods—whereas the newspaper was founded in 1910—and treat only specific aspects whose importance and recurrence at times is difficult to assess in the absence of more substantive points of reference. Other researchers did not seem to pay sufficient attention to making a fine distinction between different kinds of texts that appeared in *Le Devoir*, and their relative importance in the overall ideological stance expressed in the newspaper. A report by an anonymous journalist appearing on the front page does not have the same explanatory worth as an editorial with the name of the writer clearly indicated. Thus, a humour column, even hostile to Jews and immigrants, needs to be viewed differently from a supposedly objective report on the same subject. In a daily, there is a hierarchy in the structure of information and opinions that it is absolutely necessary to take into account or risk gaining a historical understanding that is only partial or impossible to validate. A newspaper is also based on specific and quantifiable political foundations, which is especially the case of *Le Devoir*, conceived by Henri Bourassa as a publication devoted to defending the ideas that he wished to promote in the public sphere. *Le Devoir*, therefore, has its own history to which the newspaper has remained faithful for long periods, a history that has guided its approach on a host of subjects that are important to the evolution of French Canada. It is difficult to extract information on the Jewish community or Judaism from *Le Devoir* without situating these texts in a broader context and without at the same time examining certain ideological declarations based on the nature of French-Canadian nationalism.

Le Devoir represents only one ideological strain among others within a complex and multi-faceted movement of ideas. Certainly, the newspaper is characterized by a quality of writing and intellectual strength that have made it a very prominent commentator in Francophone society. However, it has not embraced all of the political and ideological thoughts expressed day after day in French Canada, regardless of the period studied. Throughout its history, *Le Devoir* has had to deal with numerous detractors who have questioned the ideological path it has taken and competed for attention to deprive it of the enviable place it has earned in public opinion. *Le Devoir*'s conservatism was criticized relentlessly by Francophone newspapers more open to social progress and its nationalism was condemned by press organs of liberal allegiance, without mentioning the existence in Montreal of mass circulation dailies not having any very specific political preferences. Too often in historiography, the influence *Le Devoir* may have exercised over certain well-defined sectors has been mistaken for influence in all of French Canada, as if this society spoke with one voice and never faced internal conflicts or splits. The texts appearing in the newspaper founded by Bourassa cannot be considered as representative of the entire Francophone elite and their impact must be assessed with a great deal of care. In many cases, it still remains to be evaluated whose attention *Le Devoir* attracted regarding certain specific subjects. With respect to the opinions it expressed on Canadian Judaism, we need to know if the newspaper really convinced a great number of readers to act one way or another towards Montreal's Jewish population. The newspaper, of course, did express hostility to Jews at times in its history. Here again, it should be asked what influence these views had and if they had a real impact on the political and social life of French Canada. If *Le Devoir* was guilty of anti-Semitism—which cannot be denied—how exactly can this attitude be understood and at what level in the hierarchy of racist ideologies? These questions have hardly been examined until now and in many cases, they have been addressed only in a superficial way.

The preceding reflections should not, however, be taken as severe criticism or any kind of blame toward researchers who have preceded us on this difficult road. The subject examined on these pages remains extremely complex and demands knowledge in several divergent fields within Canadian studies. It is only after a long examination of the broad evolution in Canada of the two great religious traditions in question—Judaism and Catholicism—that it is possible to tackle this hard core of Canadian Jewish history. Furthermore, the contact between *Le Devoir* and the Montreal Jewish community has been influenced by several elements that complicate its study, including mutual incomprehension, a sentiment of exclusion, and the impression felt at certain times by the main historical figures of being duped by their counterparts. In this clash of two different cultures and pressure groups, accusations of racism, bias, and ethnocentrism poured forth from both sides, at times with very damaging insensitivity that still remains an obstacle. The researchers who have ventured onto these confusing pathways have often themselves been weighed down by the historic confrontation which they are trying to fathom. At times it has been difficult for them to maintain sufficient distance or a position of well-intentioned neutrality respecting the pre-war context. In this search for meaning and balance, I must confess my initial analysis of this extremely difficult issue, published in the 1988 volume *Le Devoir, les Juifs et l'immigration, de Bourassa à Laurendeau*, was really only a partial analysis of a subject that is more pertinent than ever. This explains my desire, twenty-five years later, to return to this unfinished project. Whatever angle is chosen to approach the issue, it is clear that the history of *Le Devoir*, considered from the point of view of Canadian Judaism, requires more thorough research. The subject also demands a better understanding of the situation in which Canadian Jews found themselves after Hitler arrived in power in Germany and the ideological leanings of the Montreal Jewish community at the time.

Methodology

The 2010 centenary of *Le Devoir*'s founding provided an opportunity to acquire more in-depth knowledge of the historical relationship between Canadian Jews and Francophones. Four years earlier, with *Le Devoir*'s editor Bernard Descôteaux, I proposed producing an anthology of the best editorials printed in the newspaper—categorized by theme and period—to gain a better understanding of the paper's long-term evolution. A newspaper of opinion, *Le Devoir* has been a vehicle of important ideas and has borne the imprint of certain dominant streams of thought in French Canada. In systematically analyzing the newspaper's editorial output, it became apparent that *Le Devoir* was marked by shifts in direction. The changes in orientation reflected ideological transformations throughout French Canada and subsequently its more specific Quebec component. The act of preparing an anthology also entailed bringing out of hiding numerous documents which had not been read in several decades and yet were representative of the evolution of ideas in the newspaper. Two volumes in this new history of *Le Devoir* appeared in 2010 under the titles *Fais ce que dois* and *À la hache et au scalpel*.[2] They covered the period during which Henri Bourassa (1910 to 1932) and Gérard Filion (1947 to 1963) led the newspaper. In 2013, a third volume was published, entitled *Soyons nos maîtres*,[3] which was devoted to Georges Pelletier's editorial direction and provided an analysis of the years from 1932 to 1947. Many of the issues treated in this latter work are eminently relevant to the discussion undertaken here.

During this research project, which entailed a close reading of each editorial printed in *Le Devoir*, the idea came to me to note systematically for the 1910 to 1947 period all sections mentioning Montreal's Jews and Judaism in general. It was during those four decades that the sharpest inter-community tensions appeared and developed — that is, while Henri Bourassa and Georges Pelletier controlled the paper's editorial direction. One of the most difficult aspects to discern had been the vehemence of *Le Devoir*'s position on the Jewish presence in Canada and the frequency of these reflections. Nor was it known exactly on what subjects the negative discourse regarding Jews was expressed, or when those views appeared most vehemently. In short, we lacked a chronological framework situating all the editorials printed in *Le Devoir* about Montreal Jews. A reading of *Le Devoir*'s editorial corpus over a period of thirty-seven years also ensured that the collected information presented a certain quantitative and methodological coherence, the lack of which until now has been the principal flaw requiring correction in this kind of study. From 1910 to 1947, at a rate of about 300 editorials printed each year, we arrived at a total of nearly 11,000 texts. Furthermore, the editorials are all signed; they were written by a very limited number of individuals and appeared in a newspaper whose broad ideological themes were well known. Until now, it had not been possible to undertake a study in such a systematic way, nor to such an extensive chronological degree. In fact, most often, historiography has recounted Jewish issues only by occasional surveys of *Le Devoir*'s pages, or in relation to certain specific events that, due to their seriousness or their emblematic significance, attracted the attention of researchers.

However, it was not enough to simply extract editorial material linked either closely or even remotely to the Jewish presence in Montreal or elsewhere in the world without providing greater specifics. To analyze the connection between Jewish themes and *Le Devoir* with appropriate rigour also required that the relevant editorials be categorized according to precise criteria. Initially all texts that mentioned, even briefly, a cultural presence, an event, or a person closely associated with Judaism were selected. At times it was a brief reference in a sentence or a single word that still provided, without a shadow of doubt, an opportunity for *Le Devoir* to address an established fact of Jewish life. Texts were not retained that related to personalities of Jewish origin recognized by historians, for example, the municipal councillor, Joseph Schubert, or the Member of Parliament, Samuel W. Jacobs, and did not contain in the newspaper a comment related to their cultural identity. In many cases, *Le Devoir* took an interest in Jews or a Jewish activity only when considering a broader issue with no particular relation to the Jewish presence in Montreal, for example, during the campaign against Hollywood films or when the newspaper attacked dubious electoral practices. On the other hand, some editorials immediately declared their intention to address in detail an issue closely associated with the interests of Canada's Jewish community, as in the case of the policy called "buy from your own," the boycott of German merchandise during the Nazi era, or the British mandatory policy in Palestine. Therefore, I decided to make a very clear distinction between two kinds of texts: those addressing Jewish issues as a secondary or passing subject and those focused on the Jewish presence in Montreal or elsewhere in the world. In the latter case, the title of the editorials often had a clearly Jewish reference and the editorialists asserted a desire to address the subject as a priority.

It should be noted that every reference in *Le Devoir* to Jewish activity or life was not necessarily an indication of a negative attitude with respect to Montreal's Jewish population or proof that the editorialist held or expressed anti-Semitic opinions. At times the newspaper's reporting to the public was done in a neutral and impartial manner and the comments on the editorial page on a matter seemed at first glance objective and without particular emphasis. For example, at certain times in *Le Devoir*'s history some editorialists commented on the vital statistics of Montreal's Francophone population to better highlight its unfavourable social and economic situation compared to the rest of Canada. Since interesting data was also available at City

Hall respecting the state of health of Montrealers of Protestant and Jewish origin, that information was also provided to readers for purposes of comparison between groups of different origins. These texts in no way added to prejudices towards Montreal Jews. On the contrary, they provided reliable data compiled from credible sources that shed light on social realities and allowed the reader to gain a better in-depth knowledge of society. On the other hand, comments regarding "Jewish financial power," "Jewish monopoly over the press," and "major immigration projects planned by Jews" were usually based on incomplete analysis or wrong information, and displayed clear hostility. That was the case regarding the malicious perception of the "Jewish republic" in France, "Jewish plots" in the world, and the supposedly "arrogant" behaviour of the German Jews in the Weimar Republic. In the present study, it was necessary to introduce a degree of balance that allowed a distinction to be made, for example, between seemingly neutral demographic and socio-economic considerations and tendentious comments regarding Jewish merchants established in Montreal or German Jewish refugees seeking a safe haven.

In addition to listing the editorials on the subject of the Canadian Jewish population and personalities, our analysis sought to determine if *Le Devoir*'s interest focused on Montreal Judaism and its most prominent representatives, or if it instead turned its attention abroad to the situation in Central Europe after 1933. The distinction is significant for a newspaper that was inclusive and all-encompassing in its editorial policy and which, despite expressing strong criticism, sought to better inform readers about Canada and to establish contact with the local Jewish population. The matter was presented differently when the newspaper turned its attention abroad and its editorialists feared an influx of Jewish immigrants and refugees hounded by openly anti-Semitic political regimes. In the first case we are witness to an exchange among Canadians of various origins and in the second we see a display of defensive measures articulated around a rejection of pluralism. This lends itself to an interesting study of each editorialist's position in *Le Devoir* respecting Jewish culture. Over a period of thirty-seven years, from 1910 to 1947, only four major voices were heard in the newspaper about the Jewish presence in Canada and elsewhere in the world: the founder, Henri Bourassa, two of its original journalists, Georges Pelletier and Omer Héroux, and Louis Dupire from the early 1920s. Therefore, among this small number of editorialists, a very precise attitude can be discerned which varies considerably from one individual to another. The information collected from *Le Devoir* reveals diverse opinions on these issues that until now have often been overlooked by academic analysis.

Like the previous volumes in this series about the history of *Le Devoir*, the purpose here is to allow the editorials themselves to be read as they were printed at different times under different signatures. These texts, which constitute documents of essential value regarding the relations between Jews and French Canadians, had not been read since their publication. With some rare exceptions, the editorials have not been used in historiography, not even in bibliographical references. In fact, until now, no researcher had succeeded in finding these texts or the exact date of their publication. The weakness of analysis carried out until now on the subject is derived mainly from the fact that the known editorials—and there were very few—were often objects of erroneous interpretation and quoted out of context. Consequently, these little-known editorials became isolated from a long sequence of similar writings published over a period of several decades that provide an explanatory historical context. An editorial often contains a fairly explicit message, but it is very difficult, if not impossible, when relying on a single text, to obtain a clear idea of *Le Devoir*'s position on circumstances as different as the Great Depression or the two world wars. Particular attention was, therefore, paid in the preparation of the anthology of these editorials to assessing their importance and subjects according to a detailed knowledge of the entire editorial corpus that appeared on the pages of *Le Devoir* between 1910 and 1947. In total, sixty editorials were selected for the present volume. Categorized according to eighteen significant themes, they constitute a rational and coherent overview of the newspaper's position regarding Jews, from its founding to the death of Georges Pelletier. To avoid giving the reader the impression of being presented with material that has not been assessed, each of the themes is preceded by a detailed commentary and an analysis within its historical context, with respect to Canada as well as in relation to the international situation. In addition to providing *Le Devoir*'s broad views on the subject, the volume also presents texts that allow the reader to obtain a more precise idea of each theme's evolution and the place it occupied in the newspaper.

Jews and French Canadians

Just as with the three preceding volumes the original series published in French (Septentrion, 2010–2013) the present book bears a title, *A Reluctant Welcome for Jewish People*, that reflects the thinking of *Le Devoir* respecting the Jewish presence in Canada and elsewhere in the world. In December 1938, following the Kristallnacht[4] pogrom, when emotions had reached their peak throughout the world regarding the persecution of Jews in Germany, Pelletier signed an editorial that very explicitly encapsulated his ideological position on the issue. The text, which is not devoid of some spontaneous sympathy towards the Jewish victims of Nazism, aimed at putting an end to any attempt to open Canada's borders to refugees from Hitler's Germany. With the title "To everyone their own Jews,"[5] the editorial categorically rejected a suggestion from the French journalist and parliamentarian, Henri de Kérillis, who, writing from Paris, proposed sending the German Jewish population to British colonies including "Western and Northern Canada." The remarks by de Kérillis, which appeared in the newspaper, *L'Époque*,[6] were general and impartial in nature regarding regions of the world capable of providing refuge to Jews threatened by the German dictatorship. Pelletier jumped on the opportunity with a plea to explain why Canada must avoid playing such a role and how the reception of new Jewish groups was contrary to the country's interests. The editorial emphasized that Canada had already done enough for Jews of European origin (thus explaining its title). The editorial also claimed this was not the case with the powers neighbouring Germany, especially since they, too, had colonies available for settlement. Pelletier ended his argument by asserting that Canada was primarily seeking farmers and, in any case, Jews resisted integration into a new homeland, regardless of its geographical position and the good intentions of its inhabitants.

The publication of a study on how *Le Devoir* covered the subject of Jews serves a broader objective of providing a more nuanced, and more exhaustive, description of the relations between Jews and Catholic Francophones in Montreal before the Quiet Revolution. Now, many decades later, we have hardly begun to examine an issue that continues to have a profound influence on Montreal's Jewish population, and on how Jewish community organizations deal with contemporary Quebec nationalism. Regarding an issue as crucial as the attitude of French-speaking Canadians towards Montreal Judaism, we were confronted by a closed book. In that context, it was difficult to make a true distinction between perceptions and established facts. Many elements of this complex problem were not publicly known until now or were revealed in a form much too incomplete and often too distorted to draw any conclusions. The following analysis is also a contribution to what the sociologist Morton Weinfeld correctly describes as a duty of collective remembrance on the part of Francophones towards a still-recent past, constituted, as often as not, of negative and harmful attitudes. The analysis includes an understanding of historic Jewish sensitivities.[7] It is extremely important to provide a true assessment of the French-Canadian stance toward Judaism during a period when the Nazi genocide was being planned and carried out in Europe, and while Canadian Jews were doing everything possible to help their co-religionists entrapped by the Nazis. Similarly, we need to better understand the perception of educated Francophones regarding their Jewish neighbours in the context of sharing the same territory in Montreal and acceptance of religious diversity during the first half of the twentieth century. This is likely to facilitate establishment of improved channels of communication and exchange between two major communities, both in their own way constituent parts of Montreal's and Quebec's identity.

It was with some apprehension that I chose to undertake a study of such emotional complexity. Jews of diverse origins and Francophones of Catholic tradition have mingled in Montreal for more than two centuries,[8] at times quite intensely. Until very recently, we did not have reliable references allowing us to gain an in-depth understanding of this complex and continually evolving cultural and political relationship. Since the beginning of the twentieth century, there has been a long evolution in the identity of Jewish and French-Canadian Montrealers that has completely transformed the image both communities have of themselves and of their future. The histories of Montreal Judaism and Quebec nationalism have been the subject of distinct studies that have examined complex ideas and notions that are now better understood. Looking at the contact and interaction between these two populations, however, requires vast linguistic, as well as cultural and religious, knowledge, which is not common in university circles. Yet this relationship has valuable knowledge to contribute regarding the treatment of minorities in the Canadian context. Furthermore, it can shed light on the development of a framework for inter-cultural exchange in the Quebec metropolis. In my analysis of the relationship between Montreal Jews and Francophones I have attempted, as much as possible, to remain detached in the description of historic facts and maintain an emotional distance. After all, one of the key qualities of a researcher is to step back from the information collected and the contemporary situation. The task of academic research is not to right wrongs committed many decades ago, nor to condemn past attitudes deemed unacceptable today. I simply hope to have been able to contribute to a better knowledge of situations clearly belonging to the past, but to which we are heirs.

Bourassa and Jacobs

Before addressing the manner in which *Le Devoir* treated the theme of the Jewish presence in Canada — and Judaism in general — it is important to look at a broader aspect of the issue. From the beginning there existed between *Le Devoir* and the Montreal Jewish community (in other words, the editors of the newspaper and institutions of Canadian Judaism) a relationship that transcends our immediate subject. In this broader context the issue is not one of actual editorial issues or ideological aspects of a normative nature, but rather the personal relationship established between individuals closely associated with *Le Devoir* and leaders of Montreal Jewish life. Before founding his daily, Bourassa's image was extremely negative among prominent Jewish personalities, based on their reaction to his positions in Canadian politics. This was partly due to Bourassa's flamboyant personality, which left no one indifferent, and partly to his visceral opposition to the policies of Wilfrid Laurier, notably with regard to British imperialism and Francophone minorities in Canada. This inevitably shocked some of the leaders of Montreal's Jewish institutions, who often were very close to the federal Liberal Party and had great admiration for its leader.

Canadian Jews had opportunities to witness Bourassa's fiery oratory before he founded *Le Devoir* — as in March 1906 in the House of Commons when Bourassa the politician formally opposed the immigration of Russian Jews to the country. The attack was delivered following serious pogroms carried out in Imperial Russia and the speech left a very negative impression on the Montreal Jewish community. In this speech to Parliament, Bourassa reiterated most of the anti-Semitic prejudices common in his era, including the claim that even when Jews were accepted they did not integrate into their new homeland. The politician was not shy either in asserting that in Russia the Jewish population supported revolutionary movements and, at the same time, practised debilitating usury in the countryside and with small savings holders. Bourassa, at the time, even claimed that Jews had only themselves to blame for the violent attacks against them in the country of czars, given how their conduct seemed contrary to the common good:

> It is a well-known fact that the Jews do not become owners of property to a large extent. In Russia especially, they have not purchased land but have lived and enriched themselves to an enormous extent by extorting from the poor people not only their money but the blood of their life [*sic*], and repeating in fact the historical example that has been illustrated over three hundred years ago by the greatest of English poets. In days of revolution, the common people simply go and strike blindly but instinctively against the people who have persecuted them for years and years.[9]

Worse still, Bourassa based his comments on the well-known opinions of Goldwin Smith, a British professor and journalist who had settled in Canada in 1871 and whose anti-Semitic declarations often made news. In the circumstances, it did not take much for the Jewish community leaders to believe the Member of Parliament from Labelle had become the propagator in French Canada of racist ideas inspired by Smith. Bourassa also expressed negative opinions about Jews during a debate in June 1906 on the subject of Sunday observance, and again in April 1907 when there was another heated exchange in the House of Commons concerning the financial means used by the Laurier government to attract immigrants. On that occasion, Bourassa insisted Canada focus its energy on improved settlement on agricultural lands of its own citizens of English and French origin and that it turn away from foreign immigration. His harangue, directed against people from diverse places and of diverse origins described as "the dregs of every nation," included this passage:

> The idea of the founding fathers of this nation was that the double current of our national and mental activity should go on, that the British civilization and the French civilization should be maintained in this country and not that we should give the better half of the our continent to people who have nothing in common with us in history, nothing in common with us in blood, nothing in common with us in education or economics, nothing in commons

with us in national sentiment—to men who have come here, not
with our inherited pride in our own land, but with the purpose
only of making money. It was no part of the idea of the fathers
of confederation that these people should be gathered from the
ends of the earth and helped to come to this country, given such
inducements as to bring them here in such number that before
twenty years are over at the present rate of movement, they will
be masters of the country and the two races that have founded the
Canadian people will be swamped by the "intruders."[10]

The peremptory declarations of 1906 and 1907, even when they were
corrected or refuted in later years, would for decades sustain a strong
hostile sentiment towards Bourassa among leaders in the Jewish community. The *Canadian Jewish Times*, the publication of well-to-do Jews
in downtown Montreal, had reflected this perception starting in 1909,
before *Le Devoir* even came into existence.[11]

When the great orator set up his newspaper in 1910, Canadian
Jews did not hesitate to regard the new publication with suspicion,
despite the little interest he took in the Jewish presence in Montreal
in his editorials. During the federal election of 1911, the first in which
Le Devoir took part, the *Canadian Jewish Times* showed no reluctance in
reminding Jewish voters of Bourassa's earlier positions: "Lest the Jews
of this country should have forgotten what occurred in the Ottawa
House of Commons in March 1906, when expressions of sympathy
for our brethren in Russia...were made by members in the House
with one exception, and that, the utterance of Mr. Henri Bourassa."[12]
A number of Montreal's Jewish personalities, who were Liberal Party
supporters, took advantage of the opportunity to attack Bourassa and
the anti-Laurier positions adopted by his daily paper. Proof can be
found in this letter, released only a few days before the 1911 election,
and the following also cited by Michel Lévesque in his 2013 publication on the history of the Quebec Liberal Party:

> Every Jew in Canada ought to cast his vote against Bourassa's
> candidates, owing to the fact that Mr. Bourassa is a pronounced
> anti-Semite, and uses his paper "Le Devoir," whenever the occa-
> sion arises, to insult our people. I can send you, if you like, dozens
> of copies of the paper in which the most uncomplimentary things
> are said about Jews. If anything was required to show what Mr.
> Bourassa's views are, it is only necessary to read the enclosed

> copy of a speech delivered by him in the House of Commons at
> the time of the Russian massacres of 1906. This will show you
> what Mr. Bourassa is, and against it you can see what Sir Wilfrid
> Laurier said on the same occasion.[13]

Le Devoir had been in existence for less than two years and it had
already drawn bitter criticism from Samuel W. Jacobs,[14] the President
of the Baron de Hirsch Institute, a Montreal community organization
dedicated to the settlement of Eastern European Jewish immigrants.
On September 5, 1912, appalled by what he read in *Le Devoir*, Jacobs
wrote directly to Bourassa:

> I enclose for your perusal a clipping from yesterday's "Devoir,"
> and I am curious to learn if the publication of items of this kind
> meets with your approval. Do you think that any good purpose
> is served by insisting upon the religious belief of every Jewish
> petty offender against a civic By-law? You and your paper have
> made yourself the champions of the rights of the Roman Catholic
> minorities in this country, and you are constantly inveigh-
> ing against what you consider a violation of the rights of these
> minorities by the English-speaking and Protestant majority of
> this country. In this Province, the French Roman Catholics are in
> a majority, and it would appear as if, in many cases, you would
> have about the same regard for the feelings of the Jewish minority
> as the larger body of Protestants, according to you, have for the
> French-Canadians of other provinces.[15]

Jacob's scathing opinion was based on the fact that *Le Devoir* had vehemently attacked the Canadian immigration policy that was implemented in 1896 by the Laurier government and that was a source of
hope for Montreal's Jews at a time when major anti-Semite persecutions
were taking place in the Russian Empire. In addition, Bourassa was a
committed proponent of an anti-imperial policy that was contrary to
the sentiments of the Canadian Jewish elite, which was strongly influenced by British culture and origins. Jacobs was especially furious to
see that the newspaper published—unbeknownst to the editor—news
and reports depicting Montreal Jews in a rather negative light. It needs
to be noted that these spiteful articles appeared at the height of the
Beilis affair,[16] while the memory of the Kishinev pogroms[17] was still
fresh throughout the Eastern European diaspora. Jacobs undoubtedly

also feared *Le Devoir* would be inspired by the virulent anti-Semitic campaigns that had taken place in the wake of the infamous Dreyfus affair, which still had very noticeable echoes in 1912 in French political life. A few days later, on September 12, Jacobs again attacked Bourassa:

> How can you explain that from the first issue of the "Devoir," to the time I wrote you, scarcely an issue was published without some mean and contemptible reference to Jews?
>
> I have in my possession hundreds of clippings from the "Devoir" similar to the one I wrote you about, all written before "the new member of the staff was appointed"...
>
> You publish quite frequently long articles copied from the notorious Drumont's "Libre parole," holding our people up to scorn and hatred, the publication being with the object of spreading the vile calumnies against our people in this Province where the "Libre parole" does not circulate.[18]

This latent hostility towards *Le Devoir* probably reached its height during the vigorous campaign that the newspaper led, in 1917–1918, against Canada's participation in the First World War and, in particular, against compulsory conscription for service overseas. That position offended the patriotic mettle of the Canadian Jewish community, which was quite supportive of Great Britain's interests. In fact, the anti-Bourassa sentiments were clearly noticeable on both sides of the House of Commons in Ottawa. That was the case, for example, when a Conservative candidate in the federal election of 1917, Charles Ballantyne, circulated a tract in Yiddish in the riding of Saint-Laurent–Saint-Georges denouncing Bourassa and the Liberal Party in the following manner: "Jews, who are you going to vote for? For Ballantyne, Palestine and freedom or for Bourassa, anti-Semitism and slavery?"[19] Because of its French-Canadian nationalism, its militant Catholicism, and its defence of conservative social values, *Le Devoir* was perceived from the beginning as a daily profoundly hostile to the legitimate interests of Canada's Jewish population or, at least, far removed from its sensitivities and its aspirations. Towards the end of the 1920s and at the beginning of the 1930s, when signs of a new form of a more assertive anti-Semitism—in part motivated by Nazism in Germany—began to appear, there was a notable reconciliation between Bourassa and Jacobs.[20] On the one hand, this was due to the fact that as of 1925 the two men were both Members of Parliament in Ottawa and they had an opportunity to get to know each other better; and on the other hand, due to the fact that Bourassa had condemned in veiled terms Adrien Arcand's primitive anti-Semitism.[21] However, this late open mindedness was not enough to undo the impression, long implanted in the Montreal Jewish community, that *Le Devoir* was a publication easily liable to resort to anti-Semitism.

The Canadian Jewish Congress

It marked the end of an era when Bourassa left as head of the newspaper in August 1932. From that moment on, the great orator turned his attention entirely to Canadian politics and left journalism behind forever. A few months later, new events came at a tragic time to cast a shadow again on relations between the Canada's Jewish community and *Le Devoir*, by then headed by Georges Pelletier. In January 1933, Adolf Hitler was asked to become chancellor by the president of the Republic, Marshal Paul von Hindenburg. Once the Nazi leader was established as head of state, it marked the start of a merciless regime of terror, particularly towards German Jews, who were immediately targeted by the new National Socialist government. In the space of only a few weeks the violence in Germany against people of Jewish origin and their institutions increased to such an extent that the severe attacks became the subject of major reports in the international press. In Montreal, Canada's Jews were alarmed by this great upsurge of anti-Semitism, which led to their desire to protest publicly against the treatment of their co-religionists under Hitler's government. In March 1933, the community mobilized under the impetus of a number of prominent figures. A decision was then taken to reactivate an institution that had become inactive since the signing of the Treaty of Versailles and the years following the end of the First World War: the Canadian Jewish Congress (CJC). Among the leaders of the revived organization was one of its early activists, H.M. Caiserman. With his allies from unions and among workers, he organized a major public demonstration in Montreal aimed at denouncing the harsh conditions inflicted on German Jews. The event took place on April 6, 1933, in the Mount Royal arena. Numerous well-known political figures from both English Canada and French Canada took to the stage to express their concerns. The meeting was but one element of a broader program aimed at stimulating activism within a population faced with complex challenges, including the education of Canada's Jewish children, immigration and the reception of refugees, the battle against anti-Semitism in the country, and a desire to make the government in Ottawa aware of community objectives.

In order to mobilize Canada's Jewish population at a time when that population was subject to various political movements dispersed over a vast territory, CJC activists came up with the idea at the end of 1933 of launching a major funding and organization campaign intended to unite community forces. This bold project took the form of an "Emergency Call" signed[22] by Member of Parliament Samuel W. Jacobs and by Peter Bercovitch, a member of the Legislative Assembly in Quebec. The document explained in detail the reasons that motivated the Jewish leadership to take up the battle.[23] The fight against National Socialism in Germany by CJC leaders was accompanied by a desire to oppose the progress of Canadian anti-Semites. The latter often conveyed a message similar to that of the Nazis and attempted to infiltrate different groups in society. Among the documents circulated by the CJC was a text marked "Confidential," that contained a list of a number of Canadian organizations and publications considered hostile to Jews. Those responsible for drafting the infamous list had taken particular care to note that the situation was particularly worrisome in the province of Quebec where various newspapers disseminated clearly anti-Semitic messages that focused on the typical stereotypes respecting Judaism. These very insistent accusations related to *Le Patriote* and *Le Restaurateur*, two periodicals published by Adrien Arcand, the dailies *L'Action catholique* and *Le Journal*[24] in Quebec City, and *Le Devoir*—"A leading French-Canadian daily in Montreal, also distinctly anti-Semitic." The CJC not only sought to place *Le Devoir* in the category of publications clearly antagonistic to Jews, but its leaders promised to attack these newspapers through a systematic campaign to condemn them and target their financial position. The CJC in fact planned to launch "a campaign of education to discourage advertising in the anti-Semitic newspapers of Quebec."[25] And if that was not enough, the organization proposed implementing an economic boycott of the newspapers. As part of this effort, the CJC told Canada's Jews:

> We are particularly compelled to defend ourselves against the venomous campaign of "yellow" Jew-baiting journals in the Province of Québec. These journals and other organized groups are conducting an active and increasing propaganda amongst the

uneducated elements of our country, which threatens our peace and welfare.[26]

Le Devoir saw in these statements a declaration of war at a time when the newspaper was staggering under the persistent effects of the economic crisis and assaults from its political opponents in the provincial Liberal Party. During this period of serious financial hardship, the CJC's threat against the newspaper's advertising raised panic among leaders at *Le Devoir*, which was reflected in Omer Héroux's editorial. In the context, no one stopped to think that advertising paid by Canada's Jews, in fact, represented only a minute percentage of the daily's revenues. However, the threat was sufficient to create in the minds at the editorial board of *Le Devoir* the spectre of powerful Jewish action that would scuttle the daily's last hopes of survival. In brief, the "Emergency Call" of 1933 confirmed Héroux's worst apprehensions respecting the capability of Canada's Jews to silence their enemies and inflict exemplary punishment on them. In the space of a few days, *Le Devoir* was shaken by irrational fears that the press would be manipulated for ideological purposes:

> However, it must be seen and it must be noted that, for minds capable of reflection, Mr. Caiserman's declaration leads to very worrisome prospects. No one is unaware that the press—since the creation of cheap newspapers—to a large extent depends on the amount of its advertising revenues, since newspapers are very often sold at below cost. Without advertising, they would, in most cases, be constantly in debt....This results in a very great danger, which should be obvious to even the least interested, if they are willing to take a moment to give it some thought.[27]

There was also the fact that *Le Devoir's* editorial board, cut off from any sustained contact with the Jewish community leadership and absorbed in its own ethnocentric attitudes, had not taken into account the visceral reaction raised by the numerous texts appearing on the editorial page that were openly hostile to the interests of Canada's Jews. From the beginning of 1933, the newspaper had opposed the proclamation of an anti-defamation law in the Parliament of Quebec, tabled by none other than Peter Bercovitch. In addition, the newspaper, on several occasions, had made known its negative opinion regarding the immigration of Jewish refugees to the country.[28] During this period, *Le Devoir* had also promoted the movement called "buy from your own" and the observance of Sunday—supposedly violated by merchants of Jewish origin—and had commented extensively on a private commercial dispute about the management of the Maurice Pollack clothing store in Quebec.[29] In addition, there were many malicious references in a humour column on the front page of the newspaper under the pseudonym, Le Grincheux (the Grump), as well as a series of tendentious reports on small scale legal or political matters involving Jews. Héroux, especially, did not seem to understand the grievances of the CJC or the reasons that incited the organization to condemn a newspaper that on its editorial pages frequently attacked Jewish merchants in the working-class neighbourhoods of Montreal.[30] The criticism by Canada's Jewish leadership had the effect of a very brutal awakening:

> Where and when have we been anti-Semitic? Where and when have we taken a position that might be described as distinctly anti-Semitic? Is it anti-Semitic to suggest to French Canadians to have as much common sense as Jews and practise the mutual economic assistance that all other groups, starting with Jews, practise regularly, without having to talk or even think about it? Is it anti-Semitic simply to want to make one's own decisions, rather than being dictated to by the press or Jewish interests, regarding events in our country or abroad?[31]

In the circumstances, the leaders at *Le Devoir* were not the only ones to be dragged onto the convoluted paths of folly and hyperbole. The difficult context of 1933–1934 also weighed on the CJC, particularly when the time came to examine with a level head the anti-Semitic currents appearing in certain sectors of Quebec society. H.M. Caiserman and his colleagues, who at the time were caught up in new examples of hostility, also had difficulty in separating the wheat from the chaff. There was a world of difference between *Le Patriote* and *Le Devoir*, which the CJC activists, without a proper knowledge of the French language, were unable to distinguish. At an exceptionally grave time for German Jews, which raised long-term fears among Canada's Jewish population, the CJC leadership lacked objective parameters to assess the prevalent sentiments in Francophone Montreal. Héroux, who grasped perfectly the gulf that had grown between Adrien Arcand's crude and obstreperous anti-Semitic press and the press based on Catholic ethical principles, took the opportunity to complain about this bias in an editorial on February 3, 1934: "Therefore, the Jewish attack is aimed against us, as much as against *Le Patriote* or any other newspaper that may be virulently hostile to Jews."[32] Lack of understanding prevailed on both sides in a period where the political and economic climate was dominated by a general bitterness that was difficult to suppress. Furthermore, the condemnation which *Le Devoir* claimed made it a victim of the CJC seemed to have come out of nowhere at a time when the daily was struggling with extremely pressing financial commitments.

The "Emergency Call" affair in 1933 lasted a few weeks on the pages of *Le Devoir*, then slowly faded away. However, the confrontation did reveal the inability of the two sides to communicate with each other. At the time, this dispute was symptomatic of the broader context in which the relations between the nationalist elites of French Canada and the Jewish community leadership of Montreal were situated. There were new outbursts during the summer of 1935 when H.M. Caiserman wished to reply on *Le Devoir*'s pages to a correspondent defending "the buy from your own"[33] policy. For a few days, the CJC's Secretary-General drew significant reaction—supposedly from unbiased readers—but the controversy never reached the editorial pages. In the end, Caiserman dropped the issue when he realized it was like confronting very well-armed opponents in an endless maze. In an internal CJC document, Caiserman wrote: "I am called upon to discuss in a language which I (love but) do not (fully) master, with a whole group of trained (and capable) French (Canadian) journalists."[34] In the same document, the CJC Secretary-General gave his own definition of anti-Semitism. The definition showed that by the mid-1930s, the CJC Secretary-General had begun to make a distinction which would have been very useful a few months earlier:

> And I have never called Anti-Semitism—the endeavour of French Canada to strengthen its national, religious, cultural and economic bonds. What I have called and do call Anti-Semitism is every calculated misrepresentation of the Jew, every false statement about him which is so published that it brings prejudice to his interests; in one word, I call Anti-Semitism Jew-baiting if done by professional scribes like the demented *"Le Patriote* gang" or by uninformed persons who are engaging in Jew-baiting.[35]

It is probable that the latter group mentioned in this paragraph, the "uninformed persons," is a reference to writers in *Le Devoir* and other Francophone newspapers close to the Catholic church. It is also possible that Caiserman at this time started to develop more sustained relations with certain liberal-minded figures among the clergy and French-language elites and that his attitude became more nuanced.[36]

In September 1935, the proclamation of the Nuremberg laws significantly worsened the life of the Jewish population in Germany. This was followed in November 1938, by a broad-scale pogrom now known as Kristallnacht. At the end of the decade, the situation of Jewish minorities was desperate throughout Central Europe and thousands of people sought to flee the continent to escape merciless persecution. These European events in conjunction with the expressions of hostility by Canadian spokespersons with fascist sympathies, put immense pressure on the leaders of the CJC. In essence, Jews in the country watched helplessly as hopes for survival of their European co-religionists deteriorated, while the Canadian government took a position of indifference and of "wait and see.[37] In the circumstances, the negative position taken by *Le Devoir* was perceived with bitterness by the CJC activists, especially since they were battling with all their energy to be heard by their Canadian compatriots. On several occasions during the second half of the 1930s, *Le Devoir* declared its opposition to the immigration of European refugees; it expressed negative views regarding cultural and religious diversity in Montreal and advocated discriminatory measures against merchants of Jewish origin. With respect to Judaism in particular, *Le Devoir*'s editorialists displayed narrow-mindedness and let themselves be influenced by negative myths that were widespread in the West. These peremptory assertions, devoid of nuance, eventually resulted in creating a certain hopelessness that comes through very clearly in the documents produced by the CJC in the mid-1930s and that, at the same time, reflected the community leadership's inability to weave ties with any of Montreal's foremost Francophone nationalist press.

This profound dismay and the numerous examples of indifference, even of hostility, gathered by H.M. Caiserman regarding French-speaking elements close to the Catholic church even now constitute a damning portrait that shocks the imagination. The CJC leadership had to wait until the end of the Second World War and the beginning of the 1950s for a new and more positive climate to be established between Montreal's Jewish population and the main representatives of French Canada. This notable improvement in inter-community relations occurred when more sustained contacts were developed between the CJC and certain Francophone university and religious milieus. Numerous Montreal Jews and Catholic intellectuals actively contributed to this development, notably with the establishment of *le Cercle juif de langue française*.[38] At the beginning of the 1950s, the tone of the CJC had changed completely:

> Although the group [le Cercle juif de langue française] was formed for purely cultural purposes and has served a very useful purpose in this connection, it has become a tribune and a platform on which educated and serious Jewish and French-Canadian citizens of this country meet at regular intervals. Friendships which have thus been formed served the [Jewish] community well.
>
> Instances of anti-Semitism among French Canadians have remained quite rare. Indeed, in terms of actual cases of hostile acts or cases such as this committee deals with from time to time, we have had scarcely any occasion to take any up in recent months although such cases involving English-speaking Canadians.[39]

The CJC's tribulations during the period immediately preceding the beginning of the Second World War, nevertheless, had left a profound mark on the institutions that maintained the collective memory of Canadian Jews. Notable in this regard were Francophone publications that had expressed anti-Semitism at that time on their pages. For present-day researchers the difficulty in gaining access to texts written in the French-language press during the 1930s, or to understand the context in which they were produced, at times increased the impression of ideological confrontation and of verbal violence that emerged from this period of Canadian Jewish history. This perception was amplified upon examination of the contribution of the most important nationalist newspaper of French Canada, *Le Devoir*, whose prestige and undeniable scope of view rendered it even more guilty according to the Jewish observers of the period. These Jewish community archives, created with great care—which, furthermore, are very valuable in assessing the views of the leadership of institutions—are also the source of descriptions of *Le Devoir* that characterize most of the works of Canadian Jewish history published over the last fifty years or more regarding *Le Devoir*.[40] This ingrained cultural heritage, which is both perceptive and documentary, raises a

fundamental problem that we shall now address by taking a different approach. In short, is there another way of judging the position
of *Le Devoir* that takes into account Jewish community sensitivity,
which was greatly exacerbated during this period, and at the same
time provides an objective analysis of the texts published in the
newspaper from 1910 to 1947?

Le Devoir's Editorial Stance on Jews

After a close reading of all editorials appearing in the newspaper for the
period under study, and according to our methodological criteria, we
were able to conclude that between 1910 and 1947 *Le Devoir* published
209 editorials devoted in varying degrees to Judaism. That constituted
1.88% of all the daily's editorials in the space of a little over 37 years, or
approximately one editorial every two months during 446 months (see
Appendix 1 for the full list of 209 editorials). In these editorials, 106
contained negative connotations or a tendency to describe the Jewish
population in Canada or elsewhere in the world in an unfavourable
light. That figure represents about 1% of the total number of editorials
in *Le Devoir*, or one-half of those devoted to Judaism. In this context,
can it be asserted that the prevalence (to borrow a term from the field
of science) of an idea or a subject on the pages of a daily newspaper
takes on particular significance? Is this notion of frequency and of repetition valid in the case of a negative perception, as in the case of anti-
Semitism, that may be deemed detrimental in one way or another to
the targeted individuals or communities? In short, at this stage of the
analysis, can a conclusion be drawn that would have general interpre-
tative value respecting the phenomenon studied? In my opinion, this
depends to a large extent on the historical context in which the hostile opinions respecting Jews were published on the editorial pages of
Le Devoir; or, more precisely, how frequently they were mentioned in
the historical framework examined. The information collected shows
Judaism did not constitute a consistent subject in the newspaper
and that other concerns clearly took editorial precedence, such as
how Canadian federalism functioned, French-Canadian nationalism,
Francophone minorities in Canada, defence of the French language,
and the maintenance of Catholic heritage. In various circumstances,
British imperialism, the fight against unemployment, conscription for
service overseas, and the bilingual schools crisis in Ontario were the
subjects of intense focus in the daily at specific times during the years

from 1910 to 1947. For each of these subjects considered separately, *Le Devoir*'s editorialists wrote hundreds of editorials.

Before classifying Jewish subjects in *Le Devoir* within a chronological framework covering nearly four decades, it is important to situate certain historical markers. The first noteworthy event is the founding of *Le Devoir*, in January 1910, which corresponds almost exactly to the beginning of the large Eastern European Jewish immigration to Canada. Starting with the Russian insurrection of 1905, several thousand immigrants of Jewish origin and Yiddish culture arrived every year in the country by sea. They headed in massive numbers to three cities: Montreal, Toronto, and Winnipeg. This migratory influx, the largest in Canadian Jewish history, lasted until the First World War and led, for the first time in the Quebec metropolis, to the emergence of a Jewish community that could be clearly seen and heard.[41] By 1911, when *Le Devoir* celebrated its first birthday, 30,000 people of Jewish origin had settled in Montreal, making it the largest concentration of Jews anywhere in Canada. Twenty years later, in 1931—just before Bourassa's sudden departure from *Le Devoir*— the Jewish population in the city had doubled to nearly 60,000 souls, mainly recent immigrants who earned their living from small businesses or in clothing factories located near Sainte-Catherine Street and Saint-Laurent Boulevard. These new arrivals raised crucial questions in a Quebec society divided primarily between Francophone Catholics and Anglophone Protestants: this was the case in education, where there was no legal basis to receive the children of Jewish immigrants.[42] Similarly, Yiddish speakers were excluded from large French-language charitable, political, and cultural networks because of their religion. They had little contact with French Canadians, except when some members of the two groups mingled at a factory or in public places. In Montreal, however, Jews established their own community structures, which reflected their cultural and religious identity. As of 1907, they had, among other things, access to a Yiddish-language press and very active union organizations.

Since Eastern European Jews had just recently settled in Montreal and constituted, from the year 1910 onward, the main immigrant community in the city, they represented a kind of radical difference from the perspective of many French-Canadian observers. This sentiment was further accentuated by the fact that Yiddish speakers were the first non-Christian community wishing to establish themselves in Montreal society, where Catholicism was considered an integral part of Francophone identity. From that situation to judging that the Jews presented a "problem" or that their presence raised fundamental issues in the context of French-Canadian nationalism, was but a short step that many observers of the time had no reluctance in taking. This was the case of journalists and editorialists at *Le Devoir* who felt compelled to comment on the Jewish presence around them. The situation was made even more difficult by the widespread perception that small Jewish merchants from Eastern Europe represented unfair competition against French-Canadian merchants because they achieved domination through dubious business practices. This negative impression was reinforced when the Depression hit Montreal and Canada, impoverishing a large portion of the population. The tension was exacerbated by the opposition of many Francophone nationalists—including those at *Le Devoir*—to international immigration, as they believed that the new citizens would destroy Montreal's fragile demographic balance and threaten the political weight of French Canada in the whole country. Before the Second World War, *Le Devoir* took no interest in the integration of the many immigrants of Catholic faith from Ukraine, Germany, and Italy; furthermore, it demonstrated a near-complete rejection of any attempt by foreigners to settle in the metropolis. The Eastern European Jews, as well as those coming from Central Europe, were especially disadvantaged in these circumstances, since they were perceived by *Le Devoir* as age-old city dwellers, inapt for work on the land and incapable of becoming members of a Francophone society still turned towards its agricultural past. Like many of their immigrant compatriots of other religions, the followers of Judaism were also described on the pages of the newspaper as people impossible to assimilate, who would soon incite xenophobic reactions and were liable to bring the political tensions of Europe to Canada.

Despite this somber summary, *Le Devoir* did display a certain kind of discretion in contrast to other Montreal publications focussing on the Jewish issue, including first and foremost the newspapers published by the duo of Arcand and Ménard. During the period from 1910 to 1947, *Le Devoir* never departed from the polite and respectful language that it used in treating all subjects. Despite disagreements and significant differences in perception, the editorialists never resorted under any pretext to disdainful or obscene language towards their counterparts of Jewish religion. This was also the case during the bitter dispute that started in January 1934 between *Le Devoir* and the

Canadian Jewish Congress. During the entire episode, Omer Héroux maintained an entirely honorable high tone and language in address-ing his Jewish counterparts:

> At last we officially know what we are dealing with! We know who to speak to! We at first received only a partial response from Mr. Jacobs, Mr. Bercovitch et al. The Secretary-General of the Canadian Jewish Congress, Mr. H.M. Caiserman, on their behalf, stated to us that these gentlemen take responsibility for the *Emergency Call* bearing their name (a copy of all these docu-ments with a French translation was published in *Le Devoir* last January 18). However, he neglected to say if these gentlemen sim-ilarly take responsibility for the document marked Confidential, that appears very logically and very integrally linked to this *Emergency Call*, which seems to be developed from and comple-mentary to the Confidential document: he neglected to tell us if they approve or disapprove of the document.[43]

In all circumstances, *Le Devoir* maintained exemplary patience and disciplined reasoning. Furthermore, at no time during this period did the newspaper refer to notorious anti-Semitic documents or crude stereotypes of Judaism. Even if Georges Pelletier and Omer Héroux seemed to believe in the excessive power of Jews in the world press and finances, *Le Devoir*'s editorial pages never mentioned "the pro-tocols of the elders of Zion" or wrote a single word aimed at con-firming the myth of ritual murder. Similarly, nowhere were there ever any defamatory remarks concerning the supposed treachery in the Talmud towards Christians, nor the kind of abundant degrading allu-sions found in the works of the Tharaud brothers, published in France in the guise of objective ethnography and patriotism. Such writings, despite being present in Quebec in the publications of the Church[44] and during the Plamondon trial of 1913–1914,[45] did not appear on the editorial pages of *Le Devoir*. The Dreyfus affair was not used either as a significant political reference or as a means to judge the conduct of Canada's Jews. Except for using documents on Jewish immigra-tion to Canada at the beginning of the 1930s that were of dubious origin, as a general rule *Le Devoir* was in possession of reliable and complete information and its editorialists were well-informed on the political situation in Europe, including on German Judaism. The shortcoming at the newspaper was that its editors maintained very limited relations with leading members of Montreal's Jewish community (except for Bourassa at the end of his tenure), with the result that they were incapable of crossing, even briefly, the imposing linguistic and denominational barrier separating Jews and French Canadians. As they developed in relatively separate worlds, the two groups progressed on roads that did not intersect.

The Situation of Jews in Germany

Let us return for a moment to a quantitative analysis of the editorials published in *Le Devoir* on the subject of Jews and Judaism. When the 209 editorials are projected chronologically over the period between 1910 and 1947, a very clear structural tendency emerges, which takes on significance in the evolution of the subject being discussed on the pages of the daily (see Diagram 1). The majority of the texts chosen, more precisely 160 (or 76% of the total), were published when Georges Pelletier was editor of *Le Devoir*, compared to only 49 when the newspaper was under the responsibility of Henri Bourassa. Out of the 106 editorials that expressed negative connotations or fundamental reticence towards Jews, 87 (or 82%) were written while Pelletier held the position of director. These figures indicate clearly that the recurrence of the Jewish theme was inversely proportional to Bourassa's influence at the head of *Le Devoir*. Until 1919, Bourassa played a major role in the ideological orientation of his newspaper and during this nine-year period, *Le Devoir* addressed the subject only three times in editorials.[46] From 1919 to Bourassa's re-election to the House of Commons

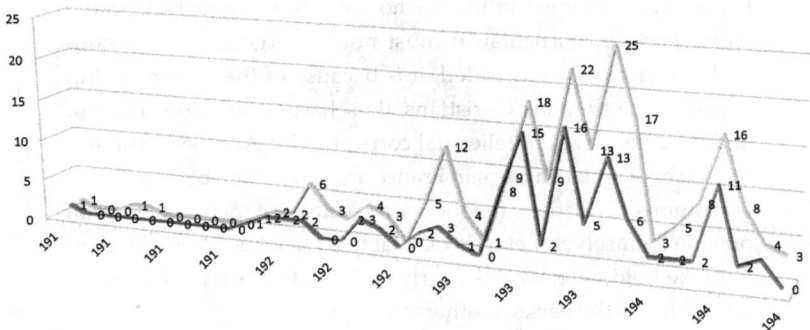

Diagram 1
Le Devoir—Number of editorials per year on the subject of Jews, 1910–1947
Negative references and total references

in November 1925, a period during which he distanced himself increasingly from his newspaper, the editorial pages addressed the issue of Judaism seventeen times. From 1926 to 1932—that is, until Bourassa resigned from his daily—*Le Devoir* took up the subject twenty-nine times, which was more often than during the first sixteen years of the newspaper's existence. Bourassa himself took an interest in Jews and Judaism only five times[47] in his entire career as editorial-ist and only twice made that the principal subject of the editorial. The most significant text in this sequence appeared on July 26, 1924. It was a detailed commentary on a volume by the abbot, Édouard-Valmore Lavergne, *Sur les remparts*, published the same year in Quebec City.[48] In this plea in support of a Catholic-inspired press, which in fact was a veiled criticism of Abbot Lavergne's essay, Bourassa challenged the Church's traditional position on Judaism and warned *Le Devoir*'s read-ers that it was not appropriate to resort to anti-Semitism to promote Christian faith or French-Canadian nationalism. This was the conse-quence of an evolution in Bourassa's thinking, based on his religious education influenced by anti-Semitism, but which had been the object of a long moral reflection before he questioned this teaching:

> Certainly, there are detestable and dangerous Jews and it is also true that the international leanings of the race, its financial power, its control of the press—due to the venality of too many Christians—increases the power of that class of Jews tenfold for evil and social upheaval. However, it is not true that all Jews or even a majority of them are like that. The bitter truth is that there are huge numbers of people of all races and every belief, including alas some Catholics who have no more merit than the worst Jews. In particular, it must not be forgotten that if anti-social Jewry is to be dreaded, it is because of the weakness and cowardice of so many Christians, their haste to swallow any bait and their moral and intellectual corruptibility. Anti-Semitism has caused enormous damage in France and elsewhere because it has accustomed Christians to look for the causes of their degradation outside themselves. Let us hope that this mistaken mentality does not take hold here; we are overly inclined to place the blame for our faults on the backs of others.[49]

Furthermore, the Jewish theme in *Le Devoir* was not prevalent during the period of large immigration at the beginning of the twentieth century which lasted, with the exception of the years of the First World War, from 1904 to 1925. As the number of Jews of Eastern European origin increased at a steady pace in the country, *Le Devoir* published only scattered comments on its editorial pages on the situation and condemned immigration in general, without going into detail. Everything continued as if the very obvious growth of the Montreal Yiddish speaking community had no effect on *Le Devoir*'s editorial board or that it did not attract the editorialists' interest. The editorials with a Jewish theme in *Le Devoir* during the years after 1910 and at the beginning of the 1920s made merely marginal references about Judaism within broader issues such as financial credit, public education, health, urban development, and Montreal's municipal administration. Other texts of a similar nature looked at Palestine and cultural life in Paris. During this period lasting nearly twenty years, Georges Pelletier mentioned the presence of new Jewish-origin arrivals among the masses entering Canada only three times[50] and then only in passing. This attitude was clearly visible, for example, in an editorial from the month of August 1910 that looks at the dealings between the Baron de Hirsch Institute and a private company:

> What have we received in return from the Company [the North Atlantic Trading Co, from 1904 to 1906], for this $403,245? Approximately 80,600 immigrants, from Russia, Germany, Austria-Hungary, Italy, Galicia and Turkey; there was no shortage of Jews, they are an indispensable part of this private immigration. Most of these people arrive here from European regions where poverty, misery and physical and intellectual degeneration have always existed for centuries.[51]

The reverse of the observation above is also true. The largest number of editorials relating to the Jewish presence in Montreal and elsewhere in the world are found in the years when immigration in general was nearly non-existent. From 1934 to 1939, when the borders of the country, for all practical purposes, were closed to the influx of immigrants, regardless of where they came from, *Le Devoir* published 104 editorials examining themes linked to the Jewish issue from various angles. Over a period of five years, this represented nearly half of the corpus analyzed in the present study. The same situation was repeated a few years later, from 1942 to 1944, when the hostilities in Europe rendered any travel across the Atlantic extremely difficult.

During that time, thirty-two editorials can be found in just three years that examine various aspects of Jewish life in Canada or in Europe. This sudden increase on the subject of Jews in *Le Devoir*'s writings, particularly in a negative tone and an anti-Semitic tendency, occurred when the newspaper was under the direction of Georges Pelletier and the country was suffering under the harsh conditions resulting from a dramatic economic slow-down. The stock market crash of 1929 and its long-term international consequences—events that could not easily be blamed on Canada's Jews alone—disrupted the editorial agenda of *Le Devoir*. Consequently, it was forced to take an interest in new subjects, including the fight against unemployment, public health, and the actions of large economic monopolies. The material hardship of families, the endlessly growing number of jobless, and the fear of foreigners convinced many Canadians at that time to oppose immigration. Similarly, French Quebec did not escape the broad impact of the political tensions in Central Europe and the spectre of another world war, which motivated the rise of isolationism in international relations. *Le Devoir*, also caught up in this toxic situation, during the 1930s advocated closing the borders, establishing a foreign policy defending only Canadian interests, and implementing measures to stimulate the economy. Why was the stance towards Jews and Judaism so important in these specific circumstances?

Diagram 1 shows four significant and clearly defined moments regarding editorials of a negative tone published in *Le Devoir*: 15 in 1934, 16 in 1936, 13 in 1938, and 11 in 1943. These 55 hostile texts reflect a strong focus in circumstances that are otherwise not very noteworthy and are not a sign of any kind of long-term coherence. The concentrated writings indicate the precise moment when a particular issue linked to Judaism or Jewish presence raised fundamental objections on the pages of the newspaper and motivated an attitude with anti-Semitic connotations repeatedly over a short period of time. Taken one by one, these anti-Judaic outbursts in the life of *Le Devoir* do indicate the presence of a systematic attitude. Three of these sudden anti-Semitic outbursts are very closely linked to the situation of Judaism in Germany, namely those of 1934, 1938, and 1943. A fourth one, that of 1936, is associated with the fall of Louis-Alexandre Taschereau's provincial government and with the fraudulent electoral machinations in Montreal of a Liberal Member of the Legislature of Jewish origin, Joseph Cohen.

The matter merits closer examination. In 1934, the writings in *Le Devoir* focused on Hitler taking power and its consequences for Canada; in 1938, the newspaper took an interest mainly in the Kristallnacht pogrom and what it meant for the fate of Jews in Germany; in 1943 it became aware of the Holocaust in Eastern Europe, a genocide that was planned and carried out by the Nazis in collaboration with some of the local populations. Each time the issue of concern expressed in *Le Devoir* was the possible immigration to the country of Jewish refugees and of victims of persecution, which circumstances in Central and Eastern Europe made more probable. In 1934, the dominant Jewish subjects on *Le Devoir's* pages were the "buy from your own" policy, the creation of the Canadian Jewish Congress, and more peripherally, respect for the Sunday law. Four years later, in 1938, the threat of war, the Czechoslovakian crisis, the persecution of Jews in Germany and the tensions in Palestine were front and centre in the news. Finally, in 1943, *Le Devoir* turned its attention to the massacres in Eastern Europe and the desperate situation of Jewish refugees in the Old World.

Le Devoir on three occasions — 1934, 1938 and 1943 — firmly rejected the possibility of Canada serving as a haven to European Jews who, each time, were exposed to extremely serious risks. While this position was not new on *Le Devoir's* editorial pages, it took on a tragic aspect after the ascension to power of the National Socialist regime in Germany, bent as it was on annihilating European Judaism. In February 1934, when German Jews were openly subjected to increasingly severe policies of harassment and spontaneous demonstrations of violence, Omer Héroux wrote:

> Do not talk to us at all of immigration right now! Wait until Canada has taken care of its jobless! Do not bring people here who would prevent our own people from taking their place in the economic life of the nation and whose presence would force them to wander again in search of work that keeps disappearing! ... Whatever care Canada's Jews wish to give the German Jews and we are certain that they will provide all possible assistance, this will not change the fact they will be settling in a country where hundreds of thousands of natives [sic] are seeking work in vain. If Jewish solidarity does succeed in finding them a suitable place, will it not be, as a general rule, directly or indirectly detrimental to those who already live in the country?[52]

What, then, were the reasons given for that rejection? First, it was the difficult economic situation and the high unemployment rate, in addition to the limited capacity of Canadian society to absorb immigrants. Added to these rational and obvious arguments were objections based more on perception. The German Jews were considered to be difficult to assimilate and to present a risk to national unity; furthermore, they had no agricultural experience and would imperil the French fact in the country. It might as well be said, *Le Devoir* warned, that they will never be able to join the ranks of Catholic French Canada. Their massive arrival would provoke an outburst of anti-Semitism — which meant blaming the newcomers for prejudices already existing in the country — and would lead to bringing the political and racial feuds of Europe to Canada. In addition, the supposed arrogance of Jews and their financial power in the world also constituted a serious problem for *Le Devoir*, as a decisive confrontation was taking shape in Germany. Pelletier asked, why become mixed up in a conflict that in no way concerned Canada and was the product of the Old World's political instability? The fact that the persecutions were becoming more severe and the Jewish population was desperately seeking support from abroad, changed nothing. Even the news of the violent acts committed during Kristallnacht, broadcast throughout the world by the international press, did not have an impact on *Le Devoir*'s determination, as demonstrated by the following excerpt from an editorial by Georges Pelletier published a few days after the pogrom:

> On the other hand, the keenest sentiment of compassion, hatred of the anti-Semite practices of the Führer and his entourage and the sincerest sympathy cannot serve as an excuse for anyone claiming to be reasonable and sensible in Canada and beyond, to demand that the borders of a young country be opened wide, without restrictions, to foreigners fleeing their land of birth and seeking asylum and refuge elsewhere.[53]

At the end of the 1930s, when the fate of German and Eastern European Jews continued to be under threat, few people in Canada foresaw that the dynamics of the persecution undertaken by the Nazis would result in an unprecedented genocide. No one at *Le Devoir*, starting with Georges Pelletier, realized the price that would soon be paid by the refusal to accept people threatened by extermination. There was also the fact that *Le Devoir*'s editor, like the Prime Minister of Canada and the Prime Minister of Great Britain, was a firm believer in peace negotiations with Hitler. In 1938, Pelletier's wish was for discussions to continue among the European powers in order to avoid another military conflagration, in which Canada would inevitably participate. To protest against the fate of German Jews, would it not raise the ire of the National Socialist regime and incite it to war? Similarly, to receive the Jewish victims of Nazism in Canada, would it not risk displeasing those who have chased them out of their own country? The claims of neutrality expressed by Pelletier regarding the tense political situation in the Old World and his isolationist discourse also contributed greatly to the newspaper ignoring the fate of Jewish refugees.[54] Even the Sudeten Germans of Christian faith who opposed Hitler at the end of 1938 received no sympathy from *Le Devoir*. The attitude of Pelletier and his colleagues remained unchanged in the summer of 1942, when *Le Devoir* and all the allied governments received the terrible news of the deliberate massacre in Eastern Europe of hundreds of thousands of Jews. The information regarding the ongoing genocide, which was clearly presented on the editorial pages of *Le Devoir*,[55] did not shake the daily's determination in opposing the acceptance of new refugees to the country, despite the cruel and tragic consequences of the Nazi Holocaust. *Le Devoir* remained true until the end to the principles that guided its founding in 1910; its position remained steadfast in the face of repeated demands by Canada's Jewish community to accept Jewish refugees, as demonstrated by this paragraph from an editorial of June 1943:

> The concern of the Canadian Jewish Congress for their co-religionists abroad and the Prime Minister's concern for the victims and the refugees of the war in general are understandable. However, that must not make us lose sight of and must not prevent us from seeing that we have here in this country, among our own people, in the Canadian population residing in Canada, victims of the war and refugees of the war in sufficiently great numbers that it constitutes a major social problem....
>
> It is all well and good to care for the victims and refugees of the war from other countries than our own and bring refugees from elsewhere to Canada. However, it would certainly be more appropriate to begin with our own victims and our own refugees of the war. Appropriate charity begins at home...[56]

It is important to note that this position was not based on any sympathy on the part of *Le Devoir* toward German fascism, which would

have convinced it to endorse the National Socialist regime in all matters. By 1935, *Le Devoir* had already condemned Hitler's regime in
very explicit terms.[57] Pelletier restated this opinion without hesitation
at the end of 1937 during a tour of continental Europe. This clearly
expressed rejection was influenced in part by the Nazi persecution of
Catholic institutions, underlined in more doctrinal terms by a Papal
encyclical in March 1937,[58] and in part by the extreme censorship
imposed on the press in Germany. In this categoric repudiation by
Le Devoir, the violence inflicted on Jews in Europe played only a negligible part. The fact is that the editorialists at *Le Devoir* realized well
before the start of the Second World War that Hitler's actions, aimed
at suppressing any independent opinions, were contrary to the ide-
als of political liberalism developed from British parliamentary tradition. Pelletier and Héroux knew also that the Church, to which the
newspaper was very attached, was being destroyed by Nazi repres-
sion and that the concordat signed with Rome in July 1933 had not
been respected. If the newspaper showed little eagerness to facilitate
the immigration of German Jews to Canada, and if its editorialists
at times displayed obstinate anti-Semitic prejudices, it must not be
thought that this was because they sympathized with the German
dictatorship. The antagonism toward Jews, in one form or another,
was not necessarily a sign of established extreme right-wing thought
having convinced *Le Devoir* to support fascism in the Old World. The
source of the anti-Jewish sentiment expressed particularly after 1934
in the daily founded by Bourassa was to be found elsewhere, such as
in essentially doctrinaire Catholic teaching and the right-wing press
in France.

Taschereau and the Provincial Election of 1935

There remains the series of editorials published in 1936, which was
an example of a very significant spike in *Le Devoir* and which was just
as full of anti-Semitism as the three other series we have just examined. This time, attention was not focused on international immigration, but rather on the political scene in Quebec. On November 25,
1935, despite extensive accusations of political corruption and administrative fraud, the Liberal Premier, Louis-Alexandre Taschereau, was
returned to power following a stormy general election. During the
campaign preceding the vote, there were acts of violence and massive
fraud, particularly in Montreal. *Le Devoir* published damning reports

about certain candidates and the methods advocated by some very active Liberal supporters. In several editorials, Pelletier and Héroux persisted in discrediting the Taschereau regime in the eyes of the electorate and in revealing its many faults, including the fact that it had lost the moral stature required of a government in a democracy.[59] The campaign waged by *Le Devoir* against the Liberals contained condemnations of a severity rarely seen on the newspaper's pages. Among the Liberal members of the legislature were two individuals of Jewish origin, Peter Bercovitch and Joseph Cohen, who, for several years, had been the targets of the scurrilous press led by Adrien Arcand. Bercovitch, who had been elected in every election since 1916 in the riding of Montréal-Saint-Louis, was a respected and irreproachable figure that *Le Devoir* refrained from attacking. The story was completely different in the case of Joseph Cohen, who had represented the electors in the neighbouring riding of Montréal-Saint-Laurent since 1927. Journalists at *Le Devoir* tracked Cohen's every move during the election campaign of November 1935 and reported every detail of the many frauds that he committed in pursuit of his re-election, including perjury, vote-rigging, physical intimidation, and the infamous use of "telegrams."[60]

Le Devoir took the opportunity to make Joseph Cohen the symbol of the disgrace befitting the Liberal regime, because of its dubious electoral tactics and for the way in which it deliberately broke the law to ensure its victory. A press campaign began immediately following the election, to condemn the dishonest means used by Cohen to achieve his objective. The reports extended over several weeks and contained numerous insinuations respecting the cultural origins of the member, his mother tongue, Yiddish,[61] and the complicity of Montreal's "Israelites" who were overly zealous in supporting one of their own.[62] An example of the malicious allusions was the labelling of the member with the first name "Josef,"[63] to make him appear more Jewish and to point a finger at the entire Jewish community. The affair created such a backlash that the CJC felt it necessary to issue a press release on December 1935—reprinted in *Le Devoir*—in which the organization condemned all illegal electoral practices, regardless of the identity of the guilty parties or their objectives:

> Our attention has been drawn to the fact that following the recent elections, statements have been made in the press and on platforms condemning particularly certain flagrant irregularities

and certain illegal acts that have been committed. Furthermore, an erroneous impression has been created that tends to link the Jewish community to these alleged illegal practices, a clearly erroneous impression that we believe it to be our duty to correct.

Along with all our fellow citizens, we condemn all irregular, dishonest or illegal procedures or acts during elections, regardless of where or by whom they may have been committed and we join them in proposing the adoption of means to ensure proper election campaigns and clean elections.[64]

The already tense situation became even worse in May 1936, when Bercovitch had to defend the Taschereau government in the Legislature during hearings of the Public Accounts Committee, where the Duplessis opposition accused the regime of using State property for personal use and giving unjustified preference to its supporters. The public in attendance, disgusted by the spectacle of corruption, shouted down Bercovitch and attacked him openly for his Jewish origins.[65] In the heat of the moment, it did not take much to link the moral collapse of the Taschereau regime and its fraudulent machinations to the two individuals identified with the Jewish community of Montreal, whereas many of the profiteering and corrupt individuals had obviously French-Canadian–sounding names. Le Devoir did not avoid the tendency and, from January to July 1936, published thirteen scathing editorials about the "Cohen affair" and the part played by the member for Montréal-Saint-Laurent in the Taschereau regime's descent into the underworld. The editorials, with an equal number written by both Pelletier and Héroux, placed heavy emphasis on the guilt of Cohen, who was eventually forced to resign his seat at the beginning of July. That incident came on the eve of a new general election which was held on August 17, 1936, in the absence of Taschereau, who had also resigned. A very clear impression emerges from these editorials: the unsavoury machinations that were deployed during the course of the preceding months were essentially matters associated with Jews. Consequently, it was thought that the removal of individuals of that origin from Quebec's political life would likely result in a distinct improvement of the situation. In Le Devoir, the whole issue was described as if the massive fraud of November 1935 was the fault of electors in the riding of Montréal-Saint-Laurent, and that the unacceptable conduct was the responsibility of Joseph Cohen, their representative in the Legislative Assembly. Pelletier even went so far as to

threaten the Jewish community itself with reprisals, as if the ills erod-
ing Quebec democracy emanated essentially from its ranks:

> Prominent members of the Israelite colony in Montreal con-
> veyed their regrets to *Le Devoir* for what happened in November
> in those two ridings. If that should be repeated—those honest
> people must be able to maintain orderly elections—and they do
> not remove right from the start those who, last autumn, as we
> know, used treachery and firearms to benefit the Cohens and the
> Plantes, *it will cost them dearly, very dearly*. They must give that
> some thought, they must act and protect themselves. *This must
> not in any way be repeated, if Jewish voters want to keep the privileges
> they now have.*[66]

Jewish Immigration from Europe

Other data allows us to understand better how Judaism and the Jewish
presence in Canada was covered on the editorial pages of *Le Devoir*
during the years from 1910 to 1947. We found that in most cases the
newspaper wrote about the issue in passing, within a broader topic,
for example, the economic situation of Francophones, the status of
the French language in the federal government, or public health in
Montreal. Often, the reference would be brief and of no particular significance, a sentence or a short paragraph, which was part of longer
review where there was no mention of issues related to individuals of
Jewish origin. There were, however, certain cases where *Le Devoir* considered it appropriate to publish a major editorial devoted entirely to
a Jewish theme and that would treat an issue closely associated with
Judaism. These editorials are easy to find, since most of them have
a title containing a recognizable Jewish issue such as anti-Semitism,
Palestine, international immigration, or the name of an individual
closely identified with Judaism in the minds of readers. In other cases,
the word "Jew" was placed prominently in one way or another to
indicate the subject of the editorial, as in the case of the dispute in 1934
regarding the Canadian Jewish Congress or when the persecutions
became more severe in Nazi Germany. Over a period of thirty-seven
years, sixty-six editorials of this nature were published in *Le Devoir*
and they closely reflected the concentration previously described
for the entire corpus of editorials (see Diagram 2). For example, in
1930, the daily published seven major editorials devoted exclusively

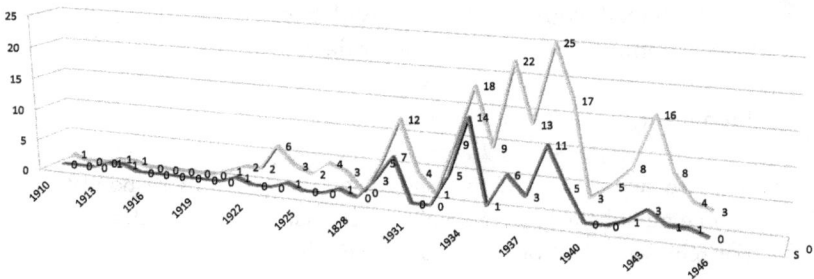

Diagram 2
Le Devoir—Number of editorials per year on Jewish subjects, 1910–1947
Major references and total references

to a Jewish subject compared to fourteen in 1934, six in 1936, eleven in 1938 and three in 1943. If we exclude 1930 from this summary since it did not have any central or identifiable subjects, the majority of editorials of 1934 were about Jewish immigration, the Canadian Jewish Congress and "buy from your own;" those of 1936 about the political corruption of Taschereau and his Member of the Legislative Assembly, Joseph Cohen; and those of 1938 about the consequences of the Kristallnacht pogrom in Germany. As for the editorials of 1943, they were focused on Jewish immigration to Canada and events connected with the Holocaust.

Of these 66 main editorials, 24 (or 36%) had an essentially factual or statistical content and consequently did not lead to any negative or unfavourable perceptions. On the other hand, 42 editorials were composed of arguments tending to prove that Jews or Judaism exercised a negative influence on Canadian society or in the world. Obviously, a total of 42 editorials does not represent an imposing mass of texts or opinions in a newspaper published daily over decades. The concentration and repetition of hostile writings at very specific times in *Le Devoir*'s history during a short period, however, does indicate that the newspaper's leaders deliberately expressed anti-Semitic views in certain significant circumstances. For example, between 1934 and 1943, *Le Devoir*'s editorialists were emphatic in wanting to reject any possibility of Jewish immigration to Canada. This interpretation can be easily verified by examining more closely the chronology and themes of the editorials chosen. From 1910 to 1928, *Le Devoir* published only five long editorials on subjects closely related to Judaism and they did not contain any unfavourable references to Montreal Jews.[67] Until March

1933, editorials with a negative connotation could be counted on the fingers of one hand. Of that total, there were four[68] on subjects having nothing to do with Canada's Jewish community; they were essentially focused on the conflict between Jews and Arabs in Palestine. From the beginning of 1933 until July 1937, all the major editorials on the subject of Judaism, without exception, were concerned essentially with immigration from Europe and were written in a negative tone. During this short period, *Le Devoir*'s editorial pages also published texts addressing "buy from your own," the cultural identity of Jewish merchants in the country, respect for the Sunday law, the Jewish protests in Canada against Hitler, and the electoral corruption perpetrated by the Member of the Legislature, Joseph Cohen. After July 1937 and until April 1945, the significant editorials on Judaism appearing on *Le Devoir*'s became more balanced, with twelve neutral texts and twelve negative ones. In the newspaper, the hostile commentary and criticisms very often centred around the conditions imposed on German Jews in Europe and the desire of Canada's Jewish community to receive refugees in this country. This latter subject became dominant particularly during the autumn of 1938, in the immediate wake of Kristallnacht, when plans on an international level were being prepared to come to the aid of the victims of Nazi persecution. The position taken by *Le Devoir* at such a tragic time caused considerable harm to its reputation up to the present day within Canada's Jewish community and has not been forgotten.

It is also possible to analyze the stance of *Le Devoir* by approaching it from another angle, namely by the daily's interest in the situation of Jewish communities abroad (see Diagram 3). During the first half of

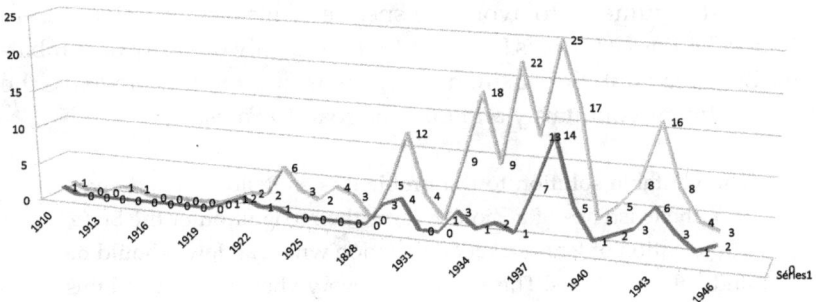

Diagram 3
Le Devoir—Number of editorials per year on Jewish subjects, 1910–1947 in relation to the situation abroad

the twentieth century, numerous dramatic events and situations linked in various ways to Jewish people made the headlines in the international press. That was the case notably of Palestine, where outbreaks of violence erupted periodically between Arab residents and the inhabitants of Jewish settlements. This was also the case, as we saw, with the increasing severity of the persecution of Jews in Germany and in Eastern Europe after Hitler's arrival in power. Consequently, it became impossible for Le Devoir to remain silent on the political conflicts and tensions capturing the attention of the entire world. During 1929 and 1930 and again from 1937 to 1939, Omer Héroux and Georges Pelletier published fifteen editorials in Le Devoir that provided in-depth treatment of developments in Palestine.[69] The issue also merited attention because the region was entrusted by the League of Nations to British administration and the newspaper took a keen interest in the political evolution of the Commonwealth, of which Canada was a member. Although the editorials were written at a critical juncture in European Jewish life, they contained, however, few negative comments since they focused mainly on Zionism, which had no direct effect on the situation in Montreal or Canada. Except for the frequent assertion made in Le Devoir that the Jewish press and finance constituted a formidable power, putting them at the forefront of the forces acting to populate the future national home foreseen by Theodor Herzl, only rare objections appeared in the newspaper to the creation in that region of the world of a Hebrew State. On the contrary, according to Le Devoir's editorial pages, the settlements in Palestine could potentially absorb German Jewish immigration and they constituted a safety valve appropriate for reducing the pressure on Canada in the matter. Pelletier was not reticent in expressing his views on the subject: in April 1937 he resorted to Zionist arguments to avoid the spectre of massive immigration to Montreal.[70] For Le Devoir's Director, there was only one way of combatting European anti-Semitism, namely by asking the Jews to leave the Old Continent voluntarily and take the road to Palestine:

> The veritable solution to the problem is as Belloc[71] stated years ago, the existence of a Zionist State, the recognition of the State, of the nation of Israel, a separate nation where all Jews should be and will be citizens. This means that everywhere else beyond this State, the Jew will be a foreigner…This State is now taking form in Palestine. Its birth created and still is creating a great many problems of all kinds, including several most serious ones—for

example, the conflict with the Arabs of the country. However, the solution to that problem will still be less difficult than the problem of the dangerous elements spread by anti-Semitism among people throughout the world. It would, in fact, be unsolvable if there were not the feasible solution of Zionism.[72]

However, in essence *Le Devoir* took no interest in Jewish life abroad and covered the subject on the news pages, often from wire services of international agencies. It was not until 1929–1930, 1937–1939, and then 1943 that the newspaper devoted editorials to the issue, specifically only 64 out of a total of 208 (30%). These editorials appeared in reaction to specific events: the inter-ethnic violence raging in Palestine, the Kristallnacht pogrom in Germany, and "the Final Solution" being carried out in Eastern Europe. In other words, unless the nature of international news interrupted the routine of the newsroom, *Le Devoir* on its editorial pages concerned itself only with Canada's Jews and those who might be tempted to ask for refuge in the country. The dominant subject in the daily was the more or less sustained relationship maintained by French Canada, or more precisely the Francophones of Montreal, with the Jewish population that had been settled in Quebec society for several decades. The issues here included the commercial presence of Jews in French-speaking neighbourhoods, the denomination of public schools, the respect for Sunday in the rural areas, and various forms of relatively radical nationalism, such as the anti-Jewish demonstration of April 20, 1933, organized by Jeune-Canada in Montreal.[73] The editorialists of *Le Devoir* also reacted to the accusations of anti-Semitism made against them: they criticized the anti-Hitler protests and the boycott of German merchandise in Canada proposed by the CJC, opposed the anti-defamation bill presented in Quebec's Parliament, and denied that they supported the racist ideology of Adrien Arcand. Pelletier and Héroux also paid very close attention to the efforts made by Canada's Jewish community to become organized, especially after Hitler took power. Both of them raised the question of the effect that immigration of German refugees might have on the country and, in particular, on French Canada. At times, the newspaper also attacked aspects of modern culture that in its view seemed to be inspired by the supposed greed or arrogance of Jews. These included American cinema, the sensational press, and popular Parisian theatre, which had many variations in Montreal, according to Georges Pelletier:

Is that French theatre? Is that French art? It is, if everything that comes from France is French. It is, if it is French because, alas! French actors and French actresses are the performers—where the author is probably some Jew, a Greek, a German Jew who has become French or a recently naturalized incomer who, ten years ago, knew not a word of French, but spoke Russian, Yiddish or pidgin French mixed with words from the ghetto. It is not, if we recall that there exists another, a true French theatre written by authentic Frenchmen for decent French people and that can be exported without splattering mud on the whole country and on the literature from which it has come.[74]

The Influence of Jews in the World

With respect to Judaism and people of Jewish origin, during the period from 1910 to 1947, *Le Devoir* took an interest mainly in aspects relating to the situation in Canada and Montreal. When events arose abroad that appealed to the conscience of the Western world, especially starting in 1933 and during the Second World War, the newspaper joined in and covered issues of international scope, but nearly always from the perspective of their impact on Montreal or Canada in general. When all was quiet or there was nothing significant to report on the subject, *Le Devoir* cared little about French, German, Polish, and Russian Jews. However, the circumstances created by Hitler's persecutions or specific events, such as Kristallnacht, drove the daily's editorialists to abandon their indifference. It seemed as if the world events of the 1930s and 1940s arrived to awaken *Le Devoir*'s curiosity and provoke a burst of interest regarding Judaism. After 1933, a series of comments and perceptions that would otherwise have remained unexpressed, filled the newspaper as well as the editorial pages. Consequently, in some years there was an over-emphasis on the Jewish issue, which corresponds almost exactly to the time of the most overt persecutions victimizing the European Jewish populations. In this context, prejudices and stereotypes that would not have been expressed openly by *Le Devoir*, for lack of relevance, were thrust to the forefront. These mainly negative notions, which were deeply entrenched in Catholic tradition, were not worthy of the editorial pages of *Le Devoir*. Among those ideas could be found the belief in a "Jewish World plot," the conviction that Judaism possessed "exceptional power," and that it exercised a "harmful" influence on Christian society, notably through the sensational press and the cinema. The editorialists had not developed these negative perceptions on their own during the 1930s, but often drew them from the French press of Catholic inspiration and from attendance at Sunday church service. The perceptions also came from a doctrinal anti-Judaism derived from centuries-old Christian custom, with which *Le Devoir*'s leaders had been in prolonged contact during their intellectual development in institutions of Catholic teaching. In summary, anti-Semitism had been an integral part of the education received by *Le Devoir*'s editorialists and of their understanding of the world in a subconscious way. Traces of this biased attitude can be found throughout the newspaper, often between the lines, as in this passage on the situation in the Middle East in 1930:

> The approximately one hundred-thousand Jews in Palestine are supported abroad by millions of magnificently organized people, displaying a tremendous spirit of solidarity throughout the world and possessing a huge amount of wealth and through the press, worldwide power.[75]

Closer to Montreal, where it would have been difficult at the time to find any hint of Jewish influence in the French-language press or in French Canada's financial institutions, other factors came into play to cause opposition to the idea of a major Jewish immigration. *Le Devoir* of the 1930s and 1940s had a concept of Quebec and Canadian society as having a fundamentally Christian nature, directly derived from the teachings of the Church and centred around the moral principles taken from the Gospel. For Pelletier and for others working at *Le Devoir* and in the major institutions that embodied French-Canadian identity, Quebec society was a territory very closely tied to the precepts and practices of Catholicism. Furthermore, Pelletier, like all of the editorialists at *Le Devoir*, paid close attention to the Pope, the spiritual leader of the Church. The newspaper, like its editor, submitted to the imperatives of disseminating and propagating a religious doctrine omnipresent in Quebec. In what could be described as a historical retrospective going back to the founding of Ville-Marie, the population of French Canada was seen by leaders at *Le Devoir* as a compact demographic group, united by the French language and by certain cultural traditions, constituting a community, menaced at times but unshakeable. Within this social structure entirely based on Christianity, there was no place for people from other cultural horizons and especially not for

Jews, who seemed to be the doctrinal opposite of everything that the Francophones were trying to preserve. In Pelletier's opinion, French Canada required its full strength to survive and keep intact its place within the Canadian federation. Consequently, its representatives believed there to be a grave danger in allowing individuals to settle in this society who were considered by Catholic thought as the enemies of the Christian spirit and who personified the complete opposite of the society's utopian plans for agricultural development.

This religious motive, which was deeply linked to French-Canadian survival and which during the same period was found in the seminal historical narrative of Canon Lionel Groulx, constituted in Pelletier's *Le Devoir* a quasi-insurmountable obstacle respecting the prospects for accepting religious diversity. This fact was still more entrenched in the case of Montreal and the eventual arrival of German Jewish people, even if in Europe they were destined to suffer the worst of abuse and merciless persecution. For Francophones, the metropolis presented a great risk of cultural desertion and assimilation that a large Jewish presence would only aggravate. In an April 1937 editorial of 2,300 words entitled "Anti-Semitism, a Growing Danger, Jews amongst Us or Jews in their Own Home?" Pelletier explained there could not be a Canadian solution to the serious difficulties suffered by the Jews living under Hitler's regime. He was of the belief that those individuals were impossible to assimilate and would never be capable of becoming members of a community founded on the principles of the Christian faith and Catholic education. Pelletier, who did not beat around the bush, ended his plea by writing as if for himself: "And we will remain alone among ourselves, among Christians."[76] The same theme was asserted in March 1939, a few months after Kristallnacht, when Czechoslovakia ceased to be an independent state. On that occasion, Pelletier wrote an editorial titled: "Is Canada Building a Tower of Babel?" The reference, taken from the book of Genesis, was clearly to the cultural and religious upheaval that would result from the arrival in the country of large numbers of refugees from Central Europe. The editorial, another long one, ended with a paragraph focused on the long-ago Middle-Eastern origins of the German Jews:

> Yes, let us take pity on refugees and exiles. Yes, let us provide help to them. Let us begin, however, by protecting Canada and old-generation Canadians, ahead of any foreign group that is more or less impossible to assimilate. That is what is most urgent.

Let us have less humanitarianism and more common sense; let us have a more realistic Canadian mindset. Are we building Babel, Babylon or Nineveh here or do we want to build a civilized nation of Christian spirit?[77]

This position, if the explicitly Jewish reference on *Le Devoir*'s editorial page that introduced the German situation at the end of the 1930s is excluded, did not, however, result from specific historical circumstances nor from a hostile attitude towards Judaism. The main constituent elements of that position can be found in politically calmer eras when the newspaper took an interest only in French Canada and its cultural loyalties. The Francophone Montreal observed by *Le Devoir* starting in 1910 was already a pluricultural society, polyglot and largely urbanized, and continued to receive large demographic additions from abroad. That, however, was not the reference point for the French-Canadian nationalism defended by Pelletier and his colleagues. From their point of view, the metropolis was a sore caused by the concentration of major commercial and industrial operations that should have been spread more evenly throughout Quebec.[78] For Pelletier, the foundation of the economic and cultural wealth of French Canada was primarily the practice of agriculture, supported by a collection of small rural communities, all similar in cultural and religious respects. In the pages of *Le Devoir* in the 1930s and 1940s, French-speaking Montreal remained a milieu where the values of solidarity and conformity to Catholicism needed to be preserved in an urban context susceptible to exogenous influences, which, therefore, became a greater menace. This strategically defensive sentiment of French Canada's traditional and historic values was expressed, for example, in a voluminous issue published on February 24, 1940, on the paper's thirtieth anniversary, and was essentially devoted to the history of Montreal. In that issue, Pelletier's editorial provided an excellent illustration of the newspaper's desire to preserve and reflect, first and foremost the Christian nature of the city and Francophone Quebec. His text helps us understand why, according to *Le Devoir*'s editors, Montreal should not be opened up to large-scale Jewish immigration:

Le Devoir has no other ambition than to see in the city of tomorrow [Montreal] a Christian population, that respects the laws of God and of men, [...] policies based on justice, reason and a Christian sensibility, [...] endeavours that at one and the same time take a profound interest in propagating the material well-being and awareness of the Christian will, the practice and spirit of faith—faith in the accomplishments—of all classes of Montreal's population.

In brief, a city that is at one and the same time Christian and Canadian, French and progressive Catholic, with a mind open to education, to common sense, to the true realities of social life [...].[79]

Bourassa Compared to Pelletier

We have seen that in the history of *Le Devoir* the 1930s constituted the peak in the number of editorials devoted to Judaism or the Jewish presence. Over half (54%) of the texts on that theme in the editorial pages were published during the years from 1933 to 1939, that is, in only six years (see Diagram 4). It was also during those years that the greatest degree of hostility could be seen in *Le Devoir*'s writings respecting Jews in general. From the time Hitler took power until the start of the Second World War, more than half (57%) of the comments made by the editorialists on the subject had a negative connotation. In

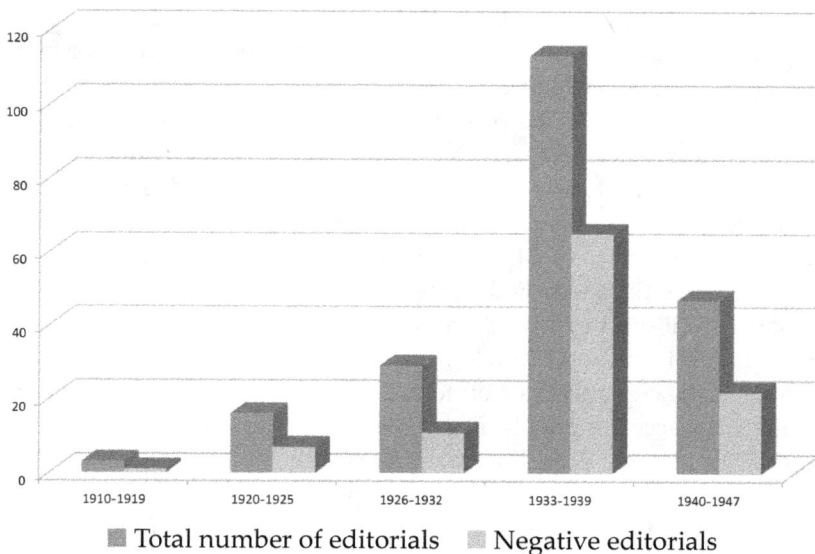

Total number of editorials   Negative editorials

Diagram 4
Le Devoir—Editorials on Jewish subjects by historical period, 1910–1947

comparison, the preceding periods, from 1910 to 1933, contained only a quarter of the editorials (22%) related to Judaism. The same proportion (21%) holds true for the years from 1940 to 1947, which were the last before Georges Pelletier's death. What is true for the chronology of the publications is true also in another way in respect to the more ideological stance taken by *Le Devoir* regarding Jewish life in Canada and in the world. The considerable differences in the newspaper respecting the tone used and the subjects addressed were based on factors other than the international situation.

Up to this point, we have analyzed the topic in a broad way, by taking into account exclusively the general perceptions expressed on *Le Devoir*'s editorial pages. However, other trends emerge when the writings of each editorialist are examined separately (see Diagram 5). We have already indicated that four figures led the way in *Le Devoir* on this subject, namely Henri Bourassa, Georges Pelletier, Omer Héroux, and Louis Dupire (see Appendix 2 for the exact numbers). Those four alone wrote 89% of the editorials that appeared between 1910 and 1947 in *Le Devoir* on the subject of Judaism. There were, nevertheless, astonishing differences in the views held by each of the writers. Upon closer examination it seems as if the newspaper presented

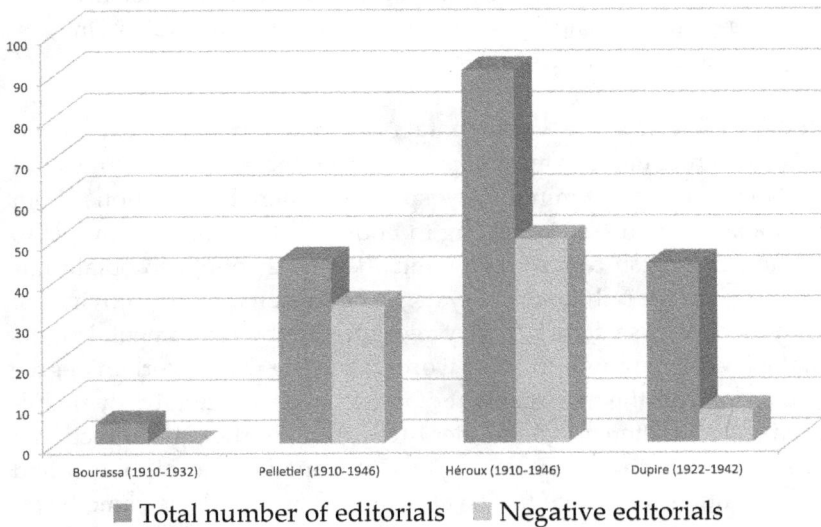

Total number of editorials   Negative editorials

Diagram 5
Le Devoir—Editorials on Jewish subjects written by the four editorialists, 1910–1947

four autonomous lines of thought, that intersected at times only very slightly. It is not an exaggeration to say Bourassa was nearly totally uninterested in the Jewish issue when he wrote in *Le Devoir*'s editorial pages. Over a period of twenty-two years he wrote on the subject only five times, twice in a very technical way that was of no consequence. The only two substantive commentaries he formulated on the theme were made, first in the 1920s, criticizing the rather widespread type of anti-Semitism found in the doctrinal teachings of the Catholic Church, and then in 1931 when he criticized the anti-Semitism beginning to appear in the pro-fascist press that Adrien Arcand was distributing. Overall, these comments constituted no more than a few sentences written at times of more general events, such as when the Taschereau government was re-elected in Quebec in August 1931:

> On another matter, we are delighted by the failure of the anti-Semitic movement initiated by some Conservatives and more or less encouraged by Mr. Houde. Mr. Taschereau endeavoured to resolve the thorny problem of Jewish schools according to the principles of our public law that recognizes, even if imperfectly, that the rights of religion and of the family have priority in all matters regarding the education of children. Some of the opposition criticism and some of the attacks on the Jewish minority resembled the language of the opponents of Catholic schools in Saskatchewan and elsewhere.[80]

In these editorials, the fundamental principle Bourassa defended was this: French Canadians must expect to be judged severely with respect to their treatment of minorities, especially where Francophones hold the balance of power. According to Bourassa, this notably applied to Montreal's Jewish community, which had long sought to obtain fair treatment in the public school system administered by the province of Quebec. Bourassa stated that by recognizing the fundamental rights of the Jewish parents—in other words, granting them a certain degree of control over the management of the schools attended by their children—the Taschereau government was going in the right direction.[81] His logic was that in other regions of Canada, Francophones had been fighting to receive fair treatment and expected the same benefits as the Anglophones. How could the Jews of Montreal be refused what French Canadians were themselves demanding for their kin in Ontario and on the Prairies? Since the issue was sufficiently important on symbolic and political levels to attract the attention of the notorious anti-Semite—Adrien Arcand—who was supported secretly by some of the Catholic clergy and conservative political forces, Bourassa took the opportunity to denounce Arcand between the lines. That already was a significant step for the founder of *Le Devoir*, someone who in his writings never stooped to mention the existence of his populist adversaries.

In the case of Georges Pelletier, the situation was very different. When he succeeded Bourassa in August 1932, Pelletier had already written eleven editorials in *Le Devoir* on the Jewish issue. With only a single exception, all contained negative connotations. Most were texts criticizing immigration in general, and specifically of people of Jewish origin, or they attacked the influence of Jews, which was deemed harmful in the Francophone cultural milieu in Montreal and in France. From 1910 to 1947, Pelletier devoted forty-five editorials to Judaism in *Le Devoir*. Three-quarters of the editorials presented a negative image of Jews and expressed a hostile attitude respecting their immigration to Canada. From a reading of these writings, it is easy to observe that Pelletier was inspired by the right-wing and Catholic press that appeared in France during the Third Republic. In short, Pelletier repeated, one after another, the earlier arguments of those who had attacked Dreyfus, specifically that Jews were impossible to assimilate—even when they had no other homeland than France or other language than French—that they weakened the French national spirit since they were guilty of maintaining multiple political loyalties and that they provoked the majority to feel disgust towards them. By receiving them, Western societies would only be letting currents of anti-Semitic thought and sentiment take root that would grow, particularly in young countries such as Canada, that were founded without the contribution of a large Jewish population. Furthermore, there was nothing to give hope that even the most educated among Jews and the most inclined to integrate, would surmount the radical difference that characterized them. This is what Pelletier wanted to prove when, in 1937, he quoted the candid remarks of a professor from a major Parisian teaching institute:

> At the Collège de France I am in contact with Israelite colleagues of remarkable mind. They sincerely believe that they no longer identify with their race, they no longer practise their religion, they are agnostic; however, there comes a certain time, when you reason

> with them, their mind no longer grasps, no longer sees, no lon-
> ger understands as a French mind or even as a mind of Christian
> training. Regardless of what they wish or think, their mind returns
> to its age-old inclination; that is exactly the Judaic mind.[82]

The anti-Semitism expressed by Pelletier in *Le Devoir* centred around
the presumed ethical superiority of Christianity and European civilization. On the other hand, his writings contained no trace of thought
based on asserting racial supremacy or categorizing humans according to biological characteristics, which at the time was very widespread
in the Anglo-British world. In short, the editorialist's comments were
very close to a pre-modern anti-Judaism, as it had been articulated by
the Church for centuries. This anti-Semitism taught that Jews must
be marginalized, with the expectation of eventually converting them
to a universal religious truth. Marginalization meant not receiving
them when they wished to settle in Canada, not giving them access
to the levers of economic and political power, and not encouraging
their social progress by purchasing goods in their stores in Montreal.
This was why, in Pelletier's opinion, the ethnic and denominational
borders that were present in the Quebec metropolis, including
between Catholics and Protestants and between Francophones and
Anglophones, despite everything, served a certain useful purpose. At
a time of an acute financial crisis, these borders helped to distinguish
people of different origins. Pelletier often reiterated the point when
it was time to ask French Canadians to exercise economic nationalism in support of their own, which was his reason for emphasizing
that Francophones should properly verify the identities claimed by
the merchants on their signs on the streets of Montreal.[83] Beyond that,
there were no calls for violence, persecution, insults, or shaming by
Pelletier. In his view, Canada had done its part at the beginning of the
century by opening its gates to destitute Eastern European Jews during a period of large immigration. That period, however, was over and
it was now time to reject any attempt to revert to that situation:

> We have our Jews and we do not persecute them. They live hap-
> pily and in wealth, without being repressed. Their presence con-
> stitutes one of the multitude of major problems that Canada needs
> to resolve quietly and without injustice first and foremost to itself.
> We have enough of our own problems, starting with our Jewish
> problem. This is not the time to make any of the problems worse...

> The solution to the issue lies elsewhere than in the mass migration
> of German Jews to Canada. The issue is really a European one and
> we old-stock Canadians refuse to suffer its consequences.[84]

From 1933 to 1939, Pelletier's writings were a perfect illustration the attitude of *Le Devoir* towards Jews. The twenty-eight editorials that he published during those six years constitute, on Judaism and the Jewish presence, an exceptionally coherent collection, which makes it possible to consider them as the standard on the subject in the newspaper. After the start of the Second World War, this theme ceased to occupy a major place in *Le Devoir*, as more significant and more urgent issues for French Canada came to the forefront, including the question of compulsory conscription for service overseas. If Pelletier was the newspaper's main spokesman on matters of Judaism and the guardian of a certain orthodox thought on the subject, other editorialists did, however, deviate from his thought or display greater sensitivity to other considerations related to *Le Devoir*'s general environment. That was the case notably of Omer Héroux: despite often reiterating Pelletier's reasoning concerning Jews in Montreal, he nevertheless introduced variations which led at times to conclusions that were different from or even contrary to those of Pelletier. Pelletier was a man of the world and, like Bourassa, he judged the issues of his time from a broad perspective, often based on the point of view of Catholic and right-wing France. Héroux was completely different, as he embodied French-Canadian nationalism in its most traditional and most pragmatic form. Héroux was concerned first and foremost with questions of organization and mobilization. Instead of mingling with European elites interested in the political debates of the moment, he wandered throughout North America where therever were Francophones communities originating from French Canada. For him, the survival of the French language was a constant battle. On the road, he never stopped reiterating that indifference and moral weakening of the troops constituted the greatest obstacle to the triumph of this cause.

Omer Héroux and Léopold Richer

During the years from 1910 to 1947, Héroux wrote twice as many editorials as Pelletier on Judaism and the situation of Jews, for a total of 91. This was not necessarily an indication of a more notable interest in the subject, but rather the fact that Héroux was the most prolific of *Le Devoir*'s editorialists. When he addressed the topic, Héroux was in general agreement with his colleague and took the same position as Pelletier in criticizing Central European Jews as having a nature that made them impossible to assimilate. Héroux also had no hesitation in questioning the Jewish contribution to Canadian life. After having strongly condemned Hitler's persecutions, starting in 1934, he supported the rejection of Jewish immigration: "Do not bring people [German Jews] here who would prevent our own people from taking their place in the economic life of the nation and whose presence would force them to wander again in search of work that keeps disappearing!"[85] However, most of the time in his writings, he vacillated between two contradictory views, which were difficult to reconcile. Since he dedicated himself body and soul to the defence of French Canada, Héroux perceived the Jews of Montreal as taking the realities and difficulties faced by Francophones in their own homeland to another sphere. After rejecting the idea that Jews would make a contribution to Canada, Héroux, nevertheless, hastened to admire their characteristics and the manner in which they led their lives. It was as if the Montreal Jewish community, which was both feared and at times hated, also represented for Héroux a persuasive model of what French Canadians could accomplish in their own cultural sphere, if they were to make the effort and apply the resources at their disposal. In short, although they deserved to be marginalized, the Jews still provided an example to be followed because of their perseverance, loyalty to their origins and community solidarity. Furthermore, they had a remarkable work ethic and an intelligence, both of which were of great benefit to them, as Héroux noted in an editorial devoted to French-Canadian nationalism in September 1937:

> How many of us, young and old, grant to work all the consideration that it deserves? How many can declare that they do not waste any of their time? Furthermore, in the success of some of our rivals, should we not recognize the quite significant part played by their powerful and tenacious willingness to work? The Jews, to name only them, arrived here with nothing. Is not their determination to work at least one of the reasons for their success? Undoubtedly to this can be added, among other things, the way they know how to help each other and support one another. Is that beyond our strength?

> Those who least like Jews and who rightly or wrongly, criticize
> them the most, would not disagree that it is worth imitating them
> with regard to what is best about them and which, furthermore,
> is not strictly a personal characteristic.[86]

Several issues, such as the inter-ethnic tensions in Palestine, the boycott of German merchandise in Canada, the re-establishment of the Canadian Jewish Congress, and that organization's campaign to support greater Jewish immigration, gave Héroux the opportunity to highlight the supposed positive characteristics of Jews. The demonstrations against Hitler in Montreal that took place after Kristallnacht provoked admiration from Héroux: "It is unquestionable proof of the indignation created by the persecution and equally strong proof, it should be noted without risking accusations of anti-Semitism, of the Jewish nation's magnificent spirit of solidarity and power of organization."[87] There are several examples of this view on the editorial pages expressed by Héroux in *Le Devoir* during the 1930s.[88] Héroux reasoned that even if Jews were victims of racism more often than French Canadians, and forced to endure discrimination and attacks published on the pages of newspapers throughout the world after 1933, they also had exceptional resources on an individual and collective level that allowed them to overcome any adversity. The plebiscite in 1942 was another event where Héroux praised the Montreal Jewish community, despite the Canadian Jewish Congress being in the opposite political camp from *Le Devoir* in that campaign:

> Once again, we are going to take the Jews as a model.
> They have decided to participate in the plebiscite to the greatest extent possible. They are, as we know,—or as we should know—superbly organized. [...] We are not criticizing the Jews on this issue; we simply regret that French Canadians have not had as much foresight and not been as active.[89]

Héroux also set himself apart by his reaction to the suffering experienced by the Jews in Germany and elsewhere in the world. Following Kristallnacht, Pelletier strongly condemned Nazi atrocities. The editor of *Le Devoir*, however, tended to take a purely logical approach and express himself on a theoretical level: "The Nazi actions against the Jews of the Reich may well be considered cruel, nevertheless it is important to contemplate any attempt at a partial solution of the

Jewish problem with reason and not by sentiment."[90] Héroux, on the contrary, felt the desperation of the Jews chased out of Germany or who, in that country, were captives of the worst kind of cruelty. He could not help but be affected by the terrible fate of the Jews during the persecutions carried out and encouraged by the National Socialist regime: "To tell the truth, we cannot help but feel great emotion at the sight of so many people forced to roam throughout the world and being rejected by a great number of those who are most aggressive in condemning their enemies."[91]

These views raise a difficult problem of interpretation in our study, since they are based on the profound and consistent ambiguity maintained by Héroux—and by part of the Francophone nationalist movement—regarding the Jewish presence in Montreal. In Héroux's thinking, the wavering is constant and the contradiction seems without solution. Héroux adhered entirely to the anti-Semitic and anti-immigration views of his colleague, Pelletier, but his nationalist sensitivities allowed him to express empathy for people of Jewish origin. Héroux understood, however confusedly at times, the vulnerability of the very small Jewish community in Canada, a community that was being kept politically isolated because of prejudices held against Jews and their religious tradition by Christians. To see in that situation a reflection of the world of Canadian Catholic Francophones, who at the time were the objects of barely disguised disdain in certain Orangemen's circles, there was a divide Héroux crossed easily at times. The man certainly held exaggerated views respecting the international power of "Jewry" and its capacity for political mobilization in Palestine, but it was for the purpose of highlighting what he saw as qualities that were often lacking in the community to which he belonged. In short, as Naïm Kattan noted in the case of post-war Quebec literature,[92] Montreal Jews, once they were removed from their principal cultural world and perceived only as individuals or a group of exceptional performance, evoked admiration from certain Francophones that was at times quite astonishing. Those Jews represented what French Canadians could become one day if they were to break with an inward looking and ignorant past. The French Canadians would become better educated and more confident people who would assert themselves in a world of broader horizons, perfectly able to succeed on a socio-economic level.

We find the same perception in the writings of Léopold Richer, a journalist who wrote his first editorial in *Le Devoir* on June 27, 1941.

In 1934, Richer had written for the front page of *Le Devoir* a series of portraits of eminent Canadian politicians; R.B. Bennett, William Lyon Mackenzie King, J.S. Woodsworth, Ernest Lapointe, and some others.[93] In a text published on September 8 of the same year, as part of this series of articles, Richer turned his attention to three Members of Parliament of Jewish origin: Samuel W. Jacobs from Montreal, Abraham Heaps from Winnipeg, and Samuel Factor from Toronto. At the time, Jews elected to the House of Commons remained a novelty. *Le Devoir* also wondered at times what to make of this arrival in parliament, provincial legislatures and in municipal councils—including in Montreal—of a first generation of politicians coming from the large wave of Eastern European immigration. It was with some reticence, and with obvious apprehension, that *Le Devoir* addressed the Jewish presence on several occasions. These fears, however, did not prevent Richer from expressing his admiration—barely disguised—for the first representatives of Canada's Jewish population in Ottawa. With respect to Jacobs, Heaps, and Factor, Richer made the effort to emphasize how seriously they took their work and their skill in establishing themselves in federal politics. He also took the time to note how the three accomplices distinguished themselves among their colleagues, even at the expense of overshadowing the Members of Parliament from French Canada, despite their greater numbers. Since they were both formidable rivals and models to be imitated by Francophones, the Jews entering public life were viewed with some apprehension by *Le Devoir*. At the same time, they also earned positive attention that emerged clearly in Richer's text:

> There are three of them [Jacobs, Heaps, and Factor]. They can be seen where we expect to see them: at the banking and trade committees, at the Stevens commission. They take the time to learn. Others attend and yawn out of boredom and ignorance. They follow the discussions and questioning with a sharp eye and enthusiastic looks. There are three of them. Only three. However, they have the intelligence of ten, work like twenty, and achieve the results of forty. The Jews have three Members of Parliament. That is sufficient for them right now. In Montreal, where their numbers are greatest, they have only Mr. Jacobs to count on. French Canadians have a large number of Members of Parliament. Many of them are sent to Ottawa from Montreal, many who are not worth two good ones. This explains why the Jews are taking on importance in Canada; and why we are losing it.[94]

This ambiguity regarding the Jewish presence in Montreal proves to be utterly complex and a challenge to analyze. At times, this ambiguity would take a bold turn as it breached very solid barriers based on religious identity in that era. In some cases, it resulted in cultural exchanges that were unexpected in the tense context of the 1930s. In this regard, there was a breakthrough when some Francophones turned their attention to the success of Jews in maintaining their cultural and religious origins, at times in situations where they were a very small minority and confronted by challenging forms of marginalization. Abbot Lionel Groulx—despite being a recognized apologist for French-Canadian nationalism—in this context, could not help but express positive and benevolent views regarding adherents of Judaism. This occurred when the writer observed the stubborn resistance of Jews in the face of assimilation, their ability to join forces against adversity, and their conviction of having a duty to bear witness to an exceptional historical destiny. Groulx, who during his lifetime, had no contact, not even a passing one, with members of the Montreal Jewish community and shared all of *Le Devoir*'s prejudices respecting that population, still managed occasionally to rise above those circumstances. Like the Israelites crossing the desert after fleeing Egypt [it was posited], do French Canadians not have a duty to remain loyal to their traditions, in a manner that is worthy of their vocation as pioneers of Christianity in North America? Groulx, with his sensitivity to this providential and messianic interpretation, at times drew astonishing parallels between Jews and Catholic Francophones. That, for example, was the message he delivered on March 3, 1938, to an audience that he wanted to convince of the need for French-Canadian "survival" in North America. In this case, the speech about Jews was only a pretext for addressing indirectly the decisive issues that Francophones themselves must face:

> Have I again exaggerated the truth, when, taking into account our exceptional situation in North America, taking measure of our small numbers and our dangerous dispersion, I have stated that we can find only one group of people in the world who live in a situation similar to ours: the Jewish people, when I said that in certain respects we are the Jews of North America?...
>
> The situations of the Jews and of ourselves present troubling similarities; can we boast to possess, like the Jews, their fierce desire for survival, their invincible spirit of solidarity, their unbreakable and proud moral armour?[95]

The Remarkable Contribution of Louis Dupire

While Héroux and other colleagues were unable to bring themselves to embrace entirely the advance of modernity and social progress conveyed by the Montreal Jewish community, another of *Le Devoir*'s editorialists proceeded very far in that direction during the 1930s and 1940s. Louis Dupire published texts that have been little analyzed and poorly known until now and offer the exact opposite of the views held by Pelletier on the pages of the newspaper. Dupire, who had been a journalist at *Le Devoir* since 1912, began his career as editorialist in 1920. In twenty-two years, until his premature death in 1942, he wrote forty-four editorials in which he mentioned Judaism or Jewish presence in Montreal; only eight (18%) contained comments of a negative nature. While Pelletier commented on the political news in Europe and Héroux covered primarily Francophone life throughout North America, Dupire commented on developments and debates driving Montreal life. Since he concentrated his energies on the metropolis and he was the only editorialist to follow the emergence of new urban and social phenomena in Quebec, Dupire described better than anyone else at *Le Devoir* the emergence of a cultural and religious diversity in Montreal heretofore unknown in the city. Dupire also had a commitment to teaching of science that, contrary to his colleagues, motivated his interest in objective facts, sociological descriptions, and public health issues. In Dupire's view, Montreal was not the excessive excrescence feared by the supporters of ruralism at *Le Devoir*. Dupire had understood for a long time that the big city was an essential area where Francophones, who would soon have to compete with people of various cultural origins, could assert themselves. For French-Canadian nationalism, Montreal, therefore, represented an opportunity to gain access to significant collective resources that could not be found anywhere else in such concentration and to scientific knowledge needed for Francophones to enter the modern era.

Among the subjects of interest to Dupire, there was economic and demographic data that helped him provide more effective support to the social progress of large sections of the Francophone population residing in the working-class neighbourhoods of East End Montreal. For the editorialist, that was the most decisive issue in the metropolis, since during the Great Depression a workforce severely affected by the industrial and commercial slowdown lived in that area. When, at the end of the 1920s, Dupire compared the situation of French Canadians to that of other ethnic communities in Montreal, he saw that the Jews, in a situation relatively similar to that of French Canadians, were much more successful in protecting their children from the ravages of infant death. In 1926, according to the statistics of the Health Services of the City of Montreal,[96] the proportion of deaths per 1,000 births was 144.62 among French Canadians and 26.31 among people of Jewish origin. Dupire observed that in a city where milk had often gone bad by the time it was delivered to homes, the situation could be explained by breast-feeding among Jews and cultural customs more focused on the well-being of the child:

> However, the most plausible explanation for the very low infant mortality rate among Israelites...is the Jewish woman's acquiescence to her essential maternal duties, the first of which is breast-feeding. She knows that a child is, so to say, but a fragile being who needs food which nature has prepared to become viable. She knows that a child deprived of this milk is physically an orphan. In her wish to care for her child in an intelligent way, she takes the means to do so and thus sets an example of maternal devotion and charity from which Christians could benefit.[97]

Dupire's observations also applied to education in science, which Jewish parents provided to their children so that they would succeed in school. Dupire responded to one of Le Devoir's readers, who had expressed opposition to the Young Men's Hebrew Association, located on Mount Royal Avenue, sending its young members to observe nature in Jeanne-Mance park in the summer: "Is there a desire to educate children, especially young Jews, about elementary ornithology and botany? Is it not desirable to do the same thing for our children, rather than criticizing those who take on the responsibility of such education for any group of children?"[98] In several respects, in Dupire's view, the Jews seemed better adapted to the big city than their Francophone counterparts. They were more concerned with the progress of their offspring and more capable of withstanding the terrible ills that affected the young generation during the Depression years. Dupire made these comments without ever offering his opinion on the situation in Germany or on whether to receive Jewish refugees from Central Europe.

Dupire, who wrote only three major editorials in Le Devoir's pages regarding the Jewish presence[99]—one of a negative nature—included in them a whole series of interesting observations regarding the health practices carried out by the Montreal Jews and their predilection for supporting the education of their youth. He also noted the benefits provided to them by vast community structures, for example, interest-free loans, philanthropy, combating unemployment, and protecting youth. At city hall, the Jewish representatives, including the very colourful Joseph Schubert, were often the most able and the most dedicated in combatting social ills. Dupire's only reticence concerned the cinema, an art that he described, like all of Le Devoir's editorialists, as a corrupting influence on the youth and blamed its growth "on Judeo-American capital."[100] This was also his attitude to the popularity of the sensational press and he accused the American journalist, Joseph Pulitzer, of being the first major distributor of such press.[101] On the other hand, there is no sign in his editorials of the doctrinaire and political anti-Semitism that stained his colleagues Pelletier and Héroux, nor any proof of visceral distrust of Jewish immigration, even during the period from 1933 to 1939.

Dupire, who was no less nationalist than Pelletier and Héroux, believed the Jewish presence in Montréal was a source of hope and presented for French Canadians an example of progress that could be an inspiration to them. What Héroux often felt in a confused way toward the Montreal Jewish community, Dupire was straightforward in expressing through a precise observation of social reality. A reading of his editorials reveals to us that from the mid-1920s onward, Dupire revealed elements of a unique Jewish culture in the metropolis, which he described without any specific prejudices and without resorting to a defensive attitude. In Dupire's view, it was clear that Montreal was in the midst of a period of intense socio-economic changes, where cultural diversity occupied an essential place as a catalyst for future transformations. At times, it is astonishing to see the extent to which Dupire's position differed from the much more traditional and conservative one of his colleagues Pelletier and Héroux, his daily associates in the newsroom of Le Devoir.

Towards New Forms of Cultural Diversity

The stance taken by Le Devoir on Judaism and Montreal's Jewish community deserved a more in-depth study, better supported by quantifiable data. As is too often the case in a complex field of research, researchers who have taken an interest in the relations between Jews and Canadian Francophones had, until now, had to make do with general impressions and second-hand accounts. The main raison d'être of a newspaper such as *Le Devoir* was to publish a coherent and valid long-term ideological position in response to specific political and social circumstances. In short, the intention of the daily founded by Henri Bourassa was to lead the way and foster systematic reflection on the major issues in twentieth-century French Canada, such as the development of Canadian federalism, the preservation of the French language, the rise of Quebec nationalism, and allegiance to a certain concept of history. *Le Devoir* also undertook to enlighten its readers on specific events, which gave it an opportunity to provide details on certain aspects of its position—events such as the bilingual school crisis in Ontario, compulsory conscription, and the consequences of the Great Depression in the 1930s. By the substance of its opinions and the scope of its views, *Le Devoir*, after 1918, became the most influential daily in French Canada. The newspaper that was liberal in orientation politically, but conservative socially, experienced serious doubts, which remained unresolved for a long time on its pages, on issues such as industrialization in Quebec, the new forms of cultural modernism, the rapid urbanization of the Montreal region, and the ethnic diversification of its population. This last subject is the focus of interest in the present study.

The Jewish presence in Montreal did not constitute a dominant theme in the pages of *Le Devoir* and it was not until 1933 that the issue began to be treated in a more systematic manner in the editorials. However, several factors led the newspaper to express hostility towards the settlement of a large population of Jewish origin in the city. The first and foremost of these was the doctrinal anti-Judaic position that had been dispensed throughout the ages by Catholic teaching institutions.[102] In those centres, Jews were perceived as the enemies of Christianity; in other words, as a presence with the power to disrupt the natural relationship that had been established in French Canada between the Church and its faithful. With respect to civil society, which was *Le Devoir*'s main field of interest, Jews were viewed as permanent foreigners in a country where the fundamental principles of public institutions were considered to be based on Christian notions. Subsequently, the newspaper also started to publish the notion that people of Jewish origin transmitted radical forms of modernism, as embodied, at the time, in the large-circulation press, the cinema, urban life, and globalization. From a more nationalist point of view, the Jewish immigrants and small merchants established in Montreal at the beginning of the twentieth century raised fears of unfair competition in commerce and the progressive Anglicization of a country where French Canadians considered themselves to be invested with inalienable rights. In *Le Devoir*, as elsewhere in Francophone Montreal, this atmosphere of mutual incomprehension fostered, until the 1940s, a defensive anti-Semitism and the maintenance of obstinate cultural prejudices, at times expressed openly and stridently.

Before 1933, these negative perceptions appeared only rarely in *Le Devoir*, which essentially reflected Bourassa's attitude in its editorial pages. However, the Great Depression of the 1930s and the deteriorating political situation in Central Europe changed this tendency. Starting in 1934, persecutions in Germany provided a context that forced *Le Devoir*'s principal editorialists to consider subjects that had received no attention until then, or that had not been considered worthy or serious interest. The possibility of new Jewish immigration closed minds and provoked a harsh rejection of immigration, accompanied by a classical anti-Semitic discourse. That sentiment was aggravated by the 1919 establishment, of the Canadian Jewish Congress and the creation of numerous community organizations throughout the country that promoted receptivity to refugees from Nazi Germany, proposed a boycott of German merchandise, and worked actively against Canadian anti-Semitic publications. It was at this time that *Le Devoir*'s editorialists began a malicious campaign of insinuations and of condemnations expressed in forty editorials devoted to a potential Jewish immigration that were published mainly in 1934 and from 1937 to 1939. There was a profound lack of comprehension between the Canadian Jewish Congress and *Le Devoir* and an inability to undertake a dialogue. The debate about the reception of refugees, which was highly emotional for the Jewish leadership and involved life-and-death issues, only resulted in pushing the two sides even further apart. At the same time, Francophone public opinion was convinced that a vast immigration of Jews was being planned that would come and inundate French Canada and potentially destroy decades of political mobilization in support of the French language. Despite being irrational and unfounded in the circumstances, these fears were clearly visible in *Le Devoir* starting in 1933. Presented on the front page, stories about vast immigration plans that had been sponsored by European Jewish organizations were, in all likelihood, entirely fictitious:

Jewish immigration from Germany, funded by a world Israelite committee, will soon be heading en masse towards Canada and South America. The plan is being prepared, under the auspices of the Zionist Union and is well under way. Mr. Aisenbud, the Secretary-General of the Fédération sioniste de Belgique, has just informed representatives of the Belgian press, who were convened on May 21 in Brussels by Mr. Kubowitsky, President of the Union sioniste de Bruxelles, to a meeting where Mr. Aisenbud revealed the present position of his co-religionists regarding Hitler's anti-Semitism...

A global committee is being constituted in Paris for the purpose of raising the initial capital (ten million pounds) that would permit the Jews to be transported to South America and to Canada. Only those German Jews who will bring their inventions and their original industrial procedures, which would be an important contribution to the country's prosperity, will remain in Belgium...

In well-informed circles here, the question is how will Canada that already has several hundred thousand Jewish immigrants from Russia, Poland, Galicia, Austria, Germany, and Romania receive this subsidized immigration, from which Belgium will have been the first to select the industrial elements.[103]

Such reports gave rise in the 1930s to the myth of a massive Jewish immigration. The myth was fostered by incoherent and unverifiable declarations, probably taken to a large extent from the French anti-Semitic press, which, at the time feared the same phenomenon would occur on its own territory. Until the end of the Second World War, *Le Devoir* continued to display hints of this entirely made-up tale:

The Jews constitute one of the most prolific races of the world, which is an acknowledged fact and they are characterized by their racial and religious uniqueness, as well as their spirit of cohesion.

It is not difficult to imagine the serious threat to our politically divided race, although numerically still strong, that would be presented by the sudden influx of a million Israelites, bringing along their emigrant's bundles, their proverbial fertility and their thousand-year-old solidarity.[104]

Maurice Duplessis, leader of the Union Nationale, had no hesitation in using this myth for the purpose of winning the provincial election of August 1944, as demonstrated by this editorial written by Roger Duhamel in *Le Devoir* on December 16, 1943:

> The issue of Jewish immigration remains in the news. Many people have an interest in keeping it in the headlines…
>
> About the same time, Mr. Maurice Duplessis, Leader of the Opposition in the Legislative Assembly of Quebec, revealed a letter at a public meeting which indicated a group's desire to settle 100,000 Jewish refugees on lands in the Province of Quebec. The statement brought an immediate denial. The truth of the matter is that no one has yet been able to demonstrate whether the document is authentic or false.[105]

By adhering to the belief that the ultimate intention of the Montreal Jewish community was to inundate French Canada with a huge Jewish demographic onslaught, first from Germany and then from Eastern Europe, *Le Devoir* deprived itself of the means to the judge the situation on the basis of rational and objective criteria. There is no doubt that the newspaper thus contributed to closing the door to Jewish refugees fleeing the German National Socialist regime between 1933 and 1939 and, subsequently, when the Nazis were preparing their genocide policy in 1942 and 1943. The fact is that during the 1930s, Pelletier and Héroux did not come to understand that the German Jews found themselves in an inextricable situation after 1938, indeed comprehend the serious risks to which Jews were exposed in the Old World. Furthermore, *Le Devoir*'s two editorialists were unable to fathom the unspeakable atrocities that would be caused by the indifference of the Western capitals respecting the torment of the Jews. *Le Devoir* was not the only nationalist organization to defend this closed-door policy. This was clearly revealed by the many petitions sent to Ottawa during this period by members of the Sociétés Saint-Jean-Baptiste from various locations. However, there is no doubt that *Le Devoir* in the Francophone press was probably the publication most zealous in promoting the idea and the most eloquent in defending it.[106]

With respect to other issues, *Le Devoir* proved to be more ambiguous and harder to categorize. Héroux did not fail to note in his editorials that the Montreal Jewish community had an extraordinary ability for mobilization and organization. He thought that he saw in these qualities cultural characteristics often lacking in French Canada, as was the case, for example, at the time of the plebiscite on conscription. Despite the reticence noted above on the subject of immigration, Héroux, in a confused way, discovered in his Jewish counterparts a logic and conduct that the Francophones should have adopted in similar circumstances. Héroux managed to do this to the extent that he detected the presence in the two groups of several shared values, such as inter-community solidarity, the desire to participate fully in Canadian society, and the will to progress socially. This realization, however, occurred only occasionally and did not really change his attitude with respect to German Jews. If that realization had been more sustained and more clearly formulated, the thoughts could have served as an opening to a dialogue between Jews and French Canadians, except that the context in the 1930s was hardly favourable in Montreal to truly overcome denominational and community barriers. Similarly, Louis Dupire clearly understood that the Jews were advancing in their integration into Montreal life and that they were making greater progress than the Francophones who suffered from less education. At this level also, between the two world wars, the possibility for exchange and an opening never really materialized, for lack of a social framework where the two groups could have met with each other. It was, finally, not until the 1950s that the Jews and Catholic Francophones engaged in a sincere and fruitful dialogue, based on new principles.

What influence did Le Devoir's editorials have on the establishment of an immigration policy in Ottawa during this period of history? The question is difficult. There is no doubt that starting in 1933, the newspaper expressed an openly hostile position towards Jews and its editorials on the subject revealed a questionable attitude both ethically and morally. Is it possible to conclude that Le Devoir's influence had a decisive impact on Prime Minister Mackenzie King and his principal Quebec lieutenant, the minister Ernest Lapointe? That is far from certain. Other strategic factors came into play before and during the war that led to Ottawa's rejection of the demands of Canada's Jewish community. Among those worth noting were the severity of the Depression in the 1930s, the desire to keep the channels of diplomatic communication open with Hitler before 1939, and the absence of political courage on the part of the federal authorities confronted by the refugee crisis. Certainly, Le Devoir also displayed narrow-mindedness on the issue and by its writings contributed to the inaction of the Canadian government. However, the extent of its influence was essentially limited to French Canada and its Francophone readers. In English Canada, only a few gifted individuals had the knowledge to read Georges Pelletier's erudite and voluble editorials on the subject. The influence of these texts needs to be looked for elsewhere, in the reassurance of a great number of French Canadians in their anti-immigration prejudices and their negative perception of Canada's Jews.

Furthermore, *Le Devoir*'s impact in Ottawa can be measured by looking at issues that were more crucial for Francophones at the time, such as increasing the use of French in the federal public service, defending provincial autonomy, and, after 1939, the planned establishment of military conscription. On all these issues, and in particular, on sending troops to Europe during the Second World War, *Le Devoir*'s views never carried the day despite an intensive press campaign lasting several years, and a very sustained call for political solidarity in French Canada. In fact, the November 1944 establishment of conscription for service overseas probably constituted the greatest failure in Pelletier's career. It was a crushing repudiation, especially since it was followed in May 1945 by the triumphant re-election in Quebec of Mackenzie King's federal Liberals. It was the end of the editorial road for Pelletier: after a long illness, he died in February 1947. In the interval, a new team led by Gérard Filion had arrived at *Le Devoir*, soon joined notably by André Laurendeau. For these new arrivals, the Jewish presence in Montréal did not have the strategic and decisive nature that had been expressed a few years earlier by Pelletier.

The war years saw the last traces on *Le Devoir*'s editorial pages of a sustained attention to the Jewish presence in Montreal. On the one hand, after the Holocaust, the myth of a large Jewish immigration from Europe no longer held up; on the other hand, Francophone Quebec was in the 1940s already heading toward a complete redefinition of its cultural identity. Within these new parameters, the role played by the Church and its teachings diminished year by year. The younger generations, who had become distanced from the main source of the anti-Semitic discourse in French Canada, would approach the fundamental issue of cultural and religious diversity from a more secular and unfettered angle. In this ideological evolution that emerged at the beginning of the 1950s, the Montreal Jewish community ceased to be a significant preoccupation and soon became part of an ever-increasing pluralism. After 1948, Montreal received the last immigrants who had survived the Holocaust; in the post-war tumult, this did not attract any attention or raise any notable reaction in French Canada. After the war and Hitler's genocide, Europe ceased to be the main focus of world Judaism. In the Middle East, the Hebrew State created in 1948 completely changed the situation and forced Francophone Quebec to view Jewish life in a different way. The perceptions defended by Pelletier and Héroux only a few years earlier were now obsolete and would never resurface in the pages of *Le Devoir*. Although anti-Semitism would not disappear entirely from Quebec society after the Quiet Revolution, it became more marginal and would often be condemned by the new Francophone political elites. It was the beginning of a new era, in which it became possible to see Jewish life from another angle than as a thinly disguised threat to the survival of the French fact in Montreal.

PIERRE ANCTIL
Jerusalem

Notes

1.   The complete list of works that have treated this theme can be found in the bibliography at the end of the book.

2.   Pierre Anctil, *Fais ce que dois, 60 éditoriaux pour comprendre* Le Devoir *sous Henri Bourassa (1910–1932)*, Sillery, Éditions du Septentrion, 2010, 392 p., translated as Do What You Must *60 Editorials to Understand* Le Devoir *under the Direction of Henri Bourassa 1910–1932*, Toronto, The Champlain Society, 2016, and Michel Lévesque, *À la hache et au scalpel, 70 éditoriaux pour comprendre* Le Devoir *sous Gérard Filion (1947–1963)*, Sillery, Éditions du Septentrion, 2010, 448 p.

3   Pierre Anctil, *Soyons nos maîtres, 60 éditoriaux pour comprendre* Le Devoir *sous Georges Pelletier (1932–1947)*, Sillery, Éditions du Septentrion, 2013, 475 p.

4.   In reprisal against the assassination in Paris of a German diplomat, a large-scale pogrom was carried out on the night of November 9–10 throughout Germany, known in English as the night of "crystal" or the "night of broken glass." With the support of the Nazi regime, organized groups burned over two hundred synagogues and ransacked a great number of stores belonging to Jews. In the ensuing hours, 30 000 German citizens of Jewish origin were arrested and sent to concentration camps. Newspapers everywhere in the world, including *Le Devoir*, made the events front-page news.

5.   Georges Pelletier, "À chacun ses Juifs," *Le Devoir*, December 3, 1938. Translated in the present volume. See p. 171 (To Everyone Their Own Jews)

6.   Between the two world wars, Kérillis belonged to a group of nationalist republicans closely identified with the right.

7.   Weinfeld, Morton, "Québec Anti-Semitism and Anti-Semitism in Québec," Jerusalem Centre for Public Affairs, Jerusalem, January 2008, http://jcpa.org/article/Quebec-anti-Semitism-and-anti-Semitism-in-Quebec/ (Consulted in June 2013).

8.   It is important to note that the first Jewish arrivals in Montreal date from the period of the English conquest, in other words from the mid-eighteenth century. Until the end of the nineteenth century, the Jewish population, however, remained very limited in size.

9. Henri Bourassa's speech during a debate in the House of Commons on the massacre of Jews in Russia, March 15, 1906, in the *Official Debates of the House of Commons of Canada*, vol. LXXIV, Ottawa, S.E. Dawson, 1906, p. 233.

10. Henri Bourassa's speech during a debate in the House of Commons on the government's immigration policy, April 9, 1907, *Official Report of the Debates of the House of Commons of Canada*, vol. LXXXI, Ottawa, S.E. Dawson, 1906–1907, column 6182 and 6183.

11. "Bourassa Again," editorial in *The Canadian Jewish Times*, March 26, 1909—See also "The French Press and the Jews," editorial of March 17, 1911 in *The Canadian Jewish Times*, that is, after the founding of *Le Devoir*.

12. "The Unholy Alliance and Anti-Semitism. Read this and see whom you can trust, Bourassa or Laurier," *The Canadian Jewish Times*, September 20, 1911, p. 2.

13. Quoted in Michel Lévesque, *Histoire du Parti libéral du Québec. La nébuleuse politique, 1867–1960*, Sillery, Éditions du Septentrion, 2013, p. 542.

14. Elected in 1917 in the Montreal riding of Cartier, S. W. Jacobs became the first Canadian parliamentarian of Jewish origin in Ottawa. He held the riding until his death in 1938.

15. Letter from Samuel W. Jacobs to Henri Bourassa, September 5, 1912. Bourassa family archives, Bibliothèque et Archives nationales du Québec, Montréal.

16. In March 1911, in Kiev, Menahem Mendel Beilis had been accused of the ritual murder of a young boy and imprisoned. The unjust and highly anti-Semitic nature of the trial made news throughout the world.

17. These were two pogroms carried out in the present capital of Moldova, the first in February 1903 and the second in October 1905. These massacres became tragically famous due to their ferocity and the indifference of the authorities in not stopping them.

18. Letter from Samuel W. Jacobs to Henri Bourassa, September 11, 1912. Bourassa family archives, Bibliothèque et Archives nationales du Québec, Montréal.

19. "Yidn, fir vemen vilt ir vuten? Far Ballantyne, Palestine un frayhayt, oder Bourassa, antisemitizm un shklaferay?" The tract was sent to Bourassa on November 23, 1917 by Louis Fitch, an associate in the law firm headed by S.W. Jacobs. Ballantyne won the election by a huge majority. Bourassa family archives, Bibliothèque et Archives nationales du Québec, Montréal.

20. See Pierre Anctil, Le Devoir, *les Juifs et l'immigration, de Bourassa à Laurendeau*, Québec, Institut québécois de recherche sur la culture, 1988, chap. 1.

21. This condemnation was made in the House of Commons on March 20, 1934. See: *Discours de M. Henri Bourassa, député de Labelle, sur les réformes économiques et sociales, prononcé à la Chambre des communes, le 20 mars, 1934*, Ottawa, J.-O. Patenaude, 1934, p. 18.

22. The other signatories of the "Emergency Call" were Lyon Cohen, Nathan Gordon, J. Levinson, Samuel Hart, Marcus Sperber, Captain Sebag-Montefiore, F. I. Spielman, Norman Viner, H. E. Hershorn, and Lieutenant-Colonel Philip Abbey, all respected individuals in the Montreal Jewish community.

23. See "Ces documents," Omer Héroux, *Le Devoir*, January 18, 1934, p. 1. All the CJC documents were reprinted in that issue of *Le Devoir*. Over the following days, five other editorials addressed the issue of relations between *Le Devoir* and the CJC: Omer Héroux, "La réponse de MM. Jacobs, Bercovitch et al.," *Le Devoir*, January 22, 1934; Omer Héroux, "L'autorité de ces documents juifs," *Le Devoir*, January 25, 1934, translated in the present volume, see p. 211 (The Status of the Jewish Documents); Louis Dupire, "Le père du journalisme jaune fut le juif Joseph Pulitzer," *Le Devoir*, January 26, 1934, translated in the present volume, see p. 214

(The Father of Yellow Journalism Was the Jew Joseph Pulitzer); Omer Héroux, "Le 'boycott' des annonces et les Juifs," *Le Devoir*, February 3, 1934, translated in the present volume, see p. 219 (The Advertising Boycott and Jews); and Omer Héroux,"Une nouvelle lettre de M. Caiserman," *Le Devoir*, February 8, 1934.

24.   The daily became *L'Événement-Journal* in October 1938.

25.   The passage is quoted by Omer Héroux in his editorial entitled: "Le 'boycott' des annonces et les Juifs," *Le Devoir*, February 3, 1934, translated in the present volume, see p. 219 (The Advertising Boycott and Jews).

26.   "Emergency Call," quoted in *Le Devoir*, January 18, 1933, p. 1.

27.   Omer Héroux, "Le 'boycott' des annonces et les Juifs," *Le Devoir*, February 3, 1934, translated in the present volume, see p. 219 (The Advertising Boycott and Jews).

28.   On this subject see Georges Pelletier, "Rien que pour plaire à M. Bercovitch? Non," *Le Devoir*, March 11, 1933, translated in the present volume, see p. 201 (Only to Satisfy Mr. Bercovitch? No) and Omer Héroux, "M. Jacobs aussi….," *Le Devoir*, October 26, 1933, translated in the present volume, see p. 102 (Mr. Jacobs also …).

29.   About this incident see Omer Héroux, "Le contrat Pollack-Renaud," *Le Devoir*, November 13, 1933.

30.   See Omer Héroux, "M. Joseph Cohen et la Saint-Jean Baptiste," *Le Devoir*, January 5, 1934, translated in the present volume, see p. 226 (Mr. Joseph Cohen and the Société Saint-Jean-Baptiste) and "De quoi au juste se plaint M. Joseph Cohen?," *Le Devoir*, January 17, 1934.

31.   Omer Héroux, "L'autorité de ces documents juifs," *Le Devoir*, January 25, 1934, translated in the present volume, see p. 211 (The Status of the Jewish Documents).

32.   Omer Héroux, "Le 'boycott' des annonces et les Juifs," *Le Devoir*, February 3, 1934, translated in the present volume, see p. 219 (The Advertising Boycott and Jews).

33.   See "Une lettre de M. H. M. Caiserman," text published in the section "Lettres au *Devoir*," *Le Devoir*, July 3, 1935.

34.   Unsigned and undated H.M. Caiserman manuscript in English. Alex Dworkin Canadian Jewish Archives (formerly known as the Canadian Jewish Congress Archives), Montreal, cote DA 1—box 8—file 15, "Notes and Reports Regarding CJC & Other Jewish Organizations." The manuscript mentions the July 1935 controversy in *Le Devoir* and undoubtedly was written on the same date.

35.   *Idem*.

36.   On this subject see Pierre Anctil, *Le rendez-vous manqué. Les Juifs de Montréal face au Québec de l'entre-deux-guerres*, Québec, Institut québécois de recherche sur la culture, 1988, chapter 6. See also H.M. Caiserman's letter to A. L. Mailman, June 21, 1935. Alex Dworkin Canadian Jewish Archives (formerly known as the Canadian Jewish Congress Archives), Montreal.

37.   On this subject see Irving Abella and Harold Troper, *None is Too Many: Canada and the Jews of Europe, 1933–1948*, Toronto, University of Toronto Press, 2012, 340 p.

38.   On this subject see Jean-Philippe Croteau, *Les relations entre les Juifs de langue française et les Canadiens français selon le Bulletin du Cercle juif, 1954–1968*, Master's thesis, Université de Montréal, 2000, 162 p.

39.   "Public Relations Program with French Canadians and Roman Catholics," undated and unsigned document. Alex Dworkin Canadian Jewish Archives (formerly known as the Canadian Jewish Congress Archives), Montréal, fonds ZA (year box) 1951, box 2, file 12. Likely a draft press release of the CJC. See also Betty Sigler, "Jewish Students at Montreal's Catholic University. Cross Over

the Open Door," Congress Bulletin, Canadian Jewish Congress, September 1950, p. 11.

40. This is particularly the case with the volume written by Abella and Troper: *None Is Too Many*, published for the first time 1983. See also David Rome, *The Jewish Biography of Henri Bourassa*, Montreal, National Archives, Canadian Jewish Congress, new series n° 39, 1988.

41. For greater detail on the subject, consult Pierre Anctil, *Jacob-Isaac Segal (1896–1954) : un poète yiddish de Montréal et son milieu*, Québec, Presses de l'Université Laval, 2012, annexes 7 et 8. (Now translated into English) *Jacob-Isaac Segal: A Montreal Yiddish Poet and His Milieu*, University of Ottawa Press, 2017.

42. See on the subject Jean-Philippe Croteau, "La communauté juive et l'éducation à Montréal : l'aménagement d'un nouvel espace scolaire (1874–1973)," in Pierre Anctil and Ira Robinson, eds., *Les communautés juives de Montréal; histoire et enjeux contemporains*, Sillery, Éditions du Septentrion, 2010, p. 65–91. See also David Fraser, *Honorary Protestants: The Jewish School Question in Montreal, 1867–1997*, University of Toronto Press, 2015.

43. Omer Héroux, "L'autorité de ces documents juifs," *Le Devoir*, January 25, 1934, translated in the present volume, see p. 211 (The Status of the Jewish Documents).

44. Our reference here is particularly to *La Semaine religieuse de Québec* and the publications of the "École sociale Populaire," supported directly by the episcopate. Newspapers such as *L'Action catholique* and the reviews *L'Action française*, *L'Action canadienne-française* and *L'Action nationale* that were strongly influenced by the Catholic Church can be placed in the same category.

45. This was a court case for defamation brought by the Jewish community against the notary, Joseph-Édouard Plamondon, who on March 30, 1910 in Quebec City had delivered an untruthful speech about the Talmud. The lead lawyer for the plaintiffs was S.W. Jacobs. Two trials held in 1913 and 1914 ruled in favour of the arguments made by Jacobs.

46. These were Georges Pelletier, "Politique anti-nationale," *Le Devoir*, August 4, 1910, translated in the present volume, see p. 90 (An Anti-national Policy); Omer Héroux, "Le crédit populaire, l'exemple des Juifs," *Le Devoir*, June 11, 1913 in *Fais Ce Que Dois* and translated in *Do What You Must* (Credit for All, the Jewish Example); and "Juifs et protestants à la commission scolaire dissidente," *Le Devoir*, April 15, 1914, translated in the present volume, p. 252 (Jews and Protestants at the Dissentient School Board).

47. The five editorials are "Résumé de session," *Le Devoir*, March 17, 1924; "Sur les remparts," *Le Devoir*, July 26, 1924 in *Fais Ce Que Dois*, translated in *Do What You Must* (On the Ramparts); "Mariage et divorce XXIV," *Le Devoir*, June 4, 1929; "Leçons et réflexions," *Le Devoir*, August 26, 1931, translated in the present volume, p. 197 Lessons and Reflections; and "Rôle capital de la charité," *Le Devoir*, September 24, 1931. Only the editorials of July 26, 1924, and August 26, 1931, deal with the issue in detail.

48. Abbé Édouard-Valmore Lavergne, *Sur les remparts*, Québec, Imprimerie de l'Action sociale, 1924, 322 p. The abbot Édouard-Valmore was the brother of the nationalist Member of Parliament, Armand Lavergne, associated with *Le Devoir* early in his career.

49. Henri Bourassa, "Sur les remparts," *Le Devoir*, July 26, 1924. In *Fais Ce Que Dois* and translated in *Do What You Must* (On the Ramparts).

50. These three editorials are "Politique anti-nationale," *Le Devoir*, August 4, 1910, translated in the present volume, see p. 90 (An Anti-national Policy); "Trucs et

réformes," *Le Devoir*, May 27, 1921, and "Ce qui importe d'abord," *Le Devoir*, April 5, 1922, translated in the present volume, see p. 93 (What Is Most Important).

51. Georges Pelletier, "Politique anti-nationale," *Le Devoir*, August 4, 1910, translated in the present volume, see p. 90 (An Anti-national Policy).

52. Omer Héroux, "Une nouvelle migration juive," *Le Devoir*, February 1, 1934. Translated in the present volume, see p. 104 (A New Jewish Immigration).

53. Georges Pelletier, "Les Juifs d'Allemagne font déraisonner le *Star*," *Le Devoir*, November 26, 1938, translated in the present volume, see p. 165 (In the Case of the German Jews, the *Star* Talks Nonsense).

54. See Georges Pelletier, "Sommes-nous des Européens ou des Nord-Américains?," *Le Devoir*, September 24, 1938, and "Libérons nos consciences," *Le Devoir*, September 27, 1938.

55. See for example: Louis Robillard, "Un mémoire judéo-américain à la conférence de Québec," *Le Devoir*, September 9, 1943, translated in the present volume, see p. 181 (A Judeo-American Brief at the Quebec Conference).

56. Émile Benoist, "Nous avons nos propres victimes et réfugiés de la guerre," *Le Devoir*, June 4, 1943, translated in the present volume, see p. 177 (We Have Our Own Victims and Refugees of the War).

57. The denouncement came from the pen of Omer Héroux in an editorial titled "Choses d'Allemagne," *Le Devoir*, August 5, 1935, translated in the present volume, see p. 125 (Events in Germany).

58. *Mit Brenender Sorge* [With Burning Concern], published by the Vatican, March 10, 1937, in German. The encyclical was the subject of an editorial analysis by Omer Héroux, published under the title "Le pape et l'Allemagne," *Le Devoir*, March 23, 1937, translated in the present volume, see p. 128 (The Pope and Germany).

59. See for example: Omer Héroux, "Que risquons-nous à voter contre le gouvernement?," *Le Devoir*, November 18, 1935.

60. This was a common term for placing a vote in a ballot box under a false identity.

61. See "Le 'yiddish' était la langue officielle dans certains polls," *Le Devoir*, January 22, 1936, p. 1.

62. See, for example: "Combien d'Israélites ont voté légalement pour Josef Cohen?," *Le Devoir*, December 20, 1935, p. 1.

63. See "L'entier support' du gouvernement à Josef Cohen," *Le Devoir*, December 4, 1935, p. 1.

64. "Déclaration du 'Canadian Jewish Congress' au sujet de la corruption électorale," *Le Devoir*, December 26, 1935, p. 1. See also "La population électorale de Saint-Laurent et la machine du 25 novembre," *Le Devoir*, November 10, 1935, p. 1.

65. See "M. Bercovitch prend la défense de M. Charles Lanctôt au comité des comptes publics," *Le Devoir*, May 16, 1936, p. 1 and "Le régime Taschereau se solidarise avec M. Charles Lanctôt," *Le Devoir*, May 20, 1936, p. 1.

66. Georges Pelletier, "Tricherie revient à son maître—avec les intérêts des intérêts," *Le Devoir*, June 13, 1936, translated in the present volume, see p. 245 (Cheating Does Return to Haunt Its Master—with Double Consequences). The italics are in the original text.

67. These were by Omer Héroux, "Le crédit populaire, l'exemple des Juifs," *Le Devoir*, June 11, 1913 and translated in *Do What You Must* (Credit for All, the Jewish Example); Omer Héroux, "Juifs et protestants à la commission scolaire dissidente," *Le Devoir*, April 15, 1914, translated in the present volume, see p. 252 (Jews and Protestants at the Dissentient School Board); Omer Héroux, "Le pape et la Palestine," *Le Devoir*, September 2, 1921; Henri Bourassa, "Sur les remparts," *Le Devoir*, July 26, 1924 in *Fais Ce Que Dois* and translated in *Do What You Must*

(On the Ramparts); and Louis Dupire, "La mortalité infantile chez les Juifs et les chrétiens," *Le Devoir*, August 5, 1927, translated in the present volume, see p. 300 (Infant Mortality Among Jews and Among Christians).

68. These were Omer Héroux, "Le pape et la Palestine," *Le Devoir*, September 2,1921; Omer Héroux, "Sur une poudrière," *Le Devoir*, August 28, 1929, translated in the present volume, see p. 317 (On Top of a Powder Keg); Georges Pelletier, "Silence au Mexique, clameurs en Palestine," *Le Devoir*, September 6, 1929, translated in the present volume, see p. 307 (Silence on Mexico, Protests for Palestine); and Omer Héroux, "Arabes, Juifs et Anglais," *Le Devoir*, February 16, 1930.

69. Of these, Pelletier wrote only one: "Silence au Mexique, clameurs en Palestine," *Le Devoir*, September 6 ,1929. Translated in the present volume, see p. 307 (Silence on Mexico, Protests for Palestine).

70. It may be worth noting that Pelletier's sympathy for the Zionist plan was also found at the same time in Poland, where the right-wing, anti-Semitic regime encouraged Polish Jews to emigrate to Palestine.

71. A reference to Hilaire Belloc (1870–1953), born in France, but a British national, a committed Catholic, a poet, and also a polemicist. Belloc was the author in 1922 of a work titled *The Jews*, from which Pelletier drew a part of his convictions on the subject.

72. Georges Pelletier, "L'antisémitisme, péril grandissant," *Le Devoir*, April 17, 1937, translated in the present volume, see p. 139 (Anti- Semitism, a Growing Danger).

73. On this subject, see Pierre Dansereau et al., *Politiciens et Juifs, discours prononcés le 20 avril 1933 à la salle du Gésu*, Montréal, Cahiers des Jeune-Canada, n° 1, 1933, 67 p. Jeune-Canada was one of the organizations targeted by the Canadian Jewish Congress in the "Emergency Call" of December 1933.

74. Georges Pelletier, "Si c'est cela de l'art français'...," *Le Devoir*, February 28, 1930, translated in the present volume, see p. 242 (If That Is "French art" ...).

75. Omer Héroux, "De Bombay à Jérusalem," *Le Devoir*, May 22, 1930, translated in the present volume, see p. 320 (From Bombay to Jerusalem).

76. Georges Pelletier, "L'antisémitisme, péril grandissant," *Le Devoir*, April 17, 1937, translated in the present volume, see p. 139 (Anti-Semitism, a Growing Danger).

77. Georges Pelletier, "Est-ce une tour de Babel que le Canada bâtit ?," *Le Devoir*, March 18, 1939, translated in the present volume, see p. 107 (Is Canada Building a Tower of Babel?).

78. See, for example: Omer Héroux, "1,028,000 personnes," *Le Devoir*, August 26, 1925, in *Fais Ce Que Dois*, and translated in *Do What You Must* (1,028,000 People); and Albert Rioux, "La vocation agricole du Canada français," *Le Devoir*, April 18, 1933.

79. Georges Pelletier, "Montréal, hier et demain...," *Le Devoir*, February 24, 1940.

80. Henri Bourassa, "Leçons et réflexions," *Le Devoir*, August 26, 1931, translated in the present volume, see p. 197 (Lessons and Reflections).

81. The reference here was to the David Law of 1931 that responded to certain grievancesof the Jewish community leadership in Montreal.

82. Georges Pelletier, "L'antisémitisme, péril grandissant," *Le Devoir*, April 17, 1937, translated in the present volume, see p. 139 (Anti-Semitism, a Growing Danger).

83. See, for example, Georges Pelletier's editorial, "Soyons logiques : estampillons le marchand comme la marchandise," *Le Devoir*, January 28, 1939, translated in the present volume, see p. 233 (We Need to be Logical: Label the Merchant Just Like the Merchandise).

84. Georges Pelletier, "À chacun ses Juifs," *Le Devoir*, December 3, 1938, translated in the present volume, see p. 171 (To Everyone Their Own Jews).

85. Omer Héroux, "Une nouvelle migration juive?," *Le Devoir*, February 1, 1934, translated in the present volume, see p. 104 (A New Jewish Immigration?).

86. Omer Héroux, "Sur les discours de Saint-Denis," *Le Devoir*, September 2, 1937, translated in the present volume, see p. 279 (The Saint-Denis Speeches).

87. Omer Héroux, "Les manifestations antihitlériennes," *Le Devoir*, November 21, 1938, translated in the present volume see p. 157 (Demonstrations Against Hitler).

88. Héroux wrote three editorials in which he suggested in the title that French Canadians imitate the Jews: June 11, 1913, December 21, 1939, and April 22, 1942.

89. Omer Héroux, "L'exemple des Juifs," *Le Devoir*, April 22, 1942, translated in the present volume, see p. 283 (The Jews as a Model).

90. Georges Pelletier, "À chacun ses Juifs," *Le Devoir*, December 3, 1938. (Translated in the present volume, see p. 171 (To Everyone Their Own Jews).

91. Omer Héroux, "Les étonnements de M. Glass, député de Toronto et organisateur du boycott juif contre la marchandise allemande," *Le Devoir*, October 26, 1938, translated in the present volume, see p. 151 (The Astonishment of Mr. Glass, Member from Toronto of the Legislative Assembly of Ontario and Organizer of the Jewish Boycott of German Merchandise).

92. Naïm Kattan, "Jews and French Canadians," (p. 104–115) in Philip Leblanc and Arnold Edinborough, *One Church, Two Nations?* Don Mills, ON, Longmans Canada, 1968, 190 p.

93. The texts were reprinted in the book *Nos chefs à Ottawa*, Montréal, Éditions Albert Lévesque, 1935, 182 p. The article about Jacobs, Heaps, and Factor can be found on pages 161–167.

94. Léopold Richer, "Trois Israélites," *Le Devoir*, September 8, 1934, p. 1.

95. Quoted in Julien Goyette, ed., *Lionel Groulx, une anthologie*, Montréal, Bibliothèque québécoise, 1998, p. 93–94. The complete speech can be found under the title "Qu'est-ce donc ?," in the Fonds Lionel Groux deposited in the Archives nationales du Québec (Fonds CLG1 / P1-B / MA250). The reference to Jewish people did not stop Groulx from mentioning favourably in the same speech the "Catholic" authoritarian regimes of Mussolini, Salazar, Pilsudski, and De Valera and suggesting them as models.

96. See on the subject: Benoît Gaumer, Georges Desrosiers, and Othmar Keel, *Histoire du Service de santé de la ville de Montréal, 1865–1975*, Québec, Éditions de l'IQRC, 2002, 277 p.

97. Louis Dupire, "La mortalité infantile chez les Juifs et les chrétiens," *Le Devoir*, August 5, 1927, translated in the present volume, see p. 300 (Infant Mortality Among Jews and Among Christians).

98. Louis Dupire, "Ne blâmons pas les Juifs : imitons-les," *Le Devoir*, June 3, 1930. Translated in the present volume, see p. 275 (Do Not Blame the Jews: Imitate Them).

99. These are "La mortalité infantile chez les Juifs et les chrétiens," *Le Devoir*, August 5, 1927. (Infant Mortality Among Jews and Among Christians); "Ne blâmons pas les Juifs : imitons-les," *Le Devoir*, June 3, 1930. (Do Not Blame the Jews: Imitate Them); and "Le père du journalisme jaune fut le Juif Joseph Pulitzer," *Le Devoir*, January 26, 1934. (The Father of Yellow Journalism Was the Jew Joseph Pulitzer); all translated in the present volume, see pp. 300, 275 and 214.

100. Louis Dupire, "Un nouveau 'scheme' : une exposition au parc Maisonneuve," *Le Devoir*, June 4, 1926, translated in the present volume, see p. 239 (A New Scheme: Fairgrounds in Parc Maisonneuve).

101. Louis Dupire, "Le père du journalisme jaune fut le Juif Joseph Pulitzer," *Le Devoir*, January 26, 1934, translated in the present volume, see p. 214 (The Father of Yellow Journalism Was the Jew Joseph Pulitzer).

102. For an analysis of the anti-Semitic discourse of the Catholic Church between the two wars, see John Connelly: *From Enemy to Brother: The Revolution in Catholic Teaching on the Jews, 1933–1965*, Cambridge, Mass., Harvard University Press, 2012, 376 p.
103. "Un bloc de Juifs allemands émigreront au Canada," *Le Devoir*, June 1, 1933, p. 1. See also "400,000 Juifs allemands en train d'émigrer," Le Devoir, August 11, 1933, p. 1; and "Au congrès juif de Prague," *Le Devoir*, September 27, 1933, p. 1. Other similar texts appeared in 1936 and in 1938 and 1939.
104. Louis Robillard, "Les problèmes d'après-guerre et la dénatalité anglosaxonne," *Le Devoir*, September 3, 1943, translated in the present volume, see p. 112 (Postwar Problems and Decline in Anglo-Saxon Birth Rate).
105. Roger Duhamel, "Le problème de l'immigration et l'animosité antiquébé-coise?," *Le Devoir*, December 16, 1943, translated in the present volume, see p. 115 (The Problem of Immigration and Anti-Quebec Animosity?). See also Louis Robillard, "Un mémoire judéo-américain à la conférence de Québec," *Le Devoir*, September 9, 1943, translated in the present volume, see p. 181 (A Judeo-American Brief at the Quebec Conference). The letter quoted by Duplessis was a false document made up to mislead the public.
106. On this subject, see Marc Hébert, "La presse de Québec et les Juifs 1925–1939, le cas du *Soleil* et du *Quebec Chronicle Telegraph*," Master's thesis, Université Laval, 1994, 138 p.

Immigration to Canada
(1913–1930)

Opposition to international immigration was one of the mainstays of Henri Bourassa's thought. The theme appeared right from the founding of *Le Devoir* and remained there at least until the 1950s. The reception of immigrants certainly was far from occupying a central place in Bourassa's thinking, but the issue was serious enough for *Le Devoir* to revisit it periodically. The reason for this hostile attitude was based on Bourassa's concept of his country. For the eminent intellectual, it was important above all for Canada to preserve its economic equilibrium and for its population, to preserve the cultural and religious characteristics passed on to it by the original inhabitants. This meant preservation of "the political hegemony and the moral and physical characteristics" of the Anglophone and Francophone majority. There is nothing surprising in such a term being found in the editorial pages of *Le Devoir* at the beginning of the century: the concept of "race" was regularly used by both Francophones and Anglophones to describe the two founding peoples of the Canadian state. Furthermore, Bourassa envisioned a French-Canadian population, from one end of the country to the other, having the same rights and privileges, particularly with respect to the French-language public school system already established under the BNA Act in Quebec and Ontario. Supporting immigrants, especially to the Canadian West, over the domestic migration of French Canadians to populate the provinces of Manitoba, Saskatchewan, and Alberta would, in Bourassa's view, encourage the arrival of exogenous forces. Since new arrivals generally adopted English as their language in Canada, proceeding along those lines also meant, de facto, promoting a policy of gradual Anglicization of Canada. The founder of *Le Devoir* viewed this as "the most serious peril threatening the future of the Canadian nation." This was the essence of the message expressed by Bourassa in the editorial of July 28, 1913.

In the broader debate on international immigration, the arrival of Jewish people did not seem worth mentioning. Between 1910 and

1920, the issue of European migration was discussed at least sixty times in the editorial pages of *Le Devoir*, but Jews were the subject only once and then under the signature of Georges Pelletier. During his twenty-two years as the head of *Le Devoir*, Bourassa found time to state his opposition vigorously to the migratory policies of the Canadian government, but without ever mentioning a single time the arrival in the country of people of Jewish origin. It must be understood that the proportion of Jews was negligible in the migratory influx to Canada during the first two decades of the twentieth century, at most 3% of the total, and Bourassa never targeted specific communities in his remarks. Rather, he was opposed generally to an unrestricted immigration policy and to administrative procedures that gave financial preference to certain private enterprises close to the federal government. These remarks of the founder were taken up by disciples. Omer Héroux took up the same ideas at length in February 1922 when the Anglophone press of Montreal indicated its support of massive new immigration from Europe, more specifically from Great Britain. The arrival of a significant number of British immigrants raised fears that Francophones would face greater pressure to assimilate over time, and see their proportion diminished in Canada as a whole. In October 1930, twenty years after the founding of *Le Devoir*, Georges Pelletier revived Bourassa's arguments in more complete form and in greater depth. Pelletier, who was writing at a time when international immigration was being reduced to a trickle, had no reluctance about resorting to a more accusatory and more apocalyptic logic than Bourassa. For Pelletier, just as for the government of Canada that strictly applied the official immigration policy, only properly identified farm workers should have been admitted to the country. Canada, in Pelletier's opinion, need not take any interest in city dwellers who were often unproductive economically, heavily left-leaning politically, and constituted "the scum of the earth." What good was it to admit the worst elements of the European continent who wallowed in filthy cities and would come and expand the number of unemployed and destitute in Canada? For Pelletier, the result of the large immigration of 1901–1914 was bad across the board. The arrival of two million new residents in that period, he asserted, cost the federal treasury a great deal and only served to increase the ranks of criminals, habitual offenders, and people affected by mental illness in the country. Worse still, Canada paid to attract, welcome, and integrate a great number of individuals, many of whom rushed to cross the American border as soon as they had the chance. It would be better to receive far fewer immigrants, but whose worth and contribution would be better guaranteed from the start. In Pelletier's mind, this would in fact close the borders of the country to any new arrivals.

The Perils of Immigration

Henri Bourassa
Le Devoir, July 28, 1913

Increasing the population of a country by immigration from abroad needs to be carefully monitored and kept within reasonable limits. The public authorities must be guided closely by the following central idea: it is less important to increase population numbers rapidly than to maintain the country's economic balance and national unity and to ensure the hegemony of the mother race and its moral and physical characteristics. If one strays from this principle, immigration may easily lead to the demise of the nation.

When immigration from abroad is centred in a specific part of the land, separated from the rest of the country by geographical obstacles and divergent economic interests, there is an even greater danger: the creation of a State within a State, with all the [attendant] risks for internal quarrels. If, in addition, the group of foreigners is composed primarily of immigrants coming from a neighbouring country that is overwhelmingly greater in number, power and wealth, it is very probable that any conflict will lead to a rupture and that the neighbouring country will absorb or dominate the territory inhabited by its citizens.

This is precisely the situation that has been created in Canada by the policy implemented in Ottawa over the last fifteen to twenty years. Far from being based on the foremost principle of preserving the nation, the federal government seems to have taken as its ultimate objective the undoing of the Canadian nation, the dislocation of the economic forces of the country and the rupture of Canadian Confederation for the benefit of the United States.

***

The statesmen who founded Confederation and annexed the vast area of the Hudson's Bay Company conceived the only policy that could inseparably link the badly connected parts of this overly vast country. They wanted to reproduce in the territories of the West the ethnic, social and political conditions existing in the provinces of the East.

Cartier and MacDonald were in agreement to make Manitoba a second province of Quebec. At the request of Blake, the two parties joined to introduce throughout the West the principle of instruction based on religion and freedom of choice in education that had prevailed in Ontario and Quebec.

Sectarians and short-sighted politicians managed to abort this policy inspired by truly national and clear-sighted thinking.

Spurred by Dalton McCarthy, fanatic demagogues undertook to turn Manitoba and the Territories, the joint possession of the Anglo-French people of the East, into an exclusively Anglophone country and then prepare its Americanization by the arbitrary and aggressive introduction of a so-called national system of schools—undoubtedly because this is the surest means of denationalization.

However, it must be recognized that the success of this anti-national undertaking, to a large extent, can be related to the little eagerness that French Canadians displayed in responding to Cartier's hopes.

If, from the beginning, a migratory flow had been initiated from Quebec to Manitoba, separate schools and the French language would never have been proscribed in the provinces of the West and the seeds of national discord would never have sprouted on those fertile lands. Furthermore, there would now be between the Canadian West and the East a moral bond, perhaps strong enough to resist separatist tendencies.

**

The results of the equally pernicious excessive immigration policy organized and directed by Mr. Sifton soon added to the work of the sectarians.

It is not reasonable to assert that access to the provinces of the West must be prohibited to foreign settlers. However, it is undeniable that it is first necessary to encourage settlement in these territories by English and French settlers transplanted from the provinces of the East or repatriated from the United States; to maintain the number of long-established Canadian settlers every year and, finally, to restrict immigration, as much as possible, to the soundest of the English-speaking and French-speaking races in order to preserve the particular nature of the native population, who must absorb the immigration.

In fact, however, it is the exact opposite that has been done.

First, in the division of land, there seems to have been an effort to discourage Canadian settlers, especially French Canadians who seek the company of kin folk. Furthermore, in granting homesteads, the government has made no distinction between Canadian settlers and foreigners.

Until recent years, at least, the government allowed shipping and railway companies to agree to transport immigrants from European ports to the lands of the Far West at a lower price than farmers from the provinces of the East.

Please note that I am not saying "at a better price" in relation to distance travelled. No, it cost *less in absolute dollars* for an emigrant from England to travel the 4,200 miles separating Liverpool from Winnipeg than for a settler from Quebec to go from Montreal to Winnipeg (1,400 miles) or one from Ontario to go from Toronto to Winnipeg (1,200 miles).

Is this despicable system, carried out with the complicity of the government, by companies heavily subsidized by the State, still in force? This is an issue that deserves the attention of commissions of inquiry as much as the tariffs for transporting wheat or cattle.

What I do know is that in 1906, the Minister of the Interior, Mr. Oliver, declared that it was not the government's intention to depopulate one part of Canada to the benefit of another and that the federal authorities have not deemed it appropriate to end this system. Through this far-reaching policy, access to the country's territories was made more difficult to sons of the land than to foreigners.

It must not be forgotten that to this appalling *discrimination* by the transport companies, an additional bonus of five dollars for each foreign immigrant was paid by the State either to maritime agencies, or to the infamous *North Atlantic Trading Company*, organized under the care of Mr. Smart, Deputy-Minister of the Interior, and Mr. Preston, Commissioner of Immigration in London, or simply directly to the immigrations agencies of the Department of the Interior.

I believe that the payment of bonuses has been pretty well ended. However, the fact remains that the policy carried out by the State, until now, was to do nothing to encourage settlement of the West by our citizens of the two official languages and to do everything to stimulate foreign immigration, without any regard for the public good and national security.

***

With regard to immigration, at least, this absurd policy was motivated, even imposed on the government by a powerful coalition

of interests and also by the stupid and narrow-minded idea of angli-
cizing the country at any price.

It is in the interest of the railway builders to bring from abroad,
especially southern Europe, armies of labourers, toughened against
misery and the sun, whom they can treat as beasts of burden. They
hire them by the thousands, bind them to what are nothing more than
contracts of slavery and when the unfortunate souls escape from their
yoke, they bring over others.

It is in the interest of the shipping companies to fill their liners
with human cattle. Nearly all of the companies are allied to railway
companies and they have no difficulty in obtaining for their passen-
gers the favourable prices that are unjust, as I have already mentioned
earlier.

Finally, real estate speculators and the owners of the land to be
settled have an essential interest in the flow of immigration, rather
than slowing down, continuing to increase and fill their coffers with
ever greater profits.

Do any of them care about the welfare of the nation?

The various categories of those interested include a considerable
number of politicians—quite probably a majority of the politicians
from the West—in the two parties, who, in various ways, exercise
enormous pressure on the two parties and on a slew of newspapers.

Two of the most powerful corporations in the country, Canadian
Pacific and Canadian Northern, are at one and the same time, owners
of the railways, transatlantic liners and vast areas to be settled. They
have, therefore, a threefold motivation to maintain the strong flow of
immigration. They have a crushing influence on public authorities, on
politicians, and on the press.

This situation alone suffices to lead governments, their supporters and their newspapers to the peculiar idea of celebrating the
increasing flow of immigration that floods the country every year as
being beneficial. This view has spread easily in the little informed
public opinion of a new country, dominated by mercenary concerns—
this applies to all of Canada—where material success and huge numbers blind so many people to fundamental realities.

It is more than time for sound public opinion to react against
this absurd notion. The truth is that the constant increase in foreign
immigration, from the British Isles or elsewhere, rather than being the
subject of congratulations in Throne Speeches, constitutes the most
serious peril threatening the future of the Canadian nation.

The *Gazette* and Immigration

Omer Héroux
Le Devoir, February 13, 1922

The front-page article about Montreal in the *Gazette* this morning under the headline, *A Time for Action*, on the issue of immigration, merits note and thought. It highlights the intensity that will drive the coming immigration campaign and the support on which it can count.

The *Gazette* does mention a couple of times the need for "*some selection as long as the economic situation has not been improved*" and for "*desirable immigrants,*" but the article, overall, indicates that those restrictive phrases cannot be given too much weight. "*We have in the past,* the *Gazette* states clearly, *received over* 400,000 *immigrants in one year and every effort should be spent to bring back those halcyon days.*" The objective of the *Gazette*, therefore, is the maximum obtained before the war by our former immigration policy. The policy, moreover, is responsible to a large extent—in the opinion of all those willing to look at reality—for our overcrowded cities and present unemployment; a policy that has burdened the provinces and cities with special expenditures for the mentally ill and police forces. The Conservative government claimed that it wished to thwart the dangerous political consequences of the policy (this is what its partisans claimed) by laws of exception. The policy was also supported by social movements, more or less revolutionary in appearance and who previously were of such great concern to the friends of the *Gazette*. (Recall especially the Winnipeg Strike, various demonstrations in Toronto, etc.).

That experience should make us wary of returning to an intensive immigration policy; however, it would be in vain, alas! to hope that it will suffice to open the eyes of many people. Such opposition would be contrary to too many interests, too many needs and illusions.

***

Who has any idea of the formidable coalition of interests that, before the war, supported and encouraged our immigration policy? Everyone with land for sale, everyone possessing means of transportation, everyone seeking cheap labour was inevitably tempted by the wish for the arrival of a great number of immigrants to the country. As long as business was good, the same temptation must have influenced manufacturers and business people, who saw in the crowds of immigrants, growth in the number of consumers. Political leaders, for their part, were delighted to see an increase in the number of taxpayers.

These factors remain and in certain cases are made worse by the harsh economic situation resulting from the war. The government, with a new burden of two billion dollars, is forced to try and find new taxpayers anywhere on whose shoulders it can place part of this debt. The railway crisis that now affects the government directly makes the temptation even greater. The government is repeatedly told that high immigration will mitigate the crisis and reduce our deficits. Furthermore, the closing of the American border, from the perspective of the supporters of intensive immigration, provides Canada with an exceptional opportunity. Finally, to top it all off, England now is making a great effort to get rid of its surplus population. England is so keen on this, that she is prepared to assume the costs of sending her unemployed to the colonies and there is significant discussion of a joint project for this task of emigration between the mother country and the Dominions. (From an economic point of view, the mother country would probably find it less costly to pay for the departure of the unemployed than to maintain them in England. At the same time, it would reduce the risk of political and social disorder).

***

It can be seen that the forces pushing for the adoption of an intensive immigration policy are significant and powerful and it would be folly to delude oneself in this regard. On the contrary, it must be recognized that the number and importance of these factors will make selection of immigrants increasingly difficult, a subject discussed only in passing. These factors will also encumber us with subjects who are less and less desirable.

Take the specific case of England, since that is where the major effort will be made. In addition to the fact that the British government is perhaps the only one, at the present time, that is glad to be rid of a part of its citizens, it must be taken into account that a certain number of supporters of excessive immigration see a huge influx of British immigrants as a means to curb or to drown out non-British elements.

Furthermore, there will obviously be a great reluctance to condemn the *undesirable* British for fear of being accused of disloyalty.

Yet one of the most senior officials of the Canadian government, our own Deputy Minister of Immigration, Mr. Black, upon his return from a trip to England, recently stated (see in the newspapers of January 28, the summary of a speech at the *Ottawa Women's Canadian Club*): "*Most of those in the British Isles clamouring to come to Canada are in the category giving preference to city life over rural life.*" We thought we had already shown that it could not be otherwise. England is probably of all large countries the one that has the least number of farmers. Its rural strength was sacrificed to its industrial development. However, the last war taught England a harsh lesson, that if she does not wish to risk suffocation in a new conflict, she must find a way to become self-reliant with respect to food supply. Consequently, it is necessary for England to restore its agriculture and, therefore, keep its qualified farmers to the greatest extent possible. This makes the situation regrettably clear for us: first, it is in England's interest to be rid of those of who will come and encumber our cities and increase the number of unemployed; second, it is in England's interest to eliminate the emigration of those who could contribute to our own agricultural progress.

***

The article in the *Gazette* indicates the amount and intensity of pressure applied on the government. It reminds those who certainly do not disdain the immediate economic interests of our country, but are even more concerned with the country's well-ordered development, that they have a duty to place at the forefront of their examination the issue of intensive immigration and to strongly oppose the pressures that they consider dangerous.

At the Monument-National [theatre], last October 19, Mr. Bourassa foresaw the present assault and stated at that time:

> After the problem of the relations to be established between the mother races of the country, the most important social issue facing Canada is undoubtedly that of immigration.
>
> You know our principles and our ideas on the subject. Well before the founding of *Le Devoir*, we expressed alarm. We indicated the danger of making the borders of the country wide open

to immigrants of any race and any social condition. On that issue, our ideas are completely opposite to those now dominant in all political parties.

They all see only an economic issue. We see first and foremost a social and national issue.

The Liberals and Conservatives want intensive immigration in order to quickly increase the number of taxpayers summoned to eliminate the appalling bankruptcy resulting from their mad railway policy and their criminal war policy. The more reasonable and more moderate Progressives mainly see an agricultural labour issue.

We are emphatic in stating that the economic issue must remain subordinate to the social issue: that we must not open the gates of the country to foreigners, the Canadian citizens of tomorrow, whose social ideas, morals and instincts would erode the foundations of Canadian nationality, which are already so deeply undermined.

An intensive immigration policy can only complicate our social problems, add to the risks of unemployment and urban life and add more consumers than producers.

It is understandable that shareholders of railway companies and large industries, thirsting for dividends and the squanderers of national resources, bewildered by the spectacle of the ruin they have created, cling to the idea of increasing the number of their dividend and tax providers. However, it is inexplicable and unpardonable that men of thought, reflection and foresight lend themselves to such sordid and self-interested calculations.

It would be better to let the economic crisis continue than to end it by an immediate remedy that will have the ultimate consequence of expanding and precipitating the social crises that are strangling the old European civilizations and already threatening the powerful American nation.

These powerful words, even now, deserve careful reflection.

We Pay Attention Finally, But Very Late...

Georges Pelletier
Le Devoir, October 23, 1930

A university professor in Manitoba has just written that the country benefited little, in terms of numbers, from the arrival of millions of immigrants to Canada from 1901 to 1929. He states that if, during this whole period, we had kept our people born here in the country, the simple excess of births over deaths would have sufficed to increase our population to its present level.

This theory, as surprising as it may seem, is based on census and immigration statistics from the beginning of the twentieth century. A quick glance at what happened between 1901 and 1911 — during the huge pre-war period of immigration — justifies in part what the Manitoba professor says and what others have already said before him around 1912 and since 1925. In 1901, the total population of our country was 5,371,315. In the 1911 census it was 7,206,643 — an increase in ten years of 1,835,328 souls. Over this period of time, according to official figures, immigrants numbering over a million and three-quarters arrived in Canada's provinces, in other words, approximately the equivalent of the total increase in population. However, the population had also increased by the excess of births over deaths during the decade; for example, the French-Canadian ethnic group, in the whole country during this period, went from 1,649,371 to 2,054,890 without the help of any significant French immigration, an increase of 405,519 — about 25 percent more than in 1901. Immigration in reality brought little benefit, in terms of numbers, to Canada during this period. The census-takers themselves in 1911 were able to track barely half of the immigrants of non-British race who entered Canada after 1901. The others had disappeared.

On the basis of well verified facts and statistics, it can now be confidently stated that if, starting in 1900, we had applied ourselves to combat, on the one hand, infant mortality and on the other, to keep our citizens of Canadian origin in the country, the millions and millions of dollars spent by our political leaders to help and encourage the immigration of millions of new arrivals, we would pretty well have the total population that we now have in the entire country. The population would be homogeneous, public and private hygiene would be better, the population would present fewer quasi-insolvable problems for the State than the mixed and cosmopolitan present population creates. In our health facilities, we would have fewer paupers, abandoned or deranged people and in our prisons fewer criminals and repeat offenders. All in all, our society and our country, as well as our finances, would be better off. Sociologists, observers and even those of our political leaders who are well informed and know how to reflect, are now forced to admit this. However, around 1900 we lost sight of the existence of the principle that the best category of citizens of a country is in general constituted by people whose origins are in that same country and the sudden arrival in a young country of hundreds of thousands of foreigners in a few years is completely undesirable and inevitably dangerous. We only began to notice this after what all our governments lived through and a world-wide crisis made its worrisome effects felt all the way here.

First from 1900 to 1914 and then from 1919 to 1926, just about everyone in the country wanted immigrants, and by the millions. The big railway companies, as well as the shipping companies, seeking to increase their revenues, wanted nothing more than the huge and continued flow of immigrants. Manufacturers thought that the more immigrants there were, the more they could produce, since they would have a domestic market guaranteed to grow endlessly. The entrepreneurs, the builders and the industrialists were the most supportive of intensive immigration: would it not ensure them of a large labour force, more submissive and less demanding than the existing labour force in the country? Furthermore, there were the land speculators, the labour market intermediaries, the importers of what was called human capital—often treated by the importers as cattle. At another level there were the large agencies, such as the *Salvation Army*, the *Church Army*, and other associations of the same nature, whose goal was to bring here the unemployed and the poor of the British Isles, first for the mother country to be rid of them, and then attempt to rehabilitate them by sending them to the colonies, the territories of social experimentation…

From 1900 to 1914, the huge European migration to Canada was uninterrupted. From July 1, 1900 to March 31, 1915, exactly 3,050,730 Europeans, Americans, Asians, etc. entered the country—two-fifths of our total population in 1901. The Great War put a brutal end to this invasion. As soon as the armistice was signed, the invasion resumed. Newspapers such as the *Montreal Star* and the *Gazette* spoke seriously of a population of 50,000,000 in Canada by 1940—millions that would be recruited for the most part in Europe. It seemed there was an intention to nearly empty Europe for the benefit of Canada. A gigantic and mad project, of doubtful benefit, thought up by great businessmen or bankers, by "captains of industry," reputedly serious people.

The millions for the most part have stayed in Europe; with the American border closed to immigration, Canada can no longer be the gateway to the United States. And it is mainly to the United States where the immigrants want to go. We already paid the price from 1900 to1915 to learn that lesson. The economic conditions became such that in our country just as in our neighbour's our political leaders were obliged to put in place a blockade of sorts against immigration for an indefinite period to deal to some extent with the plague of unemployment. Our large cities are burdened with the unemployed. There are thousands of people who have come from abroad and would like work to have at least something to eat and find neither food nor work.

No one any longer talks of immigration except to denounce it. The folly of the policy carried out over two and a half decades has become obvious to everyone—finally but too late.

It is incredible that we are ending where we should have started—by thinking about the consequences of a policy of excessive immigration. Why didn't we think about that first?

Jewish Immigration to Canada (1910–1929)

B efore Hitler came to power in January 1933, *Le Devoir* referred to the presence of Jews only four times in editorials dealing with immigration to Canada, specifically in 1910, in 1921–1922 and in 1929. Essentially, these were passing references in texts of broader scope that condemned the entire policy of Canadian immigration. In this section the three examples, all above Georges Pelletier's signature, lambaste, in passing, the alleged tendency of East European Jews to force their way into Canada by buying their way into the good graces of the government. Pelletier does not hesitate to state that immigrants of this kind remain "undesirable," since they do not meet the highest standards of admission established by the public service of Canada. From the editorialist's point of view, these new arrivals should have been farmers and not escapees from "the confines of Russia," where their situation was "miserable." Pelletier claimed to be knowledgeable on the subject, since in 1913 in the pages of *Le Devoir*, he had written a long series of reports which were later published in the form of a pamphlet titled *L'immigration canadienne* (Canadian Immigration). With his own eyes, he had seen ocean liners unload their human cargo in the port of Quebec and witnessed the superficial manner in which the formalities for admission were carried out in most cases. Between 1905 and 1913, the arrival of immigrants reached historic proportions and in a few years the country was inhabited by hundreds of thousands of new residents. Paradoxically this massive movement raised only very little anti-Semitism in *Le Devoir*'s editorials. In fact, it was not until the 1930s that the pages of the newspaper became filled with hostile commentary on Jewish immigrants, in other words, at a time when the gates to Canada were already closed by double locks against new arrivals and the immigrant flow had been reduced to a mere trickle.

An Anti-national Policy

Georges Pelletier
Le Devoir, August 4, 1910

The principal requirement of an immigration policy is that it be elastic; do not laugh, a daily favourable to the government just made that discovery.

Even if we accept that an immigration policy must be elastic; it first still needs to be reasonable. If it is not so in any way, what use is its "elasticity!"

It is perhaps due to this aspect of the Laurier Cabinet's immigration policy that Canada has had to pay more than four hundred thousand dollars to the North Atlantic Trading Company, which formerly was in the business of the immigration trade under the high and powerful protection of Mr. Sifton, Minister of the Interior, at the time, and Mr. Smart, his assistant, who from his position as Deputy-Minister of the Interior became manager of this noteworthy company.

A whole book could be written about the circumstances and consequences of the contract drawn up on November 4, 1899 between the North Atlantic Trading Company on the one side and the Canadian authorities on the other. That operation is a good illustration of the regime under which we live.

It was at this time that immigrants began to flow into the country; in the three previous years, twenty-five thousand landed in the country, in addition to the Doukhobors and the Galicians. They cost us nothing and the immigrant flow was established between Europe and Canada.

A certain Mr. Preston, a Liberal Party organizer in Ontario, appointed European immigration agent in London, thought it a good idea in 1899 to ally himself with Mr. Smart, Deputy-Minister of the Interior and close friend of Mr. Sifton; despite the advice of Lord Strathcona, Canada's representative in London. Mr. Preston was given a mandate from the Department of the Interior, without the knowledge of the Houses of Parliament, to negotiate a strange contract with the North Atlantic Trading Company — a mysterious organization for which the government was never willing to make public the names of shareholders.

For each farmer, twelve years old and older, coming from continental Europe—this excluded Great Britain from the company's field
of operations—Canada committed itself to paying the company's
agents a large cash bonus. It was not necessary for the North Atlantic
Trading Co. to incite them to come here.

It was sufficient that the farmers arrived for the company to
receive its compensation. On November 4, 1899, Mr. Sifton and the
Laurier Cabinet ratified the agreement for a term of five years.

The original contract did not provide for the payment of a bonus
for child immigrants; it was paid just the same from 1901 on, as shown
by the testimony of Mr. Smart before a committee of inquiry in 1906.

Mr. Smart answered Mr. Barker: (page 67 and following of evidence given before the Public Accounts Committee, 1906)

Question.—Do you consider a breast-fed child to be included
in the phrase: "who comes here as an immigrant farmer?" Response.
—Yes.

Q. — And domestic staff? R. — I certainly believe so.

Q. — With the intention of living in Canada? R.—I certainly
think so.

Q. — Now, Mr. Smart, do you believe it to be a proper interpretation of the clauses in the contract to pay a bonus for a child who has
arrived in his mother's arms? R.—Yes.

Q. — Just as for an immigrant farmer in good faith?—Yes.

Q. — With the intention of settling in Canada? R.—Yes.

Q. — So you think that, for example, a 24-hour old baby would,
therefore, have the clear intention of settling in Canada? R.—Yes,
I don't know why he would come if that were not his intention.

Q. — Therefore, every child arriving in this way to the country
was worth five dollars for the company? R. — Yes.

That was not all. The Hirsch Association, responsible for protecting
Jews, sent several hundred here. The Association paid their travel
expenses; the North Atlantic Trading Co. did not spend a cent for
the undertaking; in the first year of its contract two hundred arrived,
and the following year over one hundred. For each one of them, the
Company received a bonus of five dollars (Smart testimony, page 78
of the 1906 Report).

On November 4, 1904, the government and the Company nego-
tiated a new contract, even more beneficial to the Company; it should

be noted that at the time, just as in 1899, the Company did not have an authorized legal existence; it did not obtain one until 1905 on the Island of Guernsey. The immigrants continued to arrive and the Company continued to receive its subsidies, with the result that on June 3, 1906 it received from the government $306,911; from that date until the termination of the contract—at the end of 1906—it received an additional amount of $61,234. When the Canadian government indicated to the Company its intention to have no further dealings with it, the government still paid the Company a balance on the account of $46,000. This came to a total of $403,245. In addition, the Company claimed $70,000 from the Canadian Treasury. The courts have not yet ruled on the validity of that claim.

What have we received in return from the Company for this $403,245? Approximately 80,600 immigrants, from Russia, Germany, Austria-Hungary, Italy, Galicia and Turkey; there was no shortage of Jews, they are an indispensable part of this private immigration. Most of these people arrive here from European regions where poverty, misery and physical and intellectual degeneration have always existed for centuries.

These 80,600 immigrants equal the population of three or four ridings in the province of Quebec; the Laurier Cabinet has taken from the taxpayers of this part of the country—they pay one-third of the taxes in Canada—one-third of this $403,000, specifically, $134,000, and used this amount to bring here people who are strangers to Anglo-Saxon and French civilization and thus reduce the influence of the French race on the soil it has discovered, settled and developed.

If we have brought here with the power of money and paid people whose names we still do not know, eighty thousand immigrants who have no language, ideas, sentiments or even morals in common with the inhabitants of the country—Anglo-Saxons and French Canadians—have we acted with prudence and good judgment?

This is one example in a thousand of the immigration methods of the present government.

The press that defends the government by praising the "elasticity" and the excellence of the immigration methods, will in no way prevent honest people from grasping the clearly anti-national characteristic of these methods that are dangerous for the future of the country and even of the Empire.

What Is Most Important

Georges Pelletier
Le Devoir, April 5, 1922

It is that time of year again, when ocean liners usually full of new arrivals reach our main seaports. It is also the time when we hear all sides debating the need to change our existing admission regulations.

A Liberal Member of Parliament from Montreal, Mr. Jacobs, plans on proposing to the House of Commons that the regulations be repealed or revised because, he states, "*they hinder the natural development of the country and are an obstacle its natural growth.*" A senior official of *Canadian Pacific*, Mr. Dennis, for his part, wants to repeal these same regulations. He says the regulations prevent the entry to Canada of sound elements, while, on the other hand, they do not protect against *undesirable* elements—that is his term—Polish, Ukrainian or Austrian Jews—again he is the one saying this—helped by foreign associations or ones established in North America, when the arrivals show the mandatory $250 required of any immigrant who does not intend to go into farming upon arrival in Canada.

On the other hand, one of the pioneers of Canada's immigration regime, some twenty years ago, Mr. Sifton, has recently stated in Toronto and elsewhere, in very frank terms, that the only immigrants that we need are English, Irish and Scottish peasants or farmers from Bohemia, Galicia, Hungary and other similar agricultural countries. Not subsidized immigration, according to him, not those European professionals of unemployment, not the *scalawags* and *ne'er-do-wells* from overseas cities who will do nothing good in Canada, where we have already received too many of them. From his perspective, it would be a disaster for the country to admit these rejects of European civilization; the Canadian West has lived through the painful experience (*Toronto Star*, April 3, summary of Mr. Sifton's speech at the Canadian Club, the same day).

***

In other words, opinion is quite divided. However, those who do not think simply of the number of immigrants to be settled here, but also of their quality, all conclude that the present regulations should be maintained and applied strictly. It is understandable that some people wish to make arrival here as easy as possible for thousands of men who live in miserable conditions on continental Europe and in the confines of Russia at the present time and whose presence in Canada would serve the goals of those who wish to reinforce, to the extent possible, the political and ethnic influence of an element concentrated nearly exclusively in five or six large cities. However, that is not a reason to eliminate all the barriers and promote this kind of invasion.

The only justifiable position is the one that Mr. Larkin, our new representative in England, presented to journalists upon his arrival in Liverpool. According to a cablegram from the *Toronto Star's* correspondent in London, he stated: "*Canada is not interested in any grand immigration plan for the time being. What Canada wants first of all is to re-establish a better balance between the urban population and the rural population, a balance eliminated since the war. Canada does not want costly immigration, carried out haphazardly, and it only wants people ready to come live and work on the land. Canada does not want to add to the urban population: it needs true farmers and only them—people of sound body and mind, trained for work on the land*" (*Toronto Star*, April 3, 1922). Moreover, what good is it to bring workers, peddlers and the unemployed here when, according to a recent article in the *Toronto Globe* (March 30, *Newcomers in Slums*), there are now in the slums of Toronto over 30,000 new arrivals from Europe, cramped into shacks? Is the situation any better in many of Montreal's neighbourhoods?

***

Go ahead and talk of the need to pour 500,000 or 600,000 immigrants into Canada every year, when your only interest is to redress the finances of our railways and of the country; try to make us believe that is the only remedy to Canada's economic health, when we know from the experience of 1901 to 1921 what a significant portion of our population poured into the United States during the period; to claim that, first and foremost, numbers are important—all of that is contrary to common sense.

Everyone admits that we have built too big. However, do you fix a mistake by making another one? If we built the foundations of our house poorly, do we make it more solid by adding to the height of the building disparate materials brought en masse from here, there and everywhere and taken from cracked walls elsewhere?

It is astonishing to see people who speak quite sensibly about political economy, railways, public finances and industry, how obviously absurd their reasoning becomes, as soon as they address the subject of immigration. They want to build still bigger. Why do they not want to begin first by making the structure solid and compact?

Twenty Years Too Many

Georges Pelletier
Le Devoir, December 19, 1929

At a meeting this week where homage was also paid to the memory of Mr. Robb, the Minister of Finance of Canada, who passed away a few months ago, a Member of Parliament, Mr. S.W. Jacobs, stated that *"in 1923, Mr. Robb, then Minister of Immigration, saved 5,000 Jewish refugees from death, by authorizing their entry to Canada under a special permit"* (see the *Gazette* of December 17, first page).

This fact, broadly unknown until now—although, around 1923 it was rumoured in circles dealing with immigration, that a minister had granted a special entry permit to Canada to a significant number of people chased out of Russia—allows us to see how one of the most important clauses of the Act on Canadian Immigration operated. The clause is not new. It does not date back to the post-war period. It can be found already in the former Act on Immigration (9–10, Edward VII, chapter 27), where it reads as follows:

> 4 — *The Minister may issue a permit in writing to authorize a person to enter Canada without being subject to the provisions of the present Act. The permit must comply with form A in the appendix to the present Act and indicate that it is in force only for a specific period, but on occasion may be extended or revoked at any time by the Minister ... "*

This section 4 first appeared in a statute of 1910. It destroys the entire substance of the Act from top to bottom. The Minister of Immigration, or a subordinate he authorizes to sign in his place, may by a single stroke of the pen remove completely all barriers to immigration. Medical examinations, examinations of the civil status of the immigrant, questions of whether the immigrant is apt to become a good Canadian citizen, all that disappears as soon as the Minister puts his signature on the special permit, since it dispenses the Minister from the formalities of any medical or civil examination. The only change made to this section in 1924, other than specification of terms, is that the Minister is now obliged to provide to

Parliament, in each session, a list of permits issued during the year with names and details.

Already in 1913, on these very pages, in an investigation on Canadian immigration, published from mid-October to mid-November of that year, we indicated that the clause was open to numerous abuses and several ministers had already used it, including Mr. Oliver, who had sponsored the bill under the Laurier regime, as well as Mr. Rogers and Mr. Roche, the two Conservatives who succeeded him at Immigration. There is no doubt that it has been applied on many occasions since that time. What Mr. Jacobs has just said about Mr. Robb demonstrates that under the King regime, just as under the Laurier and Borden governments, ministers have signed numerous special permits under the provisions of section 4. As for Mr. Robb, did he not, in effect, by a stroke of the pen remove the barriers to 5,000 immigrants, all at once in 1923? Something to make us think.

In recent weeks, there has been talk of bringing into the country — obviously under the provisions of the clause in the special permit — several thousand Mennonites. It is said that the Russian government persecutes them, seeks to eliminate them and has crammed them into railway wagons in poor condition, without any material assistance, while waiting for them to find a way to leave the land of the Soviets. Mr. Forke, the Minister of Immigration, before signing the requested permit, consulted the governments of Alberta, Saskatchewan and Manitoba. All three refused to share Ottawa's responsibility and accept that the new arrivals settle within the borders of their provinces under their protection and with their consent. In this case, at least, the Minister conferred with the provincial authorities and informed them beforehand of what he intended to do. However, nothing in the Act obliges him to do so; it was simply a friendly gesture on his part — there is no trace of such a gesture in relation to the entry to Canada in 1923 of five thousand immigrants at once. Neither Mr. Taschereau nor Mr. Ferguson nor any other Canadian premiers at the time seem to have been consulted on the matter. It is only now, after an accidental remark by a Member of Parliament from Montreal, that the public has learned of what happened.

It is not a matter here of examining or debating the ethnic origin or source, no more than the rural or urban characteristics and the capacity to adapt of the bloc of immigrants of 1923. That is not the question. We are raising a question of principle. Is it acceptable, is it just to leave in our statutes, at a time when all countries are tightening the rules in their immigration laws, a provision that grants politicians an excessive discretionary power: that of dumping into a country at any given time, five or six thousand or twenty thousand foreigners, exempt from any civil or medical examination and entering here just as if they were going to their village of birth?

To leave a similar clause in our laws any longer is unjust to the minister himself. The existence of the permit confronts him with a difficult choice, either displease a group of influential citizens, financiers or voters who will seek to make the department for which he is responsible, pay for his decision not to admit certain immigrants or yield to them without any publicity and thus add to the already difficult Canadian immigration problems. It is equally unjust to the mass of Canadian citizens who must have the right, to some extent, to learn who are the people wishing to come and live beside them in Canada.

At a time when in some countries regulations are becoming increasingly strict, with immigration even being restricted to a given number over a specific period of time and immigrants required to submit to serious examinations of all kinds, it is urgent that in our country we finally dare to delete the special permits from the Act and eliminate the practice. This abusive regime has now existed for twenty years, twenty years that it should not have existed.

Jewish Immigration to Canada
(1933–1943)

After January 1933, once Hitler was in power, the perception regarding Jewish immigration to Canada changed completely on the pages of *Le Devoir*. After that date, the German government set in motion brutal forms of oppression that forced tens of thousands of people of Jewish origin to flee their country, a situation that continued to worsen until the end of the 1930s and culminated with the start of the Second World War. Faced with an unsupportable, if not desperate situation, many of the victims turned to Canada to find shelter. In Canada, numerous Jewish organizations, realizing the gravity of the situation of the German Jews, demanded the government accept Jewish refuges for humanitarian reasons. From 1933 to 1943, that is, after Bourassa's departure, *Le Devoir* addressed the issue of Jewish immigration to Canada eighteen times, sixteen times in a clearly negative tone. The views of this nature were most often found in the years 1933–34, 1938–39, and 1943, which correspond in European history to the worst periods of persecution committed against the Jewish population and included the implementation of the "Final Solution." Several other factors explain the increase in the hostile opinions in *Le Devoir*, including the fact that after 1933 several Jewish spokespersons made their views known openly on the subject in Canada and that community leadership acted more effectively. Canadian Jews could not remain indifferent to the suffering of those who shared their faith and they led major public opinion campaigns to convince the Canadian government authorities to come to the assistance of German and East European refugees. Furthermore, there were members of Jewish origin in the federal and provincial parliaments, such as S.W. Jacobs in Ottawa and Peter Bercovitch in Quebec, who made numerous efforts to raise the issue in public. *Le Devoir*'s position often contradicted their efforts or flatly rejected them.

The attack in *Le Devoir* was led mainly by Georges Pelletier and Omer Héroux. Starting in 1934, Héroux raised objections of a more practical nature, for example, the absorption capacity of a country in the throes of a serious economic depression. The refugee crisis, particularly during 1933–1934, occurred when unemployment had reached unparalleled heights and public opinion was in general much opposed to the arrival of new citizens, whatever their origin. To these more immediate and practical arguments, Pelletier, in March 1939, added ideological considerations based on the notion the editorialist had of his country. Following the *Anschluss* of Austria, the Kristallnacht pogrom, and Germany's annexation of Czechoslovakia—all events seriously threatening the future of Jews living in Central Europe— Pelletier determined it was now time to consider Canada as a country of Christian tradition that could not support the acceptance to its bosom of immigrants "impossible to assimilate," if not alien to its fundamental values. The rejection was now placed into the more abstract spheres of national identity and religious beliefs. Pelletier did not consider German Jews farmers and thought they obtained special entry permits through political machinations. His opinion in March 1939 was that they were incapable of becoming Canadians mainly because of their ethnic and religious origins, and that accepting them ran counter to the idea Canadian citizens held of their country and would make Canada vulnerable. Throughout these years, *Le Devoir* did not seem to realize the seriousness of threats faced by German, Austrian, and Czechoslovak Jews—and, later, Polish, Russian, and Hungarian Jews. In fact, Héroux and Pelletier were incapable of judging the price that would soon be paid for having left the situation of refugees fleeing National Socialism during the 1930s to deteriorate with impunity. No one at *Le Devoir* understood that the Nazis were already planning the destruction of European Judaism, nor that a world-wide conflict of unheard-of scope would soon give them the opportunity to execute their plan.

Another explanation for *Le Devoir*'s defensive stance is that it was influenced by ideas, spread skilfully by anti-Semitic propaganda, that Jewish immigration would be a major wave capable of drowning French Canada. There are hints of these concerns in two editorials published in *Le Devoir* at the end of 1943, that speak of a "massive invasion" by Jewish people of "notorious fertility" and liable to become a "serious rival" to Francophones. At the time, European Judaism was perishing under the double onslaught of Nazi genocidal policies and the appalling conditions imposed by the war. This incredible misinformation was even repeated by Premier Duplessis in

1943 who, while electioneering, suggested tens of thousands of Jewish refugees from Europe would soon be directed to Quebec's farmlands. Such talk, by playing on the profound fears of Francophones, was instrumental in leading Quebec nationalist groups to reject without any further examination, an understanding of the European situation. It is not hard to see that the fear of an uncontrolled influx of Jews had an impact, as early as 1933, on the imagination of several observers and commentators on the Quebec political scene, including those at *Le Devoir*. This sentiment of urgency and irrational panic did much to prevent French Canada from expressing some empathy towards the Jewish victims of Nazism.

Recognizing that pressure from the Jewish community was not sufficient to loosen the Canadian government's restrictive policy regarding refugees, and that it had become essential to form a multi-faith coalition to make oneself heard in Ottawa, immediately after Kristallnacht the leadership of the Canadian Jewish Congress (CJC) undertook to seek allies among various Christian sectors in the country. Thanks to Senator Cairine Wilson, the Canadian National Committee on Refugees and Victims of Political Persecution (NCRVPP) was set up at the end of 1938. The organization immediately started speaking tours, as well as contacting numerous newspapers and publishing a pamphlet titled *Should Canada Admit Refugees?* Lobbyists supporting refugees, however, neglected to include Francophones among the main activists of the NCRVPP and, even in Montreal, all its activities were carried out in English. Among those wanting to provide assistance to the refugees from Germany was a minister of the United Church, the Reverend Claris Edwin Silcox, who in 1940 became the director of the Canadian Conference of Christians and Jews. Silcox was keen on inter-faith dialogue, but, as soon as he had the chance, launched into an anti-Catholic tirade and made particularly hostile remarks about French Canadians. Instead of opening useful lines of communication with the French-language newspapers, the NCRVPP succeeded in doing exactly the contrary and thus aggravated the disagreements between Protestants and Catholics, as can be seen in the editorial signed by Roger Duhamel on December 16, 1943. This gave additional ammunition to those in French Canada who believed that the immigration to the country of European refugees would be at the expense of the legitimate interests of Francophones.

Mr. Jacobs Also…

Omer Héroux
Le Devoir, October 26, 1933

M r. S.W. Jacobs, a Member of Parliament from Montreal, gave a speech yesterday evening in support of immigration. This morning's *Gazette* provides us with a very brief summary under the heading: *S.W. Jacobs, M.P., Declares More People Needed—Would Help Pay Debt.* Mr. Jacobs was speaking under the auspices of a society of young Israelites, the *B'nai Jacob Young People's Society.*

> One definite way of reducing the heavy burden of weekly interest on Canada's public debt is to invite a greater number of people to live in Canada… Mr. Jacobs stated (This morning's *Gazette*, page 14, bottom of the 5th column). *He notes that Canada, with a land area greater than the United States, has a population of only 10,000,000 while it could easily accommodate 100,000,000. The national debt is three and a half billion dollars, with a weekly interest of $4,000,000, specifically $200 per person.* [sic]

This speech of Mr. Jacobs will surprise no one. It is in line with his previous statements; it corresponds to the state of mind of many people; it coincides with the profound sentiments and interests of the speaker's ethnic group, with which he knows, on occasion, how to identify proudly.

On immigration, Mr. Jacobs is a declared partisan of the *open-door* principle. This principle, which reflects his cast of mind is, furthermore, the only one that would allow the entry to the country of a great number of people of Mr. Jacobs' origin, in the best sense of the word. No one would dare invoke in support of that group, the argument that the members would not at all add to the already excessive population of large cities and that they would strengthen the number and power of our rural population.

The argument that is invoked—we in no way are discussing its merit right now—support of the planned British immigration and some non-English European immigration, will not dare be used by anyone or by Mr. Jacobs, even less than anyone else, to support Israelite immigration.

On the other hand, it is perfectly understandable that our concern with preserving the traditional characteristics of the country to the extent possible, is of no interest to Mr. Jacobs. As the old French proverb says, *he is not of the parish…*

This is in no way an accusation: it's an observation. Right now, we are not starting the essence of the discussion. We do not have the space this morning and we shall have an opportunity to come back to the subject. Furthermore, no one is unaware of where we stand on the issue. With regard to immigration policy, more precisely the policy that must guide the settlement of our country, for twenty years we have said and repeated in this newspaper what is essential. The Canadian experience has simply confirmed our opinion inspired by reflection and the experience of other countries.

What we want to highlight once again today is the development of a methodical campaign, which we can see finds members in widely different sectors, that despite circumstances should paralyze the campaign.

Special interests, racial interests and false or incomplete views are coalescing in support of resuming a policy that obviously had failed.

It is up to those who want a settlement policy in accordance with the highest interests of the country and its permanent and long-term interests to become organized and become vigilant.

If not, tomorrow they risk being overwhelmed once again.

Editorial N° 8

A New Jewish Immigration?

The "Absorption Capacity" of the Dominion — Simple Conclusions

Omer Héroux
Le Devoir, February 1, 1934

W hat is going on? Or at least, what is being planned?
To be more clear or more exact: Is a new Jewish immigration to Canada being planned? If we were to take the rumours in the street seriously, it should be added: Has this immigration already begun? Is it true that a few hundred Jewish refugees from Germany have entered the country in the last few weeks?

Open this morning's *Gazette*, page 2, column 2. There you will see that the commission established by the League of Nations for assistance to Jewish refugees from Germany has just decided (the dispatch is dated January 31 from London) to institute an information office whose work will focus particularly on this issue of refugee immigration and settlement. You will also see that the head of the Commission, Mr. McDonald, has been authorized to negotiate with governments for the admission into any country of groups of exiles and that he will work in cooperation with the private societies most qualified to act in each case. The dispatch adds that there will also be a general information office responsible for all professors, speakers and workers in the field of science who have been deprived of their livelihood by Nazi Germany.

Now go to Toronto's newspapers from Tuesday (the fact was noted in a dispatch from the *Canadian Press*, which reports from across the country) and you will see that the *Jewish Congress*, that brought delegates from all the Jewish groups in the country to Toronto, stated (we quote the *Mail and Empire*) that "the Jews of Canada will accept responsibility for the proper maintenance in Canada of any German refugee that the government in Ottawa deems appropriate to be allowed to enter the country upon the recommendation of the League of Nations."

At the congress, in a speech on the situation in Germany, one of Toronto's prominent Jews, Rabbi Eisendrath, proclaimed (see the text in Tuesday's *Globe*): "Let Canada receive these German refugees (it is still German Jews being discussed here) who would be able to raise our prosperity and extend our culture. Let us institute a national committee that will examine the Dominion's capacity of absorption. Let us insist on drafting on behalf of the Canadian people a national protest resolution against Hitlerism."

If these texts are taken together, if account is taken of what has happened in the country in the last thirty years and the normal reaction of the Jewish people, is it too much to think that, if it has not begun already, a new immigration is being planned?

***

The energy, the spirit of solidarity of the Jewish people and the care with which they defend their own people everywhere must be admired.

However, whatever emotions may be created by the events in Germany, it also necessary to look at what is happening here.

Rabbi Eisendrath put his finger on one of the most serious aspects of the Canadian situation when he proposed the establishment of a committee to examine the Dominion's *capacity of absorption*. This implies that there is a limit to this *capacity of absorption*, a limit that it is not reasonable to exceed.

Now, when a country has reached a point that it can no longer provide work for hundreds of thousands of its children, that it is forced to have thousands and thousands of men live at the expense of the State, that thousands of young people, having reached the age when they should be able to earn a living, anxiously wonder where they can find work, when a country has reached that point, is it not plainly obvious that its capacity for absorption has been exhausted?

This is the cry even of people who ordinarily support a large immigrant flow. Do not talk to us at all of immigration right now! Do not bring people here who would prevent our own people from taking their place in the economic life of the nation and whose presence would force them to wander again in search of work that keeps disappearing!

The truth is that it is no more agreeable not to have any work in one's own country than it is not to have any work in Germany; it is no more agreeable to be deprived of one's work by the economic crisis than by Hitler's policies.

This objection that our fellow English-speaking citizens raise occasionally against their own counterparts from England, does it carry any less weight against German Jews?

Whatever care Canada's Jews wish to give the German Jews, and we are certain that they will provide all possible assistance, this will not change the fact they will be settling in a country where hundreds of thousands of *natives*, are seeking work in vain. If Jewish solidarity does succeed in finding them a suitable place, will it not be, as a general rule, directly or indirectly detrimental to those who already live in the country?

***

To deal with these immigration questions is quite tedious. It is always unpleasant to appear to be opposed to works of aid and assistance; but for peoples as for individuals, it is necessary in the final analysis, to remember that *Charity begins at home...*

Is Canada Building a Tower of Babel?

Expected Consequences
of Central European Immigration

Georges Pelletier
Le Devoir, March 18, 1939

Should we accept in the country this year several thousand of the Europeans who are fleeing Hitler's regime? It is claimed that in Central Europe they number over one and a half million. That was before the events of the last few days. Should we not be talking about at least two million now?

***

We have already begun to receive a few groups of these fugitives. For example, a Quebec daily last Monday reported that five hundred immigrants from Sudetenland passed through Lévis. It is on the subject of these people that Mr. Crerar, minister in Ottawa, a few days earlier made a statement (newspapers of March 10) where the following sections can be seen: "We have not made any commitment to a specific number ... The number that we shall accept will depend on those deemed physically and in other ways qualified to enter the country. However, we have also notified these people that each family (we established the average at four people per family) should possess upon arrival in Canada at least $1,500 dollars in capital ... and that we would not raise any objections if the refugees identify themselves as farming families ..."

Therefore, provided that a family is qualified to pass the medical examination, that it identifies itself as farming family and that it possesses at least $1,500—Mr. Crerar does not say "that it must own $1,500," but that it possesses $1,500, which, it will be noted, does not mean the same thing—Canada will admit the family. Whether two thousand or ten thousand families of this type arrive, Canada may receive them. Mr. Crerar states that: "We have not made any commitment as to the exact number." Therefore, he has complete flexibility to accept a greater or lesser number.

Where will the $1,500 come from that each eligible family must bring? That does not seem to concern the minister overly. According to a dispatch from London, the Czech government has consented "to put at the disposition of the heads of these families the amount of $1,500 that they will bring to Canada to settle in farming regions. The funds come from loans and donations made by the French and British governments according to the Munich Agreement" (*Canadian Press*, March 3). There is no longer a government in Prague. London (see the dispatch of the *Associated Press* in *Le Devoir* of March 15, page 3) in the last few days has notified the Bank of England to block the balance of $33 million on deposit in the Bank as part of the $46 million promised to the Czech government. That cuts the funds available for these immigrants by an equal amount.

Where will the advances for these new immigrants come from, since there will be other immigrants from Central Europe? We know that Berlin, now the master of Bohemia's and Moravia's fate, has begun to apply to their residents the regulation prohibiting any export of capital by citizens of the Reich. The Czechs mentioned by Mr. Crerar come from provinces that in the past few days have come under the regime in Berlin. Are we to believe that, on the one hand, the *Alliance israélite* or Baron Hirsch's services, for the Jews of Bohemia, Moravia and Slovakia and on the other hand, England and France, will from now on provide the necessary capital to people who have already left Central Europe and wish to come to Canada? In the first case, certainly, especially since funds already come from this source. In the second case, it remains to be determined and it is significant. Basically, most of these people are coming or will come to our country supplied with capital borrowed or received while passing through London. Who is lending them the capital? On what conditions? Would it be in compliance with the spirit of our immigration law that new arrivals can enter the country with money that is not in reality theirs? Might we call it financing of convenience, especially when the objective is to evade certain laws, whether the immigration law or many others?

***

Canada itself does not seem to know exactly what the expected immigrants will do nor, first and foremost, what those who have already arrived will do; where will they settle; how will they establish themselves? Mr. Crerar states that the railway settlement services will be responsible for all that. Then what? And what if things do not work out?

On that point, Mr. Pouliot asked this relevant question: "If some of these immigrants turn out to be unacceptable, where will we deport them?" Mr. Crerar did not have an answer. The fine man did not know what to say. These people, in fact, no longer have a country. Czechoslovakia no longer exists. There no longer is a government in Prague. A Czechoslovak passport no longer has any value in the eyes of Germany. As for the Jews among the immigrants—according to serious information there are some—where can they be deported later for one reason or another? Germany will never want to take them back. There is nothing to do with Prague, which has become just another German city. Palestine is becoming closed. If Canada decides not to admit all these people, it would not know where to send those that it will want to deport. Through force of circumstances, it will have to keep them, unable to return them anywhere—their country of origin having been abolished for all practical intents and purposes. We shall inevitably inherit those who *cannot be deported*.

Is this what certain elements, recently established in Canada, would count on? The names of the representatives of these elements can be found on a recent leaflet dated March 11 of this year and distributed by the *Montreal Conference to Aid Victims of Nazi-Fascist Persecution*. The group's president is Mr. N.M. Benjamin and the treasurer Mr. J.K. Mergler, two very "Canadian" names. The association's goal, according to the text, is "to have a large number of exiles admitted to Canada"; and furthermore—the March 11 leaflet states it in unambiguous terms—to oppose old generation Canadians, particularly in Quebec, "who are solidly opposed to admitting this category of refugee"; this Quebec "that may be the main obstacle to the entry of refugees to Canada." We know that Messrs. Silverstone, Steinberg, Rosen, Wilford, Kerbs, Ellias, Aranoff, Gold, Greenspon, Sigda, Plawucki and other members of the executive of the *Montreal Conference*, have already set everything in motion to quell the reluctant Québécois whose thoughts naturally turn to the thousands of young and old unemployed of Canadian origin who seek aid, assistance and work here and to whom is thrown, at regular intervals, a bone of vain promises, when the slightest paid task would be better for them and the country.

Since we are talking about liberal and humanitarian sentiments, why can we not begin to show these sentiments at home and toward our own people? It is true that they have the defect of not coming from Bohemia, Moravia, Slovakia or the Carpathian Ukraine and not even the historic ghetto of Prague; therefore, any practical sympathy in their regard can wait. As to the others, "it is easier to pity he who comes from afar." Forget about those who are close by and think about those from Central Europe. ... They would be our brothers more than our blood brothers could be. It is "humanitarianism" founded on a weakness of mind!

***

Therefore, we shall witness an increase in immigration, if we do not pay attention, if we give *carte blanche* to this minister passionate about humanitarianism, when what we need first is charity and pity for our own people. Immigration, as such, is not an evil, during normal times in a young country, if it is well controlled by the government and the citizens. We have never monitored it adequately, even before the war when it would have been crucial, since 350,000 to 400,000 immigrants came through our ports each year, a great number of whom—which was a good thing, we discovered afterward—quickly headed to the United States.

Since the end of the war, we have again begun to admit thousands of immigrants each year. In 1930 nearly 105,000 came here. In 1935, immigration fell to its lowest level, for a total of 11,227. Then things resumed with the start of another increase. In 1938, close to 17,250 arrived. This year, the first quarter is more than promising, with the influx of the refugees from Central Europe already started. As long as Mr. Crerar lets things go, the arrivals will exceed 25,000 and may reach 30,000, if not more, especially since, in Central Europe, there are two million wishing to come to North America. Furthermore, in addition to the "farmers" from Sudetenland, Mr. Crerar leads us to believe that we shall receive "professors, scholars and musicians, people of exceptional merit deemed likely to make a contribution to the country." The existing regulations clearly exclude them from the eligible category; but the government may, by cabinet decree, authorize the entry of such people. Of this kind of immigrant admitted by cabinet decree, who totalled 6,502 during the last seven years, over 2,565 were of Hebrew origin, according to the official statistics tabled by Mr. Crerar himself in the House of Commons (see *Le Devoir* of February 20). Therefore, the "people of exceptional merit" abound in the Israelite group. A close look at the work of the *Montreal Conference to Aid Victims of Nazi-Fascist Persecution*, will show that we shall receive many more of these people of "exceptional merit" in 1939, whose first merit is to have very enthusiastic friends.

***

The time seems more than appropriate to demand a revision of our immigration law. It is especially important to insist that it must not be left up to the Minister of Immigration alone to issue special permits authorizing the entry of any particular individual, exempt from the general regulations. Such permits are of an abusive nature. The minister has until now been able to grant in all good faith, we would like to believe, hundreds every year: 1,360 in 1933, nearly 1,060 in 1935, over 1,240 in 1938. This state of things cannot continue. The government has a duty, a duty to all native-born Canadians not to entrust to one man, as conscientious as he may be, the responsibility for an issue of this importance. A special commission should have the responsibility—a commission constituted from people outside politics, analogous to the commission that manages the *CBC*. Provided with full powers, it would be able, better than a minister, to resist the pressure in support of various individuals, various groups, pressure coming from Members of Parliament, parliamentary agents, behind-the-scenes players, lawyers, even people paid to try and have admitted to Canada men from Europe or elsewhere who, without this paid intervention, could not enter the country and should never be residents of Canada ... and who become so too easily. A thorough and impartial investigation would quickly bring to light the abuses being committed in the area, significant abuses, for which Canada is already paying a price and for which it will suffer long-term consequences if certain men make their fortune by obtaining "permits."

Yes, let us take pity on refugees and exiles. Yes, let us provide help to them. Let us begin, however, by protecting Canada and old-generation Canadians, before any foreign group that is more or less impossible to assimilate. That is what is most urgent. Let us have less humanitarianism and more common sense; let us a have a more realistic Canadian mindset. Are we building Babel, Babylon or Nineveh here or do we want to build a civilized nation of Christian spirit?

Post-war Problems and Decline in Anglo-Saxon Birth Rate

Australia with Low Immigration, Counted on Increasing Its Numbers on Its Own and Failed — The Case of the United Kingdom — French Canadians Remain Prolific — Threat of a Major Jewish Migration from Europe to North America

Louis Robillard
Le Devoir, September 3, 1943

Australia is slowly being depopulated; the political leaders in Canberra are worried by the decline in the birth rate; over the last ten years, the population of this British Commonwealth has decreased by twenty percent.

Until now, the Australians had counted on their own fertility to maintain their numbers. The population of this southern land is estimated at 7,000,000. The country is mainly agricultural; it provides a great deal of wheat and wool to the rest of the world.

Australia would prefer to maintain a small population and not open its gates too wide to immigration for two reasons: an overly great number of immigrants would have caused a drop in salaries and wages, which are particularly high in the country; in addition, the living standard has reached a height that the citizens boast about and an influx of new arrivals would have created the risk of lowering the standard; also, the Australians were willing to admit a certain number of foreigners, but on condition that they were of British blood.

The Curtin government, returned to power following the last general election, is concerned by post-war immigration, according to a dispatch from down under.

"There is a question of whether Australia will resort to immigration to increase its population or, the dispatch adds, *whether it will take other*

measures. As of now, the Australian authorities have not yet invited the British government to send emigrants to Australia. There are reports, however, that two other Dominions, Canada and South Africa, have made such offers to London."

On the other hand, we know that the United Kingdom is threatened by an ever greater decrease in births; the British mother county will not be able to feed its dependents with Anglo-Saxon blood and the news transmitted from Sydney, that we quoted in part, notes in that regard: *"In Australia the political leaders complain about the drop in the birth rate and the risk of extinction of the Anglo-Saxon race in the colonies. The adoption of all possible means has been proposed to increase births; there will not be a more important issue after the war than that of the decline in the birth rate in the British Empire."*

Too bad for sterile peoples; they are the cause of their own decline; as for French Canadians, their numerical survival is guaranteed; over the last decade, they increased by 19% and now constitute 30% of the Canadian population, while people of British origin diminished by 2.2% and account for 49.7% or less than one-half, of Canadians; furthermore, the other European races increased by 11.9% during the 1931–1941 period.

French-Canadian households have generously ensured our ethnic survival and by the grace of God we have not been marked by the decline in birth rate bemoaned by the Anglo-Saxons, who are wealthy in ambition and gold but increasingly poor in numbers.

The great difficulty remains the prolific migration from Europe, notably of Jews. Preparations are underway for their massive invasion on our continent. It is up to us to adopt defensive measures against this gigantic peaceful aggression, which is perhaps more formidable than an armed attack, since it is more subtle.

In the open and with great fanfare, the American Israelites are now organizing the settlement of some five million of those who share their faith, threatened by extermination and exile in countries under Hitler's domination; the plan would operate under the aegis of the United Nations. Great Britain, the United States and Canada would be asked to provide asylum to this mass of Hebrews in the name of humanity and the principles set out in the Atlantic Charter.

The Jews constitute one of the most prolific races of the world, which is an acknowledged fact, and they are characterized by their racial and religious uniqueness, as well as their spirit of cohesion.

It is not difficult to imagine the serious threat to our politically divided race, although numerically still strong, that would be presented by the sudden influx of a million Israelites, bringing with their emigrant's bundles, their proverbial fertility and their thousand-year-old solidarity.

The Problem of Immigration and Anti-Quebec Animosity?

A Public Issue on which French Canadians Have the Right as Much as Anyone to Express Themselves — A Speech and a Letter from Reverend Silcox — An Accusation against Our Bishops — The Myth of a Fascist Quebec

Roger Duhamel
Le Devoir, December 16, 1943

The issue of Jewish immigration remains in the news. Many people have an interest in keeping it in the headlines.

Recently, we learned in a news release from Ottawa that the federal government has established a Canadian immigration bureau in Lisbon to facilitate obtaining a visa for Europeans wishing to settle here.

About the same time, Mr. Maurice Duplessis, Leader of the Opposition in the Legislative Assembly of Quebec, revealed a letter at a public meeting that indicated a group's desire to settle 100,000 Jewish refugees on lands in the Province of Quebec. The statement brought an immediate denial. The truth of the matter is that no one has yet been able to demonstrate whether the document is authentic or false. At the same time, there was even a former Israelite Member of Parliament, who on his own initiative and in opposition to his former political leader, spoke in the debate to insult French Canadians.

Regardless of this matter that has not yet been clarified, the fact remains that influential figures and groups are working incessantly to organize large-scale major immigration after the war and in certain cases even before the end of hostilities.

In this regard, the sentiment of French Canadians is known, a sentiment based on a comprehension of Canadian reality and inspired by a concern to ensure a minimum of political and psychological harmony and economic and social stability in our country.

There are others who want to transform Canada into a land of asylum. It is their opinion and they have the right to defend it. However, they need to do so without insulting elements of the Canadian population who intend to preserve the Canadian character of the country. French Canadians, for a multitude of reasons which need not be repeated here, are opposed to mass immigration, as has been carried out since the beginning of the twentieth century and that has to a large measure contributed to the economic imbalance of recent years, after having painfully burdened government finances with debt.

***

Last November 14, a protestant pastor who has already made some noise in the press, Reverend C.E. Silcox, secretary of the *World Alliance for International Friendship through the Churches*, of which Reverend W.W. Judd is the president, gave a speech in Cornwall on the Jewish situation and Judeo-Christian relations. Mr. Silcox, according to a dispatch from the *British United Press*, stated that Mr. Duplessis did not know what he was talking about when he claimed that there was a proposal to bring 100,000 Jews from Europe to Canada. In addition, "Reverend Silcox criticized the attitude of the Société Saint-Jean Baptiste that, in a petition with 125,000 signatures, demanded that the government in Ottawa not admit Jewish refugees to Canada. He said that this was a stain on Canada's image." There were further insults, which there is no point in repeating here.

A person outraged by this insolence, wrote to Reverend Silcox to express very politely a contrary opinion. A few days later, the pastor responded with a letter full of insults and threats to the province of Quebec. We have reproduced here two paragraphs that reveal unequivocally the sentiments of Mr. Silcox and his friends in our regard:

> *Beyond the matter of political or constitutional right, as a clergyman and a Christian, I wish my country to assume a Christian attitude on the large issue of providing sanctuary for refugees from the most infamous persecution in the last two hundred years. Canada has largely been prevented from doing what it ought to have done by the opposition of Quebec. This was made evident in the latter part of 1938 and the early part of 1939 when the petition was sent to Parliament with the backing of the St. John the Baptist societies. I consider that petition the most unChristian, the most damnable piece of smug prejudice and fanaticism due to crooked thinking — religious, social, economic and political — that*

> *has darkened our country's life. St. John the Baptist would himself dis-*
> *own the people who signed it and warn them of the day of judgement*
> *that would follow. But to the best of my knowledge, the religious leaders*
> *of Quebec made no protest and acquiesced in the position. This shall be*
> *remembered whenever the three million murdered Jews of Europe are*
> *recalled, and to their everlasting disgrace.*
>
> *This latest statement of Duplessis is of a piece with the whole pre-war*
> *fascist sentiment too vocal in Quebec, encouraged as is well-known by*
> *Nazi propaganda and hostile to sound democratic principles and to any*
> *real understanding of essential Christianity. I KNOW that many eyes*
> *outside of this country are watching every step she takes, and if she takes*
> *the wrong step, the day of reckoning will come. The day of appeasement*
> *is past! !*

We shall dispense with the translation of the text since its meaning will not escape any of our readers.

We ask that Reverend Silcox first allow us not to turn to his interpretation to know the opinion of St. John the Baptist in the circumstances. There are many people who may believe themselves to be at least as qualified as him to interpret the thoughts of the Precursor.

The quoted text contains a serious accusation against Quebec's religious leaders. An opinion is attributed to our bishops, completely gratuitously, with regard to the petition against immigration. Mr. Silcox should know that the Catholic religious authorities express their opinion on questions of dogma and morals and speak every time that principles are at stake. Contrary to certain troublemakers, they do not feel obliged to enter the fray and give their opinion, for example, to support or oppose immigration. As Canadian citizens, bishops have the right to their opinion, they even have the right to express it, but they are not obliged to do so. It is up to their wisdom and their prudence to make the decision.

As for the threat contained in the last paragraph of the letter, it would make only the very spineless tremble. Who does not know that Canada's English provinces collectively are more powerful than Quebec? However, it does not appear to be democratic or Christian in spirit to indicate that force may eventually take precedence over law. Mr. Silcox gets carried away by his universal zeal and has little concern for Canada's permanent interests. That is his business. However, he needs to respect the equally legitimate sentiment of the province of Quebec to think differently from him. He would do well to revise his arsenal of arguments, which are particularly outdated and have hints of racial prejudice. The myth of a fascist Quebec submitted to Nazi propaganda has served dubious ... and more than dubious interests for far too long.

Nazi Germany
(1933–1937)

The historic and notional roots of anti-Semitism propagated by *Le Devoir* during the 1930s can be found in the doctrinal teachings of the Catholic Church. The proof is in the fact that *Le Devoir* frequently evoked the fundamentally Christian nature of Canadian and Quebec society in order to declare people of Jewish origin impossible to assimilate and, therefore, inadmissible. Before the Second World War, integration into the French-Canadian world meant devotion to the Catholic tradition in heart and mind—as much as, if not more than, identifying with French culture. Starting with Henri Bourassa and Georges Pelletier, who led the daily from 1910 to 1947, all the editorialists at *Le Devoir* who wrote about the Jewish presence in Montreal during the period examined here were fervently religious and had received an intensive Catholic education. *Le Devoir*'s opinion on the issue adhered very closely to the traditional position of the Vatican. This did not mean that open-mindedness regarding Jews was unthinkable, as shown by the statements of Pope Pius XI at the end of his life, but the theological gulf between Catholics and supporters of Judaism was deemed insurmountable and thoughts of any meaningful change were rejected. In this regard, Bourassa, following his personal audience with Pope Pius XI in November 1926, was undoubtedly the most liberal tendency in *Le Devoir,* while Pelletier represented the least receptive. The fact is, *Le Devoir* was not a daily with a religious vocation; other factors of a more political nature had an impact on the understanding its editorialists had of the Montreal Jewish community. It should be noted that among those factors was the influence of the right-wing Catholic press in France, which was closely reflected in the newsroom of *Le Devoir.*

Bourassa—and especially Pelletier—read what was published about Jews under the Third Republic, and they took in all news about the Dreyfus affair. They also paid attention to the views expressed in *La Libre Parole,* influenced by Édouard Drumont, and the views expressed in *L'Action française* led by Charles Maurras. Anti-Semitism predominated in the Third Republic, a society clearly more removed from Catholicism than French Canada, and aimed to marginalize those Jews considered to be overly influential at the higher echelons of French cultural life and in State institutions. This was a harsh condemnation of the social coarseness and a strategy of monopolization of which Jews were supposedly guilty, especially the immigrants who were half assimilated or barely settled in France. This position had an impact on the way *Le Devoir* reacted to Jewish immigration in Montreal during the 1930s. Pelletier, especially, often in short texts published under a pseudonym, made abundant use of Maurras's approach to radical nationalism by highlighting the supposedly negative attitudes and behaviour of Jews. The tone is the same in certain editorials on the cinema, on French language theatre and on the social context in Montreal, which contain sardonic humour and cynical expressions regarding Jewish immigrants. On the other hand, in these often scornful condemnations, there is nowhere to be found an understanding of Judaism based on racial considerations or any direct calls for physical violence.

Anti-Semitic writings appeared in *Le Devoir* well before the rise of Hitler in Germany and, for this reason, it may be hypothesized that there was no direct connection between the two currents of thought. On the one hand, the influence of Germanic culture was nearly non-existent in French Canada while, on the other, the notion of an inherently racial anti-Semitism was unable to assert itself in a society dominated by doctrinal Catholicism. Furthermore, *Le Devoir's* opposition to National Socialism would only come in 1933 with the persecution inflicted on the Church and Catholic teaching institutions in Germany. Despite the concordat signed with the Vatican, when hostile acts intensified across the Rhine against the faithful of Rome by August 1935, Omer Héroux would qualify Hitler's regime as a "dictatorship." Faced with these facts, which were troubling for a profoundly Catholic-oriented newspaper, *Le Devoir* in March 1937— again under the signature of Héroux—expressed even greater resistance with the appearance of the *Mit Brenender Sorge* encyclical, which contained an unequivocal condemnation of Nazism. This forceful sentiment respecting a "very serious situation" in Germany did not, however, take into account the even more brutal discrimination suffered at the same time by the Jews, which Héroux hardly mentions. Rejection of Hitlerism was reiterated at the end of 1937 in the editorial pages of *Le Devoir*, specifically when Pelletier undertook a European tour that lasted several weeks. In several articles devoted to the political situation in Germany and in Italy, Pelletier very clearly condemns the control exercised by the Nazi and fascist regimes over the press and freedom of speech. This time the break was final.

Editorial N° 12

As Dispatches Keep Arriving …

*The Rise of Dictatorships — News from Germany
and the United States — Yesterday's Elections —
Mr. Roosevelt's Speech*

Omer Héroux
Le Devoir, March 6, 1933

E vents are accelerating to such an extent, especially with our neighbours, that it would be quite difficult to note their nature and scope in the few sentences that we must jot quickly, while dispatches keep arriving. We are witnessing major historical events and it is only in the rather distant future that, for the most part, we shall be able to judge their importance.

However, we are struck by one thing, which applies to both the events in Germany and the United States: it is the rise of dictatorship.

In Germany, the point requires no discussion. Dictatorship has existed in fact for several months already. The election that just gave a clear majority to Hitler and to the parties supporting him will only result in solidifying absolute power in the hands of the new chancellor and his group.

In the United States, in a different form, Mr. Roosevelt similarly demanded sovereign powers. He spoke as a leader, aware of the very heavy responsibilities imposed on him by the Depression, and ready to confront every difficulty. The event alone may characterize him definitively, but he immediately adopted the tone of a leader fearing nothing and ready to govern. The emphasis was more personal, even more authoritarian than what has been heard in a long time from the lips of any political leader. Mr. Roosevelt does not hesitate to recall the memories of the war and state that, if necessary, he will demand the same powers as if the country were physically facing the enemy.

It is probable that all of the American people will applaud this tone. Already foreign journalists can be seen who openly regret that their political leaders do not speak with the same emphasis.

In a time of crisis, people particularly want to be governed and feel above them a firm and precise will.

The United States and Germany, who, in fact, are following several other countries, perhaps will not be the last countries where in one form or another, a dictatorial regime will be implemented.

Even in France the expression can be heard in the streets and in newspapers.

***

The numbers from the German election, when compared to those of last November are more than interesting.

Neither the Centre Party, the parliamentary group constituted mainly by Catholics outside Bavaria, nor the Bavarian People's Party, bringing together most of the Bavarian Catholics, lost ground in the last campaign. The Centre, on the contrary, received a total of 4,289,000 votes compared to 4,228,000 last November, the Bavarian People's Party 1,206,000 compared to 1,081,000 in the last elections. More precisely, those two parties increased their support by a combined total of 200,000 votes.

It is the parties that may be called more specifically of the left that lost ground; the Socialists fell from 7,231,000 to 7,175,000 votes and the Communists from 5,970,000 to 4,746,000. The enormous gains made by the Nazis, Hitler's party, that went from 11,705,000 to 17,264,000 votes, seems to have been made at the expense of these same left-wing parties and for the people who did not participate at all in the last election.

The main argument presented to these latter voters seems to have been the spectre of Bolshevism and the need for a strong government to oppose it.

It is to be hoped that the triumph of the Nazis, who still represent only a minority of the nation, will not justify any of the fears it has created in many Catholic centres.

***

We should take the time to have another look at Mr. Roosevelt's inauguration speech and at the program he presented, especially respecting what he said about the unfortunate ruptured balance between the urban and rural elements of the nation.

However, immediate note must be made that following the authoritarian tone of the speech, perhaps nothing was more remarkable than his condemnation of a certain category of speculators. Some have said that this Roosevelt, so perfectly brought up and of such distinguished appearance, was nothing more than a high society copy, dare we say, of the other Roosevelt, also very well educated, whose cowboy image is still remembered by everyone. We cannot remember that *Teddy* ever spoke in a more virile tone, that he attacked any plutocrats more aggressively or asserted a more clear or more personal determination.

Let us hope—and this is not only important for his country, it is important for the entire world—that the new leader of the American government achieve his dreams.

… Even the most indifferent and the most cold-hearted could not have listened or read without emotion the very simple few dozen words with which the President finished his authoritarian speech: …. *We humbly ask the blessing of God. May He protect each and every one of us. May He guide me in the days to come.*

It was simple and grandiose at one and the same time. The speech was truly that of a high and noble soul.

Events in Germany

The Assault on Catholics — A Few Quick Notes

Omer Héroux
Le Devoir, August 5, 1935

We do not yet have in hand complete information on happenings in Germany, but, as of now, one thing appears certain. The situation concerning Catholics is becoming very serious. In that respect, the recent articles in the *Osservatore Romano* (we reprinted an entire article recently) and a Catholic review in Berlin, said to be of an official nature, have left no doubt.

The reports from these two publications are all the more impressive since neither one is inclined to speak before it is absolutely necessary. This is obviously the case for the *Osservatore Romano*, which must reflect the thoughts of the Supreme Pontiff and must avoid interfering with the actions of the Pope, who recently concluded a very detailed concordat with Germany, which is quite probably the subject of ongoing negotiations. This is no less the case for the Berlin review, since right now, Hitler, according to an expression in a French newspaper, is a near God-like figure in Germany and an attack on his regime or those around him—especially by representatives of minorities with no particular political interests to pursue—should be considered only if it appears strictly, and in all conscience, necessary.

***

There must be very varied reasons behind the campaign being carried out right now in Germany.

First and foremost, which might explain both the actions against the Protestants and those aimed especially at the Catholics and still others, is the desire for domination—perhaps more accurately for survival (but, in fact, the two are one and the same, since Nazism can only survive on the condition that it dominates)—of the National Socialist Party that claims to identify itself with the German state.

We have quoted, more than once, a saying by a Canadian politician. All parties fear independent forces. This is a truth that can be
verified daily right here. Parties everywhere can be seen, when they
have recovered from an election and once they hold the power of government, to be determined to increase their activities and their support in order to remain in power.

Think what this desire for domination may do in the case, as in
Germany, of a dictatorship that came to power due to exceptional circumstances and knows full well that still millions of men are secretly
hostile to it.

Any semblance of local power, that could have possibly served
as a basis for autonomous action, was crushed. An absolutely unified
Reich was created out of the Germany of the multitude countries of
the past. The emperors of the past never possessed power equal to
that of Adolf Hitler.

Churches (and even the Freemasons) may occasionally represent
a small island of independence. There is a desire to bear down on all of
them also, with whatever means are at hand. There was a desire to *regu-
late* Protestant churches and there is an attempt to paralyze the activities
of the Catholic Church in an entire field. This is nothing new, since the
similarity between the campaign against sectarian *clericalism* in Latin
countries and the Nazi assault on *political Catholicism* is striking.

Logic and passion may lead to extremes when embarking on
a similar road with similar ideas. This explains why *Nazism*, which
claims it will dominate the future, as it does the present, tries to extend
its heavy hand over as much of the German youth as possible.

***

This is the broad reason that may explain, in part, all the attacks
against those lumped together and described as *enemies of the State*.

Furthermore, this obsession for domination is based on a multitude of factors. Against Jews, for example, there are old resentments
of an ethnic, economic and social nature. Against the Catholics, there
is the old *anti-Roman* sentiment that so profoundly troubled the
Germany of the past. Against those, whether Catholic or Protestant,
who identify as Christian, there exists a radical hostile movement.

It is clear that in Germany, as in many other countries, there is
an obvious and brutal anti-Christian current that may be asserted in a
variety of forms, but fundamentally remains the same.

In observing what is happening in Germany and noting the particular and painful aspects of the German situation, it must not be forgotten that the battle between good and evil is neither recent nor specific to one part of the world. Take a simple example: we fortunately are not subject to the German violence, but if you read some of the German speeches demanding elimination of denominational schools that still exist legally, you would think you are hearing some of the pleas made here against our own schools and in favour of so-called *national* schools.

***

These are some very rapid remarks and therefore, quite incomplete on a very serious and most complex situation. We shall return to the subject as soon as we receive reliable information on the matter.

Right now, we shall only add to these remarks the observation of a French writer, Mr. Robert d'Harcourt, who is well versed to the German events and who devoted a painfully moving article to them in the Études of July 20: if there is every possibility that the persecution will lead to *"a detachment and a shift away from everything in German Catholicism that only exists through tradition and by force of habit,"* it has already created *admirable* devotion.

Mr. d'Harcourt states that the persecution of the Church has, *filled the churches. Religious calling has never been stronger, to the extent that, faced with the unprecedented influx of applications to seminaries, registration had to be closed temporarily. An invincible and magnificent protest of souls against force: it suffices for persecution to emerge on the horizon and candidates for martyrdom come forward.*

The Pope and Germany

Omer Héroux
Le Devoir, March 23, 1937

The broad outlines of the letter of His Holiness to German Catholics are known. The simple publication of this letter indicates the seriousness of the religious situation in Germany. At the same time that the German bishops were increasing their protests, the Pope for a long time had already taken every appropriate opportunity to support them, to remind German Catholics of their essential duty and to encourage them very directly. These public declarations have been accompanied by less visible steps, since the Holy See still maintains diplomatic relations with the *Reich*. Diplomatic approaches by the Nuncio undoubtedly must have preceded the most solemn message written by the Pope today.

In a dispatch this morning where he is criticized specifically for having waited too long to intervene so clearly, new evidence can be found that the Holy Father has done everything possible to avoid worsening a very grievous situation and that he has spared no effort to find a compromise.

After all, the Pope is a father. He does not wish to extinguish a flickering flame. Today he is again leaving the door open to negotiations.

At the same time, he proclaims in a most solemn and moving tone the rights of the Church and the duties of the faithful. He states that he is prepared to do everything necessary to defend the responsibilities entrusted to him.

Even if looking at the issue from a strictly humane point of view, one can feel only the deepest and most respectful admiration for this aged man who just narrowly avoided death and who with such virile energy asserts the eternal rights of God and His people, confronted by the most terrible powers now in existence.

At nearly the same time, the Pope has condemned both the monstrous errors of Communism and the misdeeds and the false guidance of those in Germany who claim to be the boldest opponents of Communism.

***

Hitler seems to have achieved an extraordinary exploit in Germany. He is in the process of breaking the last chains imposed on his people by the defeat of 1918.

From a simple tactical point of view, it is hard to understand that he would let or want profound religious difficulties complicate an undertaking that was already major and difficult. He really did need his country's unity and harmony!

However, it seems that the men who still remain at the top now and hold the levers of power in Germany, (more than one observer has claimed that Hitler is not the absolute master that he appears to be from afar) have had a monstrous dream. They have imagined that they would be able to dominate minds and hearts at the same time and mould them to their fantasy. They sought a kind of mechanical unity, through submission to a code that they themselves decreed. To achieve this, they wanted to govern everything, especially the youth, the promise and guardian of the future. They systematically practised the art of controlling or paralyzing everything that was not theirs.

In the field of pure politics, such a dream would probably not be achievable. It would be confronted by overly powerful and overly formidable instincts.

In the field of religion, the dream may increase destruction, but it is condemned to failure in advance. Regardless of any individual losses it might suffer, the foundations of Catholic resistance will remain unshakeable. Nazism, in all likelihood, already belongs to ancient history and Catholicism in Germany will always remain alive. Even if through misfortune, which alas, has happened, Catholicism should disappear from Germany, it will reign in other countries.

One Christendom or another may collapse; the Church possesses eternal hope.

As for the Nazi leaders, unwittingly they are preparing their own demise, since, to the extent that they manage to succeed to weaken the spiritual forces of the country, they will in all likelihood prepare the revenge of their Communist opponents.

***

The dispatches of recent days cannot be read without recalling another period of German persecution, the one called *Kulturkampf*, the battle for culture.

That time, it was a politician basking in all the glory of a great triumph, Bismarck, the *Iron Chancellor*, who led the assault on Catholicism. He seemed to have enormous forces on his side. He was counting on triumphing. To ensure triumph, he did not hesitate to resort to any and all violent means. The bishop of Posen, the future Cardinal Ledochowski, was imprisoned.

After years of battle, Bismarck, had to concede defeat to a power greater than himself.

This justifies great hope.

… However, in the meantime, the battle remains difficult; it will obviously be very hard. Our hearts and our brotherly prayers need to be sent with particular fervour to the Catholics of Germany, as to those of Spain, of Russia and of Mexico.

Our filial piety will lavish with most fervent affection the illustrious Pontiff whose recent days have been burdened by such great pain and who has demonstrated such apostolic courage in adversity.

Editorial N° 15

In Hitler's Germany

*The Press System — Extreme Regulation — Newspapers
that Appear to Be Free — How the Foreign Press Is Watched
and Treated — Free Thought No Longer Exists in Germany
— The Religious Issue — The Domineering Cult of Power*

Georges Pelletier
Le Devoir, December 18, 1937

Vienna, November 23,

T he press as we understand it in countries of the English or
American democratic system—such as Canada, the United States,
England and the British Dominions—no longer exists in Germany.
There are many newspapers, major ones, even if there are not as
many as before 1933. There is only a controlled press. There is no longer a free press. Every newspaper takes and receives its instructions
through the propaganda bureau headed by Minister Goebbels; this
propaganda bureau, in turn, takes its instructions from the offices
of the Chancellor on *Wilhelmstrasse*, where nearly all ministries are
grouped together in the immediate vicinity of the heart of the *Reich.*

There is in Germany an unofficial press agency or, in reality, official, the *D. N. B.*, which centralizes the news that the State wants the
press to publish; it distributes the news and watches over its publication,
just as it watches over foreign newspapers, notably those from England,
France, Switzerland and Belgium, the *Reich's* neighbouring countries.

The German press has complete freedom to publish insignificant
news—what we call *dog hit by car* stories—purely local news in no
way tendentious. For anything related to the actions of the government, State politics, statements of officials and especially news that
the State deems harmful to the German cause, detrimental to it, for all
news from abroad liable to be the least bit political in nature, with the
least bit of impact on German minds, the press of the *Reich* is given
one, central and consistent direction to follow, which the press would
be ill-advised to attempt to evade.

A journalist who has served at length in Germany recently told a colleague from abroad: "In all of Germany, there remain only two newspapers with any appearance of writing frankly: one in Cologne and the other in Frankfurt. *Wilhelmstrasse* willingly lets them be quoted in press articles that the *D. N. B.* transmits abroad in order to give people outside Germany the impression that a free press and newspapers exist in Germany. In reality, there are none and I do not know of any. Those two newspapers receive their official instructions like the others. The only difference is that they are sent to France and England more than any other German newspaper; furthermore, the instruction to them is slightly different. They must give the appearance of being free. That is the instruction given to them and they obey it. Nevertheless, there are things that they do not have the freedom to print. This they know and they practise self-censorship. They know, for example, that they must not exceed certain limits in their commentary, even if they pretend to have some appearance of freedom. It is a given that they will take care not to step over that limit."

This single direction imposed on the entire German press explains why there is no opposition press in the country, no freedom of opinion in the press, no completely informed press; furthermore, the German press now does not have the large circulation it had formerly. In nearly all the cities of the *Reich*, newspaper circulation is stagnant, if not diminishing significantly. Exact and precise statistics about German newspapers would show this—according to someone knowledgeable about the situation—if there were an office to verify newspaper circulation such as the *Audit Bureau of Circulation*, where nearly all daily newspapers in the United States and Canada are registered.

—Someone might say, "The Germans can still get news from the foreign press." That remains to be seen. Beyond the fact that the great majority of Germans know only their own language and read no others, there is also the fact that hardly any foreign press can be found in Germany. The foreign newspapers arrive late and are also always expensive—the *Temps* of Paris or the *Times* of London costs three or four times as much in Berlin as in Paris or in London. Furthermore, the foreign press is also very closely checked in Berlin. Often certain editions of one foreign daily or another do not reach Germany. Someone in authority at the embassy or elsewhere in Paris or in London will have indicated by an urgent coded dispatch to *Wilhelmstrasse* that there is a certain article or certain information of a troublesome nature in the

Temps, the *Times*, the *Écho de Paris* or the *Telegraph*. When the newspaper in question arrives at the border, it is confiscated or destroyed. There are also cases of a foreign newspaper being prohibited in Germany for a specific period. This happens quite often with French newspapers and with English dailies. It is especially common for correspondents of foreign newspapers posted Berlin or in Germany to be severely reprimanded by the Ministry of Propaganda, by Dr. Goebbels, by one of his collaborators or even by the press section of the Ministry of Foreign Affairs for having called or telegraphed to their daily or their press agency with information that has irritated, troubled or upset the Ministry, one of the ministers or senior officials. The correspondent had better watch himself or else … The unofficial press tells him directly. He may feel watched or practise self-censorship — in which case he no longer has the freedom of mind to carry out his role of foreign observer — or he may well continue to be free and one morning he will experience what happened to a personal acquaintance of the undersigned last week, Mr. Paul Ravoux, representative of the French agency *Havas* in Berlin since 1933, and what also happened to Mr. Hermann Boschenstein, the Berlin correspondent of the German-language Swiss newspaper the *Basler Nachrichten* of Basel. Mr. Ravoux received an order to leave Germany and his position within three days (extended later to eight days) for having attributed the hoof-and-mouth disease epidemic that has been raging for some time in herds in certain provinces of the *Reich* to the poor feed given German cattle because of the four-year plan. Mr. Boschenstein has just been notified by the German authorities that his residency permit, which expires on the 25th of this month, will not be extended, since he has sent information to his newspaper that irritated *Wilhelmstrasse*. He can do nothing but return to Switzerland. These two cases from recent days are not exceptional. Only two or three months ago, a correspondent of the *Times* of London was forced to leave Berlin. He was no longer welcome. Over the last four or five years there have been countless numbers of these kinds of expulsions. This clearly shows that the foreign press is as free to tell its readers what is happening in Germany as it is to tell them what is happening in Italy or Russia. With respect to the press, the countries of anti-Communist dictatorships resemble Stalin's regime, despite expressing hatred of its methods and mentality.

***

As for freedom of expression in Germany, it does not exist. There cannot be a spirited opposition press, given the system put in place for the press. It is just as impossible as someone trying to express in public, either in writing or orally, their opposition to the regime, without being assaulted or reduced to silence. An inquisitive Canadian journalist was told, "You perhaps express surprise to see that certain men whose names were often quoted in dispatches and elsewhere less than two years ago and who were nearly part of the *Führer's* entourage or even one of his collaborators, seem to have disappeared. You no longer see their names anywhere. Nevertheless, they are alive, they work, they are free but in the shadows. They are out of favour, even though they are still part of the regime. On one occasion or another they expressed reservations; a reservation about a detail, about one plan or another or a criticism based on reason about a specific point. From that day on they became an annoyance. They could not be expelled from the party because their past was such that their orthodoxy remained resounding. However, they made the mistake of thinking and speaking when they were asked for and expected to give only their approval to one plan or another—a total and absolute approval, obedience without discussion, without reservation and not lukewarm. The choice is blind faith or withdrawal. It is difficult to follow all the changes of a party that walks on a tightrope and must sway, bend, straighten up, dance on one foot then the other and twist its head to keep its balance. They were not able to follow and you no longer hear of them."

The journalist was also told: "Serious opposition anywhere is impossible, since each person wants to keep the little individual freedom he has left and does not want to risk losing it definitively. Those who do dare, lose their freedom. Take for example the German clergy, Protestant as well as Catholic. They are no longer at home in the pulpit. It does not mean that they do not speak. It means that right now no fewer than 60 German Protestant pastors and a much greater number of Catholic priests who have spoken in tones offending the State are in concentration camps, work camps or even in jail, in any case imprisoned for an indefinite time. There is a law, passed several months ago, with the clear objective of preventing freedom of speech all the way to the pulpit ...—However, Cardinal Schulte in Cologne, Cardinal Faulhaber in Munich and the Archbishop of Berlin, Count von Preysing, did raise their voices and are not in prison.—They are not because the government at the present time wants to avoid any attention on the issue of religion for reasons of foreign policy and in order not to raise greater opposition against it from Catholics across the whole world. Furthermore, if the government attacked the leaders of the Church in Germany, it would be going too far; people have not lost their Christian faith to the point of not being deeply affected if the leaders of German Christianity are personally persecuted. However, there are associates, the parish priests and the pastors in the provinces. The State throws them in prison without a second thought, if they protest from the height of the pulpit and want to speak freely."

***

A regime that deprives its citizens of their basic freedoms, does not allow them to receive information about what is happening by any other means than officially controlled sources, prevents them from having free newspapers, from holding meetings in order to examine public issues freely, does not tolerate the existence of publications and works of free political will, does not allow the pastors of souls to present, from the pulpit, their opinion on subjects related to the teaching and development of minds and the conscience, that regime, whatever it has done and may still do for the well-being of the nation, is it not a regime that presents an intellectual or moral danger to the country it governs? Is it not a regime about which the least that can be said is that it has embarked on a dangerous slope, that of a dictatorship turning into a tyranny? There may at times exist dictatorships that do good, especially good: for example, Salazar in Portugal. However, the gap between Salazar and Stalin is great—between a veritable statesman and an absolute tyrant. Hitler and his regime are deviating from Salazar's ideal; are they heading toward Stalin's brutal ways? The domineering cult of power leads to all sorts of abuses. Power is the great goddess of Germany right now. Hitler is its prophet.

Anti-Semitism in Europe
(1937–1938)

Once Hitler's power was well-established, a number of opinions could be found in *Le Devoir* regarding the increasing hostility felt towards Jews in various countries of Europe. After the Nuremberg laws were adopted in September 1935, the Nazi regime systematically persecuted and expelled increasing numbers of German Jews or seriously restricted their freedom. In the professions, and especially in the public service, a series of measures drove a great number of people—whose only sin was to be of Jewish origin—to the margins of German society. Pelletier noted in his European trip of 1937–1938 that several Central European countries, including some which were beyond Nazi influence, also subjected Jews to legal and political harassment, thereby making their lives increasingly difficult. It was an opportunity for Pelletier to begin reflecting on the presence of Jews in the Western world and reread the works of Hilaire Belloc and Herman de Vries de Heeklingen. Underlying these thoughts was his preoccupation with opposition to new Jewish immigration to Canada that was fuelled by anti-Semitic violence in the Old World. In Pelletier's opinion, protection against this immigration could be difficult. The time then was for *Le Devoir* to take a studious tone, to anticipate worsening or irreparable events that would trigger a climate of urgency instead of calm reflection. In October 1938, Héroux pursued the same logic, but with greater sensitivity to the extent of Jewish suffering in Europe and to the ultimate outcome of the anti-Semitic measures adopted in Germany.

At the forefront of considerations proposed by *Le Devoir* was the idea that Jews were fundamentally impossible to assimilate in the countries that received them and resistant to changing their behaviour. Pelletier even doubted that the loyalty of French Jews and German Jews, who had lived for centuries in their respective societies, could be guaranteed. *Le Devoir* believed belonging to a specific people was based on innate features that could not be transmitted and acquired by new arrivals. This was even more the case taking into account the religious and ethical values of Judaism as it had been transplanted to the West. If European countries were unable to convince the Jews living among them to join forces with them, this was even more true for a new society like Canada which lacked strong arguments or long traditions regarding national unity. *Le Devoir* felt Jews constituted a separate element, but they also possessed a power of resistance derived from their internal cohesion and accumulated wealth. In Europe, the large circulation press was often in their hands and large-scale financial solidarity allowed them to manipulate governments and political parties for their benefit, as in France, for example, under the Blum government. This view was held especially forcefully by Héroux, who admired Jewish solidarity as much as he feared it. In all matters, Héroux imagined that Jews dominated the world, intervened as they pleased in any circumstances, and that even in Canada, where they constituted a small, recently arrived minority, their power was unstoppable. Faced with these facts, which he considered irrefutable, and which were corroborated by numerous writers, Pelletier in 1937–38 proposed that the best solution would be to grant the European Jewish population a national home in the Middle East. Pelletier, following the lead of Charles Maurras, thought that the Jews could not find a respectable place in France, in Germany, and especially not in Canada, where enough Jews had already been received at the beginning of the twentieth century. They could only exist as a community and as individuals on a land that had already belonged to them for a long time: Palestine. Faced with the upheaval ahead, Pelletier suggested it would be better for Jews to leave Europe once and for all, and to rebuild their national identity on another continent. *Le Devoir*'s editorialists were not the only ones thinking along those lines. During the 1930s, several extreme right-wing nationalist currents in Germany and Poland also promoted settlements in Palestine for Jewish people considered undesirable in their own country.

Anti-Semitism, a Growing Danger

Jews Amongst Us or Jews in Their Own Home?

Georges Pelletier
Le Devoir, April 17, 1937

A business lawyer, after returning from Europe, said recently "What struck me most in Europe, other than the sounds of war? What struck me most? The widespread growth of anti-Semitism. — However, the Jews are doing well everywhere except in Germany. — Yes indeed! And that is what may lead to their undoing. They are too prominent for who they are. In France and even in England, two European nations where Jews seem best assimilated, where they are a factor in politics and dominate in finance, I was shocked by the growth of anti-Semitic ideas. Everyone admits behind the scenes that there is a serious danger. Here, we have no idea of the situation. In Europe, the soundest elements are becoming alarmed. Only the Jews seem not to suspect anything. They dominate and believe themselves to be deeply rooted. — But what is happening in Germany should have put them on guard. — What is happening in Germany? — It is not so much the Jews that the situation has put on guard, as the people where the German Jews have been driven. In those countries, a few important Jews, assimilated at least in appearance, foresee serious consequences from this forced movement; but they are not the masses. And the new arrivals — the Jews of Central Europe, of Poland, of Galatia and the Baltic provinces — settled in Paris or in London, believe that they are definitively sheltered. Well, they are not. And their behaviour exasperates people in France and even in the United Kingdom to the point that there is a fear of seeing the German doings and even worse being repeated very soon. — What to do? — There seems to be no other solution to all that than the return of Jews to Palestine — their settlement in Transjordan and in Mesopotamia. — Would that be Zionism? — That's it. And anyone not wishing violent anti-Semitism will need to opt for that solution sooner or later, despite its complications. Zionism could resolve the anti-Semitic crisis and prevent a terrible campaign of hatred. Without Zionism, Jews will pay a high price for their presence, their economic and political power nearly throughout the world. It will be regrettable, but it's coming, even if the sons of Israel do not see the storm coming."

***

This is the opinion of a level-headed, important business lawyer without racial prejudice; it is the opinion that was expressed already fifteen years ago in a book, too little read (*The Jews*), by the Anglo-French Catholic historian, Hilaire Belloc, who has not changed his opinion since. Belloc writes in the preface to the book: "It is the thesis of this book that the continued presence of the Jewish nation intermixed with other nations alien to it presents a permanent problem of the gravest character: that the wholly different culture, tradition, race and religion of Europe make Europe a permanent antagonist to Israel, and that the recent and rapid intensification of that antagonism gives to the discovery of a solution immediate and highly practical importance. *For if the quarrel is allowed to rise unchecked and to proceed unappeased, we shall come, unexpectedly and soon, upon one of these tragedies which have marked for centuries the relations between this peculiar nation and ourselves.*" (*The Jews*, page 3).

The reality is that since the publication of those quasi-prophetic pages, we have witnessed Hitler's Germany deport hundreds of thousands of Jews, dispossess thousands, imprison a great number, hundreds of whom have died or have disappeared without a trace. Those still kept by the Nazis in Germany have practically no right to seek work to avoid starving to death or even get milk to feed their children. These are ultra-racist cruelties, which are not the first inscribed in the annals of the Jewish people since their captivity in Babylon.

Belloc noted already in 1922 (*The Jews*, page 22) "We already have a formidable minority prepared to act against the interest of the Jew. *It will in all probability become, and that shortly, a majority.* It may appear at any moment, on some critical occasion, on some new provocation, as an overwhelming flood of exasperated opinion."

There are reasons of a broad nature and of a special nature for this dangerous movement of public opinion that has grown since Belloc wrote the above. Belloc noted that the former, "are always present and are ineradicable. Their substance may be summed up in the truth that *the whole texture of the Jewish nation, their corporate tradition, their social mind, is at odds with the people among whom they live."* (*The Jews*, page 71). As for the special reasons, they depend on the countries and centres where the Jews have immigrated and assembled, their very nature of people impossible to assimilate and who display their pride through a keen feeling of superiority which they rarely fail to show and which brings on them increasing hostility nearly everywhere. This is true to such an extent that it can be said, without being self-contradictory, that *the worst enemy of the Jew is the Jew*, because of his lack of tact and psychology.

Belloc attributes the development of the Jewish problem since the end of the Great War to the ideological Franco-Anglo-American authors of a text, with harmful consequences that increasingly trouble and overwhelm Europe, in the Treaty of Versailles and subsequent treaties, under the pretext of protecting the minorities of Central Europe, since "the Jews of Eastern Europe were put under a sort of special protection, but not in a straightforward and positive fashion. The word "Jew" was never blurted out—it was replaced by the word "minority"—but the intention was obvious. The underlying implication was ... *the position that there is no Jewish nation when the position of it may inconvenience the Jew, but very much of a Jewish nation when it can advantage him."* (*The Jews*, page 19). Subsequently there was silence with the indulgence of the major press: "the Jew acquired in all the larger communities, and especially in France, Italy, Germany and England, a power out of all proportion to his numbers, and I may add, without, I hope, offending any Jewish reader, out of proportion to his abilities; certainly out of proportion to any right of his to interfere in our affairs." (*The Jews*, pages 198 and 199).

Belloc, who is not an anti-Semite and from 1922 onward sought, since it was necessary and is still necessary, a solution to the thorny problem of anti-Semitism without violence and sentiments, stated, "that can only be done by a frank admission of reality, by the open and continued admission everywhere that Israel is a nation apart, is not and cannot be of us and shall not be confounded with ourselves... *there is a Jewish nation.* Jews are citizens of that nation; and recognition means not only telling of this truth on special occasions but the use of it as a regular habit in our relations on both sides." (*The Jews*, pages 302–305).

Wickham Steed once wrote: "No man, writer, politician or diplomat may be considered mature as long as he has not directly tackled the Jewish problem." Belloc, on his part, concluded back in 1922:

"That is why the thing seems to me urgent, although there are still large areas of Western society in which its urgency is masked and half-forgotten." (*The Jews*, page 307).

***

Anti-Semitism has become widespread since 1922; it has exploded in many countries, such as Germany, Poland and Romania; it has grown because of the fact that Jews have gained far too much influence and power, for example in Soviet Russia and in the France of the Common Front. For the last year has France not had, in addition to a Prime Minister of Semite origin—Blum is the first of his race ever to have held the position in France—a whole host of senior civil servants of the same origin? This constitutes an additional danger for the Jews, because of the resentment created just about everywhere in centres of Christian origin, if not of mind, by the presence of numerous Jews, some slightly assimilated, others impossible to assimilate.

Recently, we have seen that anti-Semitism has spread in a more disturbing way than fifteen or twenty years ago. This has led the author of a very recent book, that is moderate in tone, full of authentic quotes, equally curious and bewildering, from the Talmud and from numerous Israelite authors in France as well in England, Germany, Austria and Russia to write: "What ... *especially worries the non-Jews, is not the religion of the Israelites, it is not always Jewish economic power, it is the sentiment of harbouring groups of a different people impossible to assimilate, with the idea of aiming at world domination and with several members fomenting revolution* ... On the one side, we see ... Jewish nationalism unwilling to assimilate at any price; on the other a non-Jewish nationalism that mistrusts Jews and that can no longer be reassured. If these two opposing nationalisms cannot be diverted, if they are not channelled, we shall be headed straight into the worst catastrophes. They will be all the more serious since there has been an attempt to delay the explosion by stop-gap measures. *The Jews will increasingly become the non-commissioned officers of all subversive parties, if not the generals. The exasperated non-Jews will resort to atrocities or expulsions.*" (*Israël, son passé, son avenir [Israel, Its Past, Its Future]*, by H. de Vries de Heekelingen, pages 3 and 4).

How can this real danger of an explosion that threatens Europe, with reverberations that may reach North America, be avoided? That is what the author of *Israël, son passé, son avenir* is seeking in all good faith. He states that not persecution, not expulsion, not emancipation, not tolerance, no more than attempts at the assimilation of Jews throughout the countries of the world, has ever led to a solution, even partially, to the Jewish problem. And the seemingly assimilated Jew — this is the case of Jews long settled in England or in France and more recently in North America, including Canada — "deep inside remains Jewish. *He remains Jewish first and foremost, to such an extent, that if at some point in time in his life he must choose between his adopted country and his Jewish nationality, his Jewish blood forces him to choose the nationality thirty centuries old over that of a few dozen years."* (*Israël, son passé, son avenir*, page 7).

Asked by a Canadian a few months ago: "The Jews in France, have they not become completely French, after the part they played during the war in your armies, where thousands of them died from 1914 to 1918 for your country?," a professor at the Collège de France, devoid of any racial prejudice, like many European intellectuals, and who had just spoken glowingly of some prominent Jews of his country, answered: "The most intelligent and the most devoid of racist sentiment may well try, but in the end, they remain Jewish ... At the Collège de France I am in contact with Israelite colleagues of remarkable mind. They sincerely believe that they no longer identify with their race, they no longer practise their religion, they are agnostic; however, there comes a certain time, when you reason with them, their mind no longer grasps, no longer sees, no longer understands as a French mind or even as a mind of Christian training. Regardless of what they wish or think, their mind returns to its secular inclination; that is exactly the Judaic mind."

***

The veritable solution to the problem is, as Belloc stated years ago, the existence of a Zionist State, the recognition of the State, of the nation of Israel, a separate nation where all Jews should be and will be citizens. This means that everywhere else beyond this State, the Jew will be a foreigner. The basic idea of Zionism is not new, even if the word is of recent origin. Théodor Herzl, who in 1895 proposed the project of a Jewish State, wrote: "The Jewish State is a necessity in the world; therefore, it will come to be. This State is now taking form in Palestine. Its birth created and still is creating a great many problems of all kinds, including several most serious ones — for example, the conflict with the Arabs of the country. However, the solution to that problem will still be less difficult than the problem of the dangerous elements spread by anti-Semitism among people throughout the world. It would, in fact, be unsolvable if there were not the feasible solution of Zionism.

Palestine and the neighbouring regions can receive from eight to ten million Jews, "that is, between 50 and 70% of the total number throughout the world." (*Israël, son passé, son avenir*, page 222). According to the author of the book, this will require the voluntary repatriation of some, the mandatory admission of others, the creation of a Jewish passport imposed on all those who want to live in other countries where they will really remain foreigners and where they would have only the rights granted to foreigners of whatever origin. Jews will have to choose: *between integral and proper Zionism or the battle against the awakening Aryan forces attempting to become organized at an international level ... They can no longer claim Jewish nationality, belonging to the Jewish people and at the same time inclusion in another nation."* (*Israël, son passé, son avenir*, page 240).

That and that alone will lead to the easing of anti-Semite sentiment, a danger that *"will not disappear until the day that the Jews will be at home."* (*Israël, son passé, son avenir*, page 242). To these words, it must be added: "And we will remain alone among ourselves, among Christians."

Anti-Semitism in Central Europe

Would Our Country Want a New Wave of Semitic Immigration?

Georges Pelletier
Le Devoir, January 22, 1938

In recent days we have seen that the government of Ecuador has notified the Jews of the country, who are not farmers, that they must leave the territory of the State within thirty days. Twenty-four hours later, dispatches told us that the Goga government of Romania intends to use, in Geneva, its right to expel half a million Jews who have settled in Romania from 1916 up to the last few months. This demonstrates that anti-Semitism has become an increasingly severe problem in a great many States. Consequently, the Canadian who visited several European countries from last September to December, having observed what is happening and seen what is coming, could not help but notice that in nearly all those countries, Jews feel increasingly threatened and their support societies are considering placing the deported and the exiled, who do not want or cannot settle in Palestine, in more receptive countries. This is matter for reflection.

***

It is clear that a growing wave of anti-Semitism is assaulting the place of Jews, almost from one end of Europe to the other. It is true that in England Jews have no problems and hardly any enemies. Part of the major press is in their hands. For example, one of the London newspapers, the *Daily Herald*, with a daily circulation of over 2,500,000, is owned by a Jewish multi-millionaire, S.J. Elias, a former peddler of printed matter, and now also the head of an increasingly large popular press business. As for the rest of the English press, it is generally at least sympathetic to the Semitic element. From that side, Jews seem to have little to fear. The average Englishman is not anti-Semitic; this explains why Oswald Mosley's *Blackshirts* and his movement opposed to Jews finds few members beyond some neighbourhoods of London.

In France, there always have been a few thousand committed anti-Semites, particularly since the Dreyfus affair that divided the nation for a period. There is also an anti-Semitic current that has been maintained for a long time by the *Libre Parole* and the revelations in the *France Juive* by Édouard Drumont. Prime Minister Léon Blum's unwise conduct, in filling the most important positions of State with an unprecedented number of Jews, including some who had been in France one or two generations, revived or rekindled anti-Semitic sentiment among many Frenchmen. The arrival in France, especially during the Blum government, of a large group of Jews expelled from Germany to the rest of Europe, did nothing to calm minds. This also causes concern amongst the Jews who have been settled in France for a long time and are assimilated in various degrees.

In Belgium, a significant Jewish problem barely exists, despite Julius Barmat, a Jewish financier who many years ago came to Belgium from Holland and whose financial escapades seriously upset lucid minds respecting the likes of the Barmat brothers, two Jews, who were closely linked to the scoundrel Stavisky. Barmat died in prison a few weeks ago and had created businesses with scandalous underpinnings that ruined the careers or the reputations of prominent citizens of Brussels.

***

In Germany, the story is altogether different. For months the Jews in the Reich have been subjected to systematic persecution by Hitler's regime, in the name of Aryanism, the theory which considers the only true German citizens to be those of pure Aryan origin. The true basis of the serious problems, that Hitler and his partisans have created for the Jews in a country where they constitute less than one percent of the population (500,000 out of 65 million people), is the determination of the Nazis to put a definitive end to the intense rivalry between Jews and Europeans or anyone else. Tens of thousands of Jews have already left Germany, permitted to take only a quarter or a fifth of their assets and their personal property.

… In Cologne, in Berlin, in Munich, in Leipzig, *Le Devoir*'s representative was able to see the signs of lawyers, doctors and dentists, with family names and first names indicating their Jewish origins, on a great many streets where professionals have their office, place of work or residence. Questioned about this and the anti-Semitic policy of the Nazis by the paper's representative, a person responded: "Jewish professionals number barely half of what they were five or six years ago. The State is gradually eliminating them. In another six months, there will be new measures taken against them. It's being prepared. You will see." Therefore, this Canadian is not surprised to read in newspapers of recent weeks (see the *Temps* of Paris, January 5) dispatches from Berlin reporting that throughout Germany 3,000 Jewish doctors have just been dismissed by the union of medical insurance funds, where they were employed. This exclusion applies even to war veterans who were established in Germany before 1914 or whose sons were killed in the war. In Berlin alone, this policy affects 800 doctors.

At the beginning of November, the author of this article, during his tour of Germany, visited an anti-Semitic exhibit in Berlin housed in the building of the former Chamber of Deputies and set up under the direction of Hitler's Ministry of Propaganda. *Jews, Communism and Bolshevism*, was the title of the exhibit, extremely tendentious and presented from a technical point of view with a wealth of documents, illustrations, graphic tables and photographs of all sorts very skilfully arranged. At the end of November in Munich, *Le Devoir*'s correspondent could see enormous posters drawing the attention of the Bavarian public to another anti-Semitic exhibition. *The Jews Through the Ages*, prepared under the personal direction of Doctor Goebbels and opened by him, was visited by Hitler with his official entourage and attended from morning until late in the evening by large numbers of the public, who were perhaps curious more than hostile regarding Jews—50,000 remain in Munich. It was a remarkable spectacle. The two exhibitions served to launch a new anti-Semitic campaign by the Nazi regime. The growing scope of the consequences are increasingly visible.

***

In Central Europe, until the past few weeks, Jews felt relatively safe. The old Jewish element of Bohemia, which for centuries has made Prague a sort of European Jerusalem, with the most ancient Jewish cemetery and the most ancient synagogue of the middle ages in Europe, occupies a first-rate place in Czechoslovakia. Masaryk, who in 1919 at Saint-Germain-en-Laye had this new republic carved out of the former Austrian Empire, and Benes, his disciple, collaborator and successor, both for nearly twenty years, have always treated the Jews settled in the region from time immemorial most generously. Czechoslovakia also has a large group of Jews, increased by several thousand in recent years, who have come quickly as they fled German territory or Poland and who have preferred to settle in cities. From there they can spread out to Austria and to Hungary, while watching what is happening across the border in neighbouring Germany. The humanitarian constitution of the Czechoslovak Republic, a thorn in the side of Germany, is such that the land has become a refuge for all of the Semite group rushing to it. Prague is also one of the European cities, in relative terms, where Jews are most numerous and feel least foreign. Did their ancestors not live there from before the year 1000? And was the old ghetto of Prague not the origin of so many of the most prominent Jewish families of Paris, London, contemporary New York, not to mention Berlin, Frankfurt and Cologne of the past?

Hungary and Austria also are overflowing with Jews, some established in Vienna or in Budapest for centuries and a great number have arrived there only recently from Germany, Poland and Russia. They who have been accumulating growing fortunes in Hungary as well as in Austria, especially since the end of the Great War and notably in recent years. In Vienna, it is said: "Out of a total population of approximately 1,800,000 souls, they number 600,000—a third of the city. And they keep coming here. You see them everywhere, at the nicest and best places (which is true). Those who have come from Germany have brought hardly any money, because nearly everything they had was frozen there. However, they could not be prevented from bringing with them their skill at making money. And they do make money. ... In the past, some of them were mixed up, either to a greater or lesser extent, with the many shady activities of their cousin from Little Russia, Stavisky, who became high and mighty in Paris. They were trained well." Vienna is full of banks, businesses, mid-size industries, brokerage offices, etc., either of Jewish capital or having Jewish support. An entire part of the press is in their hands, including the *Neue Frei Presse*. They are also at the forefront of the socialist movement, just as they occupy the main positions in capitalism. How long will this last? Who knows; however, a latent anti-Semitism, fed on the one hand by German propaganda, on the other, by the lack of tact, the arrogance and the insolence of the neo-Austrian Jewish population, is coming to light and rising.

Hungary also has its share of refugees from Poland and Germany, who are making themselves wealthy, particularly in Budapest, in business, industry and banking or by purchasing, at ridiculously low prices, what remains of big landed estates, owned by old Magyar families, nearly completely ruined by the last war or by wild extravagance. In Budapest, Jews will soon, if they do not already, constitute two-fifths of the residents and are hated, especially since their co-religionist, Bela Kun, in 1920 imposed a bloody Communist regime on Hungary for months. Simply mentioning this regime makes the whole population shudder. In Budapest as in Vienna, the Jews behave as if they were in a conquered country. Until recent months, they believed that all was well for them; however, they have become worried over the last few weeks. In Romania the arrival in power of the Goga government—the leader has clearly stated the need in his country for a quick purge of the Jewish element that numbers over a million men in Bessarabia, Bucovina, Transylvania and in the other provinces—is not reassuring.

***

In Austria, Hungary, Germany and Poland, anti-Semitism is growing, is on the rise, is becoming worse and is being expressed openly. Neither Vienna, Budapest, Berlin nor Warsaw have any desire to receive additional Jews. In Ankara, the Turkish government has already signalled that its borders will not be opened for the outcasts of tomorrow. As for Italy, where there are few Jews, its alliance with Hitler forces it to take a completely cold-hearted policy with respect to a group that, even from only an economic perspective, it does not have the means to accept.

There is also France—where the Judeo-German group that has been expelled in the last few years has been greeted coolly, even by the Jews who have been in France for a long time, and already fear outbursts of anti-Semitism as much as the arrival of future rivals, if, for example, the number of refugees in Paris were to increase.

There is England ... England that is already seeking to lodge its excess population somewhere in the Dominions. In the present circumstances, confronted by the disorder created in Palestine by Arabs, who are violently hostile to the Zionist invasion, England will want to skip its turn and, who knows, send to these same Dominions those Jews from Central Europe, from Romania, from Poland and from Germany who will undoubtedly demand England to accept them and give them asylum. Steps in this respect are already being taken.

Canada is one of these Dominions. Would it want a new Jewish immigration, regardless of where it came from? You can count on it soon being proposed to us. It was being discussed in Germany in November and it was being discussed in London last December. Less than two weeks ago, the *Montreal Star* expressed a discreet wish on the subject. We can expect the subject to become current again by next June, if not earlier. What will we do? What will our political leaders do?

The Astonishment of Mr. Glass, Member from Toronto of the Legislative Assembly of Ontario, and Organizer of the Jewish Boycott of German Merchandise

---

A Declaration Calling for a Quick Comment — The Possible Consequences of This Jewish Policy — Are We Going to Risk and Compromise Our Economic Life for European Feuds? — The Eternal Question of Immigration — The Jews Should Not Lose Sight of This Point

Omer Héroux
Le Devoir, October 26, 1938

This recent dispatch from the Canadian Press deserves attention. It stated:

> *Toronto, October 24 October (C. P.). — John J. Glass, a Liberal Member of the Legislative Assembly for Toronto-St. Andrew, yesterday stated that Jews in Toronto are being refused the right to obtain work and rent apartments as a direct result of an anti-Semitic campaign led by agents paid by Germany.*
>
> *Glass, who arrived from Hamilton, where he was elected chairman of a committee of the Canadian Jewish Congress responsible for leading the boycott of German merchandise, said that the discrimination against Jewish workers is increasing with great rapidity in Toronto and in the rest of Canada.*
>
> *He believes that the growth of anti-Semitism in Canada is not a "pure accident, but the result of high-pressure Nazi activity."*

***

First, it remains to be proved that such mistrust and such hostility really does in fact threaten the Jews in Toronto and elsewhere; and if that is the case, that the hostility and mistrust is directly linked to propaganda by paid agents of Nazi origin.

Whether true or false, the statements by Mr. Glass raise a very interesting and even most serious question.

***

Mr. Glass is Jewish, a most active Jew, such an active Jew that while a lawyer and member of the legislature, he is also at the head of a committee with the prime objective of *boycotting* German products. By that effort, he and his fellows intend to strike their German adversaries in their closest material interests.

From an economic point of view, their position is equivalent to an act of belligerence and a declaration of war.

It is astonishing that such an intelligent man, with no lack of experience, seems scandalized by the idea that such actions might be met by a counter attack.

If this counter campaign against Jews does exist, even if organized and paid, how does it differ in essence from the *boycott* in which Mr. Glass has accepted to be the grand director?

***

If the Jews and Nazis were fighting in a cage and in isolation, the battle might be only of rather slight interest to us; however, that is not how such troubles unfold.

A boycott against the merchandise of a country can certainly not be organized without determining how your own merchandise will be boycotted and without provoking a broad paralysis of trade.

Are we to believe that if through dislike of German policy and by vengeance against the anti-Jewish position of the Nazis, the Jews here succeed in paralyzing the imports of German merchandise, are we to believe that there would remain much chance of the Germans buying our wheat?

Who would suffer as a consequence and who would cover the cost of this war-like policy?

Italy is another example. We know what the application of economic sanctions decreed by the League of Nations cost us and what it cost the fishermen of Gaspésie. Do we want to repeat this experience? Do we want to sacrifice the interests of the Gaspé fishermen because the government in Rome pursues an anti-Semitic policy?

Today Germany, tomorrow perhaps Italy, and the day after tomorrow, who? Romania, Czechoslovakia, Poland?... for reasons that may be worth something or worth nothing at all. It seems obvious that several other European countries are heading toward anti-Semitism.

At the risk of a broad paralysis of our own trade, are we going to organize a boycott of all the people who fear or do not like Jews?

In other words, are we going to let our country's economic life be dictated and are we going to let the material interests of Canadian citizens be compromised by a group pursuing a self-interested policy, motivated by its specific interests, its own resentment, regardless of how justified the policy may be?

***

These are some of the thoughts raised by Mr. Glass' statements. There are some others that are perhaps useful to note immediately; the first are of a general nature and the second concern the Israelite world specifically.

First, we cannot allow immigrants, here or elsewhere to bring to our country and pursue their personal quarrels and transform it into a never-ending battle ground. We cannot allow any group to try and submit Canadian life in general to its own interests.

We already have enough conflict between those who put Canada's interests first and those who put the well-being of the Empire in that honorable place—or who imagine that serving the Empire is the best way of promoting the interests of Canada.

This then, from a purely political perspective, is one the strongest reasons possible to screen immigration and admit only people who really do wish to make Canada *their* country, the country that henceforth takes precedence in their thoughts and in their actions.

***

As for the Jews...

We are not professing to be anti-Semitic here. And we do not feel hatred towards Israelites, since it, just like all hatred, would be both obnoxious and stupid. To tell the truth, we cannot help but feel great emotion at the sight of so many people who are forced to roam throughout the world and are being rejected by a great number of those who are most aggressive in condemning their enemies.

However, certain things must be said in the interests of the Jews themselves.

A few days ago, a Canadian newspaper noted that Mussolini can strike the Jews only in Italy, while the Jews can retaliate from one end of the world to the other. This demonstrates the great power of the Jews and the influence they exercise in many countries.

There is no question of criticizing this influence. Jews are very intelligent and very active; they are highly placed, especially in the press and in finance. They know how to hold together, carry out hard work, side by side across borders.

It is clear that they are able to inflict harsh blows on their adversaries, even as powerful as Mussolini.

However, as strong as they are, Jews everywhere are a minority. It is here that a danger arises and they must be warned.

If they undertake to submit the countries where they live to their own interests and their self-interested politics, they will risk a violent reaction. This is not because these countries are in any degree sympathetic to Hitler or to Mussolini, but because they intend to govern their own political life and they will in no way accept that their economic life be disrupted for no reason and that it become part of the battle between Jews and their opponents.

Jews are not the only ones who have a sense of solidarity, concern for their independence and for their self-interest.

Israelites would do well to think about this point before broadening the boycott policy.

Kristallnacht
(1938)

The events of the Kristallnacht pogrom were so violent they drew the attention of the whole world to the persecution of German Jews. The Nazis' acts of violence also drove Jewish communities around the globe, including those in Montreal, to openly protest the treatment of their co-religionists. The suddenly-worsening situation spurred *Le Devoir* to take a stand on the suffering inflicted on believers of Judaism in Central Europe. This time it was no longer possible to turn a blind eye to events and *Le Devoir* had to admit that the anti-Semitic attacks had reached unparalleled heights in Germany. In the space of less than a month, five major editorials appeared in the newspaper above the signatures of Georges Pelletier and Omer Héroux, three of which were very negative in tone towards Jews. Both Héroux and Pelletier, in the name of Christian values swept aside by the National Socialist regime, were very explicit in condemning the injustices and the aggression committed against Jews on the night of November 9–10, 1938. This, in fact, was the first time since 1933 that *Le Devoir* went to such lengths in denouncing the situation. Pelletier even stated that the unpardonable excesses were the product of a racist ideology and "cruel" means. The sight of streets littered with glass and burned synagogues did not, however, succeed in shaking *Le Devoir*'s determination to maintain its refusal to give Jewish refugees access to Canada. In fact, the paper's determination to close the country's gates to the victims of Nazism intensified as terror in Germany increased. In brief, *Le Devoir* may have been angered by the treatment of the Jews in Europe, but it nonetheless continued to reject any possibility of immigration.

All the reasons spurring *Le Devoir* to reject appeals for assistance are assembled in the following four editorials. The first and foremost of these reasons was the fact that Canada was a country in a difficult economic situation that prevented it from providing foreigners with even temporary refuge. Why give "foreigners," Héroux asked, what the sons and daughters of the country itself are unable to receive. Pelletier, in his reasoning, went even a farther by describing Jews as "an ethnic group more or less impossible to assimilate," meaning that Canada should be reserved for people of Christian tradition. Pelletier asked, how can you justify receiving a large number of people without any affinity with the majority of the country's residents and who would never integrate with them? There was the additional fact that the great majority of the Jewish refugees were city dwellers, "alien to working the land," and therefore could not participate in French Canada's grand plan of agricultural settlement. Pelletier even took the trouble, on November 26, 1938, to provide a list of all the professions in which Montreal's Jews excelled and occupied a position that was disproportionate to their numbers. What was the point of giving them a long-term opportunity to consolidate their dominance in urban centres, often at the expense of Francophones? If Pelletier saw any solution to the suffering of the German Jews, it was far from Canada in far-off Palestine under the British mandate, where a future Jewish State was waiting for them. This suggestion, repeated twice in these four editorials, clearly demonstrates that the editor of *Le Devoir* was unable to view the difficulties of the German Jews from any angle other than where their religious identity plays a major factor: the Jews must go to a Jewish country, which in his eyes Canada clearly was not.

Editorial N° 19
Demonstrations Against Hitler

Their Significance and Nature — Tribute to the Jewish Minority — The Boycott, Breaking Off Trade Relations and Possible Repercussions — The Problem of Immigration — Where It Is Important Not to Confuse Issues

Omer Héroux
Le Devoir, November 21, 1938

This morning's dispatches tell us of a major event; literally from the Atlantic to the Pacific, from Halifax to Vancouver, thousands of people in more than thirty different cities assembled to protest against Hitler's policy respecting Jews in particular, as well as Catholics and certain Protestants.

It is unquestionable proof of the indignation created by the persecution and equally strong proof, it should be noted without risking accusations of anti-Semitism, of the Jewish nation's magnificent spirit of solidarity and power of organization.

After all, it unfortunately is not the first time, in our lifetime, that people have been persecuted.

When and where have we seen demonstrations of equal size in our country?

Do you believe that these demonstrations would have been developed to such an extent and with such force if there had not been a relatively small, but solid, compact and marvellously active group to facilitate the protestors' spectacular public expression of anger and indignation?

Once again, the Jews have given us a striking example of energy and of productive action.

***

This being said and having paid this tribute to the Jewish minority, it is worthwhile examining in some detail what occurred on Sunday in the large public gatherings.

First, the persecutions were condemned and on that nearly everyone feels and thinks like the protesters.

Second, the wish was expressed that Canada do its part to help the refugees in their situation.—This raises a not unimportant question: in what way exactly is Canada to intervene?

Third, some centres responded to the question ahead of time and clearly proposed—either in exhortations or in the form of a positive *resolution*—that the gates of the country be opened more widely to these refugees. This proposition, just like the others, on boycotting German merchandise, and breaking off diplomatic and trade relations with Germany, put forward by the Canadian League for Peace and Democracy, calls for some comments.

***

Let us first address the *boycott* and the extreme measures the government is asked to take to support it (ending all diplomatic and trade relations); is it certain, first of all, that the political impact will be significant? In addition, the proposition seems rather strange at a time when England appears to be negotiating a trade treaty with Germany.

It is asserted that if all the *democratic* nations were willing to cooperate and *boycott* Germany they would quickly bring Hitler to reason. ... The approach remains questionable, especially after the failure of economic sanctions against Italy, and would the *democratic* nations work together? In the meantime, who would be the first victims of the *boycott*, the German government or the people?

In the case that the *boycott* would effectively paralyze the German economy, would not the Jews, Catholics and Protestants, whom we claim to protect, be victims to the same degree as the *Nazis*, or even perhaps more? The Nazis would be angry at the persecuted since they would be seen as the reason for the difficulties the boycott creates for the Nazis.

Therefore, is it really certain that the idea of a *boycott* would be acceptable to the very people for whose benefit we are claiming to implement it?

That is the first aspect of the question. There is another, which is one that affects us immediately.

***

The *boycott* is a double edged-sword: prohibition incites prohibition. Furthermore, if trade relations are interrupted, it means that we shall not sell more to the Germans than they sell us. In that case, will it be the members of the *Canadian League for Peace and Democracy* who compensate the farmers of the West for their unsold wheat, as well as the railways for money not earned for the wheat not transported?

On a more modest level, will it be these gentlemen who compensate the brave people of the Île d'Orléans for the eels they will have been prevented from selling to Germany? And what about the people of the south shore of the St. Lawrence for the pulpwood that they will be prohibited from exporting to Germany, when this summer, that export specifically was one of their main sources of revenue?

Close examination of the issue would yield a multitude of these questions. We do know what the economic *sanctions* did cost the fishermen of Gaspésie, who used to sell to the Italian market.

The little we have said about the issue is sufficient to indicate that before demanding a widespread *boycott* and breaking off trade relations, it would be good to think twice.

It is worth remembering the proverb not to cut off your nose to spite your face.

***

However, the major problem is that of immigration; it was probably also the principal objective of the demonstrations organized yesterday. It comes through in very many of the speeches and is asserted clearly, as in Quebec and Vancouver, in specific *resolutions*. It is easy to understand why this is the case. Furthermore, it should be noted that this aspect of the issue is of interest nearly exclusively to the Jews. This explains particularly the large participation of our country's Jewish minority in all the demonstrations.

However, on that issue it would be good to look at it a little more closely before jumping into the venture.

The situation of the refugees appears tragic; but—let us look at the issue, first, from their point of view—will they be much better off, if they are thrown into a community where their arrival risks raising quite strong animosity against them and their kind families?

This is regrettable, but can it be denied that this is the case? Is this not what explains, to a large extent, the reluctance of Australia and so many other countries to open their gates to these immigrants?

The other day, in a working-class neighbourhood of Montreal, where the issue of refugees was raised, objections immediately came up; where will we put them? what will they do? will they have to live at public expense? will they add to the number of unemployed or will they take jobs that so many of the country's residents are seeking in vain?

Those who demand that Canada's gates be opened quite wide, if not completely to immigrants, should give thought to these questions.

***

In all matters, it is worthwhile clarifying what is necessary. In this case, particularly, it would be very useful not to mix up the anger, more than rightly created by Hitler's persecutions and a new policy; a policy that, in the final analysis, may not serve the interests of the Jewish refugees any better than the interests of our own country.

The Enduring Question of Jewish Refugees

Two American Opinions: The Call for a Boycott and the Response — The Debate in the British House of Commons — The German Violence Is Forcefully and Justifiably Condemned, Infinite Sympathy Is Expressed for the Victims, but Asserted That It Is Not Possible to Receive a Large Number of Them in England — Why? England Has Too Many Unemployed — The Risk of an Increase in Anti-Semitism in North America — Urgent Questions Here: Where Will You Put the immigrants and What Will You Do with Them?

Omer Héroux
Le Devoir, November 22, 1938

D ispatches this morning tell us that twenty thousand people at Madison Square Garden in New York demanded the boycott of German merchandise. It follows a campaign that seems to be developing methodically in the United States and has a counterpart in this country. There is a belief that cutting Germans off from all trade relations with other countries will lead the Germans to change their tactics.

But the issue has more than one side.

***

For example, at the very time that the demonstrators in New York were taking the position we just described, a professor in Boston noted that during the first nine months of 1938 the Germans sold goods in the amount of only $40,000,000 to the United States, while they purchased for $75,000,000. He concludes by asking, if bridges are burned, who will suffer the most?

The suffering will be reflected in discontent, lost earnings and job losses that will have repercussions on a very wide range of worker and business sectors. This raises the question we mentioned yesterday: who will compensate the indirect victims of this policy of reprisal? Who will put the salaries and benefits sacrificed back into the pockets of Americans?

Will it be the demonstrators at Madison Square Garden and their peers?

Permit us to be doubtful.

***

In fact, behind the boycott campaign, as behind that of massive immigration, it is perhaps useful to note immediately a looming danger, that the Jews should be the first to fear.

Let us look at the facts a little more closely. Yesterday, in the British House of Commons, everyone was in agreement (justifiably so) in condemning the German persecutions; however, just about everyone seemed in agreement on another point also. It was that England cannot accept a significant number of the people persecuted by the Germans.

Sir Samuel Hoare, after having noted the importance of the refugee problem and after having said that England will do everything possible to find an acceptable solution to the problem, he, a minister of the government, stated formally that as far as the United Kingdom is concerned, massive immigration is not possible.

Why? Sir Samuel said it very clearly: first, because of the great number of unemployed and second, the serious opposition being expressed against foreign immigration. Sir Samuel declared that he was willing to examine individual cases with the greatest of sympathy, but added that it is impossible to promise that England will accept a specific number of Jews.

The Labour M.P., Philip J. Noel-Baker, who proposed the motion passed unanimously in the Commons, made an equally remarkable and significant declaration. After having condemned the Germans' conduct in the fiercest of terms, after having said that the governments could submit protests to Berlin, etc., Mr. Noel-Baker stated: Third, *we may have to examine whether we should not take measures of active self-protection.* Mr. Noel-Baker spoke of these measures in terms that left no doubt as to their meaning.

Mr. Noel-Baker, according to the Canadian Press dispatch, *claimed that Great Britain may soon have to halt the flow of refugees seeking asylum ...*

This brings us to the grim observation made in this morning's *Gazette* by its Ottawa correspondent, Mr. F.C. Mears: *All the democratic countries demand that the refugees be treated generously, but when they are asked what exactly is to be done, their voices fall silent. Each country wants the other to do the giving.*

***

It is an agonizing problem. From an economic point of view, it is tied to a harsh fact: the Jewish nation, probably more than any other, suffers from an extreme ill: the absence of a rural class of any significance.

The Jews undoubtedly could provide interesting explanations regarding this situation; they could claim to be victims of a long-standing state of affairs. However, this would in no way change the fact itself.

The Jews could add that other peoples also, among them the English, the Americans and the Canadians have regrettably distanced themselves from working the land. This, however, unfortunately changes nothing with respect to their own case; it only makes their present situation more difficult; since everywhere, except for countries to be colonized, they risk being confronted by urban masses that are already too large and see Jews as dangerous rivals.

This is a point, understandably, given less attention than the demonstrations of the protesters, but that does not escape the notice of serious observers. Again, Mr. Mears writes from Ottawa: "... *American workers' associations, as well as other associations, have warned the (American) government that no one in the country now should be deprived of employment by granting employment or the opportunity of employment to Jewish refugees.*"

The manner in which some of the propositions were received last week by a group of Montreal workers leads us to believe that the sentiment of local workers is likely not much different than that of their American neighbours.

***

This brings us face to face with the danger we spoke of earlier: an increase in anti-Semitism.

In North America there are some people who have only a luke-warm regard for Jews; the number of open anti-Semites is not signifi-cant and they do not possess the means of voicing their views available to the Jews and their friends. Furthermore, the horror raised right now by the conduct of the German anti-Semites in no way serves the cause of rabid anti-Semites. However, what would happen if they were able to arouse the sentiments (more or less noble and more or less justified) of thousands and thousands of people who believe their means of sur-vival to be threatened by the massive arrival of newcomers?

This is a point to which politicians must give thought—in the interests of the Jews themselves; the point was probably not unknown yesterday in the thoughts of men such as Sir Samuel Hoare and Mr. Philip J. Noel-Baker.

***

The problem is formidable and agonizing.

However, just like the English government, we need to look at it from the perspective of its repercussion on our own country.

Sir Samuel Hoare, to oppose the massive immigration of Jewish refugees, despite feeling such keen sympathy for them, invokes the extent of unemployment in Great Britain. Is the argument less valid in our country?

We finally come back to the enduring question that we cannot avoid asking the supporters of mass immigration: Where will you put these refugees? What will you do? Will they be added to the people the country already must support or will they take the places that the resi-dents of the country occupy or count on occupying in the near future?

All these questions call for an urgent and clear response ...

In the Case of the German Jews, the *Star* Talks Nonsense

It Sees Rural Settlers Where There Are Only City Dwellers

Georges Pelletier
Le Devoir, November 26, 1938

O ver the past few weeks there have been as many mindless comments as factual news items written and published on the issue of the hour: the cruelty and distress inflicted on the Jews in Germany.

Anyone with the least bit of humanity, regardless of his sentiments towards Jews here or elsewhere, cannot remain indifferent to the methodical acts of brutality suffered by the German Jews. A truly strong, civilized and Christian nation does not hound, for whatever reason, shopkeepers, merchants, small or mid-size industrialists, professors and professionals, does not throw them into concentration camps, does not take their property, does not strip them of their possessions, separate them from their families and does not expatriate women, children and old people into complete destitution. There are no valid reasons for such conduct. The murder of a young diplomat by a panic-stricken Jewish adolescent does not justify the racist excesses carried out by the political leaders of the Reich against an entire defenceless ethnic group. It is clear that those political leaders have turned their backs on Christ to worship an Aryan idol.

***

On the other hand, the keenest sentiment of compassion, hatred of the anti-Semitic practices of the Führer and his entourage and the sincerest sympathy cannot serve as an excuse for anyone claiming to be reasonable and sensible, in Canada and beyond, to demand that the borders of a young country be opened wide, without restrictions, to foreigners fleeing their land of birth and seeking asylum and refuge elsewhere. There are all kinds of reasons to oppose the abolition of the regulations imposed on the mass entry of ethnic groups that are only somewhat possible to assimilate. Furthermore, there is no excuse for a newspaper in this country, one that claims to be serious and posing as an oracle, to list falsehoods such as below, varnished by cheap sentimentalism. Such publication can only be explained by all sorts of reasons that have nothing to do with logic and common sense:

> The newspaper writes: *It is a sad comment on our modern society that we are so badly organized when confronted with totalitarian nations that we consider new arrivals as a liability and not as an asset. Consequently, hundreds of thousands of industrious, thrifty and intelligent Jews are condemned to destitution. One would think that nations possessing vast stretches of open land, protected by their immense borders, would move heaven and earth to try and incite these potential citizens to come and settle on the vacant lands. We expected to see intense publicity campaigns to convince these people, condemned to wander in the desert, that various countries would offer them the best chance in the world to restart their lives. We see the opposite. It was not always so. There was a time when Canada spent good money to attract settlers to the country. That era is over. We do not even admit British immigrants anymore. ... If we had the genius, the organizational force of Germany or even of Russia, we could establish in our vast spaces settlements that would cover their costs and would soon become profitable clients for our railways, our industries and contributors to the public wealth and not leeches stuck on our anaemic economy ... If we had settlers who would be willing to stay in one place, they would be worth their weight in gold.* — "Gentiles or Jews" (*Montreal Star*, November 22: *Why Tanganyika?*)

In other terms, why would Mr. Chamberlain make Tanganyika the refuge for Jews, when Canada would ask no more than to welcome them, according to the *Star*, that is interested, among other things, with pleasing its present-day Judeo-Montreal readers and advertisers—they are numerous—and recruiting new ones for the future.

***

The Jews as rural settlers? They are everything but that. They have many qualities we recognize, including determination in work, persistent effort, solidarity of race and family spirit, which are not the least of those that we should copy. However, neither the desire nor the sense for rural settlement are part of their race and their history, if we mean by rural settlement the aptitude to populate and develop vast stretches of new territories that have not yet been opened by manual labour for work in fields, agriculture and industries linked to the land.

In Canada and the United States, the Jews number in the hundreds of thousands, even millions—approximately 3,400,000 Jews have been counted in the United States and 157,000 in Canada, in the 1930–31 census. In other words, at the very least, realistically 4,000,000 from Texas to Québec. Can someone show us significant Jewish rural settlements in North America that live, have been developed and survive on agriculture? There are claims of some small groups in the Canadian West. They are negligible and microscopic. The Jews are city dwellers; they are essentially migrants. They accompany and follow business. The proof? In 1931, of the 3,400,000 Jews living in our neighbouring country, New York alone, the biggest Jewish city in the world, had 1,765,000, more than one-half of the total Jewish population of the United States. In 1931, of the approximately 60,000 Jews in our province of Quebec alone, 58,000 resided on the Island of Montreal, according to the 1931 census figures. Almost all the rest resided in Quebec, Sherbrooke, Hull, Trois-Rivières, etc. There have not been and there are not more than 1,000 out of 60,000 who work the land here in Quebec. Those who have pitched their tents in our rural communities are just about all small merchants or peddlers. A veritable Jewish farmer here is more than a rarity; he is, if the term may be used, a rare exception. Are there Jews farming in Palestine? Let him go there.

***

Furthermore, the Jews of Germany, of old Austria and of the regions of Czechoslovakia recently annexed by Germany, some of whom were supposed to come here, what were they and what have they become? Middlemen. Small shopkeepers. Small industrialists. A few thousand are professionals, technicians, chemists, professors and intellectuals. They will never come here. The United States and England will take them. In any case, these Jews are nearly all residents of mid-size or big cities, with populations ranging from 25,000 to 4 million—for example, Berlin.

Have you read the most recent dispatches regarding the assaults and terribly cruelty inflicted by young Germans on their country's Jews, under the complicit watch of the Reich's police? All the abuses mentioned in these dispatches have been committed in the suburbs or neighbourhoods of big cities—Berlin, Frankfurt, Munich, Leipzig, in Germany; Vienna and Salzburg, in the annexed provinces of Austria. It seems that anti-Semitic excess occurs only in major cities. Why? Because German or Austrian Jews gather in cities and, there as here, they seek large agglomerations of people. The *New York Times* is the best-informed American newspaper on German events, even with respect to the anti-Semitic campaign. The newspaper is most sympathetic to Jews, which is understandable since it is owned by the Alfred Ochs family, whose son-in-law manages the *Times* and is also of Israelite origin. His name is Sutzberger. The dispatches from the *New York Times* on the subject are extremely conclusive. Equally so, are the photographs published by the *Times* of ravaged and devasted establishments and display windows smashed by young Nazis inebriated with racism. Where have you read or where have you seen that farms and rural establishments belonging to Jews have been sacked, pillaged or burned? Nowhere. What to conclude? That the German Jews, like Jews here, usually reside in urban centres.

According to the *Toronto Star* (page 2, 1st column, November 22), the approximately five thousand German Jews that Canada would be committed to receiving annually, starting now and for an indefinite period (*The quota for Jewish refugees will be set at 5,000*), would be constituted of special cases or professionals—lawyers, doctors, etc.—or peddlers, small shopkeepers, merchants and undoubtedly some technicians. The settlers that we have demanded, that we want to see, where does the *Star* claim to see them? It is laughable. Everyone knows that even if we can accept farmers with funds to settle here, it will be completely impossible for us to receive workers—we have thousands who are quasi-perpetually unemployed—peddlers, clerks, small shopkeepers, middlemen, city dwellers, even professionals. This is because, with respect to the general population, all the people we have already and whose origins are here, are unable or are hardly able to earn a living and the liberal professions are overcrowded with residents of the country. *Le Droit* reiterated this the other evening (Mr. Charles Gautier's article, November 22): we have here 240,000 young unemployed people, including 70,000 who have yet to find work. Faced with these statistics and this reality, is there not but one solution: that of Canadian gates remaining hermetically sealed?

***

At the present time, out of a population of less than 12 million in Canada, the number of Jews can be calculated at over 175,000 — there were nearly 157,000 counted in 1931. Since then, there has been a natural growth and some immigration, either from Europe or from the United States. The 175,000 Jews, all things being equal, is more than double the proportion that were in Germany and in Austria in those years; many more than in France and in England; ten times more than in Italy, where their expulsion has begun. Furthermore, how many Jews are members, for example, of the Quebec bar alone? There are 206 on a list of 1,656 registered lawyers. That represents 1 out of 8, while Jews represent 1 out of 60 in the population of Quebec (1937 figures). On the Island of Montreal alone, out of 1,100 lawyers, there are 200 Jews, in other words, more than one-sixth of the Montreal Bar, whereas the Jews constitute barely one-seventeenth of the total population. And what about doctors? There are approximately 225 Jewish doctors out of a total of 1,500; their proportion is much greater than it should be. The same applies in other professions. For example, in pharmacy, out of 400 pharmacists registered in Montreal, there are at least 75 Jewish pharmacists; and out of 350 pharmacies here, 62 are owned by Jews. That is more than one-sixth. Do not even mention small and mid-size businesses, as well as small and mid-size industries, where Jews are abundant.

It bears repeating: It is on the land that there are few Jews, that one hardly sees them or, indeed, encounters them at all. This is true all across the country, but especially in Quebec.

***

The facts prove, and it can never be repeated enough, that Jews are neither settlers nor farmers. Any settlements they establish are only in cities. Whatever the worth, the misery and suffering of German Jews, with which the civilized world must certainly sympathize, those Jews will not become rural settlers in Canada any more than the Polish, Galacian and Russian Jews were who came here in such great numbers from 1901 to 1931. The fact is that there were 16,131 Jews in the country according to the 1901 census and 156,726 in 1931. That already represents a tenfold increase in thirty years. All of these Jews settled and established settlements on the populous streets of Montreal, Toronto, Hamilton, Winnipeg... In thirty or fifty years they have not cleared a quarter of a single one of our 245 Canadian ridings. That is the true story of Jewish "settlements" in Canada.

If the gates of the country are to be opened wide to this new foreign element of German or Austrian Jews, why not state it clearly? Authentic Canadians should not be subjected to false and absurd declarations and ruses that will be quickly uncovered. The potential risks should be foreseen. Canadians would quickly become disenchanted by the influx of such new arrivals in our cities where some groups, losing their patience—the unemployed tired of seeking work in vain, young people without work, wanting work, unhappy to see new arrivals taking jobs everywhere—may be tempted to resort to regrettable abuses, that yet are understandable in the circumstances. They should not be provoked. That must not be what Jews already settled here want, where we let them live in peace, prosper and grow rich. If they persist, they can expect an onerous responsibility instead of an enduring paradise. There is such a thing as lack of perceptiveness. It is a characteristic of their clever race, sometimes too clever... Excess cleverness has in the past led to other excesses. Let this be a warning, before it is too late.

Editorial N° 22

To Everyone Their Own Jews

In the Past We Received Thousands from Russia and Central Europe — Why Receive More — From Nazi Germany? Whether Mr. De Kerillis Likes It or Not ...

Georges Pelletier
Le Devoir, December 3, 1938

The director, of a nationalist daily in Paris, Mr. Henri de Kerillis of *l'Époque*, in agreement with the *Montreal Star* (November 22, *Why Tanganyika?*), wants Canada to accept and keep in the country thousands of Jews expelled from Germany. The Nazi actions against the Jews of the Reich may well be considered cruel, nevertheless, it is important to contemplate any attempt at a partial solution of the Jewish problem with reason and not by sentiment. Mr. de Kerillis, like the *Star*, approaches the problem with some sentiment, but forgets reason which is also necessary. In other words, before suggesting that Canada accept these Jews and provide asylum to them, he should have asked whether the French government could not give them wide-open access to French colonies. After all, there are French colonies in great need of settlers. If the German Jews, according to Mr. de Kerillis, are likely to become such good settlers, why does he not invite the political leaders of his country to provide them with broad refuge in Madagascar, Cameroun or French Equatorial Africa?

The tragedy in this affair of finding asylum for Germany's banned Jews, is that none of the European nations, where the press laments over the fate of these exiled people, seem keen to receive them anywhere in their own country. All these nations say: "What harshness! Poor Jews! Go knock on the neighbour's door. They will be very happy to accept you." Nice words of welcome ... but a token that leads the Jews nowhere. It would obviously be simpler and more hospitable for all those European nations, who show such pity, to open a door to the wandering Jews: not the neighbour's door, not the North American door, but their own.

***

Mr. de Kerillis, Member of the French National Assembly from Paris and a journalist, writes in an article with the title, *A Solution for the German Jews?* (Époque of November 16), where, after recalling various persecutions suffered by the Jews since the year 586 B.C., he takes a quick bird's eye view, as befits an experienced political commentator such as himself, and seeks countries of refuge for the Jews. Mr. de Kerillis, among other things, writes: "*It is not a question of lamenting, it is not a question of becoming angry, it is a question of the honour of the human race and finding a solution to put an end to the tragedy. The Anglo-Saxons, masters of the last open lands of the world and of the necessary capital to exploit them, they alone or nearly alone are the ones able to provide the solution. On the high, healthy plateaux of Uganda—that, instead of Palestine, some clearsighted Jews demanded from Lord Balfour in 1922—on the high plateaux of Kenya, in the less welcoming regions of the Canadian West and the North and in New Zealand, there is still vast space where hounded men can work the land, breathe and live in peace. Why not try to direct the massive emigration of German Jews to these far-off lands?*"

Why not first send these poor Jews to populate, colonize and develop the French colonies of Africa? Mr. de Kerillis says nothing in this regard.

Why must it be preferably the territories of the British Empire, rather than the French colonies, that receive the German Jews banned by Hitler? Mr. de Kerillis does not seem to be aware that it is not only in England and the British Empire where there are "open lands" and "capital to exploit them."

Why send these German Jews to "the Canadian West and North"? Mr. de Kerillis has no explanation. He might say the country is vast. Are there no vast regions to be populated in the French colonial territories? Really!

If Mr. de Kerillis were as well informed as he appears, does he not remember that, for all intents and purposes, Canada is a free country and that Great Britain would not wish, know how or be able to impose any massive immigration on us—not even massive immigration of British subjects from England or Scotland? Does he not also remember that Canada alone, as the absolute master of controlling its borders with respect to the people of England and the United Kingdom, must agree to give its prior consent to receive this Jewish immigration? London may do as it wants with its colonies, but not with the Empire's autonomous countries.

If Mr. de Kerillis knows this, why is he proposing to London the "massive immigration" of German Jews to the Canadian West and North? If Mr. de Kerillis does not know this, would it not be time to learn and make it known to his readers of *l'Époque*? In this respect, he would find it useful and beneficial to read and learn or be reminded of the situation, in one of the most recent works published in France on Canada: *Le Canada, puissance internationale*, by his compatriot, Mr. André Siegfried (Librairie Armand Colin, Paris, 1937). Mr. de Kerillis would then know better than to place Canada among the British colonies at the level of Uganda and Kenya, as he did without hesitation — without even appearing to suspect that Canada, from a political and constitutional perspective, is farther from Great Britain than Togo, Cameroun, the Island of Madagascar and the Comoros Archipelago are from France.

Is a parliamentarian from Paris expected to know all of the above specifically about Canada's political status? No. Nevertheless, he can be expected not to speak about it and write about it as if he does know, whereas he seems not to know. Fifteen minutes of reading at the Canadian Legation, 1, rue François 1er in Paris — it is not that far from the Palais-Bourbon or the newsroom of *l'Époque* — would have sufficed for Mr. de Kerillis to become informed on the subject. Why does he not spend some time there between two articles on anti-Semitism from Nebuchadnezzar to Goebbels? That would perhaps make him understand that neither Mr. Chamberlain nor London holds the key, as he states, *"to the Canadian West and North,"* nor can they accommodate anyone there, not even twenty Englishmen from England, who are penniless and unable to till the soil. The soil of the Canadian North, furthermore, is not easy to farm. The Jews of Germany, these urban "settlers," run the risk of starving if they settle there, to the same extent as they do right now in Nuremberg, Cologne, Koblenz, Frankfurt, Berlin or Breslau.

***

Mr. Henri de Kerillis, full of unthinking pity asks, *"Why not try and send the massive emigration of German Jews to these far-off lands?"* Why? Because Canada actually only accepts immigration that is measured and not massive immigration; because Canada has no use for elements that are only somewhat possible to assimilate, alien to work on the land anywhere in the world, except perhaps in Palestine; and because it is Palestine, their original homeland, which is the right place to send the Jewish expatriates. If Palestine, a Jewish State, cannot or does not want to accept the Jews of Germany, on soil that was the cradle of their race and remains the cradle of their faith, why should Canada accept them rather than Madagascar, Togo, French Equatorial Africa, Morocco, Algeria or even Tunisia?

Hilaire Belloc has already written, "The whole texture of the Jewish nation, their corporate tradition, their social mind, is at odds with the people among whom they live" (*The Jews*, Constable & Co., London, 1922, page 71). This is true in Europe and even more so in Canada. Regardless of the compassion that may be felt here toward the dispossessed and brutalized Jews of Germany, Canada cannot and will not forget that if the presence of Jews, whoever they are, constitutes a profoundly grave problem for Europe, it is not a valid reason to inflict the problem on a young country, in the form of a massive immigration of fifteen to twenty thousand German Jews who speak neither French nor English. At the same time, all things being equal, Canada already shelters two or three times or even five times more Jews [in proportion] than England, France and Germany. Between 1896 and 1914, did we not receive tens of thousands of Jews invited here following the pogroms in Russia and Central Europe? Enough is enough.

We have our Jews and we do not persecute them. They live happily and in wealth, without being repressed. Their presence constitutes one of the multitude of major problems that Canada needs to resolve quietly and without injustice first and foremost to itself. We have enough of our own problems, starting with our Jewish problem. This is not the time to make any of the problems worse. The propositions such as those of the *Star*, and still less that of Mr. de Kerillis, who has no business in Canada's affairs, solve nothing. To listen and want to follow up on these propositions—London cannot follow up on them, this is Canada's business alone—would lead to a dead end. The solution to the issue lies elsewhere than in the mass migration of German Jews to Canada. The issue is really a European one and we old-stock Canadians refuse to suffer its consequences.

To everyone their own Jews, whether Mr. de Kerillis likes it or not.

The Holocaust
(1943–1945)

The profound impact of Kristallnacht lasted only a few weeks and *Le Devoir* soon stopped writing on its editorial pages about the situation of the Jews of Central Europe. The one and only time Pelletier took up the subject again was during the Czechoslovakian crisis in March 1939, in the same vein as before. The start of the Second World War put the issue of Jewish immigration into an entirely different perspective. After September 1939, lack of preparation, geographic distance, and considerations of military strategy prevented the Allies from assisting Jewish populations that had fallen under the control of German armies in Eastern Europe. The opportunity to accept great numbers of refugees in Canada was gone, never to return. In addition, the beginning of hostilities in Europe raised much more immediate issues and concerns for Canadians, including the establishment of a war economy, defence of the nation's territory and the possibility of mandatory conscription. *Le Devoir* opposed the sending of recruits overseas with all its might and from the end of the 1930s, initiated a major anti-conscription campaign. Pelletier devoted most of his energy to the campaign until 1944 and relegated many issues that were dominant before the war to the background. The subject of Jewish immigration did not appear again until June 1943, when news appeared throughout the world's media that the Nazis were actively wiping out Europe's Jewish population. From that date on, damning evidence began to circulate in the West about a deliberate genocide taking place in specially-built camps, particularly in occupied Poland.

Le Devoir was well aware of these facts, described in the editorial by Louis Robillard in September 1943, since they had been raised a few weeks earlier at the Quebec Conference attended by Winston Churchill and President Franklin D. Roosevelt. However, the newspaper did not change its position in light of these new facts and maintained its opposition to the arrival in Canada of Jewish victims of Nazism. The irrefutable information gathered in 1943, far from affecting *Le Devoir*, instead incited it to maintain its pre-war position, except this time the opinions were softened by more practical considerations. This was largely due to the fact a new generation of editorialists writing in the daily did not have the same attitude of dogmatic rejection held a few years earlier by the tandem of Pelletier-Héroux. In September 1943, *Le Devoir* instead raised objections related to the situation of Francophones in Canada, such as the fear that the refugees would assimilate with the English language community. Louis Robillard also believed that the new arrivals, regardless of origin, would increase the influx of people heading to big cities and would bring serious economic competition to small Francophones businesses. If the victims of Nazism neglected to learn French, the national unity of the country would be affected and as a consequence, the political power of French Canada. These views, as seen in the editorial of November 26, 1943, were partially justified by lobbying of the Canadian National Committee on Refugees that neglected to take into account the linguistic and political sensitivities of French Canadians. In the spring of 1945, Pelletier, for the last time in his career, picked up his pen to write about the issue of Jewish immigration in the country. By that time the war was nearly over and the atrocities committed by the Nazis were becoming better known, including the genocide of several million European Jews. Despite this, Pelletier maintained his position and thought, all in all, that it was not a sign of anti-Semitism to have been opposed to the arrival of Jewish refugees in the previous years. However, the debate was about to come to an end for once and for all. Pelletier would pass away a few months later and the issue of Jewish immigration would be raised in a completely different manner in *Le Devoir* of the 1950s and 1960s.

We Have Our Own Victims and Refugees of the War

They Are the Ones We Should Care for First — The Housing Crisis in Montreal and Its Consequences — Migration from the Countryside to Big Cities — A Past Reminder from Her Royal Highness Princess Alice to the Canadians of the Province of Quebec

Émile Benoist
Le Devoir, June 4, 1943

It can be said that Canadian generosity toward the war, toward the works and the consequences of the war, has been limitless. In that regard, at a financial level, the little gifts one after another and the accumulation of billions spent provide sufficient proof. We do more still; the fate of the victims of the war in countries other than our own, as well as the fate of refugees of the war who seek asylum in our country, including some who have already found asylum, has aroused the pity of the population and of the Canadian government. A few days ago, Prime Minister Mackenzie King announced in the House of Commons that he would soon make a statement regarding the refugees. A CCF Member of Parliament from Winnipeg, questioned him on the subject and wanted to know if his government intended to take into account a request from the Canadian Jewish Congress in Winnipeg, to admit to Canada Jewish refugees now in European territories occupied by the Nazis, but who expect to obtain exit permits in proper and due form from the Nazis.

The concern of the Canadian Jewish Congress for their co-religionists abroad and the Prime Minister's concern for the victims and the refugees of the war in general are understandable. However, that must not make us lose sight of and must not prevent us from seeing that we have here in the country, among our own people, in the Canadian population residing in Canada, victims of the war and refugees of the war in sufficiently great numbers that it constitutes a major social problem.

The two big Montreal English evening dailies, the *Star* and the *Herald*, last Friday published full page photographs of refugees, of Canadian refugees who have come to the big city from the country-side, subsisting by the hundreds in squalid hovels on Lemoyne Street near McGill Street. The texts that accompany the pictures further high-light the extreme poverty of these needy men and women. A ware-house, no longer fit to serve as a warehouse, long ago condemned by the authorities for reasons of both hygiene and safety, house, if the word can be used, shelter would be more appropriate, over two hundred people; thirteen families, including some very large families with twelve, fourteen, and even sixteen children.

The squalor of the site is in no doubt, as has been admitted by officials at city hall. If that building is allowed to be used for housing human beings in an urban agglomeration the size of Montreal, despite not being equipped with anything needed for such purposes, it means that there is no possibility of doing otherwise. The big city has for a long time not had the accommodations necessary for its population. This is more true than ever now that the population has increased significantly due to the war and wartime industries.

This makes the Lemoyne Street refugees truly refugees of the war. They are people who have come from nearly every part of the province with the hope of finding employment in munitions factories and other similar factories. The Herald noted this fact very explicitly: *the majority of these people left their rural homes for the city attracted by the lure of well-paid jobs.*

Furthermore, has not the goal of pages of publicity in the major press for months and months, been to make this lure shinier? Have not the publicity and the propaganda of the National Selective Service said sufficiently and reiterated everywhere that all able-bodied and available labour must be devoted to the essential tasks of the war? These tasks obviously are found primarily in the war industries fac-tories. In fact, are these tasks not those which command the highest financial remuneration?

People from the countryside and small centres believed all this and convinced themselves that it was true, that it must be true. Entire families surged to the big city that now does not know what to do with them and cannot receive them in a decent way, even those among them, apparently most, who arrive with money. The Lemoyne Street refugees each pay a monthly rent of $15 for the right to occupy their community slum. For the moment, these refugees are not jobless, but with the end of the war and assuming they remain in the city and if the authorities do not have the common sense to encourage them to take the road back to their former homes, they will inevitably become jobless. They are already a major problem for the authorities, who are unable to cope with issue.

The case of the approximately two hundred people of the thirteen families on Lemoyne Street is not unique in Montreal. The same two English newspapers, the *Star* and the *Herald*, in addition to the *Gazette*, have recounted to their readers the findings made by investigators and by the Secretary-General of the Family Welfare Association, Mr. G.B. Clark. According to Mr. Clark, in Montreal there are over five hundred families living in impossible conditions, in facilities that have not been made for human occupation, which are completely unhygienic and where children are exposed to all sorts of contamination. The municipal health service provides still more alarming figures: about four hundred families living in facilities that were not built for habitation and seven hundred more families living in overcrowded lodgings and in areas that "could not be more unsuitable." Other families live haphazardly and some disperse and are forced to store their furniture in city warehouses.

It can be seen that the number of Canadian victims and refugees of the war, in the city of Montreal alone, is starting to become of significant size.

The municipal authorities say they are overwhelmed; they would be even if the problem were smaller. One year ago, the city of Montreal apparently lacked five thousand lodgings; it probably lacks ten thousand now. The city representatives, perhaps because they did not apply the necessary energy and perseverance to the problem, turned in vain to Ottawa to obtain assistance in one form or another.

An English newspaper, the *Star*, directed sharp and bitter criticism at the city hall authorities; it also provided well-meant advice: *The army finds quarters for its men, it lodges them in easily built barracks. Would it not be possible for the city to lodge these families in barracks until actual houses can be found for them?*

Our colleague forgets that what is possible and feasible for the army and what is done for it, is not and cannot be done for civilians. The mess in Montreal is a perfect example of that. Furthermore, would lodging families in barracks really be suitable? They certainly would not have a family atmosphere.

The solution to Montreal's great housing problem, instead, would consist of sending back to their rural homes, their small villages and their small towns the hundreds of families who came and added to urban overcrowding, without benefiting anyone or any cause. Farming lacks workers, as does forestry; they should be given workers as soon as possible and given back the workers who were so foolishly taken away from them.

In Montreal, not only in the city itself but in all of greater Montreal, there is a severe housing problem. However, it is even more urgent to alleviate and curb the existing ill: the elimination of migration to the big city and making people who find themselves in the big city leave it, since it has no place for them and in any case, it is not in their own interest to be there.

It is fine and good to care for the victims and refugees of the war from other countries than our own and bring refugees from elsewhere to Canada. However, it would certainly be more appropriate to begin with our own victims and our own refugees of the war. Appropriate charity begins at home … Her Royal Highness Princess Alice, the wife of His Excellency, the Governor General, has already reminded the Canadians of the province of Quebec that their first duty was not to the foreign needy, but to the needy settlers and fishermen of Abitibi and the Îles de la Madeleine. Her Royal Highness said so more than three years ago. Unfortunately, over time her words have been forgotten.

A Judeo-American Brief at the Quebec Conference

"To Save the Jewish People of Europe" — An Urgent Appeal to Roosevelt and Churchill — A Reprimanding Tone — Evacuation and Settlement Plan for Millions of Jews — Which Countries Will Accept This New "Diaspora"?

Louis Robillard
Le Devoir, September 9, 1943

The Jewish world is going through new torment. Its tragic destiny continues. The sons of the *diaspora* are threatened by a new dispersion, perhaps the most massive in their history, following the pogroms carried out on an unprecedented scale in the countries occupied by the Nazis.

The extermination of Israelites in Poland, Germany and Romania is apparently continuing in such fury that it would amount to nearly a complete extinction of the Israelite race in Europe.

According to figures provided by American Jewish associations, two million Hebrews have already been massacred and five million have been marked who will probably suffer the same fate. This would mean the brutal and systematic elimination, in a short time, of seven million Jews.

If the Jews are not inflating figures in the Western or Talmudic way, this massacre of a race constitutes an event of such magnitude that we must stop for a moment to fathom its unbelievable scope.

Seven million Jews eliminated nearly at once? The number represents most of Judaism in continental Europe, estimated at nine million followers.

The Semite population of the world is estimated to be fifteen to seventeen million (the official figures vary), with nine and a half million in Europe and over five million in North America. The greatest number have chosen residence especially in Poland, Russia, Romania,

Germany and Hungary. France, England, Palestine and North Africa lodge the rest in lesser numbers.

However, the new Judea is indisputably the United States, where more than five million sons of Shem have settled. The messianic people's modern Jerusalem has built its temple in New York, where it has 2,500,000 faithful and hundreds of Solomons of capitalism and political influence. It is easy to imagine that it is from this twentieth century Zion that the greatest assistance will come in support of the European Semites, who are said to be destined for massacre.

The Emergency Committee to Save the Jewish People of Europe has stated that if the United Nations does not intervene immediately, it will mean the complete extinction of the Jewish people of the West and the allied armies in their next victory march will walk into the midst of an avenue of Semite corpses, "a veritable continental graveyard," since "the Germans have sworn to exterminate the entire Israelite race, before facing their own death."

The Emergency Committee established its headquarters in the American metropolis, which, at the same time, is the bastion of Judaism in America. It is one of the three most active Judeo-American organizations in the United States right now. The two others are the American Council for Judaism and the American Jewish Conference, whose deliberations at the Waldorf-Astoria Hotel were hard to miss in the newspapers over the last few days.

This emergency committee, uniting the Molochs of finance and politics, even brought its urgent request and action plan to Mr. Roosevelt and Mr. Churchill, who met in Québec. This we learned from an announcement in the *New York Times* published two days after Anglo-American discussions at the Quèbec Citadelle. That is actually good news that had been kept from us until then.

The document is of immense interest since Canada will suffer the repercussions if it is implemented. The reprimanding tone used by the Committee in addressing the two leaders of the United Nations can be seen below. The imperious phrases are customary in Jewish arrogance when it is supported by the power of numbers and money.

The following is a succinct presentation of the facts, plans and arguments put forward at the Quèbec Conference to save the Israelites in part of Europe, it is claimed, from complete and certain annihilation:

— Two million European Jews have already been massacred; five million more are doomed to mass extermination by the German hordes;

— The United Nations remains indifferent to this part of humanity subject to massacre; the political leaders meet frequently, consult each other, elaborate assistance plans for the oppressed or starving populations; their functionaries make plans for after the war, but these strategists have not yet developed any programs to help the tortured sons of Jerusalem;

— The Judeo-American brief adds that the United Nations has created an agency aimed at preserving art treasures in bombarded countries, but they have established no humanitarian agency to rescue Israelites from the Nazi hell; they have also recognized the *Comité français de libération nationale*, without appearing to be concerned about the liberation of millions of Semites dying from murder, famine and deportations;

— Roosevelt and Churchill, champions of the "four freedoms," are the last hope of the European Jews;

— Immediate action is necessary; later will be too late.

What method does the Emergency Committee propose for the evacuation of the five million Jews under Hitler's domination and to lead them to safety?

The allied governments would appoint an official agency responsible, first, to feed and then transport the legions of Jewish immigrants. The Red Cross, neutral countries and the Vatican would be asked for support. These columns of refugees would take the following route: by railway or by road to Turkey, then to Palestine or toward other allied territories. Sweden, Ireland, Portugal, Spain, Switzerland and Turkey would be asked to grant them temporary asylum. Palestine would receive the majority of the exodus and neutral ships tied up in ports would be provided for this gigantic movement of people; these ships could transport 50,000 people a month.

The Jews have offered to mobilize an anti-Nazi retaliation army composed of 100,000 of their co-religionists, taken from outside American territory and not subject to military service; these revenge and expiatory troops would be reinforced by 23,000 Jews from the Palestinian military.

Roosevelt and Churchill have not yet made public their decision with respect to this Jewish emigration plan, but Israelite tenacity, solidarity and influence can be counted on to ensure that the plan is achieved.

Where will these evacuees be sent? To Palestine? The territory received only three million Hebrews before the dispersion; furthermore, the country is impoverished and its situation is complicated by Arab antagonism, which the United Nations takes into account; moreover, Jewish leaders themselves are divided on the Palestinian issue and the English, in consultation with the Americans, recently decided to close the territory to massive Judaic immigration.

Will the evacuees be sent to the United States, which seems to be their new promised land and next to Canada? Our Semite population must already exceed 300,000 (official figures set it at 200,000), out of a total population 12 million. That is more than our share, when you stop to think that England only houses approximately 300,000 in a country of 47 million. Sociologists and the best-informed Jews have warned nations about a saturation point for the Israelite element, a point than cannot be exceeded without serious risk.

The Campaign to Admit Refugees to Canada

The Canadian National Committee's Plea — Where Would the Flood of Immigrants Come from and Who Are They? — No One French? — A Warning

Louis Robillard
Le Devoir, November 26, 1943

The refugees from Europe have vigilant friends in Canada. An organization called the Canadian National Committee on Refugees, with headquarters in Toronto and an office in Montréal, in the last few weeks has devoted itself to convincing Canadian public opinion to support the entry of a significant number of "anti-Nazis" through our ports. These thousands of candidates for Canadian life—there is no mention of a specific number—are waiting for the visas necessary, some in Lisbon, others in Spain, in Sweden or in North Africa.

Our Minister of Immigration, Mr. Crerar, has already announced that Canada just opened an office in Portugal to facilitate their entry. Nevertheless, the Toronto Committee is actively continuing its publicity through pamphlets and letters. Readers are being asked to petition our Members of Parliament and the King government to broaden immigration regulations for the benefit of these "guests."

Since the war of 1914, which led to so many changes to the borders of Europe, the name refugee designates people who do not possess a recognized nationality, have neither home nor homeland, and seek to settle in a new country. The immigrants called "refugees" constitute the majority of Europeans transplanted to Canada in the last twenty years. It goes without saying, that the migratory current has grown since 1939, following Hitler's invasions and conquests.

"The largest and most significant group" of refugees to whom we have opened our doors recently is composed of *"individuals or families bringing new industries to the country and the capital necessary for their establishment"* (Canada Year Book, 1942). Further down, we can see

how the publicists of the Committee on Refugees emphasize this category of new Canadians who have settled here during the war and whose activities can be seen around us.

However, the Canadian National Committee on Refugees is still not completely satisfied with the reception that we have given these recent immigrants, estimated by the Committee to number 15,000, from 1933 to 1943. The Committee asks us to double or triple the number at the risk of "not deserving the title of Christian country" if we refuse asylum in our vast, sparsely populated and rich in natural resources country to "*the victims of brutal persecution.*"

The Soviet Union apparently has already lodged millions from Poland, Romania and the Baltic States; Great Britain over 150,000; Palestine, 280,000; the United States, 260,000 and Australia, about 15,000 (particularly Austrians and Germans). That, at least, is the calculation made by the Canadian Committee, whose membership, among others, includes Mr. Henri Groulx, the Quebec Minister of Health. The publicists use these figures to contrast "the hospitality" of sparsely populated nations such as Australia with the little eagerness shown by Canadians with respect to the European peoples fleeing "Nazi terror."

The pages of the pamphlet, *Does Canada Want Refugees?* repeat the aggressive tone found in similar petitions of Israelite committees.

Where do these people who we are asked to accept come from, and what is their race or nationality? Who are they?

According to the Committee, they are Poles, Czechs, Dutch, Austrians, Germans, Lithuanians, Yugoslavians and Belgians who refuse to submit to fascist or Nazi ideology. This list, undoubtedly, cannot be considered exhaustive. Nevertheless, the absence of French nationality refugees is noticeable.

The pamphlet at hand does raise the question: "*Are all the refugees Jewish?*" This is its response: "*No.* The victims of Nazism include people of all religions: Catholic, Protestant and Jewish." However, Jews, particularly, have been targeted by Hitler's persecutions and executions, especially since the autumn of 1942. "Over two million have already been killed and the massacres continue. Each day delayed will bring certain death to a greater number of human beings."

In all probability, the hospitality that we shall grant to these thousands of Europeans would eventually become permanent. Their stay, in most cases, will become definitive. The so-called "refugees" will quickly forget any idea of returning to their former countries;

nearly all will settle here for good. The Committee foresees this and encourages it. It would be massive immigration under the guise of temporary refuge. Now is the time to consider all the consequences and all the serious hazards of this immigration.

Can we properly accept this influx of new arrivals taking into account the space available in our country? The Committee's answer is yes, since Canada is nearly empty and can easily accommodate 250 million people just within the limits of the regions fit for living. The Committee has published a graph to support its claim, where the author draws a parallel between the regions of northern Europe on the same latitude as our usable lands and that, according to him, sustain more than 160 million humans.

What is not mentioned is that northern continental Europe enjoys the warm breezes of ocean currents from the South Atlantic, while we suffer the cold breath of polar ice. We live in a mainly boreal country; the fault lies with nature and our explorers.

Geographers frankly state: *"Despite its size as large as Europe, Canada is little populated because of difficult geographic conditions, soil and climate. The fertile parts are limited plains around the south west and south east of the rocky mass of the Canadian Shield. The harsh climate restricts agriculture to the south. Consequently, habitable Canada is hardly more than a narrow fringe along the United States border. Taking into account the high mountains and the sparse forests, only a quarter of the land is suitable for veritable exploitation by people."* (in volume two of *Géographie générale* by Raoul Blanchard, a classic work by an undisputed specialist).

There you have the description of the extremely limited area available for our population and consequently for potential immigration.

The migrants whose arrival is being prepared by a group of sympathizers will inevitably be sent to our already well-populated provinces and where the most usable spaces should be reserved for the longest occupants of the country or their children. *"The province of Ontario has received the greatest number of immigrants every year since 1905. In 1929 and in 1930, Manitoba was in second place, while for the last nine years, Québec has occupied second place as the immediate destination of new arrivals."* (Canada Year Book, 1942). Consequently, it would be our province, that would inherit a large part of the next European migration. We already complain about the imbalance in numbers between rural centres and urban centres, as much as about foreign economic competition and dictatorship, as well as the changing of the French-Canadian population into a working-class mass.

More specifically, it is claimed that these "refugees" will make a significant contribution to the economic development of Canada and it is also emphasized, without causing harm to the long-time occupants of the country. There are lists of the fields in which the recent arrivals on our shores have been active, have applied their European experience and their capital; veneer factories, diamond cutting, glass trade, ceramics, woollens, new farming of paprika, goat farming for leather used in glove-making, laboratory research, etc., etc. This entire plea by the Committee should sound like a warning to us.

Furthermore, this tide of "unexpected arrivals" recruited from among elements deemed the hardest to assimilate, those from southern and eastern Europe, will aggravate the challenge of much advocated national unity, which has not been attained, despite the slowing down of immigration and the subsequent development of a larger base of long-time citizens who are more Canadianized. A true nation is built slowly and not by the continual addition of new layers; it is *the custom of living together* that characterizes a nation.

To the legitimate apprehensions we may have regarding the economic aspect of intensive immigration for the entire country—during this time of unusual movement of our people due to forced departures for work far away and the war—French Canadians are quite justified in adding an ethnic aspect. The immigrant invasion invariably will be detrimental to French Canadians at a time when they have barely reasserted their growth in numbers through their birth rate and from the decline in immigration over the last few years. Furthermore, the absence of French-origin immigrants among the expected refugees provides us with no reassurance.

The sudden admission of several thousand Europeans of extremely disparate characteristics creates a multi-faceted problem and every one of us, upon reflection, may assess the impact on his community.

The promoters of the government petition have displayed tenacious action; those with an interest in counterbalancing them, should not be less alert.

Inhumane Dictatorships

Georges Pelletier
Le Devoir, April 7, 1945

Neither Germany nor Russia has shown any particular consideration for the people of the territories that they have occupied during the present war.

The Russian government is accused of having dealt harshly especially with the Catholics of the Baltic countries. The Polish government, in exile, in London has made the grave accusation against Moscow of having, among other things, executed and eliminated ten thousand Polish officers after the division of Poland between Russia and Germany in September and October 1939. Moscow's response on the subject was far from convincing. On the contrary, the details about the deaths of the ten thousand officers are quite unequivocal. There are questions here that need to be clarified after the war. This is of particular interest to Polish patriots and it is not the government in Lublin, clearly friendly to the one in Moscow, that will attempt to resolve the question.

Germany, for its part, dealt harshly with the people and patriots in the regions it occupied starting in September 1939, whether in Poland or elsewhere throughout Europe. The dictatorships in Moscow and in Berlin arrogated to themselves the power to commit acts that can only be described as tyrannical against minorities in the Baltic and occupied countries. Human rights count for nothing to these dictatorships; just as it is true that Moscow and Berlin fundamentally resemble each other and have derived their rules of conduct from the same source: disdain for human beings and individual rights.

Moscow and Berlin have similarly committed intolerable acts against anything Catholic throughout Europe. Berlin imprisoned and executed hundreds of members of religious orders; Moscow, on its part, dealt severely with anything Catholic in the regions it occupied. There is a simple explanation for Moscow's conduct. It displayed complete contempt toward the Vatican under the pretext that the latter had not made a distinction among the mistreated peoples and that it had condemned the cruel conduct of both Moscow and Berlin, and their inhumanity.

***

One group especially has suffered at the hands of the Germans; the Jews established in Central Europe, notably in Poland, Czechoslovakia and the Balkans. For example, in Poland when the war started there were about three and a half million Jews. There were about a million in Romania and large groups in the Baltic countries, as well as in Hungary, Austria and Czechoslovakia. All these countries at some point in time found themselves under Hitler's occupation. Now, about the only Jews remaining are those who found refuge in Russia, where in the past under the Czarist regime towards the end of the nineteenth century, as we know, mass slaughters took place. The present government of Russia has changed its position, which allowed some of the Jews in the country to survive the war. The Jews who were in Poland, on the contrary, were massacred during the entire length of the German occupation. Furthermore, wherever the Nazis went, they tried to inflame anti-Semitism among the people. The Russian government opened its borders to the Jewish refugees from Poland and from elsewhere who wanted to go to Russia. However, a great many did not want to settle there, since they feared the campaign undertaken by Russia against the bourgeoisie and small capitalists. Those who did go to the Soviet Republics were taken into the war industries or transported east of the Urals.

In France, Hitler's regime dealt severely with the Jews. In Holland, the Jews suffered at the hands of the Degrelle and Mussert administrations, which were under Hitler's boot and followed his lead. Hungary and Romania followed Hitler's policy, although Catholics and Protestants did their best to help Jews in their anguish. We know that Catholics in France came to the assistance of Jews in all sorts of ways. In short, there was a nearly complete destruction of Jewish culture and community life in regions occupied by Hitler. There were deportations, forced labour and mass killings. There is no point in talking about Jewish centres in Germany for the simple reason that nearly all of them had already been destroyed before the war. Hitler's policy was to eliminate just about the entire Jewish population.

In Poland, especially since 1939, the situation of the Jews has been extremely cruel. Nearly all of the Jews have been eliminated. Barely a quarter remain of those who used to live there. It is appalling to read the details of the persecution inflicted on the Jews and of the ill-treatment they have received. Eastern Europe, from the seventeenth century until the middle of the twentieth century, had a large Jewish population. It was a major source of emigration; a portion of the Jews now living in the United States and Canada have come from the Baltic States and Poland, as well as Romania and the Balkans. The eight to ten million Jews who lived in those countries have provided a large contingent to the United States, where the Jews constitute, at the present time, one of the biggest groups of foreign arrivals. Where there were over ten million Jews in Central Europe, now perhaps only a few hundred thousand remain. The others have disappeared through deportation or been slaughtered.

***

An Englishman who has specialized in the study of Jewish issues in Europe, Dr. J.W. Parkes, writes in the London review, *International Affairs*, January 1945 issue, vol. 21, that in pre-war Poland approximately 10% of the population was of Jewish origin. He states that now, in Poland, barely 3% of the population is Jewish; similarly, in Romania where nine hundred thousand Jews constituted 7% of the population, the majority have died at the hands of the Germans and the Romanians. The Romanian Jewish population has fallen to perhaps to 2 or 3%. In Hungary and other European countries, there are almost no more Jews. At the present time in the United States, there are at least five million Jews. Three million remain in Soviet Russia. There are perhaps half a million in Palestine. Therefore, the Jews of the United States are now the most numerous and richest in the world. It is there that assimilation is in full force. A great number of American Jews have forsaken all religion, even if they sympathize with the Jews of other countries, assist them financially and in other ways. However, Dr. Parkes claims that the political ambitions of Jews in Europe and the United States, are pretty well alien to the assimilated American Jews. As for the Jews in Russia, they must comply with instructions issued by the government and by Soviet institutions. The author of the article in *International Affairs* writes that the Jews in the Soviet Union live in districts that have never had synagogues; and the elimination of Polish Jewry is not something that has increased the influence of Jews in Eastern Europe. Doctor Parkes believes that after the war, very few Jews will want to return to Germany where, under the Kaiser's regime, they exerted considerable influence.

The author of the article in *International Affairs* reviews the Jewish situation in different countries outside Europe. He believes that there is no sign or indication of anti-Semitism receding in the world. He states that it remains a potential danger especially in the regions of Canada where Catholics are predominant; and that anti-Semitism is also a force in South Africa and in several South American republics. Yet Catholics are not predominant in South Africa. Incidentally, with regard to Canada, especially in regions where Catholics are more numerous, Dr. Parkes is mistaken. There may have been some anti-Semitic demonstrations in such areas, but they have not become widespread. If in fact Dr. Parkes is targeting the province of Quebec, he is mistaken. In what other province have Canadian Jews grown as wealthy as in Quebec, especially in the region of Montreal? Nowhere. Whether desirable or not, the Jews have significant influence here. People increase the wealth of the Jews by purchasing from them. They now control or at least dominate in several industries, for example, distilleries, food supply and manufacture of clothing. A long list can be drawn up of Jews who have arrived in Canada and settled in the province of Quebec, fifteen or twenty-five years ago or perhaps less, and today are in the ranks of Montreal's millionaires. If there had been widespread anti-Semitism here, would it have been possible for these Jews to grow wealthy and acquire the capital that they invest everywhere and which they did not bring from Europe, since most of them arrived here from Lithuania or elsewhere very poor? Anti-Semitic countries do not allow Jews to grow wealthy as quickly as the Jews have grown wealthy here. Because people are Catholic does not make them hostile to Jews; if they do become hostile towards Jews, it is because the Jews are often overly arrogant and insolent.

***

What will be the solution after the war to the Jewish problem? Dr. Parkes believes that the Jews have unquestionable rights in Palestine and that if the Arabs in the country are unable to agree with them, the Allied nations should declare that Palestine will be a country reserved for Jews, and that the Arabs should withdraw from the country and abandon it as compensation to the Jews from Germany, Poland and elsewhere.

In opposition to Dr. James Parkes, Sir John Hope Simpson, in the same issue of *International Affairs* (London, January 1945), expresses his sympathy for the Jews and condemns "the diabolical extermination of Eastern European Jews" that has reduced its population of six million to less than one million. This contrary view points out that if Jews are fighting against the German army, they are not fighting as Jews, but as English, American, Russian or Canadian citizens, exactly like the Catholics of these various groups. The proof, he says, is that Jewish officers enlisted in the English army have already written a letter of protest to the *Times* of London, asserting that they are not fighting against Hitler as Jews, but as citizens of British countries.

Dr. Parkes somewhere talks of the unquestionable right of Jews to Palestine. He claims to base this right on the Jewish occupation of Palestine two thousand years ago. John Hope Simpson replies that if there is anyone who should give up rights to the Jews, it is the Allied powers which, after the conclusion of the First World War, wanted to turn Poland into a almost entirely Jewish territory or state. He states that the major nations must provide some administrative services and some assistance to the Jews; however, they do not have a duty to chase the Arabs out of Palestine, nor do they have the right to do so. That would be an abuse of power. Regardless of the strength of the Zionist movement, the solution to the Jewish problem does not lie in that direction. It would be much better to ask Russia to admit Jews to its vast territory. The most that Jews may demand in Palestine would be equal rights to those of the Arabs.

Anti-Semitism in Canada
(1931–1933)

E urope was far from alone in holding anti-Semitic ideologies. On
several occasions during the 1930s, *Le Devoir*'s editorialists can-
didly admitted Judeophobic sentiments also existed in Canada that
were disseminated in various ways by citizens born in the country.
Among others, the newspaper noted the publication, by Adrien
Arcand, of extremely crude newspapers and documents which, in
particular, attacked well-known members of the Montreal Jewish
community and their political allies in the parliament on Grande-
Allée. In August 1931, Henri Bourassa unreservedly condemned this
type of anti-Semitic discourse without ever naming its main instiga-
tor, Camillien Houde—an accusation notably used for electoral goals
by Prime Minister Bennett and by his lieutenant in Québec City. The
editorial was written immediately after the re-election of Taschereau's
Liberals and marked Bourassa's last interjection on the subject in
Le Devoir. The remarks of the newspaper's founder also confirmed
that the proclamation of the David law by the Taschereau government
in 1930, and the creation of an autonomous Jewish school board, had
sparked the Judeophobic remarks. Members of the clergy and certain Catholic activists were outraged to see equal benefits granted to
Jews respecting education and thus deemed it appropriate to promote
anti-Jewish propaganda by calling on Adrien Arcand. Out of respect
for minorities and for the preservation of French-Canadian political
liberalism, Bourassa opposed the manoeuvre and he compared the
struggle of Montreal Jews for their own public school to the struggle
of Francophones in Western Canada fighting for Catholic teaching
institutions in their own language.

Bourassa's magnanimous views, which he would reiterate a
few years later in the House of Commons, did not end Arcand's anti-
Semitic campaign. Montreal Jews were perturbed by the campaign
and, in the summer of 1932, a Lachine merchant named E. Abugov
sued *Le Goglu*, *Le Chameau* and *Le Miroir* for defamation. The case

came to an end in September 1932 when Justice Gonzalve Desaulniers condemned Arcand's views on moral grounds, but otherwise claimed he was powerless to silence the anti-Semitic newspapers. This outcome led a member of the Legislative Assembly, Peter Bercovitch, to demand it draft a new anti-defamation bill that would set stricter limits on hate speech targeting specific minorities. That is where the case stood when Pelletier turned his interest to the debate in an editorial published in March 1933. By this time Bourassa was no longer at the helm of *Le Devoir* and a different climate reigned in the newsroom. Instead of pursuing Bourassa's broad-minded views and denouncing intolerance, Pelletier advocated abandoning the legislative procedures underway on the pretext that they were initiated only to satisfy the Jewish population of Montreal. Furthermore, he suggested the risk of diminishing freedom of the press was greater than the potential benefit of protecting minorities from racist abuse. *Le Devoir*'s position changed again following the riots in Toronto in August 1933, popularly known as the Christie Pits Riots, when young Jewish athletes confronted gangs wearing swastikas. This time, Pelletier put the responsibility for these violent events on immigrants themselves. In his view, the presence of a great number of newly arrived residents in some cities would lead to a growth in the crime rate, increase the number of misfits of all kinds and create racist sentiments among Canadians. These were the first echoes of a position Pelletier would defend forcefully until the mid-1940s. For *Le Devoir* and its editor, it was better to keep Canada sheltered from such ills by restricting the entry of undesirable elements to the country. In doing so, the government would admit only those immigrants whose cultural and religious profile resembled that of Canadians and the country would keep out people quick to carry political feuds to the new continent from the old one.

Lessons and Reflections

Henri Bourassa
Le Devoir, August 26, 1931

P ost-electoral explanations are usually pointless and vainly irritat-
ing for the vanquished—except when they contain useful lessons
for everyone. Are there any to be drawn from Monday's election? Yes;
and we are especially at ease in seeking them without bias since we
are neither among the victorious nor among the vanquished.

***

It is a waste of time to dwell on the first point. The lesson is harsh and
irrefutable. The young people who, in the last few years, have taken
over the leadership of the provincial Conservative Party and are the
driving force of its newspapers, may and should learn from the lesson. If they object to some of the crude actions of their opponents, the
answer is easy. Other than two wrongs not making a right, the young
conservatives who are so eager to identify with their great ancestors,
should not forget that their party has always claimed to be, at times
justifiably, as the party of order, tradition, as the pillar of the throne
and the altar. For some obscure reason of justice, people forgive parties calling themselves liberal more easily for using strong language.
If the Quebec Conservatives want to win back the ground they have
lost, instead of chasing and imitating the least respectable features of
their opponents, they should oppose them by a contrary tone as much
as by contrary ideas and programs.

***

What is true regarding the form is even more so regarding the
substance.

During this past campaign, the opposition leaders put forward
valid ideas, notably that of focusing all social and economic legislation on support for the family. Mr. Héroux, yesterday, expressed the
hope that the idea would progress, regardless of the men or parties in

power. This hope will be achieved only if all the forces and actors with an interest in the policy do not get lost in detail, but devote themselves to demonstrating that the salvation of society lies there and only there.

On the other hand, we hope that the defeat of the opposition will eliminate, from the provincial stage, two propositions, or rather, a proposition and a particularly harmful position.

Mr. Houde's plan, supported by Mr. Barré, to lend money to farmers at the rate of 2%, would, in practice, have led the province to a dead end as disastrous as the one in which England is now struggling.

On another matter, we are delighted by the failure of the anti-Semitic movement initiated by some Conservatives and more or less encouraged by Mr. Houde. Mr. Taschereau endeavoured to resolve the thorny problem of Jewish schools according to the principles of our public law that recognizes, even if imperfectly, that the rights of religion and of the family have priority in all matters regarding the education of children. Some of the opposition criticism and some of the attacks on the Jewish minority resembled the language of the opponents of Catholic schools in Saskatchewan and elsewhere. It must never be forgotten that the province of Quebec's legislation and traditions constitute the only rampart providing protection, as best it can, to all minorities.

***

However, we have already said the main reason and the best justification for the Conservative rout is the unpopularity of the Tory government in Ottawa.

In my capacity as a simple voter, I made my decision to vote for the Liberal candidate in my riding on the day that Mr. Bennett hung around Mr. Houde's neck the millstone that drowned him; and, I believe, many others did so for the same reason.

No bias should be seen here. In many respects, I have a profound admiration for the Prime Minister of Canada, his courage, his talent, his hard work and his very real devotion to public life. While many of the sycophants who now praise him, sought to block him from the party leadership and supported either Mr. Meighen, Mr. Ferguson or even Dr. Manion, in my view, he was the right person to hold the top position. Since he has governed, I have approved of several of his initiatives, or rather his ideas, which are better than his policies.

If he is able to overcome his two major faults — vanity and impatience with any contradiction — he will be remembered as a significant figure in the political history of the country. Unfortunately, his dangerous tendencies, encouraged by the subservience of his supporters and exacerbated by his habits and his connections to men of wealth, may lead the country to disaster. I have noted the disturbing nature of the dictatorial conduct he assumed at the end of the parliamentary session. Most of the provincial governments seem to want to become instruments or accomplices of this dictatorship, some because of their financial difficulties, others out of a partisan spirit. If the government of Quebec had entered the federal Jupiter's orbit, there would have been no counterweight left to its omnipotence.

***

It may be asked, why was this not written before the battle? Our position appeared discreet. The reason is actually quite simple, certainly honest and unbiased. In any case, I am expressing it in all frankness to the thoughtful minds that have confidence in us.

On the one hand, the reasons and facts that I have just indicated seemed to us sufficient not to oppose the government. On the other hand, it seemed to us, as to many others, even to Liberals, that a strengthened opposition would render service to the province and even to the government. Since we were unable to make a distinction between the respective strengths of the opposing views, it seemed more equitable to give them free rein, and provide our readers, in an impartial way, with summaries of speeches and public meetings and abstain from any tendentious commentary. The position, I reiterate, was not brilliant; it was necessary in our mind and to our way of viewing the specific situation of the province, taking into account all aspects of the country.

***

However, what is much more important than the success of parties and the views of individuals, is the economic and social crisis that the province is going through with the rest of Canada and the world. The Liberal government in Quebec, by itself, cannot resolve the crisis any more than the Tory government in Ottawa or the present municipal regime in Montreal.

Now that the electoral battle is over, it is our hope that everyone, Liberals and Conservatives in Ottawa, in Quebec and in Montreal, know how to repress the intoxication of victory, the bitterness of defeat and petty revenge. There is not a minute to lose to give work to the jobless, stimulate the sale of farm and forestry products and organize effective aid programs, now needed to relieve the hardship that work alone cannot eliminate. This arduous task requires the active and faithful efforts of all existing authorities and of all individual and common good intentions.

We must stop being for a few months *Grits* or *Tories* and remember that we are or should be, first of all, Christians, Canadians and united members of human society.

Editorial N° 28

Only to Satisfy Mr. Bercovitch? No

Georges Pelletier
Le Devoir, March 11, 1933

The Bercovitch Bill (Bill 167) from last year regarding publication of defamation should still be fresh in our memories. The bill was conceived to stop the campaign of the rare weeklies opposed to Jews. If the bill had become law, it would have given the right to a person of any race, nationality or religion who claimed to be offended by the repeated publication of an article or some printed matter, to demand a provisional, interlocutory or final injunction from a court to prevent the further publication of the defamation or any written defamation of a similar nature (category 4). This exceptional law was extraordinary; its nature was such that it would have encouraged anti-Semitism in our province instead of restricting it. The Chamber referred the Bercovitch Bill to a committee and that was the last we heard of it.

Well-informed people knew that the issue would return. They were right. In the summer of 1932, following a series of articles published in an anti-Semitic weekly, an Israelite merchant in Lachine initiated proceedings against the owner of the paper. In a decision that was met by divided opinion at the time, a Superior Court magistrate rejected the application of the Lachine merchant; however, he expressed regret that in our Code of Civil Procedure there was not a section that could be used to prohibit campaigns of this sort. It was a wish to see the Bercovitch Bill resuscitated in another form in the coming months.

Therefore, the content of Bill 28 (with the title, *An Act to Amend the Code of Civil Procedure Regarding Libel*) is hardly surprising; Mr. Taschereau himself presented it in February in the Legislature and the members will study it before the end of the session. It is our hope that they will not vote on it without having studied it; if they study it properly, they will give it the same fate as the Bercovitch Bill.

***

What is the essence of the Taschereau Bill? A section that gives magistrates of the Superior Court the right to grant an interlocutory injunction when a subpoena is issued or even during proceedings, *"when a newspaper, publication, pamphlet or other printed matter continually or repeatedly publishes or when someone distributes written material or articles, which in the opinion of the judge constitute an offence under the provisions of the Criminal Code of Canada regarding libel"* (section 1, paragraph *a* of Bill 28).

An example will give a better understanding of the spirit of the text; a newspaper starts publishing information related to a businessman's and politician's involvement in a shady affair. The newspaper publishes three or four articles, provides details, reveals facts, gives names and numbers and pursues the issue. The businessman, as well as the politician, consider this to be embarrassing. Without giving the newspaper advance notice to put an end to the series of articles, retract or give an explanation, the people implicated make an application to a judge. The judge deems that the articles on first sight appear libelous and issues an interlocutory injunction. The newspaper in question must immediately stop its articles, short of disobeying the court order and consequently facing various heavy penalties. The newspaper may be justified in having decided to publish the series of articles for reasons of public order and interest. The newspaper during the final proceedings of the case may even establish the validity of its assertions and justify its conduct by arguing and proving that it was motivated only by public interest and therefore, in fact did not commit libel. The judge may even rule in its favour. It would change nothing. Bill 28 will have clearly benefited shady individuals in silencing the press, preventing the public from knowing at the proper time about their machinations and their reprehensible and blameworthy actions contrary to public interest. The businessman, in the meantime, will have had time to swindle people. Since the time from the interlocutory injunction to the final proceedings of the case may take months, sometimes even a year or two, the politician could, in that period, be elected as a member of the Legislature, even be appointed to the Legislative Council or the Senate. Anything may happen... And the public would find out too late.

This is only one example of what could happen under Bill 28, if our parliamentarians adopt it. It would do more than just put a halt to campaigns dictated by anti-Semitism and racist or religious fanaticism. It could be an exceptional weapon in the hands of unscrupulous politicians or business wheeler-dealers, denounced by a press whose only motivation is the public interest. How can the population be informed of the fraudulent and dishonest machinations of the people implicated, if from a simple reading of such articles written in a relatively aggressive tone to attract the attention of the taxpayers, they could block a campaign for political reform for weeks by means only of an interlocutory procedure? That is the danger of Bill 28, which makes it more dreadful, if that is possible, than Bill 167 of last year.

***

Furthermore, this Bill 28 in fact removes a part of the rights properly granted to the press of our province in 1929 by our legislators in Quebec, led by Mr. Taschereau, and incorporated in a chapter of the provincial statutes of that year (19, George V, chapter 72, Press Act).

According to this law (sections 3 and 4), any person who believes himself to be wronged by a newspaper article and wishes to claim damages must first give three days notice to the office of the newspaper or to the residence of its owner, in order for the newspaper to be able publish a retraction in an issue no later than the day after having received the notice. If the retraction is complete and in good faith, the individual who believed himself to be wronged may only obtain actual and real damages. Obviously, if the individual implicated is accused of a criminal offence, the newspaper does not have the right to an advance notice. Is that not sufficient protection for an honest citizen who is unjustly attacked? Bill 28 does not take this into account at all. It adds to the possibility of suing without notice, the granting of an interlocutory injunction. Consequently, this could allow and even cover up the fraudulent machinations of a person who has been denounced simply out of a concern for the public interest. The person, by using section 957 of the Code of Civil Procedure amended by the Taschereau Bill, would succeed in preventing or in any case delaying for months and months revelations clearly of public interest.

***

That would be one of the consequences of Bill 167, if it is incorporated into our laws. Should laws not exist first of all to protect the public, the public interest and honest people? As written, Bill 167 in 90% of cases, will serve mainly to protect embezzlers, politicians and dishonest business wheeler-dealers. It would be quite the weapon in the hands of one of our Insulls or a sub-Insulls.

That certainly is not what Mr. Taschereau wants. He wants the opposite. That cannot be what Mr. Bercovitch wants. However, that is what the new paragraph in section 967 of the Code of Civil Procedure will be used for; to muzzle the press, regardless of party, group or ideas, whereas the first and foremost concern of the press is to serve the public and public interest.

Is there a desire to restrict an irresponsible press? We are in agreement. However, under the guise of fighting irresponsibility, we are not going to hand dubious elements a muzzle that would allow them to stop the telling of truth. Is it necessary, in order to satisfy Mr. Bercovitch's ethnic group, to disrupt the entire order of our laws? Is there any province willing to resort to that? Does ours, where there already is a large measure of freedom extended to all, for Israelites as much as for the races long-settled in Canada?

The Brawls in Toronto

Georges Pelletier
Le Devoir, August 19, 1933

The Recent Incidents in Toronto — Brawls Between Young Jews and Young Canadians of Various Origins over the Swastika that Hitler's Followers Use and Abuse in Germany — Encourage Reflection on Certain Aspects of Our Badly Written Immigration Law and Our Badly Oriented Immigration System

***

For about the last thirty years—except during the war, when the flow dried up—we have received, without distinction, immigrants from all parts of the world. We wanted numbers, we received them. During this period, more new arrivals entered the country than there were native-born Canadians in the 1900 census. We paid hardly any attention to this rising tide. Whoever wanted to enter, nearly always succeeded. What saved native-born Canadians, to some extent, from being completely submerged, was that a great many of these people only passed through our country and went to the United States, five, ten or twenty months after disembarking in Quebec, Montreal or Saint-Jean. Still, a significant number remained here. Sometimes it was a desirable element; at other times hardly at all.

What has been the result of this haphazardly developed policy? There have been all sorts of consequences and not all have been beneficial to us. Demographic statistics show that this badly developed influx has increased crime; the number of feeble-minded interned at the expense of the federal government and the provinces in all kinds of health care facilities has grown. While we have received excellent immigrants, the mass has been of an average or pretty mediocre nature—below that of native-born Canadians who were forced to leave for the United States or other foreign destinations.

There is need for a vast inquiry and an important document to be written on the various aspects of our immigration in the past. It is of immediate importance now that support to initiate a new immigration policy is being promoted by influential figures who are primarily seeking their personal interest. We need a person well-informed on the issue and with the time to prepare, as quickly as possible, a complete overview of our experience on the subject. That may perhaps lead us to decide never again to attempt a similar venture.

**

The inevitable conclusion regarding the recent brawls in Toronto is similar to the conclusions that could have been drawn during the last Great War. The presence in the country of immigrant groups from countries where racist sentiments were prominent brought all sorts of problems to Canada from 1911 to 1918. There were numerous clashes between these various groups. The strongest tried to reduce the weaker to an inferior status of citizenship. The jingoes did not miss the opportunity to try and impose on everyone a loud and obnoxious loyalty more at home in the outskirts of London and Belfast than on the streets of Montreal, Toronto and Winnipeg.

This time in Toronto, two groups of youths came to blows; one was a group of Jews who were born or arrived here less than thirty years ago and whose families came from Russia, Germany, Poland or Galicia. The sight of the swastika is shocking to this group, because of what it represents in Europe. The other group was one of young Canadians, mostly of German or Anglo-Saxon origin, who claimed that they had the right to display whatever symbols they wanted, regardless of what they represented in Europe. This was the source of the serious brawls in the last few days between these two rowdy groups. These brawls may soon lead to an aggressive anti-Semitic movement, which would be impossible to suppress and extremely dangerous for all sides, if the present situation continues to spread.

The Jews in Canada have not given up being Jewish. Canadians of German or Anglo-Saxon origin do not accept being overwhelmed, displaced or surpassed by Jews. The present events add to the explicable sensitivity of the Jews established in Canada, just as the events add fuel to the racism of a segment in this country. We are not in

Germany, but young Germans in Toronto act in the same way as their friends in Berlin or Munich. Where will this lead?

**

The quarrels from Europe, therefore, once again risk spreading in our country because of the lack of tact on one side and exasperation on the other side. This would not happen if our cities did not have large colonies of foreigners resistant to assimilation, who act as if Canada was a country belonging to them more than it might belong to fourth-, sixth- or tenth-generation Canadians.

This is one of the numerous examples of the lack of foresight by our political leaders when they invited all of Europe and part of Asia to cross the sea and make of Canada a sort of Promised Land. They did not take the time to think at the time that the various categories of immigrants would bring here, with their baggage, the complex issues of race and civilization being confronted from the Channel to the Black Sea and from Scotland to Palestine. If they did think about that, they were excessively optimistic. The cracked heads in Toronto clearly prove it. We hope that, God willing, this sudden small spark does not flare up into a huge conflagration.

Le Devoir and the
Canadian Jewish Congress (1934)

The first sustained relations between *Le Devoir*'s leadership and Jewish community organizations took place in January 1934. This period closely corresponds to the arrival in power of the National Socialist Party in Germany and this re-establishment of the Canadian Jewish Congress (CJC) in this country. Alarmed by Hitler's extreme anti-Semitic discourse and by the first discriminatory measures against German Jews, Montreal's Jewish community leaders quickly became mobilized. In April 1933, to protest against the events in Germany, a group of militants had organized a large anti-Hitler demonstration to which people of all origins and political tendencies were invited. In the weeks that followed, these people considered re-establishing a unifying pan-Canadian organization founded in 1919, which had been left inactive in the 1920s, the CJC. The initiators of the movement, led by its Secretary-General, H.M. Caiserman, faced several very challenging issues. There was a need to consider receiving refugees from Nazi Germany in the community, to seek the Canadian government's support of the refugees and to organize a boycott of German merchandise. Numerous problems had arisen on the Canadian front, the most troubling of which was the growth in the Canadian population of currents of thought supporting fascism and also the publication of leaflets preaching virulent anti-Semitism.

To counter these troubling tendencies in the country, the goodwill of Canadian Jews was urgently called upon to enlist their personal financial contributions. It was in this difficult and worrisome context at the end of 1933 that leaflets were distributed calling for the creation of a united front in the Jewish community. To achieve their objectives, CJC leaders drew up a list of all issues needing to be addressed in coming months, including the existence of a strongly anti-Semitic French-language press in Quebec. *Le Devoir* was mistakenly added to this list. While it certainly was not a shining example of openness to Canadian Jews, it could not be put in the same category as the weekly or monthly publications led by Adrien Arcand. And, at a time when *Le Devoir* was faced with serious financial problems, Jewish leaders threatened to take action against the advertising revenues of anti-Semitic newspapers. These threats, and the ensuing editorial tempest, created a wall of incomprehension and hostility between *Le Devoir* and the Montreal Jewish community that wouldn't be eliminated until after the Second World War. The depth of the crisis and its political ramifications can be seen from a reading of the following three editorials published during one week at the beginning of 1934. These three editorials alone help us understand how difficult it was for *Le Devoir*'s leadership, and for the community leadership of the CJC, to maintain cordial relations at this troubled time in global affairs. The Jewish community's lack of knowledge of French and its few personal contacts with Francophones, combined with the deeply anchored anti-Semitic stereotypes that were a persistent feature of the French-speaking community, made constructive dialogue between the two very challenging.

The Status of the Jewish Documents — The Responsibility of the Canadian Jewish Congress

A New Letter from Mr. Caiserman — We Now Know Who to Speak to — What Are Mr. Jacobs, Mr. Bercovitch et al. Complaining About? And Why Is the Newsletter "Confidential"? — Why Is There Fear to Make it Public?

Omer Héroux
Le Devoir, January 25, 1934

At last we officially know what we are dealing with. We know who to speak to.

We at first received only a partial response from Mr. Jacobs, Mr. Bercovitch et al. The Secretary-General of the Canadian Jewish Congress, Mr. H.M. Caiserman, on their behalf, stated to us that these gentlemen take responsibility for the *Emergency Call* bearing their name (a copy of all these documents with a French translation was published in *Le Devoir* last January 18). However, he neglected to say if these gentlemen similarly take responsibility for the document marked Confidential, that appears very logically and very integrally linked to this Emergency Call, which seems to be developed from and complementary to the Confidential document: he neglected to tell us if they approve or disapprove of the document.

A second letter from Mr. Caiserman resolves the last point. It absolves some of the signatories from personal responsibility for the Emergency Call and affirms the responsibility of the Canadian Jewish Congress.

Mr. Caiserman wrote to us (the letter is dated January 23):

Dear sir: —
All the circulars referred to, were prepared by the office of the Canadian Jewish Congress with the knowledge of its officers.

We note the press reports of last night's meeting of *Jeune-Canada*, and the disavowal by its officers of anti-Semitism and anti-Semitic aims.

We take exception, however, to the insulting remarks that were made on their platform at the same time concerning us.

The addresses delivered last April by the speakers of *Jeune-Canada* were without doubt anti-Semitic. These have been widely published, and speak for themselves. Yours truly.

***

We shall leave aside, for the moment at least, the case of *Jeune-Canada*. Our readers are aware of the statements made by that group Monday evening. Furthermore, if *Jeune-Canada* wishes to return to the subject, we certainly would not refuse appropriate publication.

We shall instead turn to our case, since we have been specifically attacked in the Confidential document.

Under the heading, *The Alarming Situation in the Province of Quebec*, the fourth of twelve paragraphs that seem to justify the broad allegation, states:

> *Le Devoir, a leading French-Canadian daily in Montreal, is also distinctly anti-Semitic.*

Where and when have we been anti-Semitic? Where and when have we taken a position that might be described as distinctly anti-Semitic?

Is it anti-Semitic to suggest to French Canadians to have as much common sense as Jews and practise the mutual economic assistance that all other groups, starting with Jews, practise regularly, without having to talk or even think about it?

Is it anti-Semitic simply to want to make one's own decisions, rather than being dictated to by the press or Jewish interests, regarding events in our country or abroad?

***

To be more specific, we have never expressed anti-Semitism for multiple reasons that our long-time readers know very well or have been able to surmise. First, as we reiterated quite recently, we take a positive approach to our work and are not *anti*-anything, except to the extent needed to lay groundwork before starting to build. Furthermore, we find it absurd and dangerous to foment racial hatred. For example, in our most fervent defence of French rights, we have always strived never to direct the anger of French Canadians at any group of our English-language compatriots, even when it was obvious that they were guilty of harsh injustices towards our group. Nor do we want to support the tendency of French Canadians to blame others for their fate, which unfortunately they share with all other humans. In fact, it would be easy to show the dozens of times that we have cited the Jews as an example to our people for their spirit of solidarity and their perseverance in work. We are not even counting the number of times our friend Dupire has praised the care that Jewish mothers take of their children!

What is the President of the Canadian Jewish Congress, Mr. S.W. Jacobs, Member of Parliament for Cartier, complaining about? What is his Vice-President, Mr. Peter Bercovitch, Member of the Legislative Assembly, complaining about? What are their colleagues from the Canadian Jewish Congress complaining about?

If they could be more specific, we would pursue the debate as long as they wish.

***

However, we first wish to ask Mr. Jacobs and Mr. Bercovitch and their colleagues from the Canadian Jewish Congress a question of major importance and one that is of interest not only to us.

Why did they mark as Confidential and why did they not wish to be completely open about the accusation that implicated us, and in the public interest, inform all newspapers and various associations?

Why did they want to organize things in such a way that the accused could not know about and, when necessary, oppose the charges?

Why did they want their Jewish kinfolk to be the only ones to read the text—which they did not take the trouble to sign and for which they did not care to take responsibility clearly and publicly?

Mr. Jacobs and Mr. Bercovitch, to name only the most well-known of the leaders of the Canadian Jewish Congress, normally never shy away from publicity.

The Father of Yellow Journalism Was the Jew Joseph Pulitzer

Mr. Leon Levinson Denies this Assertion that Appeared in Le Devoir — *We Shall Prove It*

Louis Dupire
Le Devoir, January 26, 1934

On January 18, *Le Devoir* published a photo of three leaflets issued by a Montreal Jewish group, including one signed by Mr. S. W. Jacobs, K. C., M.P., Mr. Lyon Cohen, Mr. Peter Bercovitch, K.C., M.L.A., Mr. Nathan Gordon, K.C., Mr. J. Levinson, Sr., Mr. Samuel Hart, Mr. Marcus Sperber, K.C., Captain Sebag-Montefiore, Mr. F. I. Spielman, Mr. Norman Viner, M.D., Mr. H. E. Hershorn, N.P., Lieut. Col. Philip Abbey.

Among other things, the leaflet contained the following: "We are particularly compelled to defend ourselves against the venomous campaign of *yellow* Jew-baiting journals in the Province of Quebec.

A confidential leaflet under the same signatures and published the same day, in section 4, added *Le Devoir* to the list of newspapers denounced: "*Le Devoir, a leading French-Canadian daily in Montreal, is also distinctly anti-Semitic.*"

On January 20, our *Carnet d'un grincheux*, contained the following:

The father of yellow journalism is Pulitzer, a Hungarian Jew who came to the United States. To call newspapers *yellow leaflets,* is the same as calling them Jewish leaflets. It would be difficult to say anything more insulting in their regard. But who makes the claim?

Also, on January 20, Mr. Leon Levinson sent the letter below to Pamphile, which *Le Devoir* received on the 23rd:

Pamphile
Le Devoir
430 rue Notre-Dame est, Montréal.

Sir,

I found your comments in last Saturday's *Le Devoir* on "yellow journalism" very amusing.

It seems that you would have your readers believe that without Jews in the United States, there would never have been "yellow newspapers."

If that was your goal — a rather amusing idea — your example was very badly chosen.

Pulitzer, born in Budapest, as you told your readers, was indeed Jewish. However, how do you manage to link him to the paternity of "yellow journalism" in America?

Joseph Pulitzer senior, as any well-informed journalist knows, was the owner of the *New York World* and of the *St. Louis Post-Dispatch* for many years. These two newspapers were never considered "yellow newspapers." Far from it. The *World* to the end of its days enjoyed an enviable reputation and the *Post-Dispatch* today is one the best American newspapers.

When the *World* was forced to shut down by yellow newspapers a few years ago, all good journalists and thousands of readers were saddened as if they had lost an old friend.

It seems rather strange to see you call Mr. Pulitzer a "yellow journalist." I can assure you that your article would make the students of the School of Journalism at Columbia University laugh — a school established from a $1,000,000 donation from Mr. Pulitzer.

How is it that you ignored the "yellow newspaper" the *New York Times*, owned by Mr. Adolph Ochs, also of the Jewish race.

I know perfectly well not to expect anything pleasant from a "grouch," particularly if the "grouch" is a journalist from *Le Devoir* and the reader is Jewish. However, as a former journalist, I expect intelligent and informed journalism from *Le Devoir*, which, in my opinion, is lacking in your little chronicle of Saturday.

I hope you will pardon the mistakes of an English-speaking person who wishes to express himself in French.

Yours truly,

4095 Côte des Neiges Rd.

Leon Levinson

We have printed the original of Mr. Levinson's letter. It should be noted that he has no need to apologize for his mistakes, which are few, as can be seen. We wish to compliment him on his knowledge of our language.

Mr. Levinson, whose good faith we do not doubt, describes Joseph Pulitzer as not the father of yellow journalism, but the father of informed journalism. When we wrote what he criticizes about us, we knew what we were saying and we were trying to be good students of Pulitzer, as viewed by Mr. Levinson.

The *Shorter Oxford English Dictionary on Historical Principles*, 1933 edition, defines the word yellow as (p. 2466): ... *applied to newspapers (or writers of newspaper articles) of a recklessly or unscrupulously sensational character (orig. U.S. from a picture in* New York World, *1895, with the central figure in a yellow dress)* 1898. (This latter date indicates that the word "yellow" came into the English language in 1898).

Mr. Levinson will have to admit that even if it is not taught (which we do not know) at the chair of journalism established by Joseph Pulitzer at Columbia University in New York, the said Joseph Pulitzer is well and truly the father of yellow journalism.

Does Mr. Levinson want further proof? He need only take the trouble to consult the authoritative work by Mr. Oswald Garrison Villard (Managing Editor, Editorial Writer and President of the *New York Evening Post 1897–1918:* Editor of the *Nation*), *Some Newspapers and Newspaper-Men*. He will find on pages 44 and 45 the following passage.

> When Mr. Pulitzer became owner of the *World* (which was originally founded as a one-cent religious daily!) it proceeded to touch even lower depths of journalism than had the *Herald* under the elder James Gordon Bennett. Mr. Pulitzer played far more directly to the base passions of the multitude than Mr. Bennett, yet his was a moving vision of a great daily of the working masses among which he had himself toiled, suffered, and almost starved, until his feet reached the road to renown and to riches. It was by this appeal to the basest passions of the crowd that Mr. Pulitzer succeeded; like many another he deliberately stooped for success, and then, having achieved it, slowly put on garments of righteousness. I am old enough to remember that forty years ago in New York it was impossible to find the *World* in any refined home; it was regarded much as Hearst's *Evening Journal* is today. It was the *World* as well as the *Journal* which Mr. Godkin had in mind when he wrote in the *Evening Post* some twenty-four years ago that "a yellow journal office is probably the nearest approach, in atmosphere, to hell existing in any Christian state, for in gambling houses, brothels, and even in brigands' caves there is a

constant exhibition of fear of the police, which is in itself a sort of homage to morality or acknowledgment of its existence." If this language seems preposterously strong today it was pretty well justified at the time by the devilish work done both by the *World* and the Hearst press in bringing on the war with Spain. Then Mr. Pulitzer was willing to outdo Hearst in shameless and unwarranted sensationalism lest Hearst inflict on his papers irrevocable injury. That chapter in the *World's* history is not one to be read with satisfaction today by anyone connected with it. To the eldest generation of intellectual New Yorkers the *World* is still anathema; to them it connotes only sensationalism and a journalism utterly without principle.

If the students at Columbia's school of journalism are still laughing, it will be ... a hollow laugh.

Is Mr. Levinson convinced?

He must be now, unless he is unwilling to accept the overwhelming evidence of the two pieces above and, along with *Le Devoir*, place the authors of the *Shorter Oxford English Dictionary* and Mr. Oswald Garrison Villard among the anti-Semites.

Regarding Mr. Villard, Mr. Levinson's task will not be easy. In the periodical that he now leads or that he led until recently, the *Nation*, Mr. Villard attacks the German dictator, Hitler, with vehemence and defends Jews with skill and passion. There is more. The same Mr. Villard, did he not come to Montreal recently and in front of a Jewish women's association denounce Hitler's regime and especially the Führer's persecutions of Mr. Levinson's co-religionists.

In short, *Le Devoir* perhaps is less deserving than any other newspaper in Canada of the label, "yellow newspaper," but when *Pamphile* claims that *to call Le Devoir a yellow newspaper, it is the same as calling it a Jewish newspaper*, he is right, even though neither label applies to *Le Devoir*.

We are prepared to be magnanimous. Pulitzer was only half Jewish, since according to the Cambridge encyclopedia, his mother was Austrian. We could then say that yellow journalism was only half Jewish if that would make Mr. Levinson happier. However, that will not make him happy since he took great care to identify himself completely as a disciple of Pulitzer in his letter to *Pamphile* ...

We were going to ignore Mr. Ochs and his two-hundred-page *Times* that Mr. Leon Levinson brandishes triumphantly.

Mr. Ochs is Jewish and the *Times* practises yellow journalism. Mr. Levinson will not agree, just as he will not agree that the *Gazette* here is yellow. However, for eyes not blindfolded, the truth is evident: yellow journalism does not entail huge headlines, but morbid, crude and spicy reports. Every great crime, every *nice* sexual affair is accompanied by this cocktail of the best of yellow journalism in both these newspapers. What is not shown in a photo, a graphic description provides with consummate art.

We would advise Mr. Levinson to take a journalism course to learn what is yellow journalism. However, he should not go to Columbia, since he claims that the school founded by the father of *yellow journalism*, Pulitzer, teaches that he is *the father of informed journalism*. If Mr. Levinson is right, the Pulitzer chair really has no relation to the chair of truth.

The Advertising Boycott and Jews

*Mr. Caiserman's Declarations — How Advertising in
"Anti-Semitic Newspapers" in the Province of Quebec
Will Be Deterred — Which Newspapers Are "Anti-Semitic"
According to the "Confidential" Document Revealed
by Us — Our Position — Some Very Simple Declarations*

Omer Héroux
Le Devoir, February 3, 1934

Some very interesting things were said at the Jewish Congress in
Toronto.

Things that are of utmost interest to us and several of our colleagues. You will excuse us for returning to the subject.

***

We quote from the report of the *Toronto Daily Star* of Monday
January 29, page 5, column 4. The Secretary-General of the Congress,
Mr. H.M. Caiserman, stated: *We were able to combat Nazi organizations
and combat anti-Semitic demonstrations in the province of Quebec. We
uncovered a certain number of anti-Semitic organizations working in the
shadows and conducted a campaign of education to discourage advertising in
anti-Semitic papers in Quebec.*

In other terms, according to the Secretary-General of the
Congress in Toronto, the Jews organized the advertising boycott of
papers that they described as anti-Semitic.

The names of the papers are known, even if they if they seem
not to have been revealed in Toronto.

The names are written in black and white in the copy of the document marked "Confidential" that *Le Devoir* published in its edition
of January 18 and that Mr. Caiserman himself claimed to have prepared at the Congress's office with the knowledge of the movement's
leaders.

This "Confidential" document intended to provide to the Jewish community details, without any names being mentioned, of the broad assertions contained in the two documents to which it was attached, did not accuse only *Le Patriote*, for example, whose anti-Semitic virulence is obvious.

The document expressly stated:

> 3. — *L'Action catholique* and *Le Journal*, two leading French news-papers that disseminate racist hatred against Jews, are published in the City of Québec, seat of the provincial government
>
> 4. — Le Devoir, *a leading French-Canadian daily in Montreal, is also distinctly anti-Semitic.*

Therefore, the Jewish attack is aimed against us, as much as against *Le Patriote* or any other newspaper that may be virulently hostile to Jews.

Therefore, the proposed advertising boycott targets newspapers that in fact have never been anti-Semitic, that have always limited themselves to advising their readers to practise—what is so magnificently carried out by the Jews themselves—mutual economic assistance and are now criticized as anti-Semitic.

Everyone suspected that this was happening or would happen; however, it is not a bad idea to note it in a public statement without any possible contradiction.

***

Mr. Caiserman's declaration in no way intimidates us personally. For our existence, we count on neither money nor Jewish advertising. We are confident that in this country there are enough men concerned with the development of a free press, and even free from Jewish influence, to protect us against direct and indirect attacks.

However, it must be seen and it must be noted that, for minds capable of reflection, Mr. Caiserman's declaration leads to very worrisome prospects.

No one is unaware that the press—since the creation of cheap newspapers—to a large extent depends on the amount of its advertising revenues, since newspapers are very often sold at below cost. Without advertising, they would, in most cases, be constantly in debt.

This is true at all times. It is true more than ever in times of crisis. As we have reiterated here many times, newspapers, probably of all large enterprises, have the largest proportion of expenses that cannot be reduced. This results in a very great danger, which should be obvious to even the least interested, if they are willing to take a moment to give it some thought.

As long as advertising represents only a fairly modest amount of a newspaper's revenues and as long as the newspaper can forgo part of them without serious consequences, the advertising revenue is only a helpful resource; however, as soon as the revenue is significant enough to become essential to the existence of the newspaper, it engenders very dangerous risks.

In practice, this puts the existence of the newspaper at the mercy, not of the readers who generally are of likemind with the editors, but of the advertisers who may be of any race, any ethnic or religious group.

***

Many people who realized the possibility of this danger in theory, however, never thought that the threat, among us, could become a harsh reality.

Mr. Caiserman's declaration should open their eyes.

In very clear and specific terms, he warned that Jews were quite determined to use the leverage they possess with advertising to pressure "anti-Semitic newspapers." The "Confidential" document indicates that not only resolutely anti-Semitic newspapers should be included, but also newspapers such as *L'Action catholique*, *Le Journal* and *Le Devoir*, that have never displayed anti-Semitic hostility, have never done anything other than preach legitimate mutual assistance and comment freely on public issues

Where will these gentlemen stop on this road? What kind of influence will they attempt to exercise, for example, over a newspaper where they control 40 or 50% of the ongoing advertising?

In Paris, using this process, they succeeded in blackmailing a Parisian daily to stop publishing the impressions from Germany of the Tharaud brothers, who were far from fierce anti-Semites.

In this case they were caught in the act and it was clearly noted, but how many other cases have there been where the threat of withdrawing their advertising—perhaps even by the simple fear raised by the possibility of a withdrawal—where they may have not elicited words of praise, but have at least achieved opportune and useful silence?

***

We have no illusions about the power of Jews and their tenacious will-power.

However, two things are certain: first that the boycott, whatever form it takes, will not lead us to practise systematic anti-Semitism, and we have already stated why; second, this same boycott will not prevent us from judging all events freely, even those most directly of interest to Jews.

Furthermore, the boycott will not prevent us from advising French Canadians to be as intelligently practical as the English and the Jews, to do like them and *pull together*.

"Buy From Your Own"
(1934–1939)

The "buy from your own" ideology deserves attention, since it reflects the attitude of a community responding to the economic slowdown of the 1930s by turning inward. The impact of massive job losses and a significant reduction in the buying power of families led several French-Canadian nationalist organizations to propose strategies for supporting local manufacturers and merchants, although the concept took various forms: some were positive and tended to emphasize the quality and variety of goods produced in Quebec or in a particular region, while others were negative and suggested verifying the cultural or religious group of the merchant and avoiding those who were not of Franco-Catholic origin. The distinction is important since, in the first case, the message did not differentiate between the various economic players present on the Quebec scene while, in the second case, the message introduced notions that were clearly ethnocentric or xenophobic and even hostile to immigration. *Le Devoir* editorials used the slogan "buy from your own" seven times between 1934 and 1936, the depths of the Great Depression. Most of the time the goal was to encourage local agricultural marketing, as in the case of Albert Rioux, or to suggest that Canadian merchants identify themselves as Canadian in their publicity to promote a sentiment of national solidarity. Louis Dupire went even further by suggesting merchants and industrialists not hesitate to make their presence known to consumers by purchasing advertising space in *Le Devoir* or other recognized Francophone media.

In January 1934 and January 1939, Héroux and Pelletier, however, proposed a different interpretation of "buy from your own." They warned against merchants of Jewish origin who had opened businesses in Montreal communities where French Canadians were in the majority—in the parish of Saint Denis, for example, where a section of the Société Saint-Jean-Baptiste was active. In this case, a finger was being pointed at people who were not of Francophone origin, and attempts were made to exclude them from the marketplace. Such declarations could only create a climate of suspicion and hostility towards small merchants from other cultural backgrounds, including Jews, and have a serious effect on their ability to protect themselves in a volatile economy. According to the 1931 census, close to one-third of Montreal`s Jewish population depended on small businesses for its existence, most often by serving a largely French-Canadian clientele. An attack on this particular link of the Jewish economic structure would doom many humble families to significant losses. It would also entail the categorization of Montreal businesses according to the ethnic identity of the owner, an action liable to lead to the kind of abuses that had become commonplace in Germany and Poland during the 1930s. When Joseph Cohen, member for the riding of Montreal–Saint-Laurent in the Legislative Assembly, complained this strategy was motivated by radical nationalism, Héroux called him "The Jewish Member of the Legislature," thus emphasizing an impression that politicians also can be labelled by ethnicity.

In January 1934, the true nature of this negative and anti-Semitic "buy from your own" campaign proposed by *Le Devoir* on its pages was made evident by Héroux. This ideological current was based completely on a perception that Jewish merchants, in certain neighbourhoods of Montreal, had achieved "an economic influence that did not reflect their numbers." In short, it was claimed that they exercised excessive control in the city and occupied too great and disproportionate a place relative to the size of their population, an impression reinforced by the general slow-down of business. There was an additional fact that Jewish merchants, often newly arrived immigrants to the country, were perceived as "foreigners" by *Le Devoir*. Héroux stressed, therefore, that his readers should transfer their buying power to French-Canadian businesses in order to "re-establish the normal state of affairs" that had been improperly changed by external factors over which Francophones had no control. This position is more complex and difficult to decipher than it seems at first, since Héroux does not go to the extent of entirely condemning the practices of the small Jewish merchants. Nor is there, in his position, any hint of profound hatred or discrimination that would turn violent. As was often the case in Héroux's views regarding relations between Jews and French Canadians, there remained an underlying admiration of the community solidarity and capacity to mobilize of Jewish people. Héroux believed that, if the Jews were successful to the point of possibly clashing with the legitimate interests of their French language counterparts, would it not be useful to imitate them and adopt their economic strategies? By doing as the Jews did in commerce, would that not also be an admission that they might be an example for French Canada?

These contradictions were never really resolved in Omer Héroux's thinking, which in the Montreal of the 1930s, continued to be influenced by irresolute ambivalence and contradiction. As the economic situation improved after 1936, anti-Semitism and "buy from your own" disappeared from *Le Devoir* editorials, although the subject returned one last time in January 1939 in a Georges Pelletier editorial. Following Kristallnacht the Canadian Jewish Congress resumed its campaign of boycotting German merchandise and, with the seriousness of the situation in central Europe, it appealed directly to Canadian authorities. *Le Devoir* did not look favourably on the action and it once more attributed to the organization a far greater capacity to organize and a power to convince than it actually had in the federal capital. Pelletier had already opposed previous attempts of this kind and viewed it as an obstacle to the development of a Quebec economy oriented to towards autonomous small and mid-size enterprises. Pelletier also thought that the German situation, despite "the stupid and brutal persecution" inflicted on religious minorities was irrelevant to Canadians. He opted instead to turn the situation against the organizers of the boycott by demanding that the ethnic and national origin of merchants who do business in Canada be indicated, so that the "foreigners" and "Israelites of Central Europe" would be openly identified. This would show that the immigrants contribute nothing to the country and that their presence "complicates Canadian life in all sorts of ways."

Mr. Joseph Cohen and the Société Saint-Jean-Baptiste

Do Jewish Boycott Activists Really Want to Complain about French Canadians Who Simply Want to Practice Mutual Aid and Express Their Gratitude?

Omer Héroux
Le Devoir, January 5, 1934

M r. Joseph Cohen, the Jewish Member of the Legislature for Saint Laurent, is not happy with the way some newspapers treat his kinfolk. That is understandable and no one will consider criticizing him for being especially sensitive on matters respecting people of his race. Mr. Cohen has stated that he will raise the issue in the Legislative Assembly and demand that a law be enacted that would allow the articles that are the subject of his complaints, to be brought before the courts. We shall have to wait for the text of the law to see what it is about and its possible consequences—and why the Jewish minority would need to be protected by a text no other minority has yet considered demanding.

We shall endeavour, when the time comes, to judge on their merit Mr. Cohen's speeches and bill.

However, he needs to be asked right now about his goal when he attacks, as he did yesterday according to this morning's *Gazette*, the Société Saint-Jean-Baptiste.

***

What we can see from the articles published until now, Mr. Cohen's entire complaint is based on a leaflet distributed by one of the parish branches of the Société Saint-Jean Baptiste, in the Saint-Denis section.

What was the objective of the leaflet—or rather one of the objectives, since it raised a number of issues?

The members of the district have witnessed the cruel fate brought by circumstances on the corner grocer, they have been struck by the dangers threatening him and have seen the many problems he has had to face. They also know of his immense services to the jobless before the implementation of all-purpose cheques and his place in our economic structure. The members of the section, therefore, asked their friends to give their complete support to this grocer and similar merchants.

The affair is explained fully in a letter from the President of the section, Mr. Bruno Côté, which Mr. Joseph Cohen may read, if he has not done so already, in *Le Devoir* of December 23.

> Mr. Côté stated clearly that *the Saint-Jean-Baptiste officers of the Saint-Denis section never had the idea and even less the intention of launching a campaign against the Jewish merchants in our parish. The objective of the leaflet in question is quite simply to invite the jobless in the parish to support our "corner grocer" and our local merchants, the very ones who came to their assistance when direct aid did not exist and who cooperated whole-heartedly with the Société Saint-Vincent-de-Paul in its charitable work. That certainly is not something to be criticized.*
>
> *As one of the speakers stated so well last Monday evening, at a meeting organized for the unemployed in the Saint-Denis parish, our national life is too precious to be wasted on "hate" and on "disparaging" those not of our race. Instead, let us take action which would be the best proof of the sincerity of our patriotism. That is actually what the program drawn up by the Saint-Denis section of the Société Saint-Jean-Baptiste is about.*

Further on:

> *No one ever hurled a "cry of race" in the parish of Saint-Denis. No one ever had the intention of launching a campaign against foreign merchants in our parish. However, we are not prepared to give up our legitimate rights for the satisfaction of some people who are offended by the good work carried out right now by the Saint-Denis section of the Saint-Jean-Baptiste society.*
>
> *We want to let everyone live, but we shall not accept that our own right to live is refused or questioned.*
>
> *We have no grievances against anyone. All we want is the well-being and success of our people and we intend to work with all our energy toward that goal, without, however, going beyond the rights we have*

acquired over the centuries, or the framework of justice that we owe to all our fellow citizens.

That should reassure Mr. Cohen, even though he was offended by one sentence in the leaflet that simply stated: *There is much talk of anti-Semitism. We sincerely believe that the most practical, the most effective and the most forceful way to combat anti-Semitism, is to encourage our "corner grocer" and our merchants. That is true patriotism …*

That should seem, all in all, less rigid than some of the articles; it means, in short, as explained in Mr. Côté's letter: *let us help each other—* that, as Mr. Cohen knows as well as anyone, is what Jews do without needing to state it or especially put it in a leaflet or even into election campaigns.

***

The question needs to be raised frankly.

We in no way profess to be anti-Semitic. Our objective is positive action. We are *anti* something only to the extent that it is necessary to combat that something in order to pave the way for action we believe to be useful.

We are not at war with anyone because of their race. However, who can blame us for wanting to put a little bit of order in the country's economic situation?

The economic influence of the French Canadians, the English and the Jews normally should be an approximate reflection of their numbers. One need only look around to see that this is far from the case. It takes only a further look and a little thought to recognize the multiple and disagreeable consequences for our ethnic group of this imbalance. Surely it is not the Jews who would question these consequences, certainly not the Jews who are so skilled at exerting their financial influence to obtain all that this influence is capable of providing.

On the other hand, the masters and practitioners of the boycott who at the present time are chasing—at the risk of disrupting the political and economic relations of the countries where they reside— German merchandise everywhere, certainly also would not question the legitimacy of mutual assistance among people of the same race.

It is primarily this sentiment that has motivated the campaign of the Saint-Denis section. There is, however, another sentiment also and its generosity should not be questioned by the Jews; gratitude towards shopkeepers who when times were hardest, provided the unemployed with their essential needs.

If foreign merchants suffer the repercussions of this very simple policy, which their kinfolk have been the first to implement, what will they have to say? After all, there is no law, nor any principle that guarantees them a special right regarding the French-Canadian clientele.

Life Is in Disarray

It Only Needs a Little Order Put into It

Omer Héroux
Le Devoir, January 19, 1934

It is a strange fact that it is necessary to suggest to French Canadians to support merchants of their own language, the grocer or the haberdasher who lives beside them, whom they meet on the steps of the church, and who is their natural companion in every religious, school and other organization.

In a normal heterogeneous country, consumers generally can be divided according to their language, customs and usual relations. As a general rule, everyone supports members of their own group. There will of course be circumstances in which exchanges take place between various groups, for example, between businessmen of various languages and origins.

However, the overall result would be to ensure that the economic influence of each ethnic group corresponds broadly to its size in numbers.

One need only look around to see that among us life is in disarray and that French Canadians, since they, specifically, are the subject of our remarks today, do not possess—really far from it—the economic influence that is rightfully theirs.

They do not possess it at all in what we could call high finance and big business; they do not possess it even in small businesses.

There are neighbourhoods in the city with large French majorities where small French-Canadian merchants are being eliminated by the thrust of foreign merchants—especially Jewish merchants.

It is plain to see and it must be admitted that this state of affairs is abnormal.

***

How has this disarray come about?

The reasons are many: one obviously is the fact that French Canadians in their day-to-day life do not follow the example of their fellow citizens not of French origin—starting with the Jews—who usually practise, without even thinking about it most of the time, mutual economic assistance, and no one would blame them for doing so.

To tell French Canadians about the usefulness of this practice—that others need not be told about, since it is part of their everyday life—in no way implies a sentiment of hostility towards others. Furthermore, it is not like the boycott of German merchandise advocated by the Jews, some sort of act of war.

It is quite simply a matter of re-establishing the normal state of affairs, which have been distorted by external factors.

***

It is strange that neither Anglo-Canadians, nor Canadians of Italian, Polish, German or any other origin seem to be offended by this campaign called *buy from your own*.

Yet, do they deprive themselves (we have never blamed them for this) from giving each other a solid and fraternal helping hand?

If, in a city where three-quarters of the population is Jewish, a group of French Canadians, who for example constitute one-tenth or one-twelfth of the total population, were imposing a place in business and industry out of all proportion to their numbers, would Jews prevent themselves from observing—perhaps even from stating—that these French Canadians definitely are taking up too much space?

Would they prevent themselves from thinking that logic and common sense require that there be a more equitable relation between economic influence, which engenders influence in so many other spheres, and size of population?

… However, our hypothesis is a fantasy. It is hard to imagine that Jews would let others occupy space that logically belongs to them; and on this point it would be appropriate to admire them and imitate them.

***

To put a little order into affairs, it is necessary first to put order back into ideas to reiterate certain principles so elementary that other people, starting with the Jews, do not even have to hear them stated, since they are in some sense so much part of their intellectual and moral essence. This is the goal of the campaign that has been pursued here for some time, without hatred and without animosity.

It is also necessary for clients to know where to find their merchants. This is the reason for directories, which are being prepared: the first ones appeared a few weeks ago in the parishes of the Côte-des-Neiges district.

Is it necessary to reiterate that none of this is motivated by hostile thought, that all of this only aims at returning to a normal state, the same state as all other groups, an ethnic group that is foolishly letting itself be dispossessed of its natural inheritance?

We Need to Be Logical: Label the Merchant Just Like the Merchandise

The Resolution of the Canadian Jewish Congress

Georges Pelletier
Le Devoir, January 28, 1939

The Canadian Jewish Congress, by a resolution, has just requested the Canadian federal government to "extend the application of sections of the law which make it compulsory to put a country of origin stamp on all imported goods in order to make it easier to identify their place of origin" (Dispatch from the Canadian Press, in Toronto, to evening newspapers, January 24). It will be recalled that goods imported from France, England, Czechoslovakia, Italy, Japan and the United States most of the time indicate their origin. The objective is to make the stamp compulsory for all countries that Canada trades with, specifically Italy and Germany. What is the reason for this step taken by the Jewish Congress? It would make it easier to organize a complete boycott in big stores and small of all German and Italian merchandise. The dispatch spells it out in black and white: "The Jewish Congress adopted a resolution yesterday declaring a boycott of all goods coming from Germany. The Congress sent to the Committee on Advance Rulings for Origin another resolution proposing to extend the boycott to merchandise from Italy."

***

The Jews of Canada whose delegates at the meeting in Toronto are supposed to represent the entire community that has come here from Europe, claim to have applied a tenacious and effective boycott against Germany, because of the way it treats its Jews. The delegates are also considering a boycott of all goods of Italian origin, because Italy has started to apply Nazi methods to Italian Jews. *Le Devoir* has already stated what it thinks of this stupid and brutal persecution, as well as of the attempts at equally foolish reprisals by Jews. Canada can simply ignore these attempts, except to deny any responsibility for them. It could cost Canada dearly if it were to recommence the mad venture of sanctions made against Italy during its conquest of Ethiopia. This rash venture led to the loss of hundreds of thousands of dollars for Gaspésie fishermen, who were selling half of their salted cod to Italy. The market even now remains closed to them, as Italy makes it, purchases elsewhere. Who is the loser in this operation, thought up to satisfy London? Our people. Are we now going to repeat similar operations against Germany and Italy, this time to satisfy Jews here, to whom we owe nothing and who are indebted to us for the shelter they now have? Are they seeking revenge for their co-religionists over there? They provide the best proof that our security and the interests of the country itself require that we no longer accept among us groups of new arrivals intent on carrying with their baggage the grievances and quarrels of old Europe, to try and implant them and impose them on us here and even to benefit from them.

Let us take a look for a moment only at the nature of the request of the Jewish Congress, namely that all merchandise imported to Canada should bear a stamp indicating its place of origin. It makes sense. We could then clearly see that a product that we should make here comes to us from France, another from England, this one from Sweden, that one from Norway or Denmark, one or another Germany, Italy, Hungary, Switzerland, the Kingdom of Belgium, the Union of Soviet Republics, India, Japan, or Iraq. In this way, we would be able to establish the nature, the extent and the diversity of our trade, the markets we buy from and that might buy from us, as well as the present state of our industries unable to supply us with everything we need or believe we need. It would indicate that we need trade agreements other than those we have already signed and also a better orientation of our industries, fewer large-scale and more medium and small-scale domestic industries.

***

Knowing more readily the places of origin of anything we buy here would certainly be excellent. We should not oppose the idea; on the contrary let us take it to its logical conclusion. What does that mean? We should demand that what is applied to products also be applied to people; from objects around us to foreigners who wish to come and live in Canada. Is it not as important to know who we are dealing with and who we shall be dealing with in the future, as to know where toothpaste, a shaving brush, perfume, a cigarette-holder, cloth, a statuette, jewelry or an art object comes from? These are all objects, while an immigrant, a new arrival, is a person. Is our neighbour not more important than the Japanese or Mexican doormat on which we wipe our shoes?

We should support the demand of the Jewish Congress but take the reasoning to its logical conclusion. If Canadian residents need to know, for whatever reason, the exact place of origin of any imported object they buy, they should at the same time and under the same law, learn the exact origins of the importer, the retailer and the merchant who sell the merchandise here or refuse to sell it because of its place of origin. Have you bought a statuette from the *Maison d'Importation du Canada*? The true name of the owner of the business, his country of origin and his ethnic background, if it is known, should be displayed on the most visible part of the store so that no one would be misled. We should know the place of origin of this immigrant. He should no longer be able to pass himself off as a Russian when that is not his ethnicity; it should no longer be possible to register on the immigration form or the decennial census as Romanian or Czechoslovak someone who in reality is an Israelite from Central Europe. We have already received too many so-called Poles, Galicians or Austrians who do not have a drop of Polish, Galician or Austrian blood; too many Russians who are not Russian; even too many Germans who, if they have come or should come from the Sudetenland, have nothing German about them. With a regulation or a law indicating the true origins of any new arrival, as for all merchandise, we would have a much better idea of the situation in Canada. If we need to know where an object we buy comes from, would it not be appropriate also to know who are the neighbours imposed on us, who will live near us, who will constitute fairly large groups and whose presence complicates Canadian life in all sorts of ways?

A well-known writer, Mr. Murray Gibbon, director of advertising services for Canadian Pacific, has just written a well-documented work on the various groups living in Canada: *Canadian Mosaic*. In this mosaic, we should know as precisely as possible where all the parts come from; what are their specific professions; what is their ethnic background; what stress each part of this human mosaic has been subjected to, etc. If for social, customs duties, commercial or other purposes, we need to know that a product has not come from an English sweatshop, a small factory in India using child labour, a Chinese or Japanese workshop where the average wage of the craftsman is equivalent to six cents Canadian for a twelve-hour work day, is it not more important to know that an immigrant has come from an oriental neighbourhood of Moscow, Kiev, Prague or Vienna rather than rural Poland or Ukraine? That would make more sense, even much more than to know the place of origin of artificial tortoiseshell buttons, Solingen razors and trinkets covered with stones from the Rhine or the Danube.

Furthermore, appropriate Canadian legislation would force people born abroad, when arriving here, to reveal their real names, the names their ancestors had in their country of birth, and be forced to keep them; to display their original names and places of origin in all their establishments. In that way we would know exactly who we are dealing with and if we are buying a product from a Canadian or a foreigner, a German or a Jew, a Pole or an Israelite, a Frenchman or an Armenian, a truly Canadian business or one with a sign as misleading as it is resolutely nationalist.

***

Let us display the place of origin of all merchandise. Let us also reveal the origins of any intermediary, any businessman, any manufacturer and any merchant having come to Canada from abroad. No one should fear revealing his place of origin. Even more, everyone should want to know this, just as they want to know where exactly the merchandise has come from that is offered to them on store shelves and counters. Otherwise, how do you explain the absurd situation of wanting one and not the other or even being opposed to doing both?

Let us label the merchandise. Let us especially label the merchant.

The "Detrimental" Influence
of Jews in Montreal
(1926–1936)

This chapter covers a certain number of topics appearing periodically in *Le Devoir* after 1926, either as editorials or as special
columns appearing on the front page. The newspaper occasionally
resorted to making anti-Semitic allusions in columns, often inspired
by populist Parisian newspapers and relating to French-language cultural life in Montreal, but not necessarily relating to current events.
The approach was always the same, and quite simple, and Georges
Pelletier's byline often led the way. *Le Devoir* would, for example, highlight the contrast between high art inspired by the grand moral and
aesthetic values of the West and the more commercial forms supposedly presented by promoters identified as being from abroad, including Jews. In so doing, the newspaper advanced the classic image of
unscrupulous Jews usurping superior artistic expression such as theatre, classical literature and painting and diminishing their status to a
degrading and salacious level of expression. At other times, the opinions focused on new forms of entertainment such as the cinema, modern dance and jazz, to show that these decadent fashions had entered
Quebec through the complicity of enterprises owned by American
Jews devoid of any moral instincts. Each time, *Le Devoir* clearly conveyed the idea that these exogenous doings were influenced in part
by Judaism. Aiming these salvos at Jews, even if they were sometimes
mere hints, created a web of negative perceptions which became profoundly anchored in Pelletier's mind.

This was not, however, the tone in the editorial of June 13, 1936,
written two days after Premier Louis-Alexandre Taschereau resigned
under the pressure of public opinion. Pelletier attempted to link the
Montreal Jewish community to the political corruption committed by
the Liberal Party of Louis-Alexandre Taschereau during the election
of November 1935. The Liberals barely won and the election battle was

marked by massive fraud and shocking strong-arm tactics in some Montreal neighbourhoods. In its criticism of these tactics, *Le Devoir* focused on Joseph Cohen, the member for the riding of Montreal–Saint-Laurent, who had been in office since 1927 and whose campaign the newspaper had followed with great interest in 1935. Cohen favoured aggressive tactics and vote rigging and was, moreover, of Jewish origin, giving Pelletier the opportunity to condemn him and to try connecting Cohen's religious persuasion with his tendency to cheat. Pelletier was emboldened by the fact Cohen was a candidate in a Montreal neighbourhood where "the Jewish voters are numerous" and that he was, according to Pelletier, "a troublemaker whose origins are not here, although he lives among us." The affair went as far as *Le Devoir* threatening the entire Montreal Jewish community with reprisals if the Cohen in question were to be a candidate again in 1936, in other words, "if the Jewish voters want to keep the privileges they now have." In this opinion, Pelletier placed the disgrace of the dishonorable conduct of a single individual, who had acted only for his own benefit, on the entire Jewish population. It was, in short, the same as treating Cohen as the perfect representative of his co-religionists in the Liberal Party and in the Legislative Assembly of Quebec. At the same time *Le Devoir* neglected to point out the many other shady characters within the Liberal Party who very clearly belonged to the French-Canadian world.

A New "Scheme": Fairgrounds in Parc Maisonneuve

What Would This Enterprise Come and Do, Operated by American Capital That Has Already Brought Foul Cinema to the Community of the Courageous Population of the East End? — We Need All Our Parks, Especially in Areas Where There Are Too Few — The Lesson of Corpus-Christi — La Presse Is Not Concerned with Logic

Louis Dupire
Le Devoir, June 7, 1926

The scheme for a tramway to the mountain seems to have been set aside for a year.

La Presse was unlucky. It said that it wanted to make the mountain accessible so that children would have a huge playground. It had little concern for how and with whom the children would get there and how they would be watched. What was necessary, first and foremost was that the road for the tramway be built.

While the good newspaper lamented seeing the mountain deserted and large numbers of children in the streets, it did not hesitate proposing an increase in the number of little loiterers, potential victims of cars and accidents in the streets—without mentioning the moral dangers they face, which have no effect on *La Presse*, the great promoter of cinema, the worst corruptive influence on youth. *La Presse*, for economic reasons, in fact wants to find a way to exclude little five-, and six-year- old children from the schools of the Catholic school board.

Such ineptitude numbs the mind. Logic, however, has never been *La Presse's* strong suit; on Saturdays it publishes the Ladébauche page or the perfect example of how not to speak while it campaigns all week long to improve our language. With its eyes covered by Ladébauche's blinders, the newspaper claims to see the mist covering the eyes of its readers.

Furthermore, *La Presse* must be commended for being consistent in its stupidity. It does not change. While for the scheme on the mountain it emphasizes the importance of playgrounds, during the same week it has no reluctance in promoting a new scheme which, if carried out, would result in closing an immense park. It is the unpardonable shame of the city for having left it unused and empty.

***

Yesterday, the Corpus Christi procession took place in the parish of Saint-Nom-de-Jésus de Maisonneuve. It was a magnificent display of faith that incited admiration from foreigners who witnessed the event, as we learned this morning. The route was long and the crowd enormous. The many Protestants, present at the east end of the parish, who were impressed by this enormous demonstration, by the contemplative and orderly crowd, by the unique show of the *popularity* of the Catholic religion, nearly all removed their hats when the Host went by. Many of them bowed, even deeply. It was impossible not to think of the vitality of the Catholic faith and of the procession in Chicago on American soil in two weeks and what a unique display that will be. A temporary altar had been erected on the beautiful grounds of the public market, where over five thousand people knelt in the dust. As the sun sank into a golden lake on the horizon, the Eucharistic Sun that never sets rose above the bowed heads ...

It is at the middle of this very Christian population that there is a plan to instal insulting mediocre *private* fairgrounds, over which the city will have no direct control and where the sideshows with their grotesque displays and their vulgar sexual appeals will be the main attraction! In the city's own(?) parks, such as on L'île Sainte-Hélène, the *Gazette* reported the other day that people dance the Charleston, an epileptic Negro dance.

What will it be on fairgrounds where the city has no control?

We are certain that the very dignified and so proudly Christian population of Maisonneuve will not tolerate such an insult. The people believed that it was in this particularly attractive community that the grand Montreal university would be established. It appears that it is not an inflexible rule that the West end should receive all of what is our very own in infrastructures. However, it would certainly go beyond all decency to make the East end the dumping ground for the shady population that lurks around the fairs run by Judeo-American capital, the same that makes its money from the most depraved curiosity, millions from cinema and pays advertising in the yellow press for amounts of two hundred thousand dollars or more a year.

What adds even more to the baseness of this scheme, is the fact that *La Presse* on this issue has turned itself into a mouthpiece for the mayor, Médéric Martin. A few days ago, in his *throne speech*, the mayor declared that he supported the fairgrounds operated by a private company. The news in Friday's *La Presse* came like a direct relay of the voice of the person it ridiculed barely two years ago regarding the infamous *departure for L'île Sainte-Hélène*.

***

We remain certain that the population of Maisonneuve and the entire population of the East end will immediately oppose this new scheme that would transform the neighbourhood and deprive the children and the population during a large part of the year, if not the entire year, of a park, the only park available to them.

There should be a demand, instead, that the park immediately be put into good condition and to use as quickly as possible.

If companies operating fairgrounds want to establish themselves, the least we can expect from them is that they acquire land and they do not deprive us of a park where it is needed.

However, before granting the desired authorization, the city should find out the nature of the fairgrounds, what they will exhibit and especially what our youth will be exposed to.

We are not so poor that for a few thousand dollars we need to be subjected to filth. Even if we were poor, better an honourable poverty than shameful earnings.

The least we can expect from the university is that it joins forces with the courageous people of the East end to prevent the emptiness left by its withdrawal to be filled by the operation of a new Judeo-American enterprise.

If That Is "French Art" …

Georges Pelletier
Le Devoir, February 28, 1930

The personnel of the operetta troupe picked up by the police a few hours ago at a theatre in the east end of Montreal for having presented a disgraceful performance are not happy, from what we hear, about having to appear in court. This incident is not so much the fault of the municipal authorities, who ordered the police raid, as it is of the scoundrels organizing the tour who were less remarkable for their intelligence than for smut bordering at times on the obscene. The public in Montreal may tolerate indecency; performances as risqué as those of the last few days disgust them. The public is fed up with them. We received dozens of telephone calls and letters denouncing the last performance from people who are not prudish but were revolted by it. Even a newspaper that strives to be the best in writing about Montreal's populist spirit—as if there were a Montreal populist spirit—La *Patrie*, to be specific, already on Monday evening wrote in its theatre column: *"It took a great deal of audacity to present as an opening performance an operetta such as* Phi-Phi *that many previous tours were reticent to stage because of its very risqué nature… Most of the songs have a double entendre …"* (La *Patrie*, February 24, page 8, article signed *Intérim*).

The editor-in-chief of the theatre section observed in the daily on the same evening that *"Montreal, the second French city in the world … does not have a French theatre … does not support French art … does not promote French performances."* Given what we have been served in the last few months, is *"the complete indifference"* of the French-Canadian public surprising? What have our impresarios done since last autumn to invite and encourage thousands of decent people who wish to experience and applaud true art, but who do not want to spend their money and their time on performances presented only for fans of vulgar debauchery, for young people and young girls already experienced in vice, and for lecherous old men? Nothing at all. Montrealers have been justified in refusing to attend, except for a couple of acceptable musicals.

Let a list be drawn up of the plays brought here under the pretense of new literature and based on the eternal and trite stories of affairs, of ménages à trois where decency, sensitivity and marriage are treated as ridiculous and ludicrous, where faithful husbands and wives are a laughing stock and where lechery is always the main theme. It is obvious that if the invasion and near monopoly in our performance halls of idiotic, materialistic and stupid American films is deplorable, there is as much reason to note and regret that what is shown here and claimed as French theatre is beneath everything from the point of view of morality, self-respect and respect for others, and even simply from a literary point of view.

Who dictates to the impresarios the choice of plays that they come and stage here by troupes recruited over in France? Ninety percent of these plays have succeeded only in attracting vulgar and unhealthy curiosity on this continent and end up falling into the gutter, where they should have remained. All in all, it leads us to believe that these impresarios do not know the public that they claim to serve and instead are looking for easy success and money with a repertory where ambiguous situations, risqué or double entendre songs, dialogues, gestures and even simply the staging—when there is staging—all lead to villainous debauchery.

Is that French theatre? Is that French art? It is, if everything that comes from France is French. It is, if it is French because, alas! French actors and French actresses are the performers—where the author is probably some Jew, a Greek, a German Jew who has become French or a recently naturalized incomer who, ten years ago, knew not a word of French, but spoke Russian, Yiddish or pidgin French mixed with words from the ghetto. It is not, if we recall that there exists another, a true French theatre written by authentic Frenchmen for decent French people and that can be exported without splattering mud on the whole country and on the literature from which it has come.

The showmen who bring us flowers from slums, under the pretext that they represent wit, good taste and contemporary art, practise a strange trade. They have only themselves to blame and their ignorance of the true sentiments of an entire public if they are losing money, as they claim, despite paid publicity in dailies that invites the public to attend shows that too often are scandalous.

If these impresarios do not cover their costs, no one will regret it except they themselves and no doubt the extras and stars they recruit abroad to perform a repertory chosen to drive away from the theatre people who seek entertainment and relaxation there and find instead only lechery, stench and filth, which there is an attempt to cover with the overly-used label of *French art*.

Cheating Does Return to Haunt Its Master — With Double Consequences

Georges Pelletier
Le Devoir, June 13, 1936

This time, the election must be clean and it must be honest.
In 1923, in 1927 and in 1935, the elections were not honest. A government as arrogant during sessions of the legislature as it is spineless when the time comes to face the electorate, called the elections only when the dice were loaded in its favour. Works for land settlement, roads, bridges, schools and public projects of all sorts served as electoral bait. Roads were clogged with instant roadworkers, the countryside with agents dispensing liquor and cash, villages with shameless wheeler-dealers, cities with crooked voting, and special police agents usually recruited from the underworld. The election officers, picked from among friends, were too lax or too reticent when faced by brazen scoundrels. Who can forget—it was not that long ago—the helping hand of gangsters and gunmen in the ridings of Saint-Laurent and Mercier in 1935, the dirty work of all kinds repeated from one end of Gaspésie to the other and the conduct of some candidates to avoid, just barely, the government's and their own defeat in thirty ridings where the result was the least bit in doubt?

This must not be repeated. The government was able to win every election from 1923 to 1931 through such tactics; it has nothing to be proud of. If, in 1935, it had not resorted to widespread violence, treachery and corruption, it would have been crushed. It won by a hair, but it had gone to such lengths that all its skill and all its tactics have led it to where it found itself in the last few days, forced to resign by the anger of the voters and by the attacks of a vigorous opposition, supported by a justifiably alerted public opinion.

The *machine* was able to steal the November election. However, it was not enough just to steal the election; it was also necessary to succeed in keeping the stolen prize. The government did not succeed because the cynicism of its people, its organizers and its henchmen knew no bounds. Public opinion developed and grew and ended up kicking out the government that used everything and abused everything. Although it may take time, *"cheating does return to haunt its master."* It did return ... with double consequences. The government had to leave and we know in what disgrace.

***

What will the Godbout government do? Hold honest elections? It would be wise to make such a decision now. There is certainly no lack of temptation—the former organizers from 1931 and 1935 have not been fired, and this time will do their utmost—to collect money from anywhere and of any kind for the election fund, make the *machine* operate full tilt in order to try and win a hopeless game that can be said, without exaggeration, is lost in advance.

However, this election is one where money will not withstand popular will. There are circumstances where even the richest election fund will be emptied without results. That time has arrived. Exasperation is too widespread to stop the movement. Government members would be wasting their money if they tried. They would be better off investing in prayers to St. Anthony of Padua and saving the interest accumulated on top of interest for later. It is well known that powerful companies linked in all manner of ways to the Taschereau regime for the last fifteen years could try again, and once more offer to finance the party to which they owe so much, confronted by a group they fear in every respect. It would be wasted money. The only risk that the new government may be justified in taking is to hold an honest election this time. The methods used from 1921 to1935 would bring it nothing. Does the government wish to redeem itself, as Mr. Godbout has indicated? Let him start now with this election. After? After, it will be too late.

***

This honesty in the coming election will be necessary for all parties; to those who think they must take power together and have public enthusiasm on their side—they do not have to buy anyone—just as the party that fears losing power, among other reasons, because it has too often stayed in power by having stolen it. Honest people—they are the majority in any party—are justifiably disgusted this time by the dishonesty of politicians, their relatives and their friends, who have taken advantage of everything to grasp everything for them-selves. This disgust has been reinforced during the entire length of the inquiry into the manner in which friends of the regime played with public funds for personal benefit or for electoral purposes. The public wants public honesty. The public must not be frustrated this time. Whoever ventures to try will pay dearly for their foolishness.

Furthermore, there must be honest candidates from one end of the province to the other who have never been involved in the dirty work of a regime destroyed by parasites. We need clean elections with leaders who do not promise "complete support" to morally corrupt individuals and former candidates impossible to whitewash, because they have been in the gang that ransacked the province, misused public funds, squandered for its own benefit tax money paid by increasingly squeezed taxpayers.

***

Finally—this concerns Montreal—something needs attention right now. A certain troublemaker whose origins are not here, although he lives among us, operated in the ridings of Mercier and Saint-Laurent in 1931 and especially in 1935, in such a cynical way and with such audacity that it scandalized honest people who are the most dis-illusioned with politics. A Cohen or a Plante has no business being a candidate anywhere. A Cohen or a Plante must not appear on the list of any party, if it claims to be respectable and respect voters. In two Montreal ridings, there are a large number of Jewish voters. If they allow one of their own or someone who professes to be among their friends and in order to win their votes resorts to electoral methods such as those that *Le Devoir* published in detail last December, along with the names and addresses of the wrongdoers, they will pay dearly for their laissez-faire attitude and their agreement, even if implicit. Prominent members of the Israelite colony in Montreal conveyed their regrets to *Le Devoir* for what happened in November in those two rid-ings. If that should be repeated—those honest people must be able to maintain orderly elections—and they do not remove right from the start those who, last autumn, as we know, used treachery and fire-arms to benefit the Cohens and the Plantes, *it will cost them dearly, very dearly*. They must give that some thought, they must act and protect themselves. *This must not in any way be repeated, if Jewish voters want to keep the privileges they now have*. Why not make them think about it by telling them clearly ahead of the battle? After, it will be too late: they will pay very dearly for maintaining as a candidate and electing a Cohen, a Plante or people of the same sort.

***

Therefore, we and all honest voters, whether they are Liberals, Conservatives, nationalists, independents or any others, want honest elections. It is up to the competing parties to deliver them to us. Will we have them? It is up to the parties to say so and at the same time they must make a firm promise to withdraw, as soon as the next session of the Legislature opens, the despicable Dillon law, protecting political crime.

If we do not have honest elections this time, into what kind of disreputable abyss will those who are supposed to govern us fall, who, to ensure governing still longer, colluded and joined forces with crooks, a partnership that just led to the demise of a regime that in wanting to seize everything from 1921 to 1935, ended up choking on gluttony!

The Jews and Montreal Schools (1914–1930)

The question of education was the most important political issue
for the Montreal Jewish community in the first half of the twentieth century. It was enshrined in the constitution that in Quebec all
the powers in the public schools system were granted exclusively to
Catholic and Protestant church authorities — a guarantee that was the
product of an historic compromise between the two major Christian
religious traditions then present in the province. Neither Catholics
nor Protestants had wanted, in 1867, a neutral education system forc-
ing children of all origins to be submitted to a common teaching program. Thus obliged to be denominational, the British North America
Act (BNA) of 1867, therefore, excluded Jews on the basis of their
religion from attendance in, and the administration of, the Quebec
public school system. Section 93 of the BNA Act was written at a time
when Jews in Montreal constituted a very small community. There
had not been an explicit intent to exclude religious minorities or to
be detrimental to followers of Judaism. Nevertheless, the situation
became untenable once there was a great increase in Jewish immigration from Eastern Europe at the turn of the century. It remained to be
determined which education system these children would enter and
what their rights would be in the denominational schools already
in place.

To remedy increasing difficulties experienced by non-Christian
children in Montreal, the Legislative Assembly of Quebec in 1903
enacted a law declaring persons of Jewish faith as Protestants for the
purpose of education. This agreement was the product of lengthy
negotiations between the best-off leaders of the Jewish community
who wanted to integrate Jewish school children into the Anglophone
public system and the senior levels of the Protestant administration.
Consequently, after 1903, attention was focused on school management by the Protestants and their willingness to provide justice to the
legitimate demands of the parents and children of Jewish origin who

wished to maintain their religious heritage. That is precisely where the situation stood when Omer Héroux took an interest in the issue in April 1914. Héroux's editorial, with its faithful and complete portrait of the Jewish education situation and its political repercussions at the time, demonstrated that the Jewish education issue did not pose any problems for *Le Devoir* as long as the rights of the Catholics were not threatened. It is particularly interesting to note how accurately Héroux perceived the internal tensions found in the Jewish community due to the presence of sharply opposed ideological trends that often resulted from the recent arrival of Yiddish-speaking immigrants from the Russian Empire. This "radical divergence of opinions," as Héroux called it, would give rise between the two wars to a clash between different visions of Jewish education and that would lead to the creation of a significant Jewish private school system in Montreal. However, in 1914 as Héroux observed, it was time for Jews to become aware of their growing political weight on the municipal council and in Montreal life in general.

When Héroux turned to the subject again nearly fifteen years later, the situation had changed completely: the influx of Jewish immigrants had inundated schools in the lower town. By 1930 the Jewish community was once again at a critical juncture. The Taschereau government in power in Quebec wanted to provide justice to the political demands of the Jews in the field of education and recommended the creation of an independent Jewish school board under the Council of Public Instruction, the exclusive fiefdom of the Catholics and the Protestants. It was a way of circumventing the BNA Act and providing Jewish parents an organization where they would constitute a majority in the management of their education institutions. The project was submitted for discussion in the spring of 1930 under the name of the David Law. Three editorials by Héroux were published in quick succession in February, March and April 1930 to give an account of how the file was progressing in the Parliament of Quebec. The most interesting aspect of these texts is that no hesitation can be found in seeing the Jewish population take control of Protestant schools where Jewish pupils were greatest in number. *Le Devoir* adhered to the principle asserted many times by Bourassa that parents had the absolute right to control the education received by their children, particularly with respect to religion. On the Francophone side, opposition to the David Bill in 1930 would come instead from the Montreal Catholic episcopate, which saw it as an intolerable attack on Christianity's dominant position within Quebec society. This position of the Church opened the door to virulent anti-Semitic demonstrations, which Adrien Arcand's press was quick to spread during the 1930s.

Jews and Protestants at the Dissentient School Board

A Problem for the Montreal of the Future

Omer Héroux
Le Devoir, April 15, 1914

The Gazette this morning reported on a candidacy that should not be a surprise to any clear-sighted mind, but does draw attention to a most interesting state of affairs. Mr. Abraham Blumenthal, who was re-elected as alderman for the ward of Saint-Louis, asked his colleagues to delegate him to represent the Jewish community in the dissentient school board, generally known as the Protestant Board.

We know that a portion of the commissioners — Catholic and dissentient — are designated by the municipal council and that a certain number of these delegates must be replaced in the next few months at the latest.

Mr. Blumenthal states that the Jewish children constitute over 50% of the school population in dissentient schools. Would it not be right that they have someone on the board specifically to look after their interests?

He adds that if the Jewish children were to leave the schools called Protestant, some classes would not even be able to exist.

We do not know if Mr. Blumenthal's figures are absolutely correct — we have already heard that the proportion of Jewish pupils is 40% — but it is certain that the Israelite school population is already quite significant and it is growing much faster in relative terms than the Protestant population.

Difficulties also lie ahead — perhaps a conflict — that for a long time have concerned the leaders of the Protestant and Jewish communities.

Mr. Blumenthal's candidacy is not simply an act of personal ambition; it is an assertion of Montreal Jews wishing to take an effective part in the management of dissentient schools.

As long as these schools were attended only by Protestants of various sects, a religious framework could be maintained, able to accommodate nearly all parents. However, that will not be the case in the future. Recent incidents have already given us a hint of inevitable clashes.

It is impossible that the Protestants, who have preserved somewhat profound Christian traditions and who believe in the need for some religious teaching in public schools, will reach agreement on the form and substance of this teaching with the Jews, who deny the divinity of Christ and the very essence of Christianity.

There is a choice; either the schools will maintain a certain Christian nature, whereupon vehement protests can be expected from the Jews, who are recognized for their skill in complaining very loudly when they have or believe they have been wronged; or the schools will be stripped of any trace and appearance of Christianity. Then what will the Protestant faithful do?

***

We have outlined here the extreme, but essential, aspects of the problem. Sooner or later the directors of the dissentient schools will need to choose one of the two formulas. In the meantime, we shall see a whole series of minor conflicts regarding the choice of books and teachers, religious holidays, etc.

This difference in interests and principles has already given rise to bitterness that found its way into the last municipal election campaign. In this regard, we can give a relevant example.

One of our friends, a Mr. Stephens supporter, a few days before the election received a visit from an influential Israelite. — During a business discussion, the Israelite said, "I am going to vote for Mr. Martin and many Jews will do the same." — Our friend asked, "Do you know Mr. Martin?" — "No." — "May I ask then the reason for your choice?" — The Israelite continued, "The Protestant English have not behaved kindly towards us on school issues and we think it is time to teach them a lesson. And since the only way to get their attention is to vote for Mr. Martin, we shall vote for Martin."

Is that not a revealing incident?

The fairest solution to the imbroglio, no doubt, would be to expand and adapt our education system to the new conditions. Our intention essentially was to ensure the minority's right to educate its children according to its wishes. Since at the time there was only one religious minority, we only provided for two categories of schools; majority schools for the Catholics and the Protestants, as the case may be, and minority schools for the dissentients. Since a third significant minority has now come into existence, it would only be fair to provide it with the means to benefit from the general principle of freedom of choice that is the foundation of our law.

However, it is our belief that an extreme difficulty will arise specifically from the fact that the Jews do not want separate schools. Another of our friends recently had a very conclusive experience in this regard. Speaking in front of very varied Jewish audience, he was able to observe in his audience a radical divergence of opinions. Some were Zionists, others internationalists; others identified themselves as orthodox Jews, others as reformed Jews, others still claimed to be atheists. Anarchists and socialist revolutionaries sitting side by side with capitalists. However, when it came time to talk about the possibility of implementing a special school system here for Jews, the uproar was unanimous; we want nothing of the sort!

If they do not want their own special school system, clearly, they would not want schools with a Christian orientation either; the consequence then, unless the Protestants agree to remove Christianity from their schools, will be more or less open, but inevitable warfare.

***

Mr. Blumenthal's candidacy also draws attention to the selection process of the two school boards and the surprises it may reserve.

According to normal practice, the religious minority and majority each choose their representatives in the two school boards and the choice is ratified by the entire council. However, this is merely a gentlemen's agreement. In theory, *all* the aldermen may participate in the selection of *all* the commissioners. The possible consequences of this state of affairs can be seen immediately.

The present municipal council is composed of thirty-one aldermen, including five Protestants and two Jews. The Catholic majority could, if it wanted, select the representatives of the minority against the wishes of most of the minority. On the other hand, it would suffice for the five Protestants and the two Jews to enlist the support of nine Catholics and impose on the fifteen other Catholic aldermen, commissioners not wanted by them.

Who can say if at some point in time, for personal interest and through skilful manoeuvring, that there will not be schemes of this sort?

This perspective must not be forgotten by those interested in the proper operation of our schools and in the possible restructuring of the two boards.

Montreal Schools

*Forthcoming Legislation — Regarding the Catholic
School Board — The Bercovitch Law — A Handful
of Statistics — Jews and Protestants Over the Last Thirty
Years — Changing Numbers — A Table for Analysis*

Omer Héroux
Le Devoir, February 20, 1930

M ontreal schools will likely be an issue of much attention during the present session of the provincial legislature, even if most of the bills have yet to be presented.

First there is a need to specify that the members of the Catholic School Board must be Catholic. There should be agreement that our observations already made on this point are valid. The omission is said to have been inadvertent. While we congratulate the Board for requesting a correction to this oversight, we wish to note that the Board will still be constituted in such a manner that the choice of chairman may, in fact, always be determined by the Government of Quebec and that a portion of the electors will represent various interests.

There will also be a bill proposed by Mr. Bercovitch for the establishment of Jewish schools. This bill may well be postponed, although it seems that the sponsor of the bill intends to proceed with it this year. However, there is another bill that cannot be delayed. It is the bill concerning the allocation of a portion of the taxes of the so-called neutrals respecting the education of children who are not Catholic or Protestant, in other words, Jews, Greeks and schismatics, etc.

It will be recalled that a bill of this nature was passed in the last days of the session in 1929. It hardly attracted any attention, although we believe that, behind the scenes, it was the subject of intense discussion. Given the agreement between the Catholic and Protestant school boards and that the Legislative Assembly hardly had any time to study the issue, it was satisfied with merely recording unanimous consent, which was quite normal.

The agreement, however, is essentially temporary. The law is specific about the fact, in terms that leave no room for ambiguity: "*The present act will remain in force for a period of one year from the first of July 1929.*" The whole issue, therefore, needs to be reconsidered in this session.

There was talk before the session began, that some Protestants would be prepared to request the extension of the present system for another year. That is not the opinion of the Catholic School Board. It would find the arrangement too onerous.

***

At this time, it is not our intention to discuss the substance of the issue. It simply seemed interesting to us to remind the public about the debates ahead—and present our readers with some figures that tend to be ignored.

How many people other than specialists, for example, have any idea of the number of children attending Montreal Protestant schools and the proportion of Jews and of Protestants in these schools?

The last report of the Protestant School Board of the city of Montreal provides us with a table in this regard that we believe appropriate to reproduce in whole and that would be useful to analyze. The table provides figures for the number of Protestant and Jewish school children established in September of each year since 1901 and the total registration in these schools. (The first column after the year gives the number of Protestant children, the second the number of Jewish children, the third number of Protestants, Jews and other pupils, which explains why the figures in the third column exceed the total of the two others.)

September	Protestants	Jews	Total
1901	6776	1526	8921
1902	6755	1775	9128
1903	6610	2144	9297
1904	7022	2443	9804
1905	7272	2881	10449
1906	7424	3302	10991
1907	6875	3583	10770
1908	7188	4374	11056
1909	7164	4763	12252

1910	8559	5331	14168
1911	9347	5951	15535
1912	9330	6858	17036
1913	10646	8081	19181
1914	11533	9194	21231
1915	12129	9642	22197
1916	12131	10027	22606
1917	12392	10208	23022
1918	15016	10580	25988
1919	15909	11015	27434
1920	15799	11275	27730
1921	18054	12142	30880
1922	18609	12432	31654
1923	18597	11974	31391
1924	18651	11567	31842
1925	18919	11202	31316
1926	19009	11007	31121
1927	19341	10918	31547
1928	19312	10613	31362
1929	19460	10194	31061

On another page of the report we see that last year in the Protestant Board schools there were 56 Catholics (namely 19 fewer than the previous year) and 1,157 schismatic Greeks, plus a certain number of residents and non-residents of various categories who, we believe, are only included in the third column of the table.—We should note in passing that according to Mr. Manning's last report, published at nearly the same time as the Protestant report, there were 106,157 pupils registered in the Catholic Board last year.

***

The figures in the Protestant report are quite interesting, first, with respect to the relative numbers of Jewish and Protestant children and second, with respect to the growth of the two student populations.

At the present time, the Jewish children constitute nearly one-third of the total number of pupils attending schools of the Protestant Board; the Jewish children equal a little over half the number of Protestant children. However, contrary to popular belief, this latter proportion of Jewish children is not growing.

From 1901 to 1929, the Protestant school population increased in a nearly regular pattern. The Jewish population, on the contrary, which increased from 1,526, in 1901, to 12,432 in 1922, reached its maximum that year. It was only 10,194 in 1929, while from 1922 to 1929, the number of Protestant children increased from 18,609 to 19,460. It is worth noting that during the pre-war years and even a little after, the number of Jewish children and of Protestant children became nearly equal; 8,081 Jews compared to 10,646 Protestants in 1913, and 9,194 Jews compared to 11,533 Protestants in 1914; 10,027 Jews and 12,131 Protestants in 1916; 10,208 Jews and 12,392 Protestants in 1917. It is probably those figures that created the impression of a continuous increase in the number of Jews.

However, this article is already too long. We shall say nothing more. This series of figures should still help to *situate* and better follow the debates that will become necessary in the next few weeks.

Under the Government's Thumb

Omer Héroux
Le Devoir March 18, 1930

All we know about the bill that will provide for the constitution of a new section (Jewish) at the Council of Public Instruction and a new Jewish School Board in Montreal, is what is contained in the dispatch of the *Gazette* of March 13.

According to the dispatch, the bill decrees that the Jewish section of the Council of Public Instruction would eventually act as a school board for one or several Jewish school districts that may be established on the Island of Montreal (where nearly the entire Jewish population of the province is located). —This means that the members of this section would combine the duties exercised in the Catholic and the Protestant communities by the Catholic and Protestant committees of the Council: such as designation of an office of inspectors, etc. and by local boards: direct administration of schools, selection of teachers, etc.

The bill also decrees that the members of this Jewish section of the Council of Public Instruction will automatically become a school board, with direct responsibility for Montreal's Jewish children (this board would have the right to establish its own schools and deal with existing school boards for the education of its pupils); but the bill decrees that the members of this section-board will be appointed by the Lieutenant-Governor in Council (in other words by the government) *at pleasure* and, therefore, revocable at will.

Conclusion: if the new bill corresponds to the information provided by the *Gazette,* the education of Montreal Jewish children will depend on a board directly appointed by the government of Quebec and whose members would be subject to recall by the government.

It should be noted, to be honest, that this goes significantly beyond the condition imposed on the Catholic School Board of our city. In the latter, through a very simple mechanism (the government restricted the choice of the chairman of the Board to the five delegates it has appointed and made an arrangement by which it is mandatory to elect the candidate of its choice), the government was content to give itself the direct selection of a certain number of commissioners and the indirect selection of the chairman. The latter, according to the terms of the law, is "the director-general of the schools," "the official and permanent representative of the corporation," "the director of the heads of service and of the entire personnel."

It can be seen that the tendency is to increase the control of the government of Quebec over Montreal schools.

In fact, it is probably the group of Protestant schools that is the least affected by this tendency. But this would require a special examination ...

Why Not a Postponement?

Omer Héroux

Le Devoir, April 1, 1930

A special dispatch from the *Gazette* this morning (page 6, column 4) reports that the bill providing for the education of Jewish children in Montreal is being revised. The amendments would pertain to one of the financial sections and to some details. The amendments have apparently resulted from comments made by the two other school boards; the Protestant board and the Catholic board. Furthermore, we know that at the end of last week, a section of the Montreal Jewish community itself criticized (Mr. Caiserman's statement in the *Gazette*) version no. 2 (We called it no. 2, because there was an earlier version that decreed: *"The Council of Public Instruction is composed of Roman Catholic members, Protestant members and of members of the Jewish faith* (section 1)" and this version consequently, by its section 3, would have amended section 22 of Chapter 133 of the Revised Statutes, which states: *"Education issues in which the interests of the entire population are of common concern come under the jurisdiction of the Council of Public Instruction and are decided by it."* We might add in passing that it can be seen that the first version applied to the entire province and the Jewish members of this tripartite council, as part of an essentially provincial council would eventually have had the right to deal with the interests of *"the entire population")*.

This second version has already provoked comments, which apparently will result in corrections that are mentioned in the *Gazette* dispatch. The second version provoked other comments, including a submission from the *Société Saint-Jean-Baptiste* council to the Premier, which can be found on page three of today's newspaper and provides an idea of the nature of the comments. We might add that a quick glance by us, which was necessarily the limited one of a person unfamiliar with the issue, was enough to raise other concerns. For example, the government retains the right to appoint, not only the members of the Jewish Board, but also the chairman. After having decreed in section 3 of the new bill that the board *"possesses all the rights and all the powers generally held by similar corporations"* and in section 4 that *"the provisions of the Education Act (Revised Statutes, 1925, chapter 133)* apply to the Board and Jewish schools, except in cases of incompatibility," which appears quite complete, the authors of the bill take the trouble to add (section 10): *"The Board possesses with respect to the education of persons of the Judaic faith all the powers possessed by the Montreal Catholic School Board and the Office of Commissioners of the Protestant Schools of the city of Montreal, regarding education in their respective schools."* If this is not a simple duplication, the future Jewish board will automatically possess all powers that may be granted to one or the other of the boards. What reason is there for binding the future in such a broad way, instead of leaving it to the future to decide on cases that may be very varied, arising under the law in general or under a specific law?

These are observations and even objections from various sources. There is another observation whose importance may have been underestimated. There is an effort to create a legal status for a community that is situated outside the two denominations that have lived side by side here for a long time and who have developed a regime of peace and harmony. This community is the largest of the non-Catholics and non-Protestants but is no longer the only one. In the schools administered by the Montreal Protestant School Board, there are already over one thousand children who are neither Catholic, it goes without saying, nor Protestant of any sect, nor Jewish. With the increase in immigration, no one knows how much this group will grow. Furthermore, no one knows if these people, in turn, will demand a special status in the future.

The present bill, which has just barely been published, has raised a variety of objections, which will probably be difficult to resolve at the end of the session, and it covers only one aspect of a problem much broader in scope. This is why we wonder if it would not be more advisable and wiser to postpone this partial solution and consider the full scope of the problem and find a principle that would allow an equitable resolution, not only for the present case of the Montreal Jews, but also, for example, for the schismatics. Time should be taken to consult the Council of Public Instruction, where there are already committees with competent people from the Catholic and Protestant groups. We already know that it is not possible to create a new system without studying the possible repercussions on existing systems.

The only objection that may be raised against this idea is that of extreme urgency and of the need to prepare immediately for an imminent crisis. This objection has been raised, but if we refer to a statement made by Dr. James Smyth, chairman of the Protestant School Board of Montreal, published in the *Gazette* of March 24 (page 4), it seems that nature of the situation has been quite seriously misjudged. The Protestants naturally want a decision as soon as possible on what will happen, in order to establish, for example, their building program, but they do not seem to have any intention of completely refusing Jewish children entry to their schools next September. In fact, no one seems to believe that the situation can be resolved before the autumn of 1931. A system of this scope cannot be improvised.

A postponement that would allow an in-depth examination of the question of principle would in no way prevent interested parties from examining, at the same time, all aspects of an eventual system and every detail of its application.

In all likelihood, it will give us a stronger and longer lasting result. Would it really be lost time?

Furthermore, this additional examination of an issue whose importance no one underestimates would be carried out in a most suitable atmosphere. No one among us contests the natural rights of the paterfamilias; respect for those rights, it can be said, is part of our tradition and of our life itself.

Observance of Sunday
(1933–1934)

The two following editorials demonstrate how difficult it was for non-Christians to integrate into dominant Francophone economic networks. In pre-war Quebec, it was difficult to establish a precise line between the precepts of Catholic faith and French-Canadian nationalism and, in many cases, religious demands took precedence over legal practices. A Quebec law in existence since 1907, which respected the observance of Sunday rest, stated: "It is prohibited on Sunday for the purpose of profit, except in cases of necessity or emergency, to carry out or have carried out any industrial work, as well as any business or trade." As the editorial written in May 1933 by the Jesuit Father Joseph-Papin Archambault demonstrates, the Catholic clergy considered that stopping all profit-making activity was a question of religious doctrine and an issue for which the State was directly responsible. At the beginning of the twentieth century, numerous Catholic organizations lobbied for a strict application of the Sunday law and publicly condemned how some enterprises broke the law. In this climate of rigid surveillance and religious militancy, it was difficult to find tolerance toward communities that did not consider Sunday a day of some significance. This was especially true regarding people of the Jewish faith, who found themselves subjected to feelings of hostility from the community, the Church and the State.

Father Joseph-Papin Archambault, who in the 1920s founded the *Semaines sociales du Canada* and the École sociale populaire, did not hesitate to refer to Jewish merchants of the city when raising the issue of Sunday observance. Although the allusion was not marked by virulent anti-Semitism, it still left the reader with the impression that Jews were among those neglecting to observe the "national holy customs" of French Canada. Consequently, the Quebec countryside on Sunday was described as being like "a Jewish neighbourhood of Montreal." These comments, although not constituting the principal aspect of Father Archambault's argument, still contributed to isolating and marginalizing people of Jewish origin in Quebec society. Since people identified as Jews were considered not particularly inclined to follow certain practices deemed essential to maintaining social order, such as Sunday rest, these comments served to marginalize Jews from the general development of French Canada. While Father Archambault at times went off on a tangent to comment on Jews doing business on Sunday, Héroux devoted an entire editorial to the issue in April 1934 in a more aggressive tone. This time, he focused not only on the marketing of farm products, but on the "mastery" of Jews in obtaining unjustified benefits and abusive privileges from the Parliaments. In short, he felt that Jews were perverting laws and regulations passed by the Legislative Assembly and with the full knowledge of the Liberal majority were introducing clauses applying only to them. This accusation of Héroux's raised much more worrisome concerns in the long term, notably with respect to issues such as libel, freedom of expression and the right of minorities to education that respects their religious convictions.

The Observance of Sunday

*The Sunday Week — The Situation in the Past and Now
— Laxness in the Countryside — An Incredible Privilege —
Blame the Consumers — Support for the Holy Year*

Joseph-Papin Archambault, Society of Jesus
Le Devoir, May 3, 1933

This year again — it has become a tradition now — a week is devoted to celebrating the observance of Sunday.

This perseverance, which characterizes the tenacity of the *Ligue du Dimanche*, at the same time highlights another less reassuring fact: the depth of the ill being tackled.

The leaders of the *Ligue* are not on a mission against windmills and ghosts. They are all burdened by onerous professional duties, also give of their time to other works and do not have time to waste on worthless tasks. If they have deemed it worthwhile to take up this task, it is because the task appears urgent to them.

And it is true that, unfortunately, our Sunday is increasingly under threat.

It would be unfair to deny that the *Ligue's* campaigns have achieved significant results. The *Ligue* has aroused public opinion, it has prevented abuses, it has put a stop to multiple blameworthy practices and it has revealed situations that, unfortunately, have been tolerated for too long and are, therefore, difficult to rectify, but which it still hopes to overcome.

The simple appointment of inspectors by the provincial government, on the recommendation of the *Ligue*, is a measure with great impact. The regions that have benefited from the measure have already been transformed to a great degree.

However, no sooner is one wound healed that another is suffered elsewhere. This fact reveals the extent to which our society is affected and the profound ill that is silently undermining it.

For a long time, efforts were focused on the worst abuse, which was the work in factories, especially pulp and paper mills. We can recall the vigorous campaign led by the fearless vicar-general of Chicoutimi, Monseigneur Lapointe. The ill was blamed on foreign industrialists who forced Canadian workers to work on Sunday. The example of farmers supported that opinion. Free to do as they pleased, they scrupulously respected the observance of Sunday.

The situation has changed. First, work in factories on Sunday has been almost entirely eliminated, except for certain repairs that, for some strange reason, are still carried out on Sunday, even when factories operate only a few days during the week. Various factors, including unemployment, obviously have contributed to this improvement of the situation.

However—it must be admitted—farmers no longer deserve the praise given them in the past.

We do not wish to descend into unfair generalizations. The rural masses, on the whole, are still faithful to our national holy traditions. It is amongst them, more than any other group, that the strong virtues of race have been preserved. They are especially attached to the Catholic faith, close to their clergy and mindful of observing their precepts. However, this observance is not as solid as previously. Cracks are starting to appear.

The desecration of Sunday is one such crack; it is recent but already deep. Some regions have still avoided it. They are rare. Most regions suffer from the general evil. It appears in the form of roadside vendors. In front of properties, owners place produce from the garden and the farm; fruit, vegetables, milk, eggs, butter, honey; even certain handicrafts; rugs, curtains, etc. They wait for passing tourists or even go to the extent of enticing them.

There are even farmers who receive their biggest clients from the city on Sunday. Trucks are filled with vegetables pulled out of the fields as the buyer watches. Did a journalist not write last year that parts of the countryside on that day have a strange similarity to Jewish neighbourhoods in Montreal?

Alas, that is often where the bad example or the reprehensible suggestion has come from. Jewish merchants travel through the countryside on Sunday to stock up for the week. Others carry on business openly right in the city. They take advantage of the unfortunate section seven of the provincial law that gives them an incredible privilege, denied by Ottawa and unknown in other provinces, but that we in Quebec have stupidly granted them.

The *Ligue du Dimanche* recently demanded the section be repealed. It invited all citizens to support the demand. We hope that the invitation will be heard. However, the best way to respond to the invitation is still to observe personally, to the best of our abilities, the law that we blame others for breaking.

We must be fair. We are not completely blameless in this regard. Our province has a poor reputation in Canada for respecting the observance of the precept for Sunday and it is not due only to the Jews. Without a doubt, there are two ways of understanding this observation; the Protestant way and the Catholic way. Our way appears broader, more human and more in accordance with a religion of love. We do not intend to replace it with Toronto's way.

However, it is also necessary to observe rigorously the substance of the precept. In that regard, since trade is considered as subservient work, it is prohibited. Only a legitimate purpose or necessity allow it. What to conclude from this rule? That a small sweets shop, goods for immediate consumption or necessities—medication, for example—are permitted. Furthermore, the nature and size of the business may vary according to the place, the circumstances and the season.

However, at the present time there is certainly a growing tendency in Quebec to eliminate Sunday as a holiday and as a holy day. Stores of all kinds sell for, no reason, all types of things. And buyers swarm everywhere. They definitely are nearly always the main culprits. The merchant opens his store to satisfy and fulfil the desires of the buyers. The buyers hold in their hands the key to the solution. They need only abstain from buying and the stores would shut their doors.

That would be the right decision to make during this year's Sunday week and one of the principal reforms to carry out during this holy year. Sunday must be better observed and made truly the Lord's Day. A day of prayer first of all, then a day of rest, a joyful day also, a day even of holy enjoyment, but with family as much as possible, in accordance with its unique holy nature.

Oh, what joy we would give to the good Lord, if all of us, political leaders and simple citizens, employers and workers, merchants in cities and farmers in the country, Catholics, Protestants and Jews, made an unselfish effort to return to our Sundays their traditional features!

Such an approach, better than any plans of economists and statesmen, would contribute to bringing a faster end to the terrible crisis that our country is suffering, since it would have a most beneficial effect on the heart of the One who holds our fate in His hands.

Dotting the I's

*Jewish Privilege and Observance of Sunday — Origins
and Extent of the Privilege — It Exists Only in Quebec
— Ottawa Refused to Grant it — The Provincial Law
of February 28, 1907*

Omer Héroux
Le Devoir, April 26, 1934

The Jews in the province, under certain specific conditions, enjoy the *right* to carry out *work* and not *to keep a store open on Sunday* (the law, on the contrary, expressly states that the place where their work is carried out must not be *"open for business that day"*). (The text of the law, as we reiterated very recently, makes a clear distinction between the words *work* and *business* for a reason.)

To repeat, despite the prohibition on *opening shops*, the right to work under specific conditions is one the Jews do not enjoy in any other province.

Why is there this difference?

Simple minds tend to believe that since the consequences have appeared at the provincial level, that is also their source.

However, it seems that it is not clear for everyone. It is time to dot the i's.

***

There exists a *federal* Sunday law and a *provincial* Sunday law.

The *federal* law, which now is Chapter 123 of the Revised Statutes of Canada 1927, and which first appeared as Chapter 153 of the Revised Statutes of 1906, dates from 1906. It was originally Chapter 27, 6 Edward VII. Men of a certain age have certainly not forgotten the long and passionate debate provoked by the drafting of this law.

The *federal* law did not refer to Jews, either in its stage as a bill or in its final version.

It was not at this time that, as small as their numbers then were, there was an attempt to grant the Jews a privilege.

The special committee of the Commons, to which the initial bill had been referred, took the time to add a section with the obvious purpose, which was published with a note in the margin, *Exception respecting Israelites*, to exempt Jews from the general application of the law.

The federal Parliament wanted nothing to do with this section.

It was quite differently—in a most interesting way—that the privilege for Jews was included in our laws.

***

The federal bill established a broad principle of prohibition, mitigated by a certain number of exceptions.

Under the avalanche of objections and criticisms provoked by the bill, the authors decided to add to all the specific exceptions listed and that had been increased during the debate, a very broad text that incorporated, so to say, in the federal list all the exceptions provided by the *"the provincial laws now in force or that may come into force."*

The federal law received assent on July 13,1906, but was not to come into force until March 1, 1907. At its next session, the provincial parliament of Quebec hastened to pass a law using the text that we just quoted with the aim of maintaining a special regime in our province.

The law was given assent on February 28, 1907, just a day before the federal law came into force. The provincial law came into force immediately.

Among other things, the law stated that all our laws in existence at the time would remain in force until repealed or amended and that it would *"be permitted for any person to carry out, on Sunday, any activity not prohibited by the laws of this Legislature in force on the date of February 28, 1907, or to exercise, on Sunday, all the freedoms acknowledged by the ACCEPTED CUSTOMS of the province respecting that person ... "*

***

That covered a great number of things, but in no way changed the situation of the Jews, since neither the law nor the customs had until then acknowledged for Jews the privilege of working on Sunday in our province.

Consequently, the famous section 6 (Chapter 42, 7 Edward VII) was enacted for the specific benefit of the Jews, and subsequently became section 4471 of the Consolidated Statutes of 1909 and then section 7 of Chapter 199 of the Consolidated Statutes of 1925:

> Notwithstanding any contrary provisions contained in the present section, any person conscientiously and customarily observing the seventh day of the week as the Sabbath and truly refrains from working on that day, is not subject to prosecution for having worked on the first day of the week. IF THE WORK DOES NOT INTERFERE WITH OTHER PERSONS IN THE OBSERVANCE OF THE FIRST DAY OF THE WEEK AS A HOLY DAY AND THE PLACE OF WORK IS NOT OPEN FOR BUSINESS ON THAT DAY.

This is the source of the Jewish privilege.

By succeeding in having the parliament of Quebec take advantage of the breach opened by the federal law to pass this exception—that the federal legislators had formally rejected—the Jews, at a time when they were only a handful, proved once again their mastery in making the parliaments do their bidding.

***

That being said, it must be remembered that the privilege granted by the provincial law to the Jews is very clearly limited and conditional, as demonstrated by the text we just quoted.

It must be remembered that repealing the text and bringing it into force are two very distinct things. While one requires an act of the provincial parliament and provokes differences of opinion between lawyers, the other presents no legal difficulties and requires not a single additional piece of paper.

… A text exists, neat and clear. It is up to the responsible authorities to demand simply that it be applied precisely and consistently.

The Success of Jews in Montreal (1930–1946)

The relations between *Le Devoir* and the Montreal Jewish community were more complex than they first may appear. Despite rather strong doctrinal criticisms and expressions of profound mistrust, especially during the 1930s, the newspaper still managed to maintain a positive discourse regarding certain very specific issues. This emerged, vaguely at times and clearly at others, in editorials describing the two groups as minorities, both of which were vulnerable to unjust treatment by the Anglo-British majority. Some of the editorialists were of the view that despite nearly insurmountable differences in perception and experience between Jews and Francophones, there were undoubtedly traces of a common historical destiny among all oppressed peoples. At least five times during this period, *Le Devoir* published texts encouraging French Canadians to be inspired by the achievements of Canadian Jews. These editorials appeared under headings that could not have been more explicit, such as "Do Not Blame the Jews: Imitate Them" and "The Example of the Jews." Why did the Jewish community deserve such recognition from the newspaper? Essentially it was because Jews were perceived as possessing characteristics and promoting behaviour lacking in Montreal's Francophone population, including the desire for education and to further one's education constantly, the ability to organize and demonstrate solidarity and a unique aptitude for productive work.

It would be wrong to see these remarks by *Le Devoir* as the result of concrete observations, or the result of sustained exchanges between the two groups. The impressions published in these editorials are very broad and the result of an analysis made from a distance. Before 1945, Jews and French Canadians interacted very little, either in the upper echelons of Montreal society or among the intellectual elite. This impacted *Le Devoir*'s editorialists, some of whom rarely stepped outside the precisely defined Francophone Catholic circles. Even in positive descriptions there is stereotyping based on widespread negative perceptions of Jews, which in other circumstances often took on a more hostile tone. Nevertheless, it is important to include texts presenting contrasting images of Jewish life at a time when *Le Devoir* sought to reject new immigration from Central Europe. It needs to be noted that the newspaper was also the proponent of a concept of a society, and of a French-Canadian nationalist ideology, that placed great emphasis on values relating to community solidarity, social progress, and surpassing one's abilities. Consequently, individuals such as Omer Héroux became aware that the metropolis was also the scene of an intense effort by some communities, including the Jews, to improve their future prospects. There were similarities that filtered through periodically, which the most engaged Francophone nationalists could not help but note in their writing. It was as if the newspaper let itself become emotional over the success of other minority groups who also faced adversity very familiar to French Canadians, such as lack of capital, lack of knowledge of the English language, and membership in a culture considered marginal.

The editorials favourable to Jews in *Le Devoir* also have the particularity of nearly always focusing on Canada's internal circumstances; in other words, they viewed the life of the Jewish community from a Montreal perspective. *Le Devoir* did not systematically oppose the Jewish presence at the local level, quite the contrary. On several occasions, the newspaper's editorialists, except for Georges Pelletier, found it interesting to observe the kind of activism promoted by certain Jewish organizations. Héroux, for example, in the tense context of the 1942 referendum, wrote a nearly admiring text about the Canadian Jewish Congress while it was lobbying energetically against the position defended by *Le Devoir*. Héroux simply could not help but observe that the strategy and the motivations of the Jews deserved to be copied by the French Canadians opposed to conscription. As long as there was no question of attracting new immigrants to Canada, or of rushing to the assistance of German refugees, *Le Devoir* found a kind of enjoyment in reporting on certain particular features for which the newspaper, to use Héroux's words, "did not wish to criticize Jews." This even went to the extent of admitting in 1946, that, all things being equal, Jews donated six times more per capita to their philanthropic organizations than French Canadians. Émile Benoist hinted that it was not difficult to imagine the beneficial effect such a level of generosity would have had on the network of Catholic charitable works.

Do Not Blame the Jews: Imitate Them

Louis Dupire
Le Devoir, June 3, 1930

A reader sent me the following letter:

Montreal, May 28,1930

To Mr. Louis Dupire
Le Devoir

Dear Sir:

Are you aware of the movement organized by the Y.M.H.A. *(published in yesterday's* Star*) to establish a campground in Fletcher Park? Could this part of the public park, therefore, be reserved for a single group? Is that part of the park not a site open without discrimination for the enjoyment of the entire population of Montreal? It seems to me that this Urban camp, under the administration of the* Y.M.H.A. *will prevent the public visiting Mount Royal from enjoying the park. If the organizers rent private land, that is their own business, but whatever good reasons they may raise, no one has the right to deprive the residents of Montreal of any area of land for the benefit of a single organization, especially during the summer months. What is your view? Etc.*

The letter was accompanied by a clipping of the article in question from the *Star*. I read the article with great interest. Here it is:

The Young Men's Hebrew Association *is planning healthy and educational recreational activities for more than one thousand young boys for the coming summer months.*

Under the name of Urban Camp, *a great number of activities have been organized which will attract many male children and provide them with a beneficial way of spending hot summer days far from the dangers of city streets. Registration has already begun and a great number of boys unable to attend rural vacation camps have been signed up. The camp will be located on* Fletcher Farm *(parc Jeanne-Mance).*

> *The collaboration of a certain number of municipal agencies has been obtained. The* Parks and Playground Association, *through the offices of Captain William Bowie and the* Boy Scouts Association, *through the offices of Russell Paterson, have promised their complete support for the* Urban Camp. *The Department of the Interior in Ottawa has agreed to support nature studies by sending speakers to lead outings on the mountai, where the children will be able to learn first-hand about the birds, trees and flowers of Canada.*

All in all, the objections to the *Urban Camp* in the parc Jeanne-Mance are weak. (The *Star* calls it *Fletcher Farm,* which actually is the parc Jeanne-Mance and proves how old names persist, even when they no longer have any meaning.) The parc Jeanne-Mance is huge; but it belongs to the entire population of the city. Is it a good idea to reserve a part of it to a single specific group? Nothing in the *Star's* article gives the impression that the organization will focus only on Jews. The organization is sponsored by a Jewish association; because of this fact, inevitably in practice, it will attract mainly young Israelites. However, is that blameworthy? Would we rather see them fill and litter the streets?

We should not be too quick to criticize something that, upon reflection, we would agree that we should imitate.

We would have a thousand children achieving love of the country in a practical way by learning to know birds, trees and flowers of their country under the guidance of specialists. It would mean a thousand children who would not invade Mont Royal, as do so many others, to vandalize and destroy trees, lawns and flowers, but instead acquire notions and subjects of natural history.

Is that really bad?

Would it not be better, instead, to criticize those who worked so hard to build a tramway on the mountain and succeeded only too well in significantly diminishing the educational value of the mountain? The mountain had been, until then, the customary refuge of the deceased and birds. Walkers wanting to enjoy some rest had only to climb toward this Mount Thabor, where in the heart of the city they found life transfigured. Soon, that will no longer exist. Nature will have been chased away from the mountain by the infernal din of the tramway. The solitude and this kind of nature reserve will be violated. We should not condemn those who wish to fully enjoy this charming place in decline. Let us hope, instead, that the much discussed botanical or natural history garden will be ready in time to replace what the invasion of modern transportation will destroy on the mountain.

Is there a desire to educate children, especially young Jews, about elementary ornithology and botany? Is it not desirable to do the same thing for our children, rather than criticizing those who take on the responsibility of such education for any group of children? Summer is the best time for children to learn about nature. In winter, they are taught between four walls only through their eyes and ears. In the summer, when they have a teacher who knows how to do so, it could be said that teaching derived from the book of nature can be conveyed through the five senses and through the pores of the skin. God knows that to rouse us from our lethargy, to become accustomed to seeing, to observing and consequently to knowing and liking our city better, we need to learn from studying nature. Adults are terribly ignorant about natural history and if we do not want children to be the same, it is more than time to begin teaching them.

We finally need to get started and that is why I do not wish the initiative to be condemned, even if it comes from others. The initiative should be adapted by us and applied throughout the province. Already, in the last two years, scouting and organized games were initiated in the parish of Immaculée-Conception.

Any association whose primary objective is to look after youth, such as the Association catholique de la jeunesse canadienne-française, should take this parish as a model and apply in all parishes what is done in that parish and add to it. Natural history excursions should be added to supervised and interesting games (without organized games, playgrounds are either deserted or as wild as the jungle).

The moral, intellectual and physical health of children will be improved. Parents will enjoy the peace that they deserve in the knowledge that their children are safe and the progress of the plague of neo-Malthusianism will be slowed, if not eliminated completely.

If associations that take such an initiative were serious and truly capable of inspiring confidence in everyone (not doing as some organizations that see education of children as handing out ice cream cones and free admission to parks that young children should never visit), they would receive the support of everyone who thinks about the seriousness of the problems confronting those responsible for families. If the associations do not succeed, and quickly, after having been surpassed in scouting and vacation camps by the English, we shall be surpassed by the Jews. It is not only national pride that will suffer, but the health of the hearts, minds, and bodies of thousands and thousands of young children.

The Saint-Denis Speeches

*An Appeal for Work and Effort — The Urgent Need for the
Appeal — Let Us Take Advantage of All the Opportunities
Presented to Us — In Montreal the Opportunities Are
Nearly Infinite — The Dignity of Manual Labour — The Best
Way to Stand Out Is to Know Your Work and Know It Well*

Omer Héroux
Le Devoir, September 2, 1937

The tone of the Saint-Denis speeches last Sunday, overall, seems to have been remarkable. They counselled work and effort. One of the speakers specified: *Talk less, act more!* Another speaker or the same one, who is very involved in politics, emphasized the need for unity and mutual assistance. Alas, he knows, as well anyone, that our political system tends to create among us a type of latent but permanent conflict.

However, it is possible to mitigate the consequences of this system to some extent. The mitigation would become nearly automatic if minds were better prepared to see problems other than the struggle for power.

The relevance and the urgency of these appeals for work are more sharply perceived and felt at times such as now, when children are seen heading or preparing for school.

What will become of this youth if they do not make a resolution to make an effort in life and if they are not taught in a methodical and sustained way?

***

We do not have illusions any greater than others regarding the obstacles on the road of the young generations and especially the French-Canadian generations. However, the youth must not think that their ancestors did not find life hard. They must not despair. It is particularly necessary that they not add the weight of inertia and negligence to the burden of these difficulties.

Is it certain that all of our youth do what they can and make every effort necessary to improve themselves and consequently their chances of success and that they do not stray, at times, onto dead end roads—simply out of habit?

Of course, all of that is not exclusively their fault and some of the mistakes are the fault of their ancestors; however, that is one more reason for everyone to make an effort to improve himself and correct his ways.

***

We, at times, wonder whether or not the most urgent task may be to bring back into fashion a very simple value, *work*, and whether it would not be especially suitable to attempt to restore to favour, which unfortunately seems necessary, a particular type of work, that which is described as manual labour.

How many of us, young and old, grant to work all the consideration that it deserves? How many can declare that they do not waste any of their time? Furthermore, in the success of some of our rivals, should we not recognize the quite significant part played by their powerful and tenacious willingness to work?

The Jews, to name only them, arrived here with nothing. Is not their determination to work at least one of the reasons for their success? Undoubtedly to this can be added, among other things, the way they know how to help each other and support one another. Is that beyond our strength?

***

Those who least like Jews and who, rightly or wrongly, criticize them the most, would not disagree that it is worth imitating them with regard to what is best about them and which, furthermore, is not strictly a personal characteristic.

***

We were once told about a significant characteristic of the Jews: one of our friends asked one of McGill's bigwigs at the time, the reason for the success, which appeared very remarkable, of certain Israelite students. The McGill man pointed at two students: he said, *Look at those little Jews. They are going to the library. At the same time, my son is probably playing tennis ... It will show at exam time ...*

There is a lesson here to be learned by all. For pupils returning to class right now, we must encourage them to make use of all their time and support them to ensure that they do so. We must also suggest to those who are not required by regulation to return to school to take advantage of every opportunity to learn. In a city such as Montreal, the opportunities are nearly infinite. They are available through evening classes for those who wish to complete an elementary education; arts and trades courses and technical schools are available to those who want to develop their manual skills; there are university courses and lectures and study groups available to anyone wishing to increase their general education.

La Fontaine would surely reiterate here: *that the means are the least of our worries...*

***

We believe that no one would dispute that we have suffered greatly from the excessive obsession with the so-called liberal professions, even by those who have attained the highest levels in those professions, such as in medicine or law.

However, we wonder whether there has not developed, parallel to this obsession, a loathing of manual labour, not only because it entails physical effort, but due to the mere fact that it is *manual*, that it requires putting on overalls, etc. It would be a great mistake.

Basically, except for certain trades that are becoming mechanized, what kind of *manual* labour does not entail a very active and constant use of mental faculties? You only have to watch a carpenter at work to see that it is not only hands that are at work.

***

It is necessary to react against the biases and highlight, not only the dignity of farm work, but also of labour in the workshop. We Christians have special reasons for this, which need only be mentioned without any particular emphasis. These reasons are on top of all those we can find in our social and economic conditions. The greatest number possible of our young people in cities need to acquire solid technical skills and the number of unskilled workers must be reduced to a minimum.

Parents and all of you who exercise any influence around you, impress on your children, not only the utility, but also the dignity of the trades. We must take advantage of everything that technical schools, arts and trade schools have to offer.

Here, as elsewhere, we must remember that the surest way to stand out and prepare the right path is to know your work and know it well.

The Jews as a Model

If Only We Knew How to Imitate Them ... When Will
We Stop Letting Ourselves Be Treated as Inferior in Our
Own Country? — The Case of the Federal Department
of Agriculture — The Comment of a Former Minister:
"I Would Kick Him Out ..." — An Old Battle — A New Year's
Resolution: To Make ... and to Keep

Omer Héroux
Le Devoir, December 21, 1939

We would be making a mistake if we did not learn from the action just taken by the Jews of Canada.

One of the commentators on *CKAC* spoke about the Jews in Russia and their role in the Revolution. The Jews of Canada determined that the comment was unjust regarding their fellow Jews over there. There were immediate protests. The *Canadian Jewish Congress* intervened. Mr. Bercovitch entered the fray. The Jews won on all points.

Is there any French Canadian the least bit concerned with our collective interests who would not have said on the issue: When will we show a similar esprit de corps and energy? When will we, not regarding the French of Europe, but regarding the French here—the oldest Canadians—know how to assert ourselves firmly?

***

Not a day goes by that does not bring news of a protest or event that would make the Jews rise up as one, if they are implicated.

Our colleague Richer in the past few days recounted how French-speaking journalists are treated in Ottawa.

The other day we repeated the complaints regarding radio, made by *La Frontière* and our friends in Temiscamingue and Abitibi. *La Terre de chez nous* has brought us equally persuasive details on another aspect of the problem.

It involves the federal Department of Agriculture. It seems that quite a major internal reorganization was just carried out in the department. In that connection, the department published a list of its 558 civil servants. *La Terre de chez nous* was curious enough to take a close look at the document. It found that out of 551 positions, barely 50 — and not the most important ones — are occupied by French-speaking Canadians. (The list here is only of civil servants directly employed by the department).

In the departmental administration, a single assistant deputy minister; in the communication services, out of the 7 officials whose names are listed, not a single French Canadian; in the scientific services, 5 French Canadians out of 157; in the Experimental Farm services, 19 out of 158; in production services, 16 out of 108; in marketing services, 10 out 122. It goes without saying that all the heads of service are English.

The disproportion between what is and what normally should be is such that it leaves no room for any quibbling.

The injustice is flagrant. It can be neither questioned nor suitably explained. Even if in one case or another it can be claimed that the appointment of an Anglo-Canadian was inevitable, it can never be proved that a similar imbalance in numbers is justified.

***

Furthermore, for a great number of these English-language civil servants, their ignorance of French is a serious professional weakness and detrimental to the common good.

These civil servants are unable to provide direct service to the French-speaking population, services to which they have a right. This leads, first, to an injustice regarding taxpayers who pay their fair share of taxes and, second, to a risk of reduced production and sales, a reduction that is detrimental not only to the people directly affected, but the entire country.

The contempt for the spirit of the Constitution and the injustice toward a part of the population is compounded by damage to all of Canada.

***

Our long-time readers know that we are not criticizing a specific minister or even a minister's staff here.

This is a campaign we have been leading for forty years now. It has been necessary to take to task, one after another, officials everywhere. The struggle (we would like to recall the names of all those who took part) has not been pointless. We have made several gains. For example, we now have French on postage stamps and on currency, when in the past our dear Armand LaVergne drew insults because he dared to demand something so simple, yet so significant in scope, since it affirmed the bilingual nature of the country. In other words, there has also been progress.

But there is still much to be accomplished!

***

If we only simply knew how to act like the Jews ... or like the English!

On our pages, Mr. Albert Rioux, who, at the time, was the President of the *Union catholique des cultivateurs*, recounted how he had asked a former Minister of Agriculture, who was a farmer:

If a civil servant came to your farm (his farm was in the West) who did not speak your language, *what would you do? —I would kick him out*, was the Minister's calm answer.

We do not want to go that far. However, we must not allow injustices or privileges to take place without immediately raising an energetic and sustained protest.

It is especially necessary not to play into the hands of the unilingual civil servants by writing to them in English and using English forms ... When have we seen an Anglo-Canadian, in his exchanges with the federal services, use a language other than his own?

That is an example we should never fail to follow.

***

We are on the eve of the holidays and well-intentioned resolutions. Could we finally make a resolution not to let ourselves be treated in our own country as second-class citizens, able to pay all taxes, but unable to enjoy the public benefits that are never denied to our English-speaking compatriots...

This means, first of all, that each one of us must strive daily to reach this goal; it also means that we need to make all the forces at our disposal strive toward the same goal, perhaps by starting with our Members of Parliament.

If only we could make the resolution and also know how to keep it!

The Jews as a Model

*They Throw Themselves Wholeheartedly Into the Battle
for the "Yes Side" — The Supporters of the "No Side"
Should Demonstrate Equal Enthusiasm — In This Case
It Would Be Good to Imitate their Example*

Omer Héroux
Le Devoir, April 22,1942

O nce again, we are going to take the Jews as an example.
They have decided to participate in the plebiscite to the great-est extent possible. They are, as we know—or as we should know—superbly organized. Their Canadian Jewish Congress has branches across the country. Right from the beginning of the war, the leaders of the Jewish Congress examined the problems presented by this new crisis for their ethnic group. They established special commit-tees to examine and look at specific aspects of the crisis. One of the committees, if memory serves us right, had as its goal to ensure that Jews received their share of the war-time contracts. Judging by the $3,800,000 in contracts obtained in Québec City, over a relatively short period of time, by Mr. Maurice Pollack, the committee could not have been very disappointed. We are not criticizing the Jews on this issue; we simply regret that French Canadians have not had as much fore-sight and have not been as active.

In any case, the Canadian Jewish Congress intends to have Jews support the *yes* group in Monday's plebiscite in the most energetic and most powerful way possible.

***

The Jewish Congress is careful to declare that it is clearly above poli-tics; but it considers that this case has nothing to do with politics. It takes for granted that all Jews support the *yes* side and that the only question of importance is to mobilize the decided voters and ensure that all these *yes* supporters vote on Monday.

To succeed, the Congress will spare no effort. To be convinced of this, one need only read the article published yesterday in the *Star* under the double heading: *Jews Urged To Vote "Yes" — Committees Organized Across Country for Big Plebiscite Vote.*

The article recounts that two weeks ago, Jewish delegates from across the entire country met in Montreal and decided to establish a special committee that, *"at the end of this week will contact all Jewish homes from one end of the continent to the other."* In addition to this main committee responsible for the overall management of the Jewish effort, the *Star* relates that special committees, *"have now been organized in all parts of the country to make Canadian Jewish voters understand the necessity of voting on Monday and men's and women's speakers committees have been established to contact voters, while the coordinating agency* [this is the main committee] *has received the support of all the rabbis, all fraternal and communal organizations across the entire country."*

***

The *Star* published large excerpts of a Canadian Jewish Congress declaration that provides details about the goal and reasons for the campaign. Among other things, it states the following: *The plebiscite will be held on April 27. The* Canadian Jewish Congress *asks that all Canadian citizens of Jewish origin answer the plebiscite question in the affirmative.*

That is not all. The Canadian Jewish Congress concerns itself with the overall interests of Jews. Another organization, called the *Zionist Organisation of Canada,* chaired by Mr. A.J. Freiman, the important Ottawa merchant, is especially interested in the establishment of a Jewish national home in Palestine. Although this particular issue is outside Canada's borders, it has not prevented the Zionists from intervening in the plebiscite. We see in this morning's *Gazette* that Mr. Freiman has addressed a letter to thousands of his members in which he urges them to vote *yes,* to ask others to do the same and to spare no effort in achieving a huge win for the *yes side.*

It will not be the fault of the Jews if the *yes side* does not win.

***

Furthermore, it can be seen that the supporters of the *yes side,* since they are probably worried about the overall result, are now multiplying their efforts. They have even succeeded in bringing the

Lieutenant-Governor of Alberta into the battle, who, it seems, should have remained in his ivory tower.

The government yesterday denied paying for publicity in support of the *yes side* in newspapers. It continues, nevertheless, to monopolize *Radio-Canada* and broadcast fervent propaganda at our expense, and send by mail, still at our expense, literature also paid for by us. This is one of the most cynical ways of proceeding that we have seen in a long time.

There is only one effective answer to this: follow the example of the Jews and spare no effort in order that all supporters of the *no side* vote on Monday.

***

Everyone knows that a *yes side* victory will mean the elimination of the only moral barrier that could be raised against the government regarding conscription.

If this barrier is eliminated, those who abstain from voting will be as guilty as those who vote *yes*.

It should be stated and should not be forgotten that all those who support the *no side* need to demonstrate at least as much effort and action as the Jews.

The *Fédération des Œuvres de Charité* Must Exceed Its Goal

The $850,000 that the Federation Requests Will Not Be Sufficient to Meet the Needs of the Thirty-eight Services It Supports — What the Anglo-Protestant, Jewish and Anglo-Catholic Federations Receive — The Case of Some of the Services, Notably the "Maison Ignace-Bourget"

Émile Benoist
Le Devoir, February 25, 1946

S haring is a duty.

That is the slogan that the French-Canadian *Fédération des Œuvres de Charité* has given its fundraising campaign this year, its fourteenth. The slogan is aimed at those who possess a great deal, as well as those who possess less, to the rich as well people of modest means, for the purpose of supporting those who have nothing, who, young and old, need society's help.

The requirements of the needy are great; they are as immense as contemporary society's shortcomings.

The Fédération set a goal that may seem huge or enormous compared to the goals of previous campaigns: $850,000, close to a million dollars. The needs are as great; in fact, they are even much greater than one dares to state.

The information sheet that the Fédération and its staff have distributed and that the press also reprinted, is unequivocal:

THE AMOUNTS REQUIRED BY OUR 38 SERVICES ARE GREATER THAN THE GOAL. THE GOAL, THEREFORE, MUST BE EXCEEDED.

This comes as a second slogan of the campaign, one that it behooves us to take into account.

It is not $850,000 that the new campaign must raise, but a full million.

When we compare what other groups in Montreal donate to their own charitable federations, we can see that French-Canadian generosity is far from overwhelming.

These are the principal services that may be compared: assistance to families, health services and child protection, vacation camps and youth protection, care for the elderly, and consultation organizations. The English and Protestant Federation, which constitutes only 16% of the population, at the present time distributes $847,197; the Jewish Federation, with 6% of the population, distributes $214,850; the English-speaking Catholic Federation, with 8% of the population, distributes $168,277; while the French-Canadian Catholic Federation, with 70% of the population, distributes no more than $761,114.

The average per capita donation by the various groups is a statistical fact that is even more persuasive.

Anglo-Protestant average	$6.15
Jewish average	$6.22
Anglo-Catholic average	$2.90
Franco-Catholic average	$1.06

It is obvious that an average donation of one dollar and a few cents cannot provide the *Fédération canadienne-française* the same means for action as donations of $6.15 and $6.22 in the Protestant and Jewish federations.

In the case of the two Catholic federations, no doubt account should be taken of the fact that a significant number of our charities are entirely or partially entrusted to religious communities that do not receive the same remuneration required by lay workers.

Nevertheless, we must not think that the devotion and charitable spirit of members of religious orders will eliminate financial necessities.

A former president of the Protestant Federation, Mr. William Birks, who was invited to speak last year at the opening ceremony of the *Fédération canadienne-française*, noted that latter would need $4,000,000 to meet the needs of its services.

The organizers of this year's campaign are not exaggerating in the least when they state that the goal of $850,000 they have established must be exceeded. Even by greatly exceeding the goal, all the existing and obvious needs cannot be satisfied. Even if all the members of the *Fédération canadienne-française* were to double last year's donation this year, it would still be far from the amount indicated by Mr. Birks.

Six services dedicated to youth protection which, last year, helped 6,058 people, are listed in the budget for the very modest sum of $100,325; eight vacation camps that lodged 3,689 campers, will have to manage to do everything for everyone with an amount of $59,760. That is more than modest.

When we know that a service such as the *Assistance Maternelle*, which helps thousands of mothers and children in need, must survive with revenues of barely $35,000, with $26,000 coming from the Fédération alone, should we not ask how this is possible? When we stop and take the time to consider the needs of such a charitable service, should it not incite a wave of greater generosity?

The space of a simple article does not allow us to enumerate all the services that depend on the Federation, that count on it to survive and that should count on it—if it is given the financial means—to develop. However, please allow us to cite the case of another service, in which *Le Devoir* has an interest for special reasons, since it was under the auspices of the newspaper that the service was created and organized in the autumn of 1930, when unemployment was at its worst and poverty, in its many forms, reigned throughout Montreal; the *Maison Ignace-Bourget*, a day refuge for the homeless elderly and handicapped. This service, which started on rue de Montigny, where it was managed by the Frères de la Charité, receives its day residents mainly from among the night residents of the Meurling refuge. The Frères de Saint-Jean-de-Dieu added it to their Notre-Dame-de-la-Merci services located on rue Notre-Dame, right opposite our offices. Although the *Maison Ignace-Bourget* has become the responsibility of the *Fédération des Œuvres de Charité canadienne-française*, we still take the time regularly to follow its activities. Over the course of a year, this day refuge serves over fifty thousand meals and provides hundreds of homeless, elderly and handicapped a shelter from the cold and bad weather. It is a necessary service in a city like Montreal and an indispensable service, which must adapt to a budget of barely over $6,000. The cost of a meal at the *Maison Ignace-Bourget*, taking into account all expenses, and despite the increase in the price of food, right now is less than eleven cents. Is there really any possibility of doing any better in providing a service and being thrifty?

The case of the *Maison Ignace-Bourget* is not unique. All services depending on the Fédération find themselves with the same need to do a great deal with very little money.

This justifies volunteers in the present fundraising campaign to be more insistent than ever in soliciting donations. Everyone whom they will approach will understand this.

Public Health in Montreal
(1925–1927)

L e Devoir's manner of covering the issue of the Jewish presence in Montreal was not entirely negative. Since Louis Dupire was responsible specifically for Montreal issues on the editorial pages of the newspaper, over the years he uncovered and published very interesting data about the local Jewish community. These observations were clearly different from the hostile comments of his colleagues who, during the 1930s, focused on writing about the political situation in Central Europe and the possible Jewish immigration to Canada. Dupire was interested in municipal administration, urban development, and public transit, and in fields that were the responsibility of city hall. He became an editorialist in 1922, and wrote a great deal about hygiene in housing, welfare and public health in the metropolis, without ignoring education in science for the working classes and Catholic philanthropy. On the subject of Jews in Montreal, his editorials were enlightened in tone, quoted reliable statistics and maintained an objective perspective rarely found elsewhere in *Le Devoir*. Dupire did not approach his subjects from a rigid position based on doctrine or ideology but researched his subject as would a sociologist or statistician. Consequently, his observations on Jews were rarely biased or weighed down by speculation.

For example, Dupire found the Jewish community possessed a highly developed network of institutions and that specialized organizations existed to provide quality services to members. A notable example was the Hebrew Free Loan Association which, for reasons of religious ethics, provided Jews with interest-free loans. Similarly, there were several organizations in Montreal promoting education in science for Jewish children during the summer months, which kept them away from the dangers on the streets. This was due to the great value placed on Jewish philanthropy, which raised large sums that were subsequently used to serve the most destitute. During the 1920s and 1930s, Dupire also came to realize the city's Jewish immigrant population had already achieved a certain degree of social progress, and that they had clearly improved their level of health. In many aspects the Jews were more successful than their French Canadian counterparts, despite their poor economic situation, recent settlement in Montreal, and low standard of life. This was especially noticeable respecting infant mortality, life expectancy, and the prevalence of certain diseases, such as tuberculosis, which was widespread in industrial centres at the time. Dupire noted that in this regard there was an "unquestionable Jewish superiority" that could serve as a model for French Canadians, who, in Montreal, suffered from a series of recurring health problems that presented a serious risk to their future as a community.

To reach this conclusion, Dupire did not simply rely on impressions gleaned haphazardly in neighbourhoods. He turned to a remarkable resource, Health Services reports of the city of Montreal, which were published annually and where all medical statistics were categorized by community in detailed tables. In fact, the municipality had been operating clinics since 1876, where doctors and nurses responsible for the prevention of the most common diseases worked, and reported in detail on the results of the treatment they provided. In these statistical compilations, Jews were listed as a "nationality" and it was possible to compare this group with the French-Canadian and English-Canadian populations, long settled in the country. In all indicators relating to public health, Montreal's Jews, who were in no better circumstances regarding housing or income, were in a much better position than their Francophone counterparts. This was particularly true respecting the number of deaths of children under the age of five and the general rate of infant mortality, which Dupire described as "a terrible waste." And what was the reason for this notable superiority? According to Dupire, it was because Jewish women breastfed their children, they had a higher and more complete concept of young children's education, and they benefited from marital life better adapted to urban circumstances. This was in addition to the fact that they received support from very efficient community organizations. In short, Dupire noted that the Jews had organized themselves on the basis of strategies for culture and health that provided them with real long-term benefits, and that had already had an impact by the 1920s.

Why Our Children Are Dying

"Stop Killing Our Children," the Star *Tells Our Municipal Council — The Responsibility of the Municipal Executive — Why Does the Health Service Not Preach Breast-feeding Now, Since the Very Low Infant Mortality Rate among Jews Proves Its Effectiveness?*

Louis Dupire
Le Devoir, January 13, 1925

S everal times a year, the *Star* compliments the municipal executive for its economical administration.

Yesterday, the front-page article of the newspaper demonstrated what an economical administration may cost at times. We have taken the following excerpt from the article:

"Forty percent of the milk delivered to Montreal is clearly dangerous. The inspection is absolutely inadequate and, in certain respects, is a pure farce. For years, the health service has asked the municipal council to adopt more severe measures to prevent the sale of contaminated milk, but in vain. Until now, the municipal council has not even taken the trouble to have the recommendations of the Health Service published, with the result that the health department is stifled by the inaction of the constituted authority. For a civilized society, this is shameful. When there are only five urban inspectors and six rural inspectors to monitor the 145 dairies that are the source of milk, it is obviously impossible to ensure the quality."

An injustice raised by the *Star* should be noted. When there are compliments to be made on the economical administration, it addresses them to the executive; when it has criticisms to make on the negligence of the health services, it addresses them to the whole council.

It is the executive that has the power to appoint inspectors in sufficient numbers; it is also the executive that alone may receive Dr. Boucher's suggestions and submit them to the council. We believe, without the least bias against the executive, that it could, if it wished, in the space of a few days, resolve the situation, *stop killing the children*, according to the *Star's* forceful expression, and have a new by-law on milk adopted.

***

However, it would be a mistake to believe that the situation would be resolved by the adoption of the Health Service's suggestions regarding the inspection and the classification of milk. We want to be clear: we believe that it would be most useful to increase the number of inspectors and also to facilitate their work by imposing the pasteurization of milk, as Dr. Boucher has asked since 1920. However, it would be a mistake to expect a significant decrease in infant mortality immediately or even in a few years; first, because pasteurized milk is not ideal milk; second, even if unprocessed milk is produced and delivered according to all the required conditions of cleanliness (which, we readily admit is theoretically possible, but in practice impossible), it still would not resolve the problem.

Pasteurization, undoubtedly, would have a beneficial effect; however, pasteurization does not guarantee that milk will be good at the time of drinking. It requires many conditions, much precaution, a great deal of intelligence and devotion to replace what is natural! Pasteurization, according to someone who carries it out on a broad scale, becomes inevitable once a city reaches a certain size and it becomes necessary to get milk from farther and farther away in the countryside and deliver it farther and farther away to the city.

The situation is no different in Montreal. Breast-feeding is popular among Eastern European peoples, especially among Jews, and produces results that should embarrass us.

Take the latest statistics, those from 1923; children under five constituted 46.21% of all children's deaths for French Canadians, since they have many children and very poor housing.

In the English-speaking population, where generally housing is better, hygiene better practised, and the number of children significantly fewer than among French Canadians, which obviously facilitates supervision and care, children under five constituted only 24.54% of children's deaths.

Particular note should be taken that among Jews who live in housing that is often terribly crowded and in hygienic conditions not at all better than those of the French-Canadian population, the mortality was only 23.81%.

And the Jews have more children than the English!

This is the spectacular success of breast-feeding.

This is understandable, since it is known that breast-feeding provides a child with the milk he needs—although it seems to be forgotten that a child is not a calf—at the desired and always even temperature, without handling, without the need for cooling on ice (a luxury unavailable to the poor), without the need for protection against flies and dirty containers.

Most mothers, *on the condition that they are ready to sacrifice going to the movies for their child,* can achieve this. There is no denying that this is the opinion of specialists on the subject right now, whether in the information provided by our federal department of health, as well as by our provincial health service. There is no need to be a great expert in medicine to claim the effectiveness of breast-feeding after seeing such observations and to be astonished that more is not done in cities to preach and disseminate it!

***

In conclusion, we wish to leave the reader with some figures below. In July 1923, the worst month for cow's milk, and consequently for children, among French Canadians, children under five constituted 50.75% of all children's deaths. For the English, a great many of whom are out of the city in the summer, the number was only 30.12%; and among the Jews, 38.84%. It can be stated that more than half of all French-Canadian deaths are from children under the age of five. In absolute numbers, in 1923, deaths among children were,

For Jews: 70
For English Canadians: 490
For French Canadians: 3,325!

Infant Mortality among Jews and among Christians

Thoughts on an Article in the Événement —
Breast-feeding, Reasons for Its Neglect and the
Fatal Consequences — *50% of Deaths Are Avoidable* —
A Small Town Lost Every Year

Louis Dupire
Le Devoir, August 5,1927

I n its issue yesterday, *Événement* devoted an excellent article to infant mortality in Montreal.

It reminds us that the metropolis contains three cities in one; an English city, a French city and a cosmopolitan city. The first one is well housed in all respects; the second not as well, but still well; the third, which includes the Jewish population, is very badly housed.

However, our colleague notes that statistics show the Jewish population avoids the plague of infant mortality better than the French community and even than the English community. The following figures provide proof:

Infant mortality in 1926

	Deaths	Proportion per 1000 births
French Canadians	2,124	144.62
English Canadians	230	55.11
Jews	41	26.31
Other Nationalities	124	143.70
Unknown	12	
Total	2,531	119.49

"*L'Événement* states that, at first glance, it may seem that the statistics contradict the teaching of hygienists. After all, there is no doubt that the English and French live in more comfortable circumstances than the children of Israel. This impression is based on the ignorance of the general level of moral and physical hygiene practised by Jews in marriage. Without going into detail, we would say Jewish men treat their wives better than Christian men do and Jewish women fulfil their duties better to children born from this love. That is the secret of the hardiness of the Jewish race and of the Montreal Israelite population's more successful battle than ours against the plague of infant mortality. Furthermore, we reiterate, in unfavourable conditions."

There is much truth in what L'*Événement* says in, at times, a slightly archaic style. L'*Événement*, whose editor undoubtedly does not live in Montreal, is mistaken about the respective situation of the Jews and French Canadians—we shall not talk about the English—regarding the sanitary conditions in housing. There was a time when the Jews lived only in old neighbourhoods where there was little sunlight, thick dust and stale air. However, there has been a noticeable change. Once they had adapted, the Jewish population little by little yielded its place to newly arrived cosmopolitan peoples and moved up to places with better air and sunlight. It is obvious that they particularly seek out areas around parks and especially streets beside squares or public gardens, such as parc LaFontaine, carré Saint-Louis and rue Esplanade across from parc Jeanne-Mance.

Furthermore, in all neighbourhoods, the Jewish population is extremely active outdoors, which is a heritage of their Eastern European customs. One has only to go by parc Jeanne-Mance at any time of the day to see this. Entire families can be seen picnicking, along with the youngest of kids.

To think that the French-Canadian population in general resides in sanitary neighbourhoods is a mistake; it is an even greater mistake than to think that they live in sanitary housing. A sanitary neighbourhood may contain unsanitary houses. It is not sufficient to have wide streets, many parks and open spaces. Houses must have enough windows in order not to have dark or semi-dark rooms and back lanes must be maintained just as well as streets and not be long and narrow garbage dumps. Our present very deficient methods of construction create narrow apartments, with a multitude of dark or semi-dark rooms, which is combined with rubbish of all kinds accumulating in alleys thanks to our slow, irregular and archaic system of household waste collection, not to mention the smoke that continually darkens the Montreal sky.

This observation and the search for the reasons of the unquestionable Jewish superiority [in health] are not recent. In its article, l'*Événement* lists several of the reasons. First, Jews are attached to their children and take all measures necessary to care for them, which is right and proper. A prominent Israelite, who is active in the free-loan association that operates successfully among his people, told me recently that it was not uncommon for a family father to borrow an amount of a hundred dollars or more to have the best specialist treat a sick baby. A clinic was not good enough. He wanted to try everything. When do we French Canadians call a doctor? The doctor is called only a little ahead of the undertaker, if both are not called at the same time, in some working-class neighbourhoods.

However, the most plausible explanation for the very low infant mortality rate among Israelites, noted by Dr. Boucher many years ago in his reports, is the Jewish woman's acquiescence to her essential maternal duties, the first of which is breast-feeding. She knows that a child is, so to say, but a fragile being who needs the food nature has prepared to become viable. She knows that a child deprived of this milk is physically an orphan.

In her wish to care for her child in an intelligent way, she takes the means to do so and thus sets an example of maternal devotion and charity from which Christians could benefit.

A few years ago, Doctor Gauvreau, at a social conference, stated that: the rate of infant mortality is in inverse proportion to the rate of maternal breast-feeding. In a recently opened clinic, a doctor confirmed that observation: the proportion of children saved at the end of the year corresponded exactly to the increase in the proportion of mothers who breast-fed their children.

It could be said that this is a question of education. True, but much more of moral education than of hygienic education. Mothers feel subconsciously that it is their duty to provide their children with all the care that they require, including the most essential. When mothers evade this duty, it is often out of selfishness. We had a great urge to shout out this message following Mr. Desrosiers' article, which gained some attention: it is not enough to bring a child into the world, it is necessary also to care for it. To care for the child, the safest, the most demanding and the most efficient means must be taken, as is shown by all the statistics from all parts of the world.

However, this simple, economical and efficient method demands sacrifices. A mother carrying out this essential duty is tied to her young child like a slave to her work. For her, long outings, theatre, movies, long evenings or excursions are out of the question. It is veritable but mild slavery. It is the narrow but glorious path of sacrifice.

This is why sociologists are right in believing that it is inopportune to transform the teaching of theologians into a university chair teaching hygiene. On the other hand, the source of our high infant mortality rate has a moral reason that could be condemned more effectively by priests than by doctors or by nurses visiting homes. Mothers must care for the body and soul of their children. It is nearly inevitable that they will lose the physical life of their children by evading certain lifesaving obligations.

We are not moved by this terrible waste of young children that every year equals the loss of a small town, because the white coffins slide into the streets without noise or ceremony, while we are so easily moved by the death of seventy-eight children at once. Just think that among French Canadians in Montreal alone, in 1926, 2,124 children under the age of one died and breast-feeding could have saved 50% of them.

Persecution of Jews, Persecution of Catholics (1929–1933)

Despite the fragile peace between the major powers, the 1930s were a decade of exceptional inter-ethnic violence. Under the impact of a pronounced economic slowdown and the rise of authoritarian regimes, certain regions in the world were scenes of unrestrained political tension, prolonged civil wars, and the merciless persecutions of specifically targeted ethnic groups. *Le Devoir*, as it observed these ever-increasing abuses, noted on several occasions that religion played a not insignificant role in the injustices seen throughout the world. Two cases, particularly, captured the newspaper's attention at the beginning of the 1930s, the massacre of the Catholic faithful in Mexico and of Jews in Palestine. Similarly, a few years later, *Le Devoir* took a close interest in the Spanish republican regime and the German National Socialist regime, for very different reasons, when they adopted discriminatory laws against the institutions of the Catholic Church and the Jewish people respectively. It was difficult for *Le Devoir* to ignore such injustices, since they were reported throughout the international press and were the subject of numerous commentaries, including in the papal encyclicals of December 1925, June 1933, and March 1937. The situation became uniquely complicated when Hitler, despite the concordat signed with the Vatican in July 1933, targeted educational institutions and schools managed by Christian churches.

The allegiance and sympathy of *Le Devoir* was with the Catholic Church, and it confessed to being moved by the extent and the ferocity of the anti-clerical persecutions in Mexico, which, toward the end of the 1920s, claimed tens of thousands of victims among the peasantry. *Le Devoir* also reported on the executions of members of the clergy and the destruction of numerous religious communities during the Spanish Civil War. At the same time, it was difficult to remain silent with respect to the increasing difficulties of the Jewish people in

Palestine and in Germany. The following two editorials, the first written by Georges Pelletier in September 1929 and the second by Omer Héroux in June 1933, clearly demonstrate how differently *Le Devoir* reacted depending on the denomination and ethnic identity of the victims. The newspaper had no hesitation in comparing the suffering of Catholics and Jews, but always commented that the misfortune of the former remained little known and was not sufficiently condemned in public. This was a return to an approach whereby the newspaper put the violence directed against the Jews in Nazi Germany and the Middle East into the background on the pretext that this minority had "an extraordinary power" of mobilization and community solidarity throughout the world. This was a way of saying that Jews were quite capable of confronting adversity, taking into account their "power" of persuasion in the international press, while the Catholics were unable to overcome this challenge and attract widespread sympathy. Viewed from this comparative angle, *Le Devoir*'s writings by 1929 and 1933 demonstrated their indifference regarding the fate of Jews in Central Europe. This perception would pave the way, a few years later, to rejecting the acceptance of the victims of these traumatic events, regardless of circumstances.

Silence on Mexico, Protests for Palestine

Georges Pelletier
Le Devoir, September 6, 1929

Yesterday on the same page of the *Montreal Star*, there was a report on the demonstration by a Jewish group in Canada against the massacre of their kind in Palestine by Arabs and right beside it a dispatch on the most recent events in Mexico. This juxtaposition of Mexico and Palestine on the same page of a daily should immediately have turned many people's attention to a comparison of the silence surrounding the martyrdom of thousands of Catholic Mexicans in recent months and the extraordinary clamour made in the world about the violent deaths of a couple of hundred Jews in Palestine in the last little while.

Undoubtedly, we remember the execution of numerous Catholics in Mexico under the regime of Plutarco Calles, the immediate predecessor of the present President, Portes Gil, and even during the first months after the latter came to power. Francis McCullagh, in his last fascinating book containing documentation that has yet to be refuted, *Red Mexico*, compiled a table of the bloody persecution of Mexican priests and members of religious congregations and their flocks. He included official photographic proof of the massacre, of the mass deportations to prisons, which no one survived, and of people banished. He branded the Mexican regime with a red iron. A few American periodicals, before him, reported on how ferocious Calles was in his battle with the Church and Faith. In Europe, some publications such as the *London Express* and *La Croix* in Paris, provided details on the events that made us shudder and that nobody has denied. In summary, it is an established historical fact that up until the last few months thousands of Catholics paid for their attachment to their faith with their life or their freedom, near the United States and, it could be said, right before their eyes.

On this subject, have there been public demonstrations where the conduct of Calles and his lieutenants has been condemned? None at all. Very few voices have been raised to denounce the Mexican murderers and executioners. Even in countries where there is much talk of humanity, people who should have been better informed, have been heard to say: "We do not know if there is any basis to these stories of executions. The stories could well be false. And furthermore, it is an issue of internal politics." People turned away and closed their eyes and ears. The massacres continued, while in the United States, for example, and also in Europe, high finance and other powerful interests imposed silence nearly everywhere, and official or friendly censorship shut down the main sources of information and muzzled the cries and gasps of Mexican Catholics behind a wall of public ignorance. In our province, just as elsewhere, except for very small groups, no voices of authority were heard in protest against the brutality of Calles and his friends. This silence lasted until the Mexican political leaders, fearing that the truth would finally break out and cause major economic damage to their country and its affairs, consented in recent months to loosen the shackles.

Mexico, it is so far away ...

And Palestine? It is certainly farther away. Yet see how the events of the last two weeks quickly raised protests, condemnation and meetings everywhere, even before the British authorities could begin an inquiry to establish responsibility for the bloody riots in Jerusalem and elsewhere. There were demonstrations in the streets of London, Paris, New York, Berlin, Montreal, and just about everywhere; sharp criticism from people sympathetic to the English regime, right in London, for not having been able to ensure peace and order in Palestine; marches in front of British consulates in the United States. Here, just as in Europe, there were appeals to the British army, the British navy and British statesmen to protect Jews in Palestine from Arabs and prevent the latter, henceforth, from being an obstacle to Zionist demands, even the most extreme ones.

If practically no one here seemed to know anything about the massacre of thousands of Mexican Catholics, a great number of our public leaders suddenly learned, if they are to be believed, every detail of the Arab atrocities in Palestine. So it was that we learned more easily about the circumstances of the deaths of two hundred Jews in Palestine than the killing of thousands of Catholics in Mexico!

An objective observer will be neither astonished nor saddened by the difference in reaction to the massacre of people. He would condemn killings regardless of where they occurred.

It could be said that if Catholics knew how to react as do Jews, the Mexican massacres would quickly have stopped. Furthermore, if there had been among Montreal voters a group of naturalized Canadian Mexican Catholics, events would have taken place differently and many public leaders would have been heard protesting against the atrocities of Calles and his friends.

But there are no Catholic voters of Mexican origin ... whereas there are Jewish voters.

The Attention Paid to Spanish Catholics and to Jews

The Incredible Contrast — Acquiring Information

Omer Héroux
Le Devoir, June 29, 1933

E ach passing day accentuates an incredible contrast: against Hitler's anti-Semitic deeds, a movement of such power and intensity has been created and cleverly developed by the press that it leaves an impression of being nearly a world-wide event. Not a day goes by without a newspaper describing the situation as a revolt of the human conscience. In contrast, details about the Masonic persecution, pillaging and elimination of the basic rights of an entire class of citizens that brings a shame on Spanish politics, seems from a distance to have but feeble coverage.

Here at home, where some attention has been given to the anti-Hitler protests, what has been done regarding the Spanish persecutors? Compared to the Montreal demonstration, where prominent Catholics supported the Jewish protests, what significance is there to the few *resolutions* regarding Spain, adopted haphazardly?

It is a new and striking example of Jewish solidarity, of the extraordinary power that this solidarity bestows on this scattered people, also alas! a new and striking example of the absence of Catholic solidarity.

***

We admit that it has not always been easy to obtain all the necessary information on the events in Spain. This demonstrates the need to improve relations between Catholic newspapers and create the equivalent of an information bureau that is such a powerful instrument of publicity in the hands of the Jews.

In this regard, when the anti-clerical campaign began, we tried in vain to obtain copies of the protest of the Spanish section of the

Society of Jesus. We read quite a lengthy analysis in the *Irish Press* of Dublin, but we hesitate to translate a text from English that has already been adapted from Spanish to English. We were unable to find a direct French translation anywhere. (It goes without saying that if we were rich, many of these difficulties would be eliminated: there would means to maintain correspondents and competent translators in Europe. However, we are not rich).

Nevertheless (we cannot ignore the efforts made by the École Sociale Populaire to disseminate as much information as possible on the subject), we now possess a document on the issue that provides an objective and precise summary of the anti-Catholic campaign.

This invaluable document is the most recent encyclical of His Holiness, *Dilectissima Nobis*, printed in *Le Devoir* and a few other news-papers and broadcast on the radio by the École Sociale Populaire.

In a case such as this, all information eventually comes into the possession of the Vatican. The information is weighed, compared and written up by a notably competent authority who has a keen concern not to draft an exceptionally dazzling pamphlet, but to prepare a bet-ter future, for which the truth exposed in this way is only a means to put an end to a deplorable state of affairs, and for that authority, the clear condemnation of evil is no more than carrying out a supreme duty.

For any person of good faith, whether Catholic or not, the word of the Pope, in similar matters, should have supreme importance. No observer is more qualified, no one has less desire to hide the truth. On the contrary, the only concern of his future actions, even if the sensi-tivity of his conscience were to be ignored, must be to avoid, to the greatest extent possible, any exaggeration, since such exaggeration, by pointlessly angering the persecutors, would diminish his prestige among the victims.

***

Everyone who has taken the trouble to read the Encyclical already know the Pope's thoughts, especially about the new Spanish law on *"religious denominations and congregations."* His Holiness writes that "We cannot avoid raising our voice again to make known Our disapproval and Our criticism of this law that is a new and very serious injustice, not only against the Church and religion, but also against the principles and institutions of civil liberty on which the new Spanish regime claims to be established." The entire Encyclical, through a tight and precise analysis, justifies the judgement that finally forces the Pope, father of all the faithful and supreme guardian of their sacred rights, to make this anguished cry:

> AFTER THE ADOPTION OF THESE DICTATES, VIRULENTLY CONTRARY AND HOSTILE TO THE RIGHTS AND FREEDOMS OF THE CHURCH, RIGHTS THAT WE MUST MAINTAIN INTACT, WE TRULY THINK WE WOULD BE REMISS IN OUR APOSTOLIC RESPONSIBILITY NOT TO CONDEMN THIS LAW THAT IS SO PROFOUNDLY OPPOSED TO THE DIVINE CONSTITUTION OF THE CHURCH.
>
> THAT IS WHY WE SOLEMNLY AND WITH ALL OUR MIGHT DENOUNCE AND CONDEMN THIS LAW THAT CAN HAVE NO EFFECT OVER THE INALIENABLE RIGHTS OF THE CATHOLIC CHURCH.

***

This judgement, this solemn reprobation, the recitation and the analyses explaining and justifying them, must be published as widely as possible.

This is the only way that the public can really come to know what has happened and is still happening in Spain and understand anything from the dispatches.

It is only this knowledge that will create and maintain in all hearts the fervent sympathy, which we must have, for the Pope and the persecuted.

… Therefore, after having publicized the Encyclical by all means at our disposal, we are reprinting it as a brochure at a price (5 cents a copy, 50 cents for a dozen, including postage; $3.50 for a hundred, $15 for five hundred, $25 for a thousand, plus postage) that should certainly facilitate its distribution. — Actually, everyone who is familiar with these things knows full well that these prices are only possible on the condition that material already prepared by the newspaper is used, as we do, and we shall cover our expenses only if we succeed in selling a large enough quantity of brochures.

Therefore, we are asking our friends who wish to participate in this publicity campaign and wish to have a text on hand to give to

ion of Catholics (1929–1933)   313

their friends that is easy to consult and easier to keep than a newspaper article, to send us their orders as soon as possible.

The earlier the better, since that could save us unnecessary costs
of reprinting.

Furthermore, the earlier the brochure reaches a vast public, the
better it will be.

Since the truth it contains can never be distributed too widely or
too soon ...

Palestine under the British Mandate (1929–1930)

Until serious riots broke out during the summer of 1929 in Jerusalem, Hebron, and Safed, *Le Devoir* paid hardly any attention to the conflict between the Jews and Arabs in Palestine. That region of the world, readers were told, was coveted by two nationalisms confronting each other under the mandate the League of Nations granted to Great Britain in 1922. The subject was of interest to *Le Devoir* at two levels: first, because Palestine was, like Canada, part of the British Empire and the events taking place there threatened the Empire's supremacy in the world; second, because it was the location of the holy sites that were the foundation of Christianity. The open conflict between Jewish and Arab residents, Héroux argued, had significant repercussions, extending as far as India, where there was a large Muslim population. The conflict also affected Great Britain's management of the Suez Canal, a waterway of prime importance for England's trade with the Indian subcontinent. *Le Devoir* published six editorials about this, all written by Omer Héroux in 1929 and 1930, making him the principal writer at the newspaper on the situation in Palestine. Essentially, Héroux wrote how the British Balfour Declaration promised in 1917 to create a national Jewish homeland in the Middle East, and that people of Arab origin were violently opposed. Tensions in August 1929 forced the British to review their policy and Lord Passfield tabled a white paper in October 1930 that proposed to limit Jewish immigration to Palestine and to give priority to Arab grievances. This official document was vehemently denounced by the world-wide Zionist movement and led to the resignation of Chaim Weizmann, the Director of the Jewish Agency.

Since there was no risk that the events in Palestine would have any direct repercussions in Canada, Héroux examined the subject with a certain detachment and looked at it from all possible points of view. It was probably the only theme related to Jewish life in *Le Devoir* of the 1930s and 1940s that did not evoke anti-Semitice emotions or racist comments. Unlike the situation in Central Europe that risked unleashing a large Jewish immigration to North America, which the newspaper wanted to prevent, the difficulties in the Middle East were based on British resistance to an overly forceful assertion of Zionism in that region of the Mediterranean. In the view of *Le Devoir*, there was little reason to oppose German or East European refugees going to Palestine rather than Canada if that was what they wished to do. The newspaper considered it preferable in such circumstances to develop a Jewish national homeland in the Middle East that eventually could receive the Jews who were victims of discrimination in Europe. Furthermore, Héroux did have some sympathy for Jewish national aspirations in Palestine and did not neglect to note efforts made by Jewish people throughout the world to support those aspirations. It was in this regard that Héroux's prejudices about Jewish nationalism emerged, which he often described as a movement possessing very extensive power and under "the influence of important Jewish bankers." During his entire career, the editorialist remained convinced that all-powerful "Judeo-American financial interests," acting in the name of Zionist interests and "possessing a significant part of the world's wealth" really and truly existed.

On Top of a Powder Keg

*The Latest News from Palestine — The Background
to the Conflict — Everyone Blames the Arbitrator —
Why England Is There and Does not Want to Leave —
Christians Are Outside the Conflict*

Omer Héroux
Le Devoir, August 28, 1929

The dispatches from this morning—when reading them, we must not forget that they have passed through a censor—lead us to believe that in Palestine the British forces will soon control the situation. It must be hoped for the cause of world peace that this is true and that the conflagration will remain inside the borders of that country.

However, this tragic venture is a reminder to everyone that Palestine really is a powder keg and that the smallest spark may light a conflagration, which may quickly threaten peace in a large part of the world.

The English newspapers from yesterday and this morning say the same thing we have said on these pages and what is obvious to all. The conflict bloodying the country may have its direct roots in the feud underway between Jews and Muslim Arabs over the Wailing Wall, but it has taken such a serious turn only because there was a background of ancient animosity, aggravated, it must be added, by the events of recent years.

The inquiry that has been called for may well determine the responsibility of one person or another, but it will leave in place the tragic basis leading to the feud, which remains such a great threat for the future.

***

There must be an attempt to get to the bottom of things. Muslim Arabs, if the stories of travellers are to be believed, hate and despise the Jews. If Palestine is the homeland of the Jewish people and the sacred land of their forefathers, it has in reality become an Arab country. The 1922 census stated (we are citing figures from the New York *Sun*) that Palestine had a total population of 757,182, of whom 580,890 were Muslim and only 83,794 Jewish. The disproportion was such that it had the effect of preventing conflicts between the communities — even more so since people had been accustomed to the situation for a long time.

However, in recent years, a new aspect was introduced. Zionism intended to reconstitute a Jewish national home in Palestine and directed to the country a large number of immigrants, supported by their co-religionists with their gold and their sympathy. England gave its support to this idea and, after having occupied the country militarily following the events of the last war, it accepted the mandate for supervision and administration accorded by the League of Nations. In reality, the country is governed by an English official.

It can immediately be seen how, under this regime, new factors would be added to the long-existing aspects of the feud. Jews feel very much at home in Palestine; their national sentiment has been whipped up by recent events and they consider it quite logical that England, after the declarations it made to them, must help them achieve their dream. In five years they have doubled their population in Palestine; in 1927, they already numbered 147,687 (compared to 648,566 Muslims) out of an approximate total of 882,000. The Arabs, on the other hand, see in this rapid increase of the Jewish population a threat to their own influence and a danger that they might be expelled from a country which they consider theirs.

In short, the two races both believe that they have a right to the same country and both seem quite in agreement in this case to blame the arbitrator, in other words the mandatory power that they accuse of not being supportive enough of them. In newspapers you can read, side by side, diametrically opposed protests by Zionists abroad and by a group of Muslims from India.

***

England did not go and meddle in this hornet's nest for its own enjoyment or to take responsibility for troubles that its statesmen should have foreseen.

An explanation was given for England's declarations of support to a Jewish national home: the influence of important Jewish bankers, notably from the United States, who supposedly made that a condition of their financial support during the war. Regarding its desire to occupy the country in some form or another, there is an explanation that can be seen on a map. England did not want to let another power, that might become hostile, rule a territory that has such direct control over the route to India.

England's presence in Palestine is one of the consequences of its imperial policy; but the difficulties that it faces also risk taking on imperial proportions.

Behind the Arab Muslims, we must not forget, there are Muslims from the rest of the Empire and neighbouring countries; behind the Jews of Palestine, there is the Jewish influence in the entire world, admirably organized and always ready to be mobilized. Furthermore, a certain number of massacred Jews were American citizens, which has already led the American government to approach the government in London. The latter has stated that it will watch over foreigners with the same care as its own citizens.

***

Regardless of what happens in the immediate future, the distant future will remain full of potential feuds. There seems to be a thought in some quarters that England should ask the League of Nations to confer the Palestinian mandate to another country; but other than the fact that, after what has just happened, the gift perhaps would not tempt many friends, British prestige is now at stake. To leave after the present drama, would be, in the opinion of most of the English, an implicit admission of weakness that would have most disastrous repercussions in the entire Middle and Far East.

... To conclude these hastily written notes, it should be added that the official statistics clearly establish that the situation is a feud restricted to Muslims and Jews.

Christians constitute only a small portion of the total dead and injured.

From Bombay to Jerusalem

England Caught between Jews and Muslims

Omer Héroux
Le Devoir, May 22, 1930

A dispatch this morning states: *Bombay, May 22. — The Council of the Muslim Federation of India today adopted a resolution declaring that if the justified demands of the Palestinian Arabs are not received favourably, the feeling among the Muslims of India will become grimmer and it will be more difficult to control the Muslim masses.*

This is one of the most important and most significant telegraphs that we have received in a long time and one that most accurately puts its finger on the extreme complexity of the problems that English politicians must confront.

No one dares question the seriousness of the situation in India. It has seen relatively few bloody clashes. Taking into account the vast size of the country, differences in characteristics, the aggressiveness of some of the groups and feelings that inevitably boil over, the small number of clashes even seems astonishing. However, it seems that the civil disobedience movement is constantly spreading and developing. It now embraces prominent politicians. Convictions and imprisonment have had no effect and the time is coming when no one will know what to do with the prisoners. Furthermore, the boycott of English products is being pursued methodically, which may be the most powerful weapon possessed by the Indians. It should be quite clear that this boycott does not affect only the capitalists of England; it also has a direct impact on the workers and seriously risks worsening unemployment, which is at the root of the domestic crisis.

Against this seemingly powerful movement, England is managing with its superb sense of governing and its long experience with foreign populations. One of England's foremost advantages is obviously the diversity of races and religious sects in India. England claims that if its moderating influence were to disappear, India would fall into anarchy and that the races and sects would clash in bloody skirmishes.

It is trying to establish links with the minorities, who see England as a protective figure against the potential tyranny of the Hindu population. (*Indian* is used to designate the entire population of the country; it is a political and geographical term; *Hindu* describes the majority of the population, other than Muslims, etc.) At the present time, it is obvious the British government and the leaders of the Gandhi movement are relentlessly courting the Muslims. They number about sixty million; the fervent attempts to seek their support are understandable.

Up to now—at least judging by the dispatches—the British side seems to have the upper hand. Few Muslims have rallied publicly to the nationalist movement. Even some who joined Gandhi in one of the previous major campaigns have now kept their distance.

However, England has other problems than India or rather, a concern to maintain its domination in India has forced it to face new problems. In order to ensure control of the Suez Canal and its connection to India, England is in Egypt and intends to remain there, at least in some form. It is with the same objective that it had the Palestinian mandate granted to it and that it is in Jerusalem.

So many problems and so many diverse situations generate new difficulties every day. Our dispatch from Bombay trains a harsh light on one these problems.

In Egypt, as in Palestine, the majority of the population is of the Muslim faith. The treatment of these Muslims naturally has quite a noticeable impact on the sentiments of the sixty million Muslims of India. In Palestine, the situation is complicated and aggravated particularly by the fact Jews and Muslims face each other in a state of latent hostility, even when the hostility is not bloody as in recent months. Probably to ensure the support of Israelite bankers of North America during the War, the English, through Mr. Balfour, promised the establishment of a *national home for the Jewish people* in Palestine; a broad formula lending itself to divergent hopes and realities.

Nevertheless, the Arabs and the Jews are there, in what could be called a fenced field, with the English as arbitrators and supervisors. The English, in addition to the difficulties that inevitably arise in similar situations, have to take into account two facts: first, that the approximately one hundred thousand Jews in Palestine are supported abroad by millions of magnificently organized people, displaying a tremendous spirit of solidarity throughout the world and possessing a huge amount of wealth and, through the press, world-wide power; and second, that the six or seven hundred thousand Arabs in Palestine are of the same faith as the sixty million Muslims of India (without counting other Muslims), whose support seems essential to maintaining British power.

English politicians are used to these difficult situations; they have untangled many during their long history; however, this in no way prevents these situations from existing and demanding new efforts, which perhaps eventually will become insufficient.

To grasp the extent and importance of these situations, it is necessary to place the dispatch from Bombay and the dispatches from Jerusalem and London side-by-side. While the Muslims of India formally warn the British government that if it does not satisfy the justified demands of the Arabs of Palestine, it will inevitably suffer the consequences in India, at the same time the Jews of Palestine—certainly supported by their co-religionists throughout the world—have declared a general strike to protest against the apparent conduct of the English towards the Jews in Palestine.

The issue is one of immigration, which, understandably, is extremely important for the Jews, just as it is for the Arabs. Right now, the Jews in Palestine are clearly outnumbered; according to even the most favourable figures, the ratio is one to four or five. If they do not receive support through immigration from abroad, they will remain a minority and perhaps become an even smaller one, and then what will become of the Zionist dream? On the other hand, the very reasons for the Jews desiring easy recruitment from abroad, incite the Arabs to oppose it. There is also a basic question: is Palestine, with its present indigenous population, capable of receiving a significant amount of immigration?

Even if the problem (the latest dispatches from London indicate that it is still unresolved) could be isolated and examined separately, it would apparently be complicated enough; but it cannot be isolated. The problem is linked to all the factors we have just listed: Jewish power, external Muslim power and the impact of one and the other, not only in India and in Egypt, but on the whole world. The long-ago words of Shakespeare should be recalled: *Uneasy lies the head that wears the crown* ... The task of governing is a harsh one and the imperial sceptre may be very heavy in the hands holding it.

This is the origin of perhaps the seemingly simplistic observation that young nations with a future to build, as a general rule, are wise to stay as far away as possible from these great struggles.

If the observation seems irrelevant, it would be well simply to remember that we already went to Africa to fight for a cause that surely had no more relevance to us than the Indian feud…

The Palestine Question

*The Issue Is Back on the Agenda — The Zionists Are
Protesting against the Attitude of the British Government
— Some of the Problems in the Situation*

Omer Héroux
Le Devoir, October 21, 1930

We had nearly lost sight of—we are referring to the ordinary reader—the Palestine question. The dispatches from this morning have brought it back to the forefront of the news. Since the question has come up right in the midst of the Imperial Conference and on the eve of the Anglo-Indian Conference, the coincidence allows us to see at a glance some of the complexities of British politics.

This issue regarding Palestine is being raised in a broad framework that is already familiar. England is acting in Palestine, on behalf of the League of Nations, as a mandatory power—which naturally means that, to some extent, it is submitted to the supervision of the Geneva association. It goes without saying that England did not seek or accept the mandate because of any enchantment with the League of Nations. Quite simply, given its interests in the world and particularly in India, England considers it necessary to watch very closely over the Suez Canal, the major route to the East.

The English statesmen, when they took responsibility for the task, were not at all unaware that they were stepping into a hornet's nest. They were dealing with a divided population where the Arabs are many times greater in number than the Jews. The bloody events of recent months have shown the sentiments driving these people. Several years ago, a man who knows the country admirably well recounted in private the problems in the situation. — Are the Arabs armed? he was asked by one of his listeners. — Oh no! he answered. If that were the case, the issue would be resolved in a day: there would be no more Jews.

This violent animosity, which is probably rooted in age-old antipathy, seems to have been inflamed by the consequences of the

Zionist movement. In the past, the Jewish minority seemed to have resigned itself to its fate and wanted nothing more than to be forgotten. Then the Zionists arrived with great hopes and enormous resources. They were convinced that they were coming home and consequently wanted to settle there. The invasion of these new elements seriously unsettled the life of the country. It appears to have over-heated racial feelings, as well as creating major economic problems. (The fact that the British authorities have proposed the temporary suspension of Jewish immigration is an indication of the seriousness of the economic problems). England was dragged into the feud simply because of its presence and its role in the country and also because of the notorious Balfour declaration. That declaration is the focus of most of the fighting. The Jews see in it a justification of their fervent actions and their greatest hopes, while the Arabs lament that its scope is being exaggerated or are revolting against the interpretation given to it by the Jews.

The conflict quickly spilled beyond Palestine's borders. It can be presumed that the famous declaration, which promised the establishment of a national home for the Jewish people in Palestine, was forced on the English in the interest of gaining the support of Jewish high finance, especially Judeo-American high finance, during the war. On the other hand, although the Arabs do not have at their disposal the support in Europe and in North America that is possessed by the Zionists, they have powerful allies in India who occupy a strategic position and whose power has been highlighted by recent events. The sixty or seventy million Muslims in India constitute a force that England at present has every interest to take into account.

The broad outlines of the problems of the situation can be summarized as follows: significant local problems, enormous external problems due to the support possessed abroad by the Arabs and the Jews. We can imagine the degree of interest England must have had to remain in Palestine and, therefore, to have accepted in advance the troubles and difficulties in such a mishmash of contradictory interests and feelings.

Particularly interesting in this morning's dispatches is the announcement that the mandatary authority, following a long inquiry, has taken a position that appears to have huge consequences. While still supporting Jewish immigration, the authority considers that in the present circumstances, it is advisable to reduce the flow of immigration. On behalf of the authority, the minister responsible explains that this appears to be in the interest, not only of Palestine in general, but of Jews in particular. According to the minister: *"As long as wide-spread suspicion exists, and it does exist, amongst the Arab population, that the economic depression, under which they undoubtedly suffer at present, is largely due to excessive Jewish immigration, and so long as some grounds exist upon which this suspicion may be plausibly represented to be well founded, there can be little hope of any improvement in the mutual relations of the two races. But it is upon such improvement that the future peace and prosperity of Palestine must largely depend."*

The first consequence of this decision by the British government (there, naturally, is a question of several other reasons) was the resignation in protest by Dr. Chaim Weizmann, President of the World Zionist Organization and the Jewish Agency for Palestine.

This will probably mean that there will be plans to mobilize all the forces at the disposal of the world's Zionists against the British government regarding its present position.

Thus, events are underway that must be given close attention.

A National Home for the Jewish People in Palestine (1937–1939)

New editorials on Palestine, again written by Omer Héroux, appeared in *Le Devoir* at the end of the 1930s. By this time the context had changed, since the Arab revolt had taken the shape of a political movement of great magnitude that threatened British dominance in Palestine. The newspaper reacted to the news and noted that by July 1937 the conflict had become an open confrontation which risked dragging the entire Commonwealth, even Canada, into it if care was not taken. It had become obvious that Great Britain had failed to convince the Jews and the Arabs to live side by side in the Middle East. The government in London, consequently, had to deal with two competing nationalisms in Palestine where it had fanned the flames with rash promises. The situation was also aggravated by the fact that in Central Europe Hitler's regime was pursuing an intensely aggressive campaign against Jewish communities, which drove many German Jews and subsequently Austrian Jews to seek refuge elsewhere in desperation. It appeared increasingly clear after 1938 that the British were resolved not to allow Jewish immigration to Palestine and risk worsening an untenable situation for the mandatory power. The political agitation in the region, to a great extent, was caused by the arrival of a constant flow of European refugees that increased the Jewish population in the Middle East and threatened to relegate the Arab peoples to minority status. Several attempts at mediation by London, including a major Judeo-Arab conference held in London in 1939, failed to produce results. The situation became so untenable that in May, 1939, the British government decided to publish a white paper advocating that the sale of farmland to Zionists be limited, significantly reduced Jewish immigration, and promised the creation of a unitary Arab state in ten years. It took the start of the Second World War for these tensions in the Middle East to be calmed.

Héroux did not express any particular sympathy for the British, who exercised an increasingly repressive control over a Palestine in turmoil. He was quick to denounce London's imperialism in Canada and elsewhere and observed that the Empire in the Middle East, as in India, was showing cracks and was at risk of breaking apart. In his mind, there was no doubt this augured profound changes for Canada, despite the British presence in the country already being more symbolic than real. Héroux thought sooner or later this would have an impact on the cause of Canada's Francophones to have their rights as a national minority in Canada recognized. For Héroux, the Middle East and India were like a barometer of the broad evolution of the Empire and he took an interest in them because the people in those situations were fighting for their independence and their dignity. He did not, however, take the side of one group or the other in Palestine, despite having a much better knowledge of Zionist aspirations from having heard about them in Montreal in the 1930s. This neutral stance did not prevent the editorialist from believing that the Jews had the right, like other people, to a national State where they would be a majority. Héroux even admitted having "all appropriate sympathy" for them. However, there was a complex ambiguity in these thoughts, which saw Jewish nationalism in the Middle East as having in some ways a power of attraction for Jews throughout the world, as was the wish of all the Zionists of the world. Héroux suggested this would at least have the benefit of asking the German Jews to head to Palestine rather than coming to Canada's gates. At the same time, this could serve to discourage Canadian Jews from claiming rights in the country that should be reserved only for Christians.

Editorial N° 57

Jews, Arabs and the English

England's New Proposals Regarding Palestine — A Broad Look at a Very Complex Situation — Canada, as a Member of the League of Nations, Will Have to State Its Opinion on the Matter

Omer Héroux
Le Devoir, July 8, 1937

O nce again, the Jewish question is at the forefront of world news. It will remain at the forefront for quite a long time, since the solution suggested by the English must receive the approval of the League of Nations.

First, this means that the English proposals will be discussed in all the countries—INCLUDING CANADA—that are members of the League and that will be called upon to judge them in Geneva.

This also means that the proposals will be discussed in the United States. Although not a member of the League of Nations, the United States, under an agreement of 1924, was recognized to have, in Palestine, equal economic rights with the nationals of governments that are members of the League, including respect for the real estate it possesses in the country and the right to maintain religious, charitable and philanthropic institutions.

The agreement respecting the Americans decrees that no change in the English mandate may affect these rights without the consent of the United States.

This is the reason why our neighbours, as Americans and generally, need to ensure that the proposed regime in no way restricts them, which raises the possibility perhaps of some Judeo-Americans opposing the changes to the mandate, by claiming American interests that cover their specific Jewish interests such as teaching institutions, etc.

***

All of this is an extraordinary matter with far-reaching repercussions.

Our readers are too intelligent to think in the least that it was for love of Arabs or Jews that the English had the League of Nations grant them the mandate for Palestine and that they established themselves throughout the country, despite all the problems they could foresee.

Look at a map: you will see that Palestine controls the route to India. That is why the English wanted to be the *de facto* masters of the place.

And that is why, despite all the changes that they may suggest, the English will endeavour to remain the true masters of the country, either by conserving a mandate over a part of Palestine, or acting in effect as a protectorate over the supposedly independent nations that they will create in the country or through a joint temporary occupation of a large port in the future Jewish State.

This desire to dominate is necessitated by their broad policy. They have taken possession of so many territories in all corners of the earth that they feel themselves forced to let nothing escape them and to hang on just about everywhere.

***

It was the severity of the world war that tossed the English into the imbroglio from which they are now endeavouring to escape.

When the fate of armies was teetering on the brink, the English (and probably their allies) told themselves that it was necessary to bring all possible forces into play.

In Palestine, the Arabs were needed against the Turks. In the rest of the world, the enormous financial and political power of the Jews was useful. Promises were lavished on the Arabs and the Jews.

The notorious Balfour declaration was drawn up for Palestine, offering a national home for Jewish people in Palestine, while guaranteeing Arabs respect for of their rights. The two groups, separated by significant interests, divided by age-old hatred and agitated by a violent surge of nationalism, naturally did not agree in any way on the scope of the notorious text. (A revealing detail: in response to someone among us who a few years ago asked one of the men who knew Palestine best; *But are the Arabs armed?* The man replied: Oh! *Sir, if the Arabs had weapons, there would be no more Jews in Palestine, since in the space of forty-eight hours the Jews would be eliminated!*) There have been numerous and bloody clashes, with the probable consequence that everyone must eventually have been upset with England. Everyone thought that England favoured one side or the other. The situation is additionally troublesome for London because the Arabs and the Jews have far-off allies: the Arabs among Muslims in neighbouring countries and India; the Jews among their co-religionists and kin throughout the world.

***

It was with a view to try and get out of this difficult situation and still maintain its means of controlling the route to India that England proposed to the League of Nations a radical change to the conditions of its mandate.

Palestine would be divided into three parts: England would keep Jerusalem and Bethlehem under a direct mandate, the Jews and the Arabs would each have their defined territory where they would exercise independent authority. It goes without saying that England would expressly give itself the right to occupy temporarily the major port of Haifa in the Jewish territory and by this tactic maintain the hope of exercising over these three small nations a significant, or more precisely major, direct influence.

It is easy to understand that the solution satisfies neither of the two groups, each of them aspiring to absolute control. England, in fact, believes it must keep a powerful force in the country to maintain order, which speaks volumes about the problems it foresees there.

Nevertheless, it may be presumed that the government in London must have played its hand in such a way as to ensure that the League of Nations will ratify its plans.

***

What remains to be seen is how long this arrangement will last.

On the one hand, the English are used to solving their problems from day to day and know how to deal with the future; on the other hand, they have come to the conclusion that the present system cannot last and that they were mistaken in attempting to have the Arabs and the Jews live together.

They will try once more and look for another solution if the undertaking shows that their new arrangement is not working.

***

The expectation of the creation of an independent Jewish State, with all the features of sovereignty, will revive a suggestion recently made in France and that Mr. Pelletier recounted a few weeks ago; granting Jewish political nationality to all Jews in the world and with Jews living in non-Jewish countries being considered as foreigners enjoying the highly courteous treatment normally given to foreigners.

It is likely that this is one of the questions that will soon be discussed in relation to the latest English proposal.

… With today's oppressive heat that discourages speculating on issues abroad, there is a slight inclination to read only half-heartedly all these dispatches from the Middle East. However, we must not forget that the plans underway in Palestine today may have great and distant consequences; we, especially, must not forget that Canada, in Geneva, will have to state its opinion on the English proposals.

We would not be surprised to see, in the meantime, the Jews in Canada become organized to influence the conduct of our government, since, if there are people who for centuries have made it a habit to look after their interests and do it thoroughly, it is certainly the Jews.

Furthermore, it must be recognized that they have every reason in the world to do so; their situation in many countries at the present time is especially tragic.

The Protestant Pastors of Lachine and Mr. Neville Chamberlain

We See that These Gentlemen Have Delivered a Stern Lesson to the Prime Minister of England — However, Since They Implicate the Commonwealth with Respect to the Matters in Palestine, It Would Be Interesting to Know What They Expect of Us — In the United States: the Borah-Wise Incident — A Significant Response

Omer Héroux
Le Devoir, October 27, 1938

The message from the Protestant pastors in Lachine to Mr. Neville Chamberlain, printed in this morning's *Gazette*, should be framed. It is a valuable document leading to extensive reflection.

It concerns matters in Palestine

Everyone knows, in general, what is happening there.

***

During the Great War, the Allies experienced more than just a single severe test. They sought to enlist powerful support everywhere.

Two forces whose collaboration was important were available and both were interested in Palestine.

On the one side, there was Jewish high finance in North America, possessing not only extraordinary financial resources, but considerable political influence.

On the other, there were Muslim Arabs in the region who could inflict very heavy damage on one of the enemy powers, the former Turkish Empire.

The *Daily Herald*, a Labour newspaper in London, in an article that yesterday's *Star* reprinted, stated quite clearly that promises were made to the Arabs and the Jews which are impossible to keep since they contradict each other.

***

Sooner or later, such machinations end in deplorable consequences.

The consequences for England are even more bitter, since it was granted the mandate for Palestine by the League of Nations in order to protect its broad interests in the Middle East.

England thus ensured its strategic position over the route to India; however, it put itself right into the middle of an awful wasp's nest, which did not take long to be perceived.

***

For obvious reasons, the Arabs and the Jews are strongly attached to Palestine. Jews say: it is our homeland. Arabs counter with: we have been here for centuries and the country has become ours.

Until the creation of *Zionism*, based on the movement that intends to re-establish a national home for Jewish people in Palestine, things remained as they were. The Jews constituted a relatively unimportant minority in the country. Their numbers hardly grew.

The Israelite immigration that followed what is called the Balfour Declaration profoundly changed the situation. We shall not try to recount here everything that has happened since the declaration or take sides with the adversaries. The only important thing to note for the moment is that the situation between the Jews and the Arabs has become very serious, that there has been and still is bloodshed and that England, in that part of the world, has on its hands a very major and troublesome matter.

It is a major matter because of its immediate consequences: to re-establish peace in the country, England has already mobilized a powerful army, and knows perfectly well that the re-establishment of physical peace will not eliminate the essential problem, the one resulting from the co-existence on Palestinian soil of these two enemy groups. Therefore, it is a major matter and takes on even more impor- tance from its possible repercussions.

The reason is that behind the Jews of Palestine, there are, as is now being noticed, all the Jews of the world; and behind the Arabs of the country, there are the feelings and thoughts and perhaps the future actions, not only of the Arabs of neighbouring regions, but of millions and millions of Muslims in India, among other places, whose support is extremely important to the English.

**

Faced with this terrible situation, people like us take a very simple position: they in no way wish Canada to be dragged into the bloody drama playing out there, nor do they believe that they have the right to impose advice or blame on the government in London.

The Protestant pastors of Lachine, all of them Presbyterian or United Church, do not consider themselves restricted by similar discretion. According to the *Gazette*, the pastors sent a telegraph to Mr. Chamberlain to protest against any plan to abandon the policy of a national home for Jewish people and demand that the United Kingdom maintain its mandate to assist Jews by all means to establish their national home. They assert that the Balfour Declaration "was accepted by the government of His Majesty as a sacred trust on behalf of the Christian world." Speaking of those who they describe as "victims persecuted by blind hatred" and who see in Palestine their main hope, they say to Mr. Chamberlain: "our solemn decision to abandon-them would be considered by the entire world a capitulation to the forces of violence and hatred; it would be a blow to Christian honour and a very damaging blow to the prestige of our Commonwealth."

In other words, this means first of all, no limit to Jewish immigration to Palestine and an open door to all refugees from Europe! The British government has just made a declaration on the subject; this morning's dispatches state that it is setting a limit. In all likelihood, it cannot do otherwise.

Second, we respectfully ask the signatories of the message a very simple question: if they consider that this restriction constitutes such a reduction in prestige for the Commonwealth, which includes us, what steps and what actions do they propose that Canada take, the only part of the Commonwealth where they may count on exercising some influence?

Do they want our country to become directly involved in this matter in Palestine? In what sense and to what extent?

We surely would not be the only ones to be grateful, if they would make a clear statement on the matter.

***

In the United States, the campaign for intensive Jewish immigration to Palestine naturally has its supporters. At the forefront there is Rabbi Stephen S. Wise, from New York. Mr. Wise and his friends have convened a large meeting for November 2 in New York, to protest against any halt to immigration. They have invited well-known Americans.

Until now, what has been most interesting seems to be the response to Mr. Wise from a senator with a very great reputation, Mr. Borah. Mr. Borah has refused to participate in the demonstration and he states why.—He wrote (and it is known that he has never been considered as pro-English) "Unless we are prepared to go much further than our country is prepared to do and assume ourselves the primary obligations regarding this issue, would it not be much more effective, in this matter, to have confidence in the patience, the wisdom and the honour of the mandatory power to resolve the problem in accordance with its obligations?" He adds, "I am quite convinced that England now finds itself put in a very delicate and very dangerous situation and we would not be helping the cause that interests you by holding a meeting which would be justified only on the assumption that England plans on doing something objectionable."

This is the first time, to our knowledge, that Mr. Wise has been addressed in such a tone by a man as highly placed as Mr. Borah. It is important to note that the time is perhaps not far off when others, despite the enormous power of Jewish Americans, will let them know that the United States cannot, for their sake, feud with other countries.

***

A Jewish voice, that of a veritable prince of Israel, the head of the English branch of the Rothschilds, has just given his kin remarkably wise and moderate advice. We intended to comment on it today, but we do not have the time and space.

It will have to wait another day.

"We Should Tend to Our Own Affairs!"

*On the Palestine Question — The Position of a Group
of American Politicians; Present and Possible Reactions
to It — And in Canada? — An Incident that Should
Put Us on Guard*

Omer Héroux
Le Devoir, November 2, 1938

I s this matter of Palestine going to take on an international aspect?
It appears so.

Now 245 members of the American Congress and 30 State governors have just asked President Roosevelt to use everything in his power to convince the government in London to keep Palestine open to Jewish refugees.

According to a dispatch from the *Associated Press*, these gentlemen insist that *"our fervent hope be signalled to the British Government that the borders of Palestine will remain open to the Jewish refugees who now suffer under cruel oppression in European countries."*

Of particular note here is that these gentlemen do not appear to be in the least hurry to open to these same refugees the borders of their own country, where in matters of immigration the laws are rather severe.

It would be surprising if some of the English do not remind them of this.

***

Our readers are familiar enough with this whole issue so there is no need to emphasize the nature and extent of the initiative of the American congressmen and governors.

England did not accept the Palestine mandate out of any love for Jews and Arabs. England saw in the occupation of Palestine a strategic benefit regarding the defence of the route to India. However, the mandate entails enormous risks, which increase with each passing day.

Arabs and Jews are fighting on Palestinian soil. England has already been forced to maintain a sizeable army there. The situation is made even more critical since, not only do the Arabs and Jews consider themselves to have equal rights to be at home on that land, they both received promises from England, which a Labour newspaper in London has frankly declared to be contradictory. Furthermore, both also are backed by very significant forces outside Palestine: Jewish finance on the one side, Arab and Muslim groups on the other.

England, in the middle of these two forces, is trying to manoeuvre to find a compromise, a *modus vivendi*, since a clash between the two would threaten England's situation, not only in Palestine, but in India and the whole world.

***

These gentlemen in the United States want, out of sympathy — sympathy that is quite understandable — for the Jews now assailed by hostile actions in so many European countries, England to open wide the borders of Palestine, regardless of the consequences.

Clearly, this means that England would bring on itself the violent resistance, not only of the Arabs of Palestine, but also of the rest of the world, that it would compromise its situation in the small Arab kingdoms and in Egypt and that it would risk provoking the 60,000,000 Muslims of India and those whole live throughout Asia and Africa.

It may be asked, what right do American politicians and especially the United States government have to ask the British government to run such a risk.?

If the war were to spill over Palestine's borders, what position would the advisors take? Would they insist that their government go in with rifles, machine guns and bombers to force entry of an unlimited number of Jewish refugees to Palestine?

Before taking such action, it would be useful to think of the possible consequences.

***

The steps taken by the American politicians have already had one effect, which highlights both the ease of present-day communication in the world and the sensitivity of the Muslim world.

We had barely learned, by telegraph, about the petition of these gentlemen when another dispatch, from Jerusalem this time, told us that a wave of anti-Americanism was sweeping across Arab communities in the Middle East and that there was already talk of "boycotting American merchandise and products in the entire Islamic world if the Americans continue to show support for the Jews to the detriment of the Arabs."

That is a first reaction. There perhaps may be another in the United States itself.

***

The initiative of the American politicians undoubtedly is testimony to their good intentions; but perhaps it is not rash to note that it also is testimony to the enormous influence wielded, through their votes and their money, by the Jews of the United States.

These Jews, as powerful as they may be, have they given thought to the harsh reaction that a similar intervention might provoke?

A Jewish conference is being held in New York right now where grievances are being raised about the apparent hostility already aimed at Jews in the United States. The Jews are intelligent people. Do they not think that this hostility will be exacerbated if defence of Jewish interests appears to compromise the political and economic interests of the United States?

They readily ascribe the hostility which targets them to Nazi propaganda. Even if this is true, do they not see what a powerful motivation for action such a defence of Jewish interests would provide to their adversaries?

***

It will not be a surprise to see us end these quick comments on a Canadian note.

The position of the nonconformist pastors in Lachine, in their statement to Mr. Chamberlain regarding this question of Palestine, is a worrisome sign. Numerous examples from the past show us that it is possible to have adopted just about anything by certain public officials, if a few see electoral benefit in it.

It, therefore, does not seem inopportune to reiterate old and very wise advice, namely: *We should tend to our own affairs!*

We should have all appropriate sympathy for the Jews; but we should let the English get out of this imbroglio with the least pain possible; we should not pointlessly worsen the worries of their government ...

We assume that no one wishes Canada to send regiments to Palestine. We should conduct ourselves with the discretion appropriate to all those who are not prepared to pay, with their blood or their gold, for the advice they give!

The Palestine Question

The Latest Aspects — Agitation in the United States
— Our Interest in the Matter — The Dissatisfaction of
the Jews and Their Campaign Plan — The Point of View
of the English — Clashing Forces throughout the World —
Are You of the Opinion that Canadians …?

Omer Héroux
Le Devoir, May 23, 1939

This matter of Palestine is gaining considerable attention. The Jews are already putting their influence on the American scene into action. Last Sunday, in the big cities of the United States, they organized meetings opposed to the British government's position. The extent of the movement demonstrates the power and impeccability of their organizations. A letter in yesterday's *Star* recounts that Mr. Brandeis, the former judge of the Supreme Court of the United States and an Israelite, as is known, stepped into the debate very clearly and stated that no English law would succeed in eliminating Jewish immigration to Palestine. This is an illustration of the level of Jewish society at which the combative spirit of solidarity is expressed.

It can be expected that the campaign will take little time to be developed in our country, for two or three obvious reasons. First, as we were just reminded in an article published in major American newspapers by Mr. Herbert Samuel, one of the Liberal leaders in England and a former British High Commissioner in Palestine, the publication of the English White Paper in no way solves the issue. This White Paper is to be followed by a debate that just began in the British Parliament, then the whole matter will go before the League of Nations, since the *mandate* under which England occupies Palestine England comes from the League of Nations.

The Jews have a natural interest to create in North America, both in Canada and the United States, powerful demonstrations in their support. The hope is that the demonstrations will produce an effect on

English opinion, with the additional hope that they will perhaps have some influence on the position of the League of Nations.

In any case, we must not forget that Canada, as discreet as it may be in the League of Nations, is a member of the League and, therefore, one day may have a say in this entire matter. This why the Palestine issue is unquestionably and directly of interest to us.

***

We understand the apprehension of the Jews. They believed that their age-old dream would become reality and that they would finally return as masters to the land of their fathers. The dream appeared even more attractive, since right now a wave of anti-Semitism is rolling across large European countries and the massive arrival of refugees in other countries risks provoking hostility that has not yet been expressed. Palestine, therefore, has never appeared as desirable and as necessary to Jews. Yet, it is at this moment that England has come to tell them: You may live in Palestine and you will be protected there, but in the next five years, you may not receive more than seventy-five thousand of your people. Subsequently, to open the borders wider, the agreement of the Arabs will be necessary. We have decided that in the country where so many of your people dreamed of creating a Jewish State, that is the master of its own destiny, you may hold only a minority status...

Despite the text of the Balfour declaration having been written in a way that England now may claim that it is respecting the letter of its promise, it does not preclude the Jews from thinking that they have been betrayed or at least feeling that the very authorities they have helped are excluding them from the refuge that would be most natural to them in their time of need.

***

However, the English side of the matter is also particularly tragic.

The English made the Balfour declaration because during the Great War they needed the gold and the influence of the Jews of the United States. However, they needed more than just that gold; they also needed for the anti-German coalition, as well as for themselves, the power and the boldness of the Arabs.

They made the promises necessary to enlist that power.

Now we have a dispute over the scope of these promises and of those in the Balfour declaration. The recipients of the two texts claim to see aspects in them that the English believe they did not include in the texts.

There is nothing surprising here; but this debate, this sophistry, is but one aspect of the issue. The other is that England intends to remain in Palestine and maintain at least a predominant influence there, since Palestine controls the route to India. But how can England remain there if it sees the hostility of the Arab world, and perhaps the entire Muslim world, rising up against it?

As an Anglo-Canadian newspaper noted in recent days, Palestine is no more than a pawn on a chessboard where world interests clash.

**

To grasp the importance of English interests in Palestine, it is only necessary to read the statement made yesterday in the English House of Commons by Mr. Malcolm MacDonald:

In our treaty with Palestine (once the mandate has ended, the British plan provides for a treaty to be concluded between England and the future independent Palestinian State, with an Arab majority), *there should be a provision to maintain a military and air force sufficient to protect our interests; there should be a provision for an appropriate consultation on all military questions and for mutual assistance in case of disorder.*

This, it seems, differs little from what is commonly called a protectorate.

England would give up a form of governance; but it would not be far removed from either the substance or the realities of power.

**

The initial Jewish reaction, not surprisingly, was quite violent. Emotional demonstrations and bloody clashes will now be replaced by methodical opposition. Dispatches bring us the outlines of the plan for a campaign, which is not uninteresting.

There is first an intention to prepare young Jews, who are being counted, for all urgent tasks; then there is an intention to organize the local economy in a way to make Jews independent from foreign products and able to replace them by products from Jewish and local work—which would be a quite an advanced form of *buying at home*;

there is also an intention to remove local Jewish municipalities, communities and councils from any link to the government of Palestine and place them under a supreme Jewish authority—which seems to be the equivalent of creating a State within a State; there is also an intention to reject the present municipal constitution of Jerusalem, where a Jewish majority would be governed by an Arab minority, and finally an intention to refuse to pay taxes and to reduce to a minimum the use of public services from which the government draws revenues.

In short, it seems to be a plan to create a kind of Jewish State on the periphery of the regular government and drain its resources as much as possible.

We shall see the effect of this tactic. It is surely more practical than armed resistance, which would have ended in a massacre, since the chances are that the Arabs would join the English troops responsible for maintaining order, in order get rid of their enemies more easily.

***

There is a question to keep in mind; if this all leads, as is possible, to a huge conflagration, are you of the opinion that Canadians should go there to get their heads smashed …?

List of editorials in *Le Devoir* on Jewish subjects, 1910–1947

The editorial titles in bold indicate major editorials on Jewish subjects.

1. « Politique anti-nationale » (Canadian immigration policy, "An Anti-national Policy," translated in present volume), Georges Pelletier, August 4, 1910, NEGATIVE.
2. **« Le credit populaire, l'exemple des Juifs » (Montreal, Hebrew Free Loan Association, "Credit for All, the Jewish example," translated in *Do What You Must*), Omer Héroux, June 11, 1913, NEUTRAL.**
3. **« Juifs et Protestants à la Commission scolaire dissidente » (Montreal, Protestant schools, "Jews and Protestants at the Dissentient School Board," translated in present volume), Omer Héroux, April 15, 1914, NEUTRAL.**
4. « Si vous avez la presse… » (Catholic press), Georges Pelletier, February 13, 1920, NEGATIVE.
5. « Une dépêche qui fait rêver » (minorities in Europe), Omer Héroux, October 22, 1920, NEUTRAL.
6. « Trucs et réformes » (fraudulent immigration), Georges Pelletier, May 27, 1921, NEGATIVE.
7. **« Le Pape et la Palestine » (Vatican), Omer Héroux, September 2, 1921, NEGATIVE.**
8. « Ce qui importe d'abord » (immigration to Canada, "What Is Most Important," translated in present volume), Georges Pelletier, April 5, 1922, NEGATIVE
9. « Pour réveiller le civisme » (Montreal, municipal charter), Louis Dupire, April 13, 1922, NEGATIVE.
10. « L'urbanisme » (Montreal urban development), Louis Dupire, April 28, 1923, NEUTRAL.

11. « Si les mères savaient » (Montreal, infant mortality), Louis Dupire, July 27, 1923, NEUTRAL.

12. « Pas trente milles : 4 000 pieds seulement » (Montreal, urbain transport), Louis Dupire, August 9, 1923, NEGATIVE.

13. « Que ferons-nous ? » (Montreal, public parks), Omer Héroux, October 22, 1923, NEUTRAL.

14. « Les étrangers à Paris » (Paris, social life), Georges Pelletier, November 6, 1923, NEGATIVE.

15. « Le tribunal des jeunes délinquants » (Montreal, youth protection), Louis Dupire, November 8, 1923, NEUTRAL.

16. « Résumé de session » (Canadian Parliament, political life), Henri Bourassa, March 17, 1924, NEUTRAL.

17. **« Sur les Remparts » (review of Abbot Édouard Lavergne's Book, "On the Ramparts," translated in *Do What You Must*), Henri Bourassa, July 26, 1924, NEUTRAL.**

18. « Pourquoi pas la paroisse ? » (education, commission of inquiry on schools), Omer Héroux, October 16, 1924, NEUTRAL.

19. « Pourquoi nos enfants meurent » (Montreal, infant mortality, "Why Our Children Are Dying," translated in present volume), Louis Dupire, January 13, 1 925 NEUTRAL.

20. « Les exemptions de taxes » (Montreal, municipal taxes), Omer Héroux, July 29, 1925, NEUTRAL.

21. « Sur une conférence par un échevin sortant » (Montreal, municipal administration), Louis Dupire, April 10, 1926, NEUTRAL.

22. « Un nouveau "scheme" : une exposition au parc Maisonneuve » (Montreal, municipal administration, "A New Scheme : Fairgrounds in Parc Maisonneuve," translated in present volume), Louis Dupire, June 4, 1926, NEGATIVE.

23. « Le cinéma américain ne boycottera pas Montréal » (Montreal, Hollywood cinema), Louis Dupire, June 15, 1926, NEGATIVE.

24. « Un règlement qui dort depuis 18 mois au conseil municipal » (Montreal, Hollywood cinema), Louis Dupire, November 20, 1926, NEGATIVE.

25. « Une once de sanction vaut mieux que cent onces de législation » (Montreal, Hollywood cinema), Louis Dupire, January 17, 1927, NEGATIVE.

26. **« La mortalité infantile chez les Juifs et les chrétiens » (Montréal, public health, "Infant Mortality Among Jews and Among Christians," translated in present volume), Louis Dupire, August 5, 1927, NEUTRAL**

27. « Rien que les Femmes Savantes… » (Montreal, theatre, "Nothing But the 'Learned Ladies'…, " translated in Do What You Must), Georges Pelletier, October 3,1927, NEGATIVE.

28. **« Mariage et divorce XXIV » (Lower Canada, 1832 law), Henri Bourassa, June 4, 1929, NEUTRAL.**

29. **« Sur une poudrière » (Palestine, British imperialism, "On Top of a Powder Keg," translated in present volume), Omer Héroux, August 28, 1929, NEGATIVE.**

30. **« Silence au Mexique, clameurs en Palestine » (Catholic persecutions in Mexico, Jewish persecutions in Palestine, "Silence on Mexico, Protests for Palestine," translated in present volume), Georges Pelletier, September 6, 1929, NEGATIVE.**

31. « De M. Taschereau et du "Journal" » (freedom of expression in Quebec), Omer Héroux, December 18, 1929, NEUTRAL.

32. « Vingt ans de trop » (immigration in Canada, "Twenty Years Too Many," translated in present volume), Georges Pelletier, December 19, 1929, NEUTRAL.

33. « Les compagnies d'assurance et le logement salubre » (Montréal, public health, "Insurance Companies and Hygienic Housing," translated in Do What You Must), Louis Dupire, January 20, 1930, NEUTRAL.

34. **« Arabes, Juifs et Anglais » (Palestine, British imperialism), Omer Héroux, February 16, 1930, NEGATIVE.**

35. « Les écoles de Montréal » (Protestant schools, "Montreal Schools," translated in the present volume), Omer Héroux, February 20, 1930, NEUTRAL.

36. « Si c'est cela de l'art français » (theatre in Montreal, "If That Is 'French art' …," translated in present volume), Georges Pelletier, February 28, 1930, NEGATIVE.

37. **« Sous la main du gouvernement » (Montreal, Jewish school board, "Under the Government's Thumb," translated in present volume), Omer Héroux, March 18, 1930, NEUTRAL.**

38. **« Pourquoi pas un ajournement ? » (Montreal, Jewish school board, "Why Not a Postponement?" translated in present volume), Omer Héroux, April 1, 1930, NEUTRAL.**

39. « 1 sur 65 » (federal student bursaries), Omer Héroux, April 3, 1930, NEGATIVE.

40. **« De Bombay à Jérusalem » (British imperialism, Palestine, "From Bombay to Jerusalem," translated in present volume), Omer Héroux, May 22, 1930, NEUTRAL.**

41. « Ne blâmons pas les Juifs : imitons-les » (Montreal, summer camps, "Do Not Blame the Jews: Imitate Them," translated in the present volume), Louis Dupire, June 3, 1930, NEUTRAL.

42. « En marge de la quête de la S.C.P.R. » (Montreal, Hebrew Free Loan Association), Louis Dupire, October 4, 1930, NEUTRAL.

43. « La question de la Palestine » (Jewish immigration, "The Palestine Question," translated in present volume), Omer Héroux, October 21, 1930, NEUTRAL.

44. « Après Baldwin, Smuts » (British imperialism, Palestine, "After Baldwin, Smuts," translated in Do What You Must), Omer Héroux, October 24, 1930, NEUTRAL.

45. « C'est l'avenir qui nous sollicite » (Jewish philanthropy in Montreal), Louis Dupire, March 24, 1931, NEUTRAL.

46. « Le théâtre d'exportation, » (theatre in Montreal), Georges Pelletier, April 23, 1931, NEGATIVE.

47. « Leçons et réflexions » (Montreal, anti-Semitism, "Lessons and Reflections," translated in present volume), Henri Bourassa, August 26, 1931, NEUTRAL.

48. « Rôle capital de la charité » (economic slowdown, Christian philanthropy), Henri Bourassa, September 24, 1931, NEUTRAL.

49. « Quelques traits de plume en marge du rapport Schubert » (Montreal, fight against unemployment), Louis Dupire, May 26, 1932, NEUTRAL.

50. « Rien que pour plaire à M. Bercovitch ? Non » (anti-defamation law, "Only to Satisfy Mr. Bercovitch? No," translated in present volume), Georges Pelletier, March 11, 1933, NEGATIVE.

51. « Le précepte dominical » ("The observance of Sunday," translated in present volume), Joseph Papin Archambault, s. j., May 3, 1933, NEGATIVE.

52. « Espagnols et Juifs » (Spain, anti-clericalism, "The Attention Paid to Spanish Catholics and to Jews," translated in present volume), Omer Héroux, June 29, 1933, NEUTRAL.

53. « En marge des bagarres à Toronto » (immigration, anti-Semitism, "The Brawls in Toronto," translated in present volume), Georges Pelletier, August 19, 1933, NEGATIVE.

54. « M. Jacobs aussi… » (immigration to Canada, "Mr. Jacobs Also," translated in present volume), Omer Héroux, October 26, 1933, NEGATIVE.

55. « Le contrat Pollack-Renaud » (Quebec, commercial dispute), Omer Héroux, November 13, 1933, NEGATIVE.

56. « Toute la jeunesse libérale dénonce les "Jeune-Canada" » (Montreal, youth movement), Omer Héroux, November 18, 1933, NEGATIVE.

57. « Vers la paix ou vers l'abîme ? » (world peace), Georges Pelletier, November 25, 1933, NEGATIVE.

58. « Le projet Barrette et la route de l'Abitibi » (Montreal, fight against unemployment), Louis Dupire, December 13, 1933, NEGATIVE.

59. « L'assemblée de ce soir à la Palestre Nationale » (Montreal, housing for workers), Louis Dupire, January 4, 1934, NEUTRAL.

60. « M. Joseph Cohen et la "Saint-Jean-Baptiste" » (buy from your own, "Mr. Joseph Cohen and the Société Saint-Jean-Baptiste," translated in present volume), Omer Héroux, January 5, 1934, NEGATIVE.

61. « De quoi au juste se plaint M. Joseph Cohen ? » (buy from your own), Omer Héroux, January 17, 1934, NEGATIVE.

62. « Ces documents » (Canadian Jewish Congress, anti-Semitism), Omer Héroux, January 18, 1934, NEGATIVE.

63. « La maison est à l'envers » (buy from your own, "Life Is in Disarray," translated in present volume), Omer Héroux, January 19, 1934, NEGATIVE.

64. « La réponse de MM. Jacobs, Bercovitch et al. » (Canadian Jewish Congress, anti-Semitism), Omer Héroux, January 22, 1934, NEGATIVE.

65. « L'autorité de ces documents juifs » (Canadian Jewish Congress, anti-Semitism, "The Status of the Jewish Documents," translated in present volume), Omer Héroux, January 25, 1934, NEGATIVE.

66. « Le père du journalisme jaune fut le Juif Joseph Pulitzer » (United States, sensationalist press, "The Father of Yellow Journalism Was the Jew Joseph Pulitzer," translated in present volume), Louis Dupire, January 26, 1934, NEGATIVE.

67. « Une nouvelle migration juive ? » (immigration to Canada, "A New Jewish Immigration?" translated in the present volume), Omer Héroux, February 1, 1934, NEGATIVE.

68. « Le boycott des annonces et les Juifs » (Montreal, anti-Semitism, "The Advertising Boycott and Jews," translated in present volume), Omer Héroux, February 3, 1934, NEGATIVE.

69. « Une nouvelle lettre de M. Caiserman » (Canadian Jewish Congress, anti-Semitism), Omer Héroux, February 8, 1934, NEGATIVE.

70. « Le mieux est l'ennemi du bien » (Montreal, housing for workers), Louis Dupire, February 14, 1934, NEUTRAL.
71. « Comment ces Goldberg se muèrent en Gordon » (Montreal, change of family name), Omer Héroux, February 15, 1934, NEGATIVE.
72. « Suite de l'affaire Goldberg-Gordon » (Montreal, change of family name), Omer Héroux, February 22, 1934, NEGATIVE.
73. « Suite au discours de M. Joseph Cohen » (Montreal, anti-Semitism), Omer Héroux, March 3, 1934, NEGATIVE.
74. « Pourquoi MM. Schwartz et Smilovitz veulent changer de nom » (Montreal, change of family name), Omer Héroux, March 15, 1934, NEGATIVE.
75. « Points sur les I » (Sunday law, "Dotting the i's," translated in present volume), Omer Héroux, April 26, 1934, NEGATIVE.
76. « La proposition Schubert » (Montreal, public transport), Louis Dupire, May 23, 1934, NEUTRAL
77. « M. Bercovitch soulève des problèmes intéressants en proposant de taxer les compensations bancaires » (Montreal, taxation), Louis Dupire, January 4, 1935, NEUTRAL.
78. « Ce dont ne parle pas le discours du Trône » (immigration, fight against unemployment), Omer Héroux, January 18, 1935, NEUTRAL.
79. « Les cinq petites Dionne » (public health, breast feeding), Louis Dupire, January 19, 1935, NEUTRAL.
80. « Un appel à M. Bennett qui sera à Montréal ce soir » (fight against unemployment), Louis Dupire, January 23, 1935, NEUTRAL.
81. « Le privilège juif » (Sunday law), Omer Héroux, May 3, 1935, NEGATIVE.
82. « Saurons-nous donner un coup de cœur ? » (Montreal, Catholic philanthropy), Louis Dupire, May 11, 1935, NEUTRAL.
83. « La commission industrielle et nous » (Montreal, industrial development), Louis Dupire, July 9, 1935, NEUTRAL.
84. « Choses d'Allemagne » (Persecution of Catholics, "Events in Germany," translated in present volume), Omer Héroux, August 5, 1935, NEUTRAL.
85. « Pour nos nouveaux lecteurs d'abord… » (Le Devoir, editorial policy), Omer Héroux, December 26, 1935, NEGATIVE.
86. « Le ministère Taschereau n'a pas qualité pour nous lier » (Quebec, political corruption), Georges Pelletier, January 18, 1936, NEGATIVE.

87. « Pour la propreté des élections à venir » (Quebec, political corruption), Georges Pelletier, January 25, 1936, NEGATIVE.

88. **« M. Cohen et la loi Dillon à quinze cents milles d'ici » (Quebec, political corruption), Omer Héroux, January 31, 1936, NEGATIVE.**

89. « Préjugés qui ont la vie dure » (agriculture), Albert Rioux, March 10, 1936, NEUTRAL.

90. « Les fonctionnaires unilingues » (bilingualism), Albert Rioux, March 17, 1936, NEGATIVE.

91. « Encore le Service civil » (bilingualism), Albert Rioux, March 24, 1936, NEGATIVE.

92. **« Le travail du Dimanche » (Sunday law), Omer Héroux, March 26, 1936, NEGATIVE.**

93. La tête sous le couperet ? » (Quebec, electoral corruption), Georges Pelletier, March 28, 1936, NEUTRAL.

94. « Ne soyons pas des autruches » (immigration to Canada), Georges Pelletier, April 4, 1936, NEGATIVE.

95. « Cinquante pour cent d'augmentation en douze mois » (Le Devoir, editorial policy), Omer Héroux, April 16, 1936, NEGATIVE.

96. « L'esprit nouveau nous garantit le succès » (Catholic philanthropy), Louis Dupire, April 17, 1936, NEUTRAL.

97. « Pourquoi pas une enquête ? » (Quebec, electoral corruption), Omer Héroux, April 23, 1936, NEGATIVE.

98. **« L'affaire de l'Emden » (Montreal, protests against Hitler's persecutions), Omer Héroux, May 1, 1936, NEGATIVE.**

99. « Ou M. Taschereau savait… ou il ne savait pas – Et alors ? » (Montreal, municipal administration), Georges Pelletier, May 16, 1936, NEUTRAL.

100. **« Au-dessus de MM. Bercovitch et Lanctôt » (Quebec, political corruption), Georges Pelletier, May 30, 1936, NEGATIVE.**

101. « Pour M. Lucien Parizeau » (Quebec, electoral corruption), Omer Héroux, June 3, 1936, NEGATIVE.

102. « Le gouvernement de l'ordre… sans ironie » (Quebec, political corruption), Georges Pelletier, June 6, 1936, NEGATIVE.

103. **« Tricherie revient à son maître — avec les intérêts des intérêts » (Quebec, political corruption, "Cheating Does Return to Haunt Its Master—With Double Consequences," translated in present volume), Georges Pelletier, June 13, 1936, NEGATIVE.**

104. « M. Josef Cohen s'en va » (Québec, electoral corruption), Omer Héroux, July 2, 1936, NEGATIVE.
105. « Pour Mtre Charles-Auguste Bertrand » (Quebec, electoral corruption), Omer Héroux, July 3, 1936, NEGATIVE.
106. « Quand allumera-t-il son fanal ! » (Quebec, political corruption), Omer Héroux, July 20, 1936, NEUTRAL.
107. « M. Macmillan a raison… » (Canadian nationalism), Omer Héroux, December 19, 1936, NEUTRAL.
108. « Avant les œuvres de guerre, les œuvres de charité » (Montreal, welfare), Louis Dupire, March 3, 1937, NEUTRAL.
109. « Le cas de la "Maison Champlain, Incorporée" » (French-Canadian nationalism), Omer Héroux, March 4, 1937, NEGATIVE.
110. **« L'antisémitisme, péril grandissant » (anti-Semitism, Zionism, "Anti-Semitism, a Growing Danger," translated in present volume) Georges Pelletier, April 17, 1937, NEGATIVE.**
111. « Ils ne savent pas ce qui se passe chez eux » (sensationalist press), Georges Pelletier, June 5, 1937, NEGATIVE.
112. « New York vs Montréal » (fight against unemployment), Louis Dupire, June 8, 1937, NEUTRAL.
113. « Deux articles du "Star" » (international relations), Omer Héroux, June 9, 1937, NEUTRAL.
114. **« Juifs, Arabes et Anglais » (Palestine, British imperialism, "Jews, Arabs and the English," translated in present volume), Omer Héroux, July 8, 1937, NEUTRAL.**
115. « Du cardinal Pacelli, de la France et de l'Allemagne » (France, Catholic Church), Omer Héroux, July 14, 1937, NEGATIVE.
116. « Sur les discours de Saint-Denis » (education, "The Saint-Denis Speeches," translated in present volume), Omer Héroux, September 2, 1937, NEUTRAL.
117. « Les inestimables richesses qu'on laisse se perdre » (education), Paul Sauriol, Sepember 15, 1937, NEUTRAL.
118. « Pour ceux qui s'intéressent aux réalités » (technical education), Omer Héroux, October 21, 1937, NEGATIVE.
119. **« Pour illustrer la sagesse du conseil de lord Tweedsmuir » (Palestine), Omer Héroux, October 22, 1937, NEUTRAL.**
120. « À travers l'Allemagne hitlérienne » (account of trip to Germany), Georges Pelletier, December 18, 1937, NEUTRAL.
121. **« De l'Angleterre, de la Palestine et de nous… » (British imperialism), Omer Héroux, January 5, 1938, NEUTRAL.**

122. « Sur l'antisémitisme en Europe centrale » (trip account, "Anti-Semitism in Central Europe," translated in present volume), Georges Pelletier, January 22, 1938, NEGATIVE.

123. « Londres s'intéresse moins à l'Europe centrale qu'à Londres » (threat of war, international relations), Georges Pelletier, March 5, 1938, NEGATIVE.

124. « Bravo ! Confrères » (United States, Francophone press), Omer Héroux, March 16, 1938, NEUTRAL.

125. « À propos du "Hobby Show" » (Montreal, youth movement), Omer Héroux, April 25, 1938, NEUTRE.

126. « Terre d'Europe à la dérive, ou pays d'Amérique » (threat of war, British imperialism), Georges Pelletier, May 14, 1938, NEUTRAL.

127. « Où est le scandale du marché Bonsecours » (Montreal, municipal administration), Louis Dupire, June 14, 1938, NEUTRAL.

128. « L'affaire Semple et les réflexions qu'elle suscite » (Montreal, municipal administration), Louis Dupire, June 21, 1938, NEUTRAL.

129. « À propos d'immigration » (Great Britain, immigration to Canada), Omer Héroux, June 30, 1938, NEGATIVE.

130. « La prison attend, chez nous, l'enfant sans soutien » (youth protection), Louis Dupire, July 27, 1938, NEGATIVE.

131. « De Lloyd George à Chamberlain » (Czechoslovakia, threat of war), Georges Pelletier, September17, 1938, NEGATIVE.

132. « Serions-nous des Canadiens de seconde zone ? » (Francophone minorities in Canada), Georges Pelletier, October 22, 1938, NEUTRAL.

133. « Les étonnements de M. Glass, député de Toronto et organisateur du boycott juif contre la marchandise allemande » (anti-Hitler protests, "The Astonishment of Mr. Glass, Member from Toronto of the Legislative Assembly of Ontario and Organizer of the Jewish Boycott of German Merchandise," translated in present volume), Omer Héroux, October 26, 1938, NEGATIVE.

134. « Les pasteurs protestants de Lachine et M. Neville Chamberlain » (Palestine, Balfour declaration, "The Protestant Pastors of Lachine and Mr. Neville Chamberlain," translated in present volume), Omer Héroux, October 27, 1938, NEUTRAL.

135. « Mêlons-nous de nos affaires ! » (Palestine, American intervention, "We Should Tend to Our Own Affairs!," translated in present volume), Omer Héroux, November 2, 1938, NEGATIVE.

136. « De Jérusalem à Londres et à Ottawa » (Palestine), Omer Héroux, November 10, 1938, NEUTRAL.

137. « Les manifestations antihitlériennes » (Germany, persecution of Jews, "Demonstrations Against Hitler," translated in present volume), Omer Héroux, November 21, 1938, NEUTRAL.

138. « L'éternelle question des réfugiés juifs » (Germany, persecution of Jews, "The Enduring Question of Jewish Refugees," translated in present volume), Omer Héroux, November 22, 1938, NEUTRAL.

139. « Qu'on en finisse avec cette histoire de "boycott" ! » (Germany, persecution of Jews), Omer Héroux, November 25, 1938, NEGATIVE.

140. « Les Juifs d'Allemagne font déraisonner le "Star" » (Germany, persecution of Jews, "In the Case of the German Jews, the *Star* Talks Nonsense," translated in the present volume), Georges Pelletier, November 26, 1938, NEGATIVE.

141. « À chacun ses Juifs » (German Jews, immigration to Canada, "To Everyone Their Own Jews," translated in present volume), Georges Pelletier, December 3, 1938, NEGATIVE.

142. « M. Gascon ou M. Houde » (Montreal, municipal elections), Louis Dupire, December 9, 1938, NEUTRAL.

143. « Où l'on commence à voir clair dans l'affaire » (civil service, bilingualism), Omer Héroux, December 27, 1938, NEGATIVE.

144. « Sur la lettre de M. Richer » (civil service, bilingualism), Omer Héroux, December 28, 1938, NEGATIVE.

145. « Nous avons gaspillé le passé — Sachons prévoir l'avenir » (French-Canadian nationalism, economy), Georges Pelletier, December 31, 1938, NEGATIVE.

146. « L'affaire Frankfurter » (United States, anti-Semitism), Omer Héroux, January 12, 1939, NEGATIVE.

147. « Soyons logiques : estampillons le marchand comme la merchandise » (immigration, international relations, "We Need to Be Logical: Label the Merchant Just Like the Merchandise," translated in present volume), Georges Pelletier, January 28, 1939, NEGATIVE.

148. « Le Dr Paquette mérite d'être applaudi » (Montreal, public health), Louis Dupire, February 7, 1939, NEUTRAL.

149. « Le "lait spécial" doit-il être condamné ? » (Montreal, public health), Louis Dupire, March 9, 1939, NEUTRAL.

150. « Lait pasteurisé contre lait special » (Montreal, public health), Louis Dupire, March 15, 1939, NEUTRAL.

151. **« Est-ce une tour de Babel que le Canada bâtit ? » (immigration, international relations, "Is Canada Building a Tower of Babel?," translated in present volume), Georges Pelletier, March 18, 1939, NEGATIVE.**

152. « Nous n'avons pas donné assez ! » (Montreal, Catholic philanthropy), Louis Dupire, March 28, 1939, NEUTRAL.

153. « Quelques vérités acides mais opportunes dites par M. Eugène L'Heureux, » (Montreal, urban development), Louis Dupire, May 6, 1939, NEUTRAL.

154. **« La question de la Palestine » (Jewish immigration, British imperialism, "The Palestine Question," translated in present volume), Omer Héroux, 23 mai 1939, NEUTRAL.**

155. « En visitant une bibliothèque » (historical documentation), Omer Héroux, June 20, 1939, NEUTRAL.

156. « Si nous étions Canadiens » (Great Britain, Canadian nationalism), Georges Pelletier, June 24, 1939, NEGATIVE.

157. « Images et Nouvelles » (sensationalist press, Catholic morals), Georges Pelletier, July 22, 1939, NEGATIVE.

158. « Nos vrais buts de guerre » (world war, Canadian participation), Georges Pelletier, September 16, 1939, NEGATIVE.

159. « La tuberculose, plaie d'argent... » (Montreal, public health), Louis Dupire, October 11, 1939, NEUTRAL.

160. « La canonisation du Québec » (Quebec, general election), Georges Pelletier, November 4, 1939, NEUTRAL.

161. « Québec tient la première place au Canada dans la mortalité par la tuberculose » (Quebec, public health), Louis Dupire, November 17, 1939, NEUTRAL.

162. **« L'exemple des Juifs » (civil service, French language, "The Jews as a Model," translated in present volume), Omer Héroux, December 21, 1939, NEUTRAL.**

163. « Cette proposition juive » (world war), Omer Héroux, January 11, 1940, NEUTRAL.

164. « Et nous continuerions pareille politique ? » (war effort, immigration), Georges Pelletier, July 6, 1940, NEGATIVE.

165. « L'Europe d'il y a trois ans ; celle d'aujourd'hui... » (world war, international relations), Georges Pelletier, November 23, 1940, NEGATIVE.

166. « Les morts qui frappent et celles qui ne frappent pas » (Montreal, public health) Louis Dupire, April 2, 1941, NEUTRAL.
167. « Des statistiques qui nous font rougir » (Montreal, public health), Louis Dupire, August 27, 1941, NEUTRAL.
168. « Le "Canada," Me Henry Torrès et l'amiral Darlan » (France, world war), Omer Héroux, September 15, 1941, NEGATIVE.
169. « Me Henry Torrès, le "Canada" et l'amiral Darlan » (France, world war), Omer Héroux, September 19, 1941, NEGATIVE.
170. « Une situation alarmante à Montréal » (public health, tuberculosis), Louis Dupire, December 10, 1941, NEUTRAL.
171. « M. Lehman et le "Médievalisme" » (world war, propaganda), Omer Héroux, February18, 1942, NEGATIVE.
172. **« L'exemple des Juifs » (world war, conscription, "The Jews as a Model," translated in present volume), Omer Héroux, April 22, 1942, NEUTRAL.**
173. « Un débat à la Commission scolaire protestante de Montréal » (education, teaching of religion), Omer Héroux, June 12, 1942, NEUTRAL.
174. « Une enquête nécessaire » (war effort, work by women), Omer Héroux, July 16, 1942, NEUTRAL.
175. « La réforme du calendrier » (civil calendar), Paul Sauriol, August 8, 1942, NEUTRAL.
176. « Les Amériques et l'avenir de la civilisation européenne » (United States, Anglo-American relations), Georges Pelletier, September 12, 1942, NEUTRAL.
177. « La résistance à l'anglicisation aux États-Unis » (United States, demography), Paul Sauriol, October 5, 1942, NEUTRAL.
178. « La "Croix-Rouge" ontarienne et notre langue » (Ontario, bilingualism), Omer Héroux, October 21, 1942, NEGATIVE.
179. « Une chose qu'il ne faut pas perdre de vue » (immigration to Canada), Omer Héroux, January 22, 1943, NEGATIVE.
180. « Les communistes à l'œuvre chez les néo-Canadiens » (immigration in Canada), Omer Héroux, February 5, 1943, NEGATIVE.
181. « Nous voilà racists ! » (anti-French-Canadian prejudices), Georges Pelletier, February 6, 1943, NEGATIVE.
182. « Il faut en finir avec ce régime » (administrative tribunals), Omer Héroux, February 18, 1943, NEGATIVE.
183. « Nous avons nos propres victimes et réfugiés de la guerre » (Montreal, workers, housing, "We Have Our Own Victims and

Refugees of the War," translated in present volume), Émile Benoist, June 4, 1943, NEUTRAL.

184. « Les élections d'hier » (Canada, general election), Omer Héroux, August 11, 1943, NEUTRAL.

185. « Le parti politique qui se fondera demain » (Canada, Communist Party), Omer Héroux, August 20, 1943, NEUTRAL.

186. « Les problèmes d'après-guerre et la dénatalité anglo-saxonne » (demography, birth rate, "Post-war Problems and Decline in Anglo-Saxon Birth Rate," translated in present volume), Louis Robillard, September 3, 1943, NEGATIVE.

187. **« Un mémoire judéo-américain à la conférence de Québec » (world war, persecution of Jews, "A Judeo-American Brief at the Quebec Conference," translated in present volume), Louis Robillard, September 9, 1943, NEGATIVE.**

188. « Le dédain du travail à l'endroit de nos gens » (civil service, bilingualism), Léopold Richer, September 13, 1943, NEUTRAL.

189. « Une fausseté de M. King » (Bloc populaire, anti-French-Canadian prejudices), Léopold Richer, October 1, 1943, NEGATIVE.

190. « Une politique démographique barbare » (world war, displacement of people), Paul Sauriol, October 13, 1943, NEUTRAL.

191. « Patriotisme ou parasitisme ? » (Bloc populaire, political program), Georges Pelletier, October16, 1943, NEGATIVE.

192. **« M. Louis Fitch et la "tolérance" » (immigration to Canada), Omer Héroux, November 19, 1943, NEGATIVE.**

193. « La campagne pour l'admission des réfugiés au Canada » (world war, immigration to Canada), Louis Robillard, November 26, 1943, NEGATIVE.

194. **« Le problème de l'immigration et l'animosité antiquébécoise » (immigration to Canada, "The Problem of Immigration and Anti-Quebec Animosity?," translated in present volume), Roger Duhamel, December 16, 1943, NEGATIVE.**

195. « Ceux qui ont de l'influence et ceux qui n'en ont pas » (immigration, refugees), Léopold Richer, April 3, 1944, NEUTRAL.

196. « Ce ne serait pas une affaire comme les autres ! » (British Commonwealth), Léopold Richer, April 12, 1944, NEUTRAL.

197. « Casse-cou ! » (hydroelectricity), Omer Héroux, April 13, 1944, NEUTRAL.

198. « En dépit du budget et de l'affaire Bouchard » (philanthropy education), Omer Héroux, June 27, 1944, NEUTRAL.

358 A RELUCTANT WELCOME FOR JEWISH PEOPLE

199. « Les bagarres sanglantes qui ont marqué le scrutin de mardi » (Quebec, general election), Émile Benoist, August 10, 1944, NEGATIVE.

200. « Coup d'œil sur la conférence de l'UNRRA » (United Nations, liberation of Europe), Louis Robillard, September 27, 1944, NEGATIVE.

201. « Si nous descendions de la stratosphere » (press publications, freedom of the press), Omer Héroux, September 28, 1944, NEUTRAL.

202. **« Après l'assassinat de lord Moyne » (Palestine, British imperialism), Omer Héroux, November 13, 1944, NEUTRAL.**

203. **« Dictatures inhumaines » (world war, persecution of Jews, "Inhumane Dictatorships," translated in present volume), Georges Pelletier, April 7, 1945, NEUTRAL.**

204. « Une candidature communiste au pays de Westmount » (Canada, general election), Émile Benoist, May 1, 1945, NEGATIVE.

205. « Ce que coûtent les élections » (democracy, electoral corruption), Omer Héroux, July 3, 1945, NEGATIVE.

206. « Comment les dépenses d'élections faussent le jeu de la démocratie » (Quebec, electoral corruption), Pierre Vigeant, July 4, 1945, NEGATIVE.

207. « La Fédération des œuvres de Charité doit dépasser son objectif » (Montreal, Catholic philanthropy, "The Fédération des Œuvres de Charité Must Exceed its Goal," translated in the present volume), Émile Benoist, February 25, 1946, NEUTRAL.

208. « Un témoignage » (Vatican, ecumenicalism), Alexis Gagnon, March 9, 1946, NEUTRAL.

209. « Les écoles confessionnelles » (education), Alexis Gagnon, October 9, 1946, NEUTRAL.

List of editorialists who wrote on the subject of Judaism on *Le Devoir*'s pages and the Jewish presence in Canada, 1910–1947

Editorialists	Negative editorials	Total number of editorials
Omer Héroux	50	91
Georges Pelletier	34	45
Louis Dupire	8	44
Henri Bourassa	0	5
Paul Sauriol	0	4
Léopold Richer	1	4
Émile Benoist	2	4
Louis Robillard	4	4
Alexis Gagnon	0	2
Albert Rioux	1	2
Joseph-Papin Archambault S.J.	1	1
Roger Duhamel	1	1
Pierre Vigeant	1	1

Bibliography

Abella, Irving and Harold Troper. *None Is Too Many: Canada and the Jews of Europe 1933–1948*, Toronto, University of Toronto Press, 2012, 340 p.

Anctil, Pierre. "Les rapports entre francophones et Juifs dans le contexte montréalais," p. 38–64, in *Les communautés juives de Montréal, histoire et enjeux contemporains*, Pierre Anctil and Ira Robinson (dir.), Sillery, éditions du Septentrion, 2010, 275 p.

Anctil, Pierre. *Le Rendez-vous manqué, les Juifs de Montréal face au Québec de l'entre-deux-guerres*, Québec, Institut québécois de recherche sur la culture, 1988, 366 p.

Anctil, Pierre. *Le Devoir, les Juifs et l'immigration, de Bourassa à Laurendeau*, Québec, Institut québécois de recherche sur la culture, 1988, 172 p.

Avery, Donald. "Canada's Response to European Refugees, 1939–1945," p. 179–216, Norman Hilmer, Bohdan Kordan and Lubomyr Luciuk, eds., *On Guard for Thee: War, Ethnicity and the Canadian State, 1939–1945*, Ottawa, Canadian Committee for the History of the Second World War, 1988, 282 p.

Belkin, Simon. *Through Narrow Gates: A Review of Jewish Immigration, Colonization and Immigrant Aid Work in Canada (1840–1940)*, Montréal, The Canadian Jewish Congress and The Jewish Colonization Association, 1966, 235 p.

Bégin-Wolff, Claudette. *L'opinion publique québécoise face à l'immigration (1906–1913)*, Master's thesis in history, Université de Montréal, 2000, 170 p.

Betcherman, Lita-Rose. *The Swastika and the Maple Leaf: Fascist Movements in Canada in the Thirties*, Toronto: Fitzhenry & Whiteside, 1975, 167 p.

Bialystok, Franklin. *Delayed Impact: The Holocaust and the Canadian Jewish Community*, Montréal, McGill-Queen's University Press, 2000, 327 p.

Birnbaum, Pierre. *"La France aux Français." Histoire des haines nationalistes*, Paris, Seuil, 1993, 395 p.

Bock, Michel. *Quand la nation débordait les frontières: les minorités françaises dans la pensée de Lionel Groulx*, Montréal, Hurtubise HMH, 2004, 452 p.

Chouinard, Denis. "Des contestataires pratiques: les Jeune Canada, 1932–1938," *Revue d'histoire de l'Amérique française*, vol. 40, n° 1, 1986, p. 5–28.

Comartin, Justin. *Humanitarian Ambitions—International Barriers: Canadian Governmental Response to the Plight of the Jewish Refugees (1933–1945)*, Ottawa, University of Ottawa, Master's thesis in history, 2013, 145 p.

Côté, Olivier. "Nouveaux regards sur l'antisémitisme. Enquête sur la position de cinq quotidiens canadiens-français au sujet de la question juive en Allemagne (1935–1939)," *Bulletin d'histoire politique*, vol. 15, n° 1, October 2006, p. 243–261.

Courtois, Charles-Philippe. "Le séparatisme québécois des années 1930 et les non-conformistes," *Bulletin d'histoire politique*, vol. 16, n° 2, Winter 2008, p. 287–302.

Croteau, Jean-Philippe. *Les relations entre les Juifs de langue française et les Canadiens français selon le* Bulletin du Cercle juif *(1954–1968)*, Montréal, Université de Montréal, Master's thesis in history, 2000, 162 p.

Davies, Alan. "Claris Edwin Silcox (1888–1961): Brave and Resolute Champion of the City of God," *Touchstone*, May 2009, p. 50–57.

Davies, Alan (dir.). *Anti-Semitism in Canada. History and Interpretation*, Waterloo, Wilfrid Laurier University Press, 1992, 304 p.

Delisle, Esther. *Le traître et le Juif : Lionel Groulx,* Le Devoir *et le délire du nationalisme d'extrême droite dans la province de Québec, 1929–1939*, Outremont, l'Étincelle, 1992, 284 p.

Dirks, Gerald E. *Canada's Refugee Policy: Indifference or Opportunism?* Montréal, McGill-Queen's University Press, 1977, 316 p.

Durance, Jonathan and Kyle Jantzen, "Our Jewish Brethren: Christian Responses to Kristallnacht in Canadian Mass Media," *Journal of Ecumenical Studies*, n° 46, vol. 4, 2011, p. 537–548.

Figler, Bernard. *Sam Jacobs, Member of Parliament 1871–1938*, Montréal, author's edition, 1970, 282 p.

Foulon, Arnaud. *Georges Pelletier et l'immigration, la pensée d'un journaliste nationaliste (1910–1939)*, Master's thesis in history, Université de Montréal, 1999, 177 p.

Goutour, David. "The Canadian Media and the "Discovery" of the Holocaust: 1944–1945," *Canadian Jewish Studies*, vol. 4–5, 1996–1997, p. 35–62.

Goyette, Julien, dir. *Lionel Groulx, une anthologie*, Montréal, Bibliothèque québécoise, 1998, 312 p.

Gunar, Daniel. *Le journal* La Presse *et l'immigration (1896–1911)*, Master's thesis in history, Université Laval, 1979, 102 p.

Hébert, Marc. *La presse de Québec et les Juifs 1925–1939 : le cas du* Soleil *et du* Quebec Chronicle Telegraph, Québec, Université Laval, Master's thesis in history, 1994, 138 p.

Kelly, Ninette and Michael J. Trebilcock. *The Making of the Mosaic: A History of Canadian Immigration Policy*, Toronto, University of Toronto Press, 2010, 689 p.

Leff, Laurel. *Buried by the Times: The Holocaust and America's Most Important Newspaper*, New York, Cambridge University Press, 2005, 426 p.

Marrus, Michael. *The Holocaust in History*, Toronto, Key Porter Books, 2000, 267 p.

Marrus, Michael. *The Unwanted: European Refugees in the Twentieth Century*, New York, Orford University Press, 1985, 414 p.

Medresh, Israël. *Le Montréal juif entre les deux guerres/Tsvishn Tsvey Velt Milkhomes (1964)*, Sillery, éditions du Septentrion, 2001, 242 p.

Nadeau, Jean-François. *Adrien Arcand, führer canadien*, Montréal, Lux, 2010, 404 p.

Nathans, Benjamin. *Beyond the Pale; the Jewish Encounter with Late Imperial Russia*, Berkley, Calif., University of California Press, 2002, 424 p.

Pontbriand, Mathieu. "L'affaire Delisle. Champ universitaire et scoop médiatique," p. 187–224, in Martin Pâquet, ed., *Faute et réparation au Canada et au Québec contemporain*, Montréal, Nota Bene, 2007, 321 p.

Rajotte, David. "Les Québécois, les Juifs et l'immigration durant la Seconde Guerre mondiale," *Bulletin d'histoire politique*, vol. 16, n° 1, automne 2007, p. 259–270.

Richer, Geneviève. "Le défenseur des Juifs au Québec: la lutte de Peter Bercovitch pour le respect et la reconnaissance de la minorité juive durant l'entre-deux-guerres," *Bulletin d'histoire politique*, vol. 17, n° 2, hiver 2009, p. 209–224.

Robin, Martin. *Le spectre de la droite. Histoire des politiques nativistes et fascistes au Canada entre 1920 et 1940*, Montréal, Balzac-Le Griot, 1998, 304 p.

Robinson, Ira (ed.), *Canada's Jews in Time, Space and Spirit*, Boston, Academic Studies' Press, 2013, 501 p.

Robinson, Ira. *Rabbis and their Community: Studies in the Eastern European Orthodox Rabbinate in Montréal, 1896–1930*, Calgary, University of Calgary Press, 2007, 166 p.

Rome, David. *The Jewish Biography of Henri Bourassa*, Montréal, Canadian Jewish Congress, new series n° 39, 1988, 2 vol.

Rome, David. *Clouds in the Thirties: On Antisemitism in Canada, 1929–1939. A Chapter on Canadian Jewish History*, Montréal, Canadian Jewish Congress, 1977–1981, 13 vol.

Rosenberg, Louis. *A Study of the Growth and Changes in the Distribution of the Jewish Population of Montreal*, Montréal, Canadian Jewish Congress, Bureau of Social and Economic Research, Canadian Jewish Population Series, n° 4, 1955, 51 p.

Rosenberg, Louis. *Canada's Jews: A Social and Economic Study of Jews in Canada in the 1930s*, Montréal, McGill-Queen's University Press, 1993, 424 p.

Rosenberg, Stuart E. *The Jewish Community in Canada*, Toronto, McClelland and Stewart, 1970, 2 vol.

Rubinstein, William D. *The Myth of Rescue: Why the Democracies Could Not Have Saved More Jews from the Nazis*, London, Routledge, 1997, 267 p.

Samson, Christian. "La peur de l'autre dans la presse de Québec: les représentations de l'immigration internationale dans *La Libre Parole*, 1905–1912," *Bulletin d'histoire politique*, vol. 19, n° 1, p. 187–196.

Sefton, Victor. "The European Holocaust – Who Knew What and When—A Canadian Aspect," *Canadian Jewish Historical Society Journal*, vol. 2, n° 2, 1978, p. 121–133.

Stingel, Janine. *Social Discredit: Anti-Semitism, Social Credit and the Jewish Response*, Montréal, McGill-Queen's University Press, 2000, 280 p.

Théorêt, Hugues. *Les chemises bleues : Adrien Arcand, journaliste antisémite canadien-français*, Québec, Septentrion, 2012, 410 p.

Tulchinsky, Gerald. *Canada's Jews: A People's Journey*, Toronto, University of Toronto Press, 2008, 630 p.

Weisbord, Merrily. *Le rêve d'une génération : les communistes canadiens, les procès d'espionnage et la guerre froide*, Montréal, VLB, 1988, 398 p.

Wyman, David S. *A Race against Death: Peter Bergson, America and the Holocaust*. New York, New Press, 2002, 269 p.

Wyman, David S. *The Abandonment of the Jews: America and the Holocaust, 1941– 1945*, New York, Pantheon Books, 1984, 444 p.

Canadian Studies

Series editor: Pierre Anctil

The *Canadian Studies* collection touches upon all aspects of Canadian society in all disciplines with a special focus on the situation of Canadian women, cultural and religious minorities, and First Nations. The collection is also devoted to regional studies, local communities, and the unique characteristics of Canadian society. Among the topics privileged in this collection are all contemporary issues, especially in the domain of the environment, with regards to large urban centres and new forms of art and communications.

Previous titles in this collection

Hugues Théorêt, *The Blue Shirts: Adrien Arcand and Fascist Anti-Semitism in Canada*, 2017.

Pierre Anctil, *Jacob Isaac Segal: A Montreal Yiddish Poet and His Milieu*, 2017.

Le Mawiomi Mi'gmawei de Gespe'gewa'gi, *Nta'tugwaqanminen Notre histoire : l'évolution des Mi'gmaqs de Gespe'gewa'gi*, 2018.

www.press.uottawa.ca